A LUST FOR LIVING

Venezuela offers beaches, mountains, rainforest and savannah,
but the real attraction is the character of its people

Venezuela: the best-kept secret in the Caribbean. This was the cunningly self-effacing theme of a promotional campaign of the national tourism corporation – and it remains true. Most potential visitors are aware that Venezuela has oil and, perhaps, have heard of Isla Margarita (virtually the only part of the country actively promoted), but beyond that… nothing. Thus, the usual reaction is one of amazement at the diversity of attractions.

After the unfortunate first image of hills covered with shanties between Maiquetía airport (where most visitors arrive) and surrounding central Caracas, the constant flow of contrasting landscapes as you explore Venezuela's interior is a marvelous surprise. You will become privy to many of its secrets: it is not just a "Caribbean country" with beaches, but a South American country, with mountains, plains and jungles; it has incredibly varied wildlife, fascinating architecture (even among humble handmade earth-walled houses); and you can observe the ancient customs of its indigenous peoples and the colorful displays of its rich folklore.

Along with these, other great parts of Venezuela's enchantment include its people: open, friendly, in love with life; and its climate: sunny and warm, with average daytime temperatures of about 25°C (77°F) year-round.

By air, no part of the country is more than two hours away. If driving from Caracas, within a few hours, or at most a full day, you can be on dazzling beaches, horseback riding, or birding on a cattle ranch in the *llanos* (plains); or you may be in the heart of the Andes dressed in a T-shirt but with snow-capped mountains in the background, visiting indigenous settlements in the Amazon jungle, or preparing to climb *tepuyes* (*mesas* of rock among the oldest on earth).

Although natives and foreigners alike pull their hair at the prevailing "*mañana*" (or "what's your hurry") attitude, there are compensations. This laid-back approach contributes to Venezuela's allure: rather than being ruled by diaries or watches, most Venezuelans are clearly guided by the principle that life is to live – now. If you have a chance to dance until dawn on a Tuesday – go for it.

There is something infectious about the flirty smiles, warm back-slapping or kissy-face welcomes, the boisterous laughter and people singing along with the radio on a bus. It makes such a refreshing change from the dominant "what's proper" norm (even in Latin America) that it makes you glad you came – and leaves you with a definite desire to return. ❏

PRECEDING PAGES: view from a light plane over the Gran Sabana; Spanish moss drapes the trees among tropical vegetation in the Andes; scarlet and white ibis over the *llanos*; Castillo de San Antonio de la Eminencia, Cumaná.
LEFT: façade of an old house in Maracaibo.

A COUNTRY OF SURPRISES

The vast array of contrasting lifestyles, cultures and architecture throughout
Venezuela are as distinct as the geographical features of each region

The witchcraft of Venezuela is undeniable. Natives may flock to Miami for vacations, but leave the country for good? *No, señor!* And, if you ask foreign residents why they settled here, the answer will invariably be that they came for a short vacation or temporary job assignment and decided to stay for good.

Just what is it that charms so many people? On the surface, the answer is easy: the wonderful climate, an immense variety of geographical features, and people with a natural warmth and joy of living. But there are countless other subtle ingredients that go into the magic potion: the music and dance, marvelous wildlife, the lack of development, an absence of racial barriers, folkloric customs lovingly preserved for centuries – the list is long.

Coastal smorgasbord

As a country with some 3,000 km (1,800 miles) of Caribbean coastline, beaches are a natural focal point for diversion. Together with myriad options along the continental shore or on its hundreds of islands and cays, these beaches may be wide swaths of snowy white sand lapped by calm crystalline water, or bays framed with dramatic rock formations and cactus, or perhaps ringed by palm trees with the backdrop of mountains covered with dense tropical forest. There are solitary spots ideal for reflection and others in lively resorts. Local residents may be reserved, light-skinned fishermen or dark-skinned descendants of slaves who celebrate at the drop of a hat with their African-style *tambores* (drums) and sensual dancing. If you tire of swimming or working on a tan, there is always outstanding deep-sea fishing, windsurfing, sailing and diving.

The majority of Venezuela's principal cities and some 80 percent of the population are also found on or near the coast: the dynamic national capital, Caracas, where you can dine in exotic restaurants and dance the night away to

LEFT: sun-worshipers at work.
RIGHT: water cacao on the Orinoco River.

the rhythms of salsa; the beach resort towns of Puerto La Cruz/Barcelona (not to mention the mega-resort haven of Isla Margarita with its duty-free shopping); Cumaná, guarded by a colonial fort; manufacturing centers of Valencia and Maracay; Coro, with nearby sand dunes and designated a World Patrimony City by

UNESCO, for its exceptional colonial architecture; Maracaibo, Venezuela's petroleum capital (with one of the world's largest oil reserves beneath South America's largest lake abutting the metropolis) and second largest city, where transplanted Texas oil tycoons rub elbows with Guajiro indian women in their traditional native dress and *gaita* music fills the air.

Deserts and mountains

Westbound from Caracas, next stop is Falcón and Lara, states with predominately desert landscapes. But, for variety, they also have "accents" of verdant mountains. And Lara, despite its arid appearance, is the county's principal source of

tomatoes, onions, peppers, and other produce. Meanwhile, Yaracuy's mountains harbor everything from ancient gold and copper mines, which belonged to Simón Bolívar's family, to followers of the bizarre María Lionza cult. Continuing to the southwest, one passes through the western plains: rich farmlands planted with sugar cane, rice and grains.

Mountains steeped in tradition

Traversing Venezuela's Andean states, another totally different set of sights and experiences awaits. The journey takes you from the coffee plantations of the foothills, through the barren but fascinating *páramo* (high moorland), and up to the country's tallest mountains (topped by Pico Bolívar, 5,000 meters/16,400 ft). Winding roads pass fields where farmers guide wooden plows pulled by teams of oxen and where glacier-fed lakes teem with trout. Due to the region's long isolation, farmhouses with pounded-earth walls, tiny villages with cobblestone streets and ancient buildings, and traditional festivals have all been preserved virtually unchanged for centuries. The way of life here remains slower and simpler.

The great plains

Moving on to the *llanos*, or central plains, you can go the easy way by road or plane – or hike across the mountains to the plains, a unique experience offered by various operators.

The *llanos*, in a belt roughly 100–150 km (60–90 miles) wide and 1,000 km (600 miles) long, extend north and west of the Orinoco River from its delta to the Andes. During the dry season the land is parched and cracked, but when the rainy season hits, because of the extreme flatness, it is almost totally flooded.

Apure and Barinas form the heart of the *llanos*, where the three most notable occupants are thousands of mainly beef cattle on sprawling *hatos* (ranches), an incredible quantity and variety of wildlife, and the *llanero*. The last of these, the Venezuelan-style cowboy, typically with bare feet instead of boots, has been famous since colonial times for his bravery and independence. When the *llanero* isn't tending the herds, more likely than not he will be strumming a *cuatro*, *bandola*, or *arpa criollo* to produce the local equivalent of country-western tunes.

Left: diamond miners await an air taxi, La Gran Sabana.

El Oriente

Northeastern Venezuela, popularly referred to as *"El Oriente"*, is best known for its beaches, but has many other attractions, including the spot on the Paria Peninsula of Sucre where Christopher Columbus first came in contact with Venezuela, declaring it to be "the land of grace" for its extraordinary beauty.

Heading inland, a favorite stop in northern Monagas is the *Cueva del Guácharo*, named for the colonies of night-flying, fruit-eating *guácharos* (oil birds), which occupy one of the chambers of this cave (the largest and best-preserved in the country).

Pushing southward, in central Anzoátegui state, you will pass over the Orinoco Belt, one of the world's largest petroleum reserves.

Last frontiers

The Guayana Region – including Delta Amacuro, Bolívar, and Amazonas states – covers some 45 percent of the national territory. The name comes from the Guayana Shield (some of the oldest rock on earth: 1.2–2.75 billion years old) which forms most of its base. Among the regions unique attractions are the *tepuyes*, or mesas of this ancient rock, their tops hosting plants and animals found nowhere else on earth.

Delta Amacuro state, almost completely comprising the delta (among the largest in the world) of the Orinoco River, is home of the Warao indians. Their name, meaning "the canoe people," is most apt, being excellent boat builders, and given that boats offer the only practical way through the maze of *caños* (channels and branches of the river). Tourist camps in its interior allow visitors a close-up view of the lifestyles of the Warao, along with observation of flora and fauna.

Bolívar state, Venezuela's largest, is also one of its richest, with vast deposits of iron, gold, diamonds, and bauxite. Moreover, harnessing the hydroelectric potential of its Caroní River, this state produces 70 percent of the nation's consumer power, plus that needed for the huge steel and aluminum plants of Ciudad Guayana.

Ultra-modern Ciudad Guayana and the state's capital Ciudad Bolívar are both located on Bolívar's northern border, the Orinoco River. Visitors can fly from these cities to Canaima (in the northwest corner of the Canaima National Park), the departure point for visiting Angel Falls, the longest free-fall of water in the world, plunging over the side of Auyantepui.

By road, visit the mostly overlapping Gran Sabana (Great Savanna) and 3 million-hectare (7.4 million-acre) Canaima National Park in the southeastern portion of the state, following an excellent paved road finished in 1991. Along the full length of the park, all the way to Santa Elena de Uairén near the frontier of Brazil, travelers can delight in the majesty of the gently rolling high savannah. There are numerous beautiful waterfalls (such as Quebrada de Jaspe, with a riverbed of semi-precious jasper), and fascinating flora, ranging from ground orchids to carnivorous plants. At the southeastern extreme is Roraima *tepuy*, made famous by Sir Arthur Conan Doyle's work, *The Lost World*.

The capital of Amazonas state, Puerto Ayacucho, can be reached by paved road, as well as commercial flights. But from there on, exploring the depths of its virgin forests, *tepuyes* sacred to the Piaroa indians, remote villages of indigenous groups that have changed little since the Stone Age, are the stuff of adventure tours by boat or small plane.

Need you ask why Venezuela casts a spell on people? ❑

LEFT: one of Guayana's colorful inhabitants.
RIGHT: a farmer from Mérida state.

Decisive Dates

PRE-HISPANIC DEVELOPMENT

14,800 BC First humans arrive in Venezuela.
14,800–5000 BC Paleoindian period of hunter-gatherers.
5000–1000 BC Bone and shell implements.
1000 BC–AD 300 Agriculture and ceramics develop.
AD 300–1500 Interchange of influence between groups, cultivation of grain spreads through territory.

PERIOD OF COLONIZATION

1498 Christopher Columbus discovers the mouth of the Orinoco River and lands on Paria Peninsula.

1499 Alfonso de Ojeda and Amerigo Vespucci sail from Orinoco Delta to Guajira Peninsula; name area Venezuela; pearl beds of Cubagua discovered.
1500 First settlement in South America, Santiago de Cubaga (later renamed Nueva Cádiz) founded.
1521 Cumaná founded, the first settlement by white men on South American mainland.
1527 Coro founded; Emperor Charles V gives indefinite lease to the Welsers – German bankers.
1546 Agreement with Welsers ended; El Tocuyo is made capital of the Province of Venezuela.
1548 First cattle introduced to central plains.
1567 Diego de Losada founds Santiago de León de Caracas, future capital of Venezuela.
1681 By order of Felipe II of Spain the Law of the Indies is created, which governs the colonies until Independence.
1728 The Guipuzcoana Company formed between King Felipe V and Basque merchants with total monopoly over the Province of Venezuela's imports, exports, economic development, exploitation (lasting until 1785).
1739 First political and military unification of Venezuela with creation of Viceroyalty of Nueva Granada.
1777 Captaincy-general of Venezuela is created, uniting provinces of Margarita, Caracas, Mérida de Maracaibo, Nueva Andalucía, Guayana, and Trinidad.

THE QUEST FOR INDEPENDENCE

1806 Francisco de Miranda mounts first expedition against the Spanish; Venezuelan flag flies for first time.
1810 Authority of captain-general is repudiated on April 19; the Junta Suprema de Caracas is formed to govern; the first Congress is convoked June 11.
1811 On July 5, Venezuela is the first colony to proclaim independence from Spain; the Confederación Americana de Venezuela is formed of the provinces of Caracas, Cumaná, Barcelona, Barinas, Margarita, Mérida and Trujillo; tri-color designed by Miranda in 1806 is adopted as Venezuela's flag.
1812 Earthquake leaves 10,000 dead in Caracas; May 19, Miranda given dictatorial powers; July 31, Miranda taken prisoner, deported to prison in Spain.
1813 Simón Bolívar invades Venezuela from Colombia, beginning the "Admirable Campaign" on March 1; establishes the Second Republic August 7; is proclaimed Liberator and given dictatorial powers.
1819 On February 15, Congress of Angostura convenes, elects Bolívar President of the Republic; the Constitution is approved.
1821 Second Battle of Carabobo – the last great battle in War of Independence – is fought on July 24.
1823 Battle of Lake Maracaibo fought on 24 July with Spanish captain-general surrendering in Maracaibo on August 3; Gen. José Antonio Páez liberates Puerto Cabello on November 8 and last Spanish troops leave.

NEW POLITICAL STRUCTURE

May 6, 1830 Constitutional Congress convenes in Valencia, ratifies separation of Venezuela from La Gran Colombia union, names José Antonio Páez first president of Venezuela, and creates Constitution.
December 17, 1830 Simón Bolívar dies in Colombia.
1831–35 First presidency of Páez; Caracas becomes the capital of Venezuela.
1839–43 Second presidency of Páez; road between Caracas-La Guaira built – first of its kind in Venezuela.
1845 Spain recognizes independence of Venezuela with the Treaty of Madrid.

1854 Slavery abolished

1858–63 The Federal Wars.

1864 New democratic constitution; the Republic becomes the Estados Unidos de Venezuela.

1870–87 General Antonio Guzmán Blanco is president (or behind-the-scenes ruler); in feud with Catholic Church, he establishes compulsory secular education (1870), civil birth and marriage registry (1872), closes convents and seminaries (1874), and inaugurates Masonic Lodge in Caracas (1875).

1878 First petroleum exploitation, in Táchira state.

1899–1908 Dictatorship of Gen. Cipriano Castro, with Gen. Juan Vicente Gómez as vice president.

1908 Gómez assumes power while Castro abroad.

1909–35 Dictatorship of Juan Vicente Gómez.

1922 Blow-out of "Los Barrosos" well in Zulia state; discovery of largest oil deposit in the world.

1926 Petroleum is Venezuela's number one export.

1936–45 Dictatorial presidencies of Gen. Eleazar López Contreras and Gen. Isías Medina.

YEARS OF TURMOIL

1945 Military dictatorship is overthrown; Rómulo Betancourt becomes provisional president of civilian Revolutionary Junta; women given the right to vote.

1948 Bloodless military coup overthrows government.

1952–58 Dictatorship of Marcos Pérez Jiménez.

DEMOCRACY

1958 On January 23, present-day democracy begins with bloodless overthrow of Pérez Jiménez; junta combined of military and civil members rules until elections; return of political exiles.

1959–64 Presidency of Acción Democrática Party candidate, Rómulo Betancourt.

1960 OPEC (Organization of Petroleum Exporting Countries) created through initiative of Venezuela.

1969–74 Presidency of Rafael Caldera, of the Democrático Cristiano party.

1974–79 Presidency of Carlos Andrés Pérez; nationalization of iron and steel industry (1975), and then the petroleum industry (1976).

DEATH OF "SAUDI VENEZUELA"

February 18, 1983 "Black Friday" – falling oil prices force devaluation of currency the "fat years" are over.

1984–89 Presidential term of Jaime Lusinchi is marked by corruption.

PRECEDING PAGES: a monument to the encounter between Europeans and Amerindians, Cumaná.
LEFT: primitive Panare indians, Amazonas state.
RIGHT: a grenadier.

1989 Carlos Andrés Pérez elected to second term, initiates severe economic reforms; popular uprising on Feb 27 sparked by Pérez's reform measures brings nationwide looting, burning, and hundreds of deaths.

1991 Privatization of national phone company, CANTV.

1992 two coup attempts, Feb 4 and Nov 27, with rebels turned back by loyal government forces.

1993 Pérez indicted by Supreme Court for corruption – the first time in Venezuela's history a serving president is tried; Senate votes to suspend him from office on May 21, and elects Ramón José Velásquez interim president.

1994 Failure of Banco Latino initiates two-year banking crisis and takeover of 18 financial institutions

representing more than half of deposit base; Rafael Caldera elected to second term as president, ordering 66 percent devaluation of the bolívar, exchange controls, return of price controls.

1996 Inflation tops 100 percent, exchange controls lifted, stock market sets record highs, oil prices hit five-year high; steel industry privatized.

1997–98 Economic crisis worsens as government fails to control fiscal expenditures; oil prices and stock market plunge; strikes for higher wages multiply in nearly every sector; political uncertainty.

1999 A new President, Hugo Chávez, failed coup leader, is inaugurated. His party, the Movimiento de la 5a República, does not have a majority, so he has to face a fractious Congress. ❑

BEGINNINGS

After the "discovery" of Venezuela by Christopher Columbus, the indians who had lived here for thousands of years put up a staunch defense of their lands

Most histories of Venezuela commence in the year 1498, when the navigator Christopher Columbus first laid eyes on the Paria Peninsula. Overwhelmed by its beauty, he called it "the land of grace." Of course, Columbus was the first European to visit South America, but it was hardly a "discovery" – native Americans had been living here for some 16,000 years, ever since the great migrations following the last Ice Age.

Dozens of unique cultures inhabited the vast region of mountains, desert, plains and jungle that the invading Spaniards would eventually bring together under the name of "Venezuela." Convinced that he had found the Orient, Columbus called these inhabitants "indians", and the misnomer has stuck (although, in Spanish, native Venezuelans now prefer to be referred to as *indígenas*, or "indigenous people").

These indian groups did not build magnificent empires or glittering cities like those later found in Mexico or Peru. Instead, they lived in semi-nomadic, hunting and gathering societies, or small agricultural villages. Although Europeans would dismiss their societies as primitive, the pre-Columbian world was in fact highly complex: each society had its own language, mythology and cultural traditions, as well as its long history of warfare and survival. Some, the Caribe indians for example, were fierce and warlike, descending on their enemies in canoes and turning their bones into flutes; others, such as the Arawaks, were sedentary, spending more time on farming than fighting.

No records

With no knowledge of writing, these pre-Columbian societies kept no records, and little is known about dozens of ancient cultures. Remote groups, such as the Guajiros around modern-day Maracaibo and the Piaroas in the Amazon, managed to survive the murderous onslaught of Europeans, but the majority were simply wiped out.

LEFT AND RIGHT: European visions of indian life.

Yet when Columbus's tiny caravels weighed anchor in the Gulf of Paria on his third voyage, there was little indication of the wholesale devastation that European contact would bring. The navigator decided that this new fruit-laden land was "the loveliest in all the world" and its people surprisingly open and friendly. Canoes full of Paria indians came out to greet the newcomers, and Columbus eagerly noted that they wore jewelry made of gold and pearls.

The virtual flood of explorers that followed soon abandoned Columbus's idea that the New World was Asia. After sailing up and down Venezuela's beach-lined coast, they were also decidedly unimpressed with what it had to offer in the way of riches. Apart from a few small baubles, the Caribbean yielded no quantities of precious metal, silk or spices. One of these first explorers, the Italian Amerigo Vespucci, gave Venezuela its name – literally, "Little Venice" – when his sailors commented, no doubt ironically, that the native villages on stilts in Lake

Maracaibo reminded them of the canals of Venice. But this growing suspicion that the Americas were hardly worth bothering about changed when Cortés con- quered Mexico in 1519. News of the great city of Tenochtitlán accompanied boatloads of gold to the royal court in Spain. It seemed that kingdoms of un- imagined wealth might lie deep in the heart of any new territory – and Venezuela, as the most accessible part of the new continent of South America, topped the list for conquest.

WILD RESISTANCE

Paradoxically, although the huge, "advanced" civilizations of Mexico and later Peru collapsed quickly under Spanish onslaught, the wilder shores of Venezuela proved most difficult to conquer and settle.

As a result, when Spaniards began to mount expeditions into the interior of Venezuela, the indian reaction was often immediately hostile.

The invasion begins

The tone for colonizing Ven- ezuela was set by the disastrous 1530 expedition led by one of Cortés's most trusted captains, Diego de Ordaz. Convinced that there was a link between the glow of the sun and the color of gold, the aging conquistador set off from Spain with more than 600 men towards

The Spaniards had set up a pearl fishery on the desolate island of Cubagua, but now they decided to found a town on Tierra Firme – "the mainland", or to foreign tongues the Spanish Main. In 1521, a few mud huts were established around a square plaza by the Caribbean and called Cumaná, the first Span- ish town in continental South America. But even this outpost had to be fought for: rela- tions with local indians had soured long before, thanks to regular Spanish slave raids. Slave traders would simply surprise indian families fishing on beaches and transport them to the miserable sugar plantations that were being set up in Trinidad.

the hottest place then known in South America: the Equator, lying between the Orinoco and Amazon rivers.

After a difficult crossing of the Atlantic, Ordaz and his men spent several months wan- dering the Orinoco Delta. Tropical diseases and hunger quickly took a bitter toll among the unacclimatized Spaniards. "There were men who, from one day to the next, had their entire feet consumed by cancer from the ankle to the toes," one chronicler recorded. Finally, the des- perate Spaniards found a large fishing village of Arawak indians: the conquistadores went straight for the native women, who were naked except for "a rag in front of their private parts, which is loose and just long enough to cover them…Thus when they sway, or in a wind, everything is revealed."

Before long, the Spaniards became convinced that the Arawaks plotted to steal their pigs and began a fight in which the whole village burned. At another village, Ordaz put hundreds of unarmed indians to the sword because they refused to give food (then burned the village to make sure none escaped by feigning death).

Only about 200 Spaniards were still alive when the expedition stumbled into the endless flat plains of the Venezuelan *llanos*. They wandered this near-deserted landscape, still more expeditions into Venezuela's inhospitable interior. Before long, Meta would blend with the enduring fantasy of "El Dorado", a fabulously wealthy land where an indian king was covered daily with gold dust.

Dozens of expeditions set off into the Venezuelan interior, often to disappear without trace in the steaming jungles of the Amazon or succumb to starvation in the *llanos*. Strangely, many of these ill-fated groups were led by Germans. Forming a new chapter in the history of the Spanish conquest, the whole of Venezuela was temporarily granted in the 1500s to the German banking house of Welser, a group of

following the Orinoco, until Ordaz finally agreed to turn back. The only good news was from an obviously terrified indian prisoner, who announced under questioning that vast gold could be found in the nearby empire of Meta, ruled by a one-eyed prince.

The German conquistadores

Although Ordaz himself died on the way back to Spain, the myth of Meta inspired dozens

LEFT: the quest for El Dorado inspired the exploration of Venezuela.
ABOVE: fanciful vision of a Spanish conquistador, mounted on a llama.

merchant adventurers who had interests from India to Africa, patronized the artist Albrecht Dürer, and to whom the Spanish king Carlos I owed thousands of ducats in debt.

Historians have been fascinated by the German expeditions mainly because of their cruelty, stunning even by the callous standards of the day, and their almost total futility. A wealthy young cloth merchant from Ulm, Ambrosius Dalfinger, led hundreds of finely equipped soldiers to the sandy wastelands near Lake Maracaibo, losing a third of his force without finding even a single gold earring. When he did find gold on another trip, the soldiers sent to transport it got lost, turned to cannibalism, then all

Aguirre the Mad

The 16th-century Venezuelan frontier was a remote and often desperate place, where Spaniards were as willing to turn on one another as to fight for any common goal. Spending months at sea, away from any instructions from Spain, conquistadores made their own self-serving law, and dozens of intrigues and civil wars were played out in the power vacuum.

Entering this chaotic scene in 1562 was perhaps the most notorious conquistador of them all, Lope de Aguirre, whose exploits were immortalized

for modern audiences in the 1972 Werner Herzog film *Aguirre, Wrath of God*. The historian John Hemming has described Aguirre as "a man of unmitigated evil, cruel, psychopathic and gripped by an obsessive grievance against the whole of Spanish society." These terms would have seemed charitable to the poor Spaniards and indians who had to face him in a voyage of destruction that ended up in Venezuela.

Expelled from Peru after joining the wrong side of a civil war, Aguirre signed up for a large expedition leaving Cuzco for the Amazon basin. The object, as ever, was to search for the chimerical El Dorado. But as the inexperienced group of 370 soldiers stumbled through the steaming jungle,

Aguirre soon found a wellspring of discontent. He incited a mutiny and had the expedition's leader, Pedro de Ursua, murdered in his hammock. Another Spanish noble was elevated to the leadership, but his rule was short-lived: Aguirre had him put to the sword as well, and his beautiful *mestizo* mistress hacked to death.

Described as a thin, scrawny man with one lame leg, Aguirre was nevertheless one of the most experienced and ruthless fighters in the New World. Now, floating down the Amazon River on a barge, he declared his intention of leading the rebels back to conquer Peru by traveling via Venezuela around the north of South America then marching back to where they had started.

En route, Aguirre began to indulge his long-standing grudges against Spanish society and some more recently acquired psychoses, turning the expedition into a floating death camp. According to chroniclers, Aguirre "determined not to carry with him any gentleman or person of quality, and therefore slew all such persons; and then departing only with the common soldiers, he left behind all the Spanish women and sick men." The surviving Andean porters were also left to die. Aguirre then began suspecting soldiers of plotting against him, and ordered so many of them to be garrotted that before long the expedition's numbers were reduced from 370 to 230.

Aguirre's rantings and paranoia were at fever pitch when the rebel barges arrived in Venezuela, weighing anchor on the palm-fringed Isla Margarita. The Spanish governor welcomed them, but he was quickly seized and executed. Aguirre instituted a reign of terror over the island – putting to death any local citizens or his own soldiers who seemed to be "lukewarm in his service."

Aguirre moved on to Barquisimeto, his forces then reduced by half. Between strong resistance organized by Diego García de Paredes and desertions by his troops, he realized the end was near. But, before surrender, he entered the room of his 18-year-old daughter, Elvira, killing her with his dagger, so she would not have to live being called "daughter of a traitor." When García de Paredes' soldiers entered and discovered his deed, they riddled him with bullets, then beheaded and quartered him, dividing severed members among the villages which had sent help to combat him, and placed his head in a cage displayed in the plaza of El Tocuyo for many years. ❑

LEFT: Spanish conquistadores.

died of starvation. Another German captain, a calculating 24-year-old named Nicolaus Federmann, became convinced that the Pacific Ocean lay not far south of Coro. He tricked tribe after indian tribe into offering his men help before turning on them and either slaughtering or enslaving them as porters.

Typical was his treatment of the Guaiquerí indians, who came to meet Federmann's men in an apparently peaceful fashion. "While I distracted them with words," the Teutonic conquistador proudly recorded, "I arranged that they should be surrounded by the horses, which would attack them.

"We took them by surprise and killed five hundred. The horsemen charged into the thick of them, knocking down as many as they could. Our footsoldiers then slaughtered these like pigs… In the end they tried to hide in the grass, or the living hid beneath the dead, but these were found and many of them beheaded after we finished with those who were fleeing."

In the end, Federmann found a race of dwarfs – only 76 cm (30 inches) tall, he reported, but perfectly proportioned – and even some golden trinkets, but little else. After about 20 years of such atrocious depredations, the Spanish Crown ordered an inquiry and revoked the German lease. With poetic justice, many of the Germans came to sticky ends: Federmann wasted the rest of his life searching for El Dorado and Dalfinger fell riddled with indian arrows in Colombia.

The frontier secured

Although no cities paved with jewels were ever found, these misdirected quests did attract the manpower needed to secure much of Venezuela for the Spanish Crown. Giving up on El Dorado in the 1540s, colonists turned to securing more towns and routes through the Andes to the rest of the empire. It was an uphill struggle: the scattered groups of Venezuelan indians were now aware of the Spaniards' cruelty and put up tenacious resistance to their advance.

In fact, Spanish colonists expected the struggle to go on for decades and ruefully looked at other American provinces, such as Peru and Bolivia, where silver mines were making penniless adventurers into grandees overnight. Then an unexpected weapon broke the indian resistance: smallpox. The disease was unknown in the Americas and wiped out entire indian communities. In the embattled Caracas valley, for example, a wave of the plague in 1580 killed no fewer than two-thirds of the native population.

The forgotten provinces

With this ignoble victory, Venezuela entered its long period of colonial control. These centuries as a dismal and forgotten backwater within the vast Spanish empire are often skipped over as an unmemorable and somewhat irrelevant period, not least by modern Venezuelans. However, the structures that were set up during the colonial

era have shaped – and distorted – the fate of Venezuela to this day.

The small outposts at Cumaná, Caracas, Mérida and Maracaibo grew to be muddy villages and then established towns as colonists began arriving in numbers from Spain. Still marking Venezuela's towns and cities is the original monotonous grid-iron street plan, spreading out from the *cabildo* (town council) and cathedral as a symbol of rational empire-building. Houses were built mainly of adobe mud, although a few of the richest settlers used brick; most were set around a patio and garden, and were kept one-story high to avoid damage by earthquakes. Attempts were made to create

RIGHT: English pirates became the scourge of Venezuela's coast.

genteel enclaves of Hispanic style in this tropical setting: children were still married off at 14, heavy imported wine went down with meals and a long siesta after lunch was *de rigueur*.

Pirates soon replaced indians as the main threat to Venezuela's new towns. Prowling the Caribbean coastline were packs of English, Dutch and French corsairs waiting for gold-laden galleons but not above pillaging a whole town for its wealth.

Cattle and cacao

After building towns as bases, the Spaniards claimed the countryside. In the grand colonial

plan, Venezuela became half plantation, half ranch. Missionaries often became the shock troops of settlement: fiery-eyed Franciscans, Capuchins and Jesuits filtered through the Venezuelan hinterland to make contact with the remaining indian groups. Many ended up martyrs, but they succeeded in setting up the missions that converted the *indígenas* and prepared for their submission to the Spanish Crown.

Across the warm valleys of the coast spread *haciendas*, semi-feudal plantations growing mostly the native South American plant cacao. Meanwhile, the grasslands of the *llanos* were opened up to cattle. *Hatos*, or ranches, began to dot this remote area and, as in the pampas of Argentina, half-wild herds were soon wandering the empty plains, unrestricted by fencing. Since beef was near-impossible to transport, *llaneros* – the breed of skilled horsemen, usually drawn from the fringes of society, who worked the *llanos* – would slaughter steers just to eat the tongue and take the hide, leaving the carcasses to rot in the wilderness.

Though there were chronic shortages of virtually every other domestic item in colonial times, leather was abundant and used for almost anything: it made the backing for chairs, replaced glass for windows, and occasionally could even be substituted for rare iron nails.

The shape of colonial society

The majority of initial settlers were young unmarried men, and coaxing Spanish women to brave the uncertainties of an Atlantic crossing and rough life in the New World would long remain a problem. Those that did come were horrified to find they might have to share their new husbands with one or more indian or black slave mistresses, and even accept a collection of bastard children.

Indeed, the mixture of races was soon to be the main feature of Venezuelan society. By 1700, "free-coloreds" or *pardos* – including everyone from freed slaves to half-castes – would make up some 45 percent of Venezuela's whole population, with black slaves and indians comprising 15 percent each. *Blancos,* or whites, made up only about 25 percent of the total (and even then, as one foreign writer observed with studied prejudice, they were "rarely free of any connection to the blood of the colored class").

This white elite – often called "Gran Cacaos" in deference to the source of its power – was acutely conscious of its vulnerability, and in a primitive form of apartheid made sure that *pardos* could not wear the same Hispanic clothes as whites, could not enter the Church or study at university. There were even attempts to have *pardos* carry a certificate denoting their racial status "to avoid doubts and confusion", while the motto *Todo blanco es caballero* ("every white man is a gentleman") became the rule.

As the colonial era progressed, the *blancos* became divided between a small group of Spanish-born newcomers and the vast bulk of creoles (whites born in the New World). Both of these social groups emulated the styles and

astonished to see aristocratic families on hot evenings pick up their chairs and carry them into nearby rivers, chatting with friends and smoking cigars as the water flowed up to their knees, quite unfazed by the many small crocodiles splashing about their feet or the playful dolphins spraying them with water.

The chocolate empire

Despite the Venezuelans' European airs, their six scattered provinces were for almost all the colonial period among the least important, successful or wealthy parts of the Spanish empire. In short, Venezuela was an unknown

manners of far-away Madrid. The visiting German scientist Alexander von Humboldt (*see page 173*) would record of Venezuela that "in no other part of Spanish America has civilization assumed a more European character," with *blancos* holding elegant soirées, dancing and earnestly discussing the latest French farce or Italian opera.

Still, the Venezuelans could hardly avoid some creole eccentricities: von Humboldt was

LEFT: chocolate in the making: cacao pods (*mazorcas*) grow directly out of the trunk and branches.
ABOVE: African slaves at work on an 18th-century cacao plantation.

tropical backwater. What changed all that was chocolate. When Europe and the United States developed a passion for this by-product of cacao in the mid 1700s, Venezuelan plantations geared up to meet the demand, and Venezuela was elevated from obscurity into the most valuable non-mining colony in the Spanish empire. The Gran Cacao *blancos* could hardly believe their luck.

But this Golden Age was the calm before the storm. The wars of independence would soon hit Venezuela with unexpected ferocity, turning its haciendas into cemeteries and pushing the country's progress back more than 100 years. ❑

INDEPENDENCE

Venezuelans paid a high price for independence, with the lengthy period of fighting leaving their liberated country in ruins

The soporific calm of colonial Venezuela was shattered at the beginning of the 19th century by the war of independence against Spain. Although Venezuela would play a key role in liberating much of South America, most Venezuelans entered the struggle hesitantly and failed to anticipate its enormous cost. Nowhere else on the continent was the fighting more cruel and destructive: after two decades of bloodshed, Venezuela would be lying in ruins and its tenuous colonial prosperity lost.

Inseparable from this dramatic conflict is the figure of Simón Bolívar, "El Libertador" (The Liberator). Every Venezuelan village, no matter how small, now has a bronze Bolívar statue along with a plaza, main street or municipal building named in honor of the romantic national hero who, despite his many victories, died a bitter and broken man. A heavy shroud of mythology lies over his memory. Bolívar is Latin America's Washington, Napoleon and Hamlet all rolled into one.

El Libertador

Bolívar was notoriously short in stature, thin and wiry, a fine horseman and swimmer. He inspired the devotion of his soldiers and the praises of everyone from South American patriots to the English poet Lord Byron. Exiled twice and escaping numerous assassination attempts, Bolívar squandered one of the greatest family fortunes in the New World pursuing his dream of a united Latin America. The dream took him on campaigns across the Andes to Colombia, Ecuador, Peru, and the nation named after him, Bolivia. Looking back from the present day, few historians deny that Bolívar was a genius.

Yet as the 19th century turned, there was no indication that Venezuela would soon push for independence or that Bolívar would be involved. The rich, white creole elite rarely questioned the basis of Spanish control that had served

them so well. More worrisome was that the black and colored population might rise up against them. Meanwhile, Simon Bolívar was simply another young man about to inherit a fortune from his Gran Cacao family, although on his travels to Europe, he had met Alexander von Humboldt (*see page 173*), and been aston-

ished by the suggestion that the Spanish American colonies were ripe for freedom.

The first push towards independence came in 1808 when sensational news arrived from the Napoleonic wars in Europe: Spain had been occupied by the French army, the Spanish king had abdicated and Napoleon's brother had been placed on the throne. But rather than declare Venezuela independent, leading *caraqueños* formed a junta in support of the Spanish king. Only by 1810 did the wealthy elite decide that Spain was in such confusion that they should try self-government. On April 19 they ousted Captain-general Vicente Emparan and constituted the Junta Suprema de Caracas.

LEFT: paying homage to Simón Bolívar at the Plaza Bolívar in Caracas.
RIGHT: the young "Liberator."

Having formed a Junta Patriótica to actively promote the cause of independence among the skeptical public, when the moment was deemed right, the date of July 5, 1811 was set to convene a National Congress. During this meeting, the Declaration of Independence was approved with only one contrary vote – not against independence, but the timing. The First Republic was formed, governed by a triumvirate. This lasted until May 19, 1812, when Francisco de Miranda was given dictatorial powers to try to save the Republic, already

> ### A MULTI-FACETED MAN
>
> "El Libertador" Simón Bolívar could discourse as easily about the works of Rousseau as he could about military strategy.

had risen to the rank of colonel in the patriot forces, but his true leadership potential had remained untapped. Now, during his first exile, Bolívar slowly began to exert his charisma and assume command of the patriots.

First of all came what the Venezuelans call *La Campaña Admirable* (or the "Admirable Campaign"), when Bolívar and other patriot generals regrouped their forces and began a "War to the Death" against the Spaniards.

Adding to the carnage was the arrival of the *llaneros*, the wild horsemen of Venezuela's

shaken by royalists' uprisings. Although Miranda's forces outnumbered those of the crown, disorganization, lack of funds discontent and desertion among patriots led him to capitulate on July 26, 1812 – which would result in his being declared a traitor. Many patriots fled into exile in the Caribbean.

The slaughter begins

One of the exiles was Bolívar, who had thrown himself into the lower echelons of the independence movement as if to help forget the tragic death of his young wife. He had gone to London as the new republic's ambassador (only to be disappointed in his pleas for support) and

interior plains who turned out to be a devastating cavalry force – initially on the side of the royalists, and later for the patriots. The *llaneros* lived off the land and took as pay what they could pillage.

By 1814, Bolívar had recaptured Caracas and declared the Second Republic. The *llaneros* mobilized against him, sweeping into Caracas and forcing the patriots, yet again, into exile, their property confiscated to add to the misery.

The *llanero* commander, José Tomás Boves, became notorious as the Spanish "butcher," personally supervising the massacre of entire villages. Boves finally met a violent end, skewered on a lance in battle.

Hiding out in Jamaica, Bolívar prepared to fight yet again. He realized the importance of the *llaneros*, and offered them land as a reward for joining his cause: the confiscated estates of royalists would be distributed among them. The *llanero* leader – a Herculean, illiterate cavalryman named José Antonio Páez agreed. And since the *llaneros* followed strong figures rather than any particular cause, Bolívar gained the backbone of a new army. The two retired to Apure and soon after Bolívar continued to Angostura for the Congress of February 15, 1819. There he was elected President of the Republic and submitted the project for the Constitution of Venezuela. Congress approved it six months later.

Meanwhile, Bolívar had returned to Apure with the idea of invading Barinas but, receiving favorable news from the west, he shifted plans to invade Nueva Granada, and led his army over the Andes into Colombia in the midst of winter. This march is considered one of the most daring strokes of Latin America's liberation. More than a quarter of the army died on the march. But, bolstered by the experienced troops of the British Legion (*see page 38*), the campaign was a success with the triumph of Boyacá and liberation of Nueva Granada.

With this victory, Bolívar's project to form a single Republic to be called Colombia, joining Venezuela and Nueva Granada, was approved by Congress on December 17, 1819, with Bolívar named provisional president of La Gran Colombia.

The war would continue for several years more, extending across the entire territory and adjacent lands, decimating the population and destroying the countryside.

The last great and deciding battle of the War of Independence was won at Carabobo on June 24, 1821. However, it was the patriot's triumph in the naval battle of Lake Maracaibo on July 24, 1823 which formally brought this chapter of history to an end with the capitulation on August 3 of Gen. Francisco Tomás Morales, Spain's captain general of the Costa Firme. Twelve days later, Morales, the last representative of Spanish power in Venezuela, was ejected

to Cuba, with 5,000 pesos given by the patriots to cover the cost of his trip.

The Liberator's dream

But Bolívar's career as El Libertador was only beginning. Forming and presiding over La Gran Colombia was hardly enough: Bolívar not only planned to extirpate the Spanish presence from Latin America, but wanted to unite all the former Spanish colonies as the world's largest nation. This vision, which drove him on to liberate the Andean nations, held together for a remarkably long time given that Bolívar may have been the only Latin American to believe in it.

Thousands of Venezuelan troops followed the general into battle among the volcanoes near Quito, the Inca ruins of Cuzco and the bleak *altiplano* beyond Lake Titicaca. After the last Spaniards had surrendered at the Andean battle of Ayacucho, Bolívar was fêted in Lima and seemed close to achieving his dream. Yet even as he danced all night through the glittering ballrooms of America's wealthiest city and gained a reputation as a Casanova (one cavalry officer reputedly moved out of the presidential palace because the shrieks of love-making ruined his sleep), things were going awry.

News soon arrived that the confederation of La Gran Colombia – which was then made up

---

LEFT: *llanero* lancers feign a retreat, only to return and attack again.

RIGHT: Simón Bolívar ponders Latin America's fate on the heights of Ecuador's Mount Chimborazo.

The British Legion

L a Legión Británica, or British Legion, is the shorthand term for the more than 5,000 English, Scottish, Irish and Hanoverian soldiers who journeyed across the Atlantic to join Simón Bolívar's revolutionary army in Venezuela. In one of the least-known aspects of the South American wars of independence, battalions drawn from far- away London, Glasgow and Dublin fought alongside *criollos* throughout Venezuela, with many following the Liberator even into the harsh Andes of Peru.

Recruiting in Britain began soon after 1815, when the battle of Waterloo finally brought the Napoleonic wars to a close. Multitudes of demobilized veterans were returning to their homes, only to find few jobs and dismal prospects.

In 1817, Bolívar ordered his agent in London to recruit any officers who wanted to serve as mercenaries in South America. The response was overwhelming. An officer named Gustavus Mathius Hippisley – who, like most officers, was chafing under a half-pay army pension – immediately came forward with an officer corps ready to form a regiment of hussars in Venezuela. They were followed by three more regiments of cavalry officers, one of rifles and an artillery unit – 1,000 soldiers in all.

Alarmed by the potential exodus, the British government decreed that any departure was prohibited. On learning the news, Hippisley ordered that the boats would leave immediately – weighing anchor so quickly, in fact, that many recruits were left behind. Although it departed unmolested, the flotilla hit a storm in the Channel and one of the troop ships was wrecked on the French coast, drowning 200 recruits.

The 800 who made it to the New World found themselves stranded in the British Antilles for months waiting for their arms. Tropical diseases hit, followed by massive desertions, and only 240 made it to Angostura (now Ciudad Bolívar) in Venezuela. They were immediately despatched to join Bolívar's army in the steaming *llanos,* where they took part in the battle of Samán. Hippisley arrived some time later, but fell out with Bolívar and soon returned to England.

Despite this inauspicious start, officers and soldiers arrived from Britain in a steady stream until the British government finally stopped the flow in August 1819. Historians estimate that some 6,500 set out for South America and 5,300 arrived. The bulk were English, although there was a battalion of Scottish highlanders and a separate "Irish Legion".

In spite of being on the winning side, very few of the British Legion would survive the gruelling years of war. The major killer was not weaponry but disease: soldiers succumbed to everything from malaria to typhoid.

The so-called "Albion Battalion", composed mostly of English soldiers, fought with distinction in Venezuela, at the battle of Boyacá in Colombia and beneath the volcano of Pichincha in Ecuador before being disbanded in 1822 for lack of numbers. The First Venezuelan Rifles continued to march with Bolívar through the royalist stronghold of Lima and up into the *altiplano* of Peru, where it took part in the climactic battle of Ayacucho in 1824.

The Irish contingents performed less gloriously; one group surrendered to the royalists and was executed *en masse,* others mutinied on Isla Margarita, seized boats and fled to Jamaica. Yet one Irishman, General Daniel O'Leary, stayed in South America and became one of Bolívar's most trusted confidantes, staying by the Liberator's side until his dying moments. He then wrote a 34-volume memoir, which remains the most important source of information on Bolívar's life. ❑

LEFT: contemporary drawing of a patriot in Bolívar's liberation army.

of modern Colombia, Venezuela and Ecuador, and a cornerstone of Bolívar's plan – was cracking up. The *llanero* Páez planned to lead Venezuela to secede. Bolívar rushed back to Caracas and patched up the confederation, but it was doomed. Local interests were too strong.

Even so, Bolívar spent the last years of his life vainly staving off the inevitable. Wracked by tuberculosis, his disillusion took on a tragic dimension (brilliantly captured by the Colombian writer Gabriel García Márquez in his novel *The General in his Labyrinth*). One by one, his supporters turned against him, and his only possible successor, Marshal Sucre, was assassi-

decades of Latin American history. "America is ungovernable," he declared. "Those who serve the revolution plow the sea. The only thing to do in America is emigrate."

Repairing the ruin

For most Venezuelans, nominal independence was secured in 1821. But Venezuela had fragmented into regions controlled by *caudillos* (strongmen) and there would be another 10 years of fighting before the country was more or less under stable rule.

Although the country remained a part of La Gran Colombia for several years out of defer-

ABOVE: the remains of Bolívar in the Panteón Nacional in Caracas.

nated on a mountain highway. In Colombia, Bolívar escaped another assassination attempt only by leaping out of his bedroom window. In his home country, Venezuela, he was finally outlawed as a traitor. Jeered at in the streets by the same people who had cheered him a few short years before, the general left Bogotá for exile in Europe, but never made it. He died in 1830, almost penniless, in the small town of Santa Marta on the Colombian coast.

Shortly before his death, Bolívar penned a bitter prophecy that has echoed through the

ence to Bolívar, Páez finally declared the sovereignty of Venezuela in 1829. A Congress was convened in Valencia on May 6, 1830, which conferred Páez with leadership of the Republic, ordered the expulsion of Bolívar from the territory of La Gran Colombia and, on September 22, approved the Constitution of Venezuela, which left it definitely separated from Colombia. The new country of Venezuela began the process of reconstruction.

By any reckoning, the independence wars had been devastating: at least 150,000 Venezuelans died in the fighting; working *haciendas* were destroyed; roads and bridges were in disrepair; livestock numbers had fallen from 4.5

million head to about 250,000. The treasury was bankrupt, and the new administration survived only on a high-interest British loan. Others besides Bolívar were beginning to wonder what it had all been for. The basic colonial social structure was still intact.

Bolívar had honored his promise to divide the lands of royalists among the *llaneros* and other veterans, on a sliding scale of size from generals down to foot-soldiers. But in a process that foreshadowed a history of failed land reform in Latin America, the impoverished soldiers sold out their smaller shares to the officers at a fraction of the real cost. The old white land-

ultimately lead to the extermination of the privileged classes." Male *blancos* tied the vote to owning property, kept important military posts and controlled everything from the presidency to the most obscure local municipal offices.

Years of chaos

The rest of the 19th century was a complicated morass of coups, civil wars and separatist movements. To some extent all these involved arguments among the white elite over who would control and profit from foreign trade. The chief participants were the educated *caraqueño* bureaucrats and a series of rougher *caudillos*

owning elite gained some new members, mostly white officers, whose descendants own much of Venezuelan agriculture to this day. Otherwise, their power was unbroken. Meanwhile, slavery continued to exist. Bolívar had freed his own slaves, but only a handful of other landowners followed suit.

It was only in the 1850s that they decided that slavery was actually unprofitable, and that slaves could be kept tied to plantations by making them nominally free but charging exorbitant rents. The mixed blooded *pardos* were also kept out of positions of power. Even Bolívar had dreaded the prospect of *pardocracia*, or rule by the colored masses, which he said "will

CAUDILLO WITH A CAUSE

The most famous caudillo was Simón Bolívar's old ally, the *llanero* José Antonio Páez. From 1830 to 1848 he established a modicum of order in Venezuela, hunting down bandits, crushing rebellions and, when he was not president himself, choosing exactly who should rule. The illiterate plainsman of old remained a figure in local politics until the 1860s, when he was finally exiled to die in New York City, far from his native world. Even so, Páez gave Venezuela a chance to rebuild some of its former prosperity – largely thanks to the coffee boom – and he gave it enough stability to survive the upheavals that would occur in the next generations.

who commanded armed bands left over from the wars of independence.

The legacy of two decades of brutality was that might was right in the politics of Venezuela. As in several other South American countries, the ruling elite split into two factions that called themselves the Liberals and the Conservatives – although, rather like the Republican and Democratic parties in the modern United States, their differences were more about the fine tuning of government than any serious social change. Transfers of power between the two groups occurred in violent fashion, but any hint of an uprising by *pardos* or blacks was met with ruthless, united action.

The Liberals and the Conservatives plunged Venezuela into five years of civil war after a period of economic decline in the 1850s. In theory, the argument was about whether Venezuela should have a federal system or be controlled directly from Caracas, but although the Liberal-Federalists had won by 1863, regional revolts and battles continued for decades.

Despite the turmoil, some changes were occurring. Most noticeably, the city of Caracas was growing farther apart from the rest of the country. With its direct links to the outside world, the capital became increasingly affluent and cosmopolitan: its streets, buildings and the dress of its educated bureaucrats mimicked the styles of Europe.

A change had even taken place in the popular view toward Simón Bolívar, who was rehabilitated in the eyes of history, and his personality cult began as a symbol of national unity. In 1842, the Liberator's remains were brought back to Caracas from Colombia and installed in a national pantheon; statues of Bolívar were erected all around the country; and Venezuela's first national currency was set up in 1879 – the bolívar.

Birth of a nation

As the 19th century stumbled to a close, the old regional *caudillo* style of politics looked increasingly outdated. Presidents could no longer be earthy and charismatic men with enough guns to fight their way to the top, but were expected to have professional credentials.

More importantly, the president was increasingly able to impose his will on the rest of the country. The central government in Caracas began to build up its armed forces and equip them with modern weapons, against which the smaller *caudillos* could no longer compete. Newly introduced communications, such as the telegraph and railroad, ensured that they could no longer plot in secrecy.

Naturally, few *caudillos* accepted these changes lying down, and the 1890s were a particularly chaotic period of regional uprisings. Eccentric presidents such as Joaquín Crespo – who built the elegant Palacio de Miraflores in

Caracas, complete with an iron-plated, earthquake-resistant bedroom – still made it to the presidency. The haphazard style of a successor, Cipriano Castro, led to such serious economic problems that the government defaulted on its European loans. Then, as today, debt default was considered the most heinous of economic crimes. In 1902–3, England, Germany and Italy began a naval blockade of Venezuela to make it pay up.

The era of the regional *caudillos* was finally coming to an end. With the discovery of oil in the early 20th century, a new technocratic president, Juan Vicente Gómez, would fling the country headlong into the modern age. ❑

LEFT: European-style buildings sprang up in Caracas during the late 19th century.
RIGHT: loyal troops during the civil wars.

THE OIL RUSH

The discovery of oil in Venezuela resulted in a boom which was to change the political and economic face of the country – not always for the better

The first Spanish explorers to land on the sun-scorched shores of Lake Maracaibo noted a thick black oil oozing from the sandy earth. Local indians used the sticky liquid to caulk their canoes; it could be made into candles, spread to trap animals and even used as a medicine. But for the Spaniards it held no interest, and for the next 400 years nobody but the indians gave the oil a second thought.

By the turn of the 20th century, the invention of the motor car had given this black fluid new value. Even so, at first Venezuelans were not enthusiastic about the costly task of crude oil extraction. Explorations around Lake Maracaibo were desultory: a few small wells were dug, a pipeline and tiny refinery built, but nobody expected much from the discoveries.

Then, in December 1922, a Venezuelan subsidiary of Shell restarted drilling at a well named Los Barrosos No. 2, near the sleepy village of La Rosa on the east coast of Lake Maracaibo. Four years earlier, drilling had been suspended in disappointment at a depth of 164 meters (538 ft). But this time the well "blew out": on the first day of drilling 100,000 barrels of oil spurted from the earth, eclipsing the entire previous Venezuelan production of 8,000 barrels a day.

A country transformed

The find was dubbed the Bolívar Coastal Field, and it made immediate world news.

For Venezuela, oil was like manna from heaven. Petrodollars would change the country's face forever, bringing to an end generations of stagnation and giving Venezuela the highest per capita income in Latin America. In what one writer dubbed "a compression of historical time," Venezuela was transformed by the 1960s from an agricultural society characterized by political chaos to a consumerist and relatively stable democracy.

PRECEDING PAGES: oil towers on Lake Maracaibo.
LEFT: the discovery of oil in the 1920s transformed Venezuela.
RIGHT: dictator Juan Vicente Gómez.

In the two years after that well's discovery, some 73 different foreign companies flocked to Lake Maracaibo to begin exploration, encouraged by the promise of enormous profits with minimal taxes. The skilled workers were mostly from the United States, the hired muscle Venezuelan. In a remarkably short time hard-

bitten engineers from Texas and Oklahoma had carved oil empires from the wilderness.

In the initial years of exploration, conditions were appalling: the lakeside was either virgin rainforest or bleak desert. Imported heavy equipment was unloaded on the docks of Maracaibo – with 75,000 inhabitants, by far the largest town in the area – and taken in small sailboats to the eastern shore. From there, machinery could only be dragged by oxen and mules to the oil sites, with workers following on foot.

Soon, more sophisticated oil camps were set up. The fields were fenced off and even had their own police. Makeshift towns sprouted from nowhere along the lake's shore, with all the hallmarks of a "black gold" rush: bars and brothels outnumbered food stores ten to one, and fortunes were gambled or drunk away overnight.

Techniques were quickly invented for off-shore drilling on Lake Maracaibo. Hundreds of towers soon appeared, forming a floating steel forest. These towers no longer function, but with their ghostly flames they are still one of the most vivid images the world has of Venezuela.

The iron fist

The oil boom coincided with the dictatorship of Juan Vicente Gómez, whose brutal 27-year rule marked Venezuela irrevocably and set the

Cipriano Castro to travel to Europe for a medical operation before declaring him an outlaw and seizing the presidency. Gómez quickly turned the army into his personal Praetorian Guard, with loyal officers from Andean states given positions of favor. For the more subtle tasks of social control a secret police was formed to track down anyone who plotted against or even bad-mouthed the dictator.

Having built this vast, corrupt apparatus of control, Gómez moved from Caracas – whose European pretensions he never felt comfortable with – to a cattle ranch in nearby Maracay. From there he could pronounce the major

scene for the country as it is today. In many ways, Gómez fits the classic caricature of a Latin American dictator. An ex-cattle rancher and accountant from the Andean state of Táchira, he was a colorless and taciturn figure who ran Venezuela like a latter-day Roman emperor. The country was treated like a private *hacienda*; its inhabitants like peons who needed to be looked after like children. The Gómez political philosophy was not complex: trusted friends and relatives would be given positions of power and wealth; enemies, real or suspected, were hunted down, tortured, exiled or murdered.

In 1908, having risen through the army to the rank of general, Gómez advised President

decisions of Venezuela's fate, while allowing the bureaucrats of Caracas to look after the day-to-day details of government. Civilian ministers, foreign diplomats and heads of local businesses all made the journey out to this rural outpost, begging cap in hand for the favors of the surly patriarch.

The carnival king

With Venezuela firmly under his control, Gómez greeted the news of the 1922 oil boom in typical imperial style. As the Uruguayan writer Eduardo Galeano has described it: "While black geysers spouted on all sides, Gómez took petroleum shares from his bursting pockets to reward his friends, relations and courtiers, the doctor who looked after his prostate, the generals who served as his bodyguard, the poets who sang his praises and the archbishop who gave him a special dispensation to eat meat on Good Friday."

Lavish tax concessions to US oil companies meant that the Venezuelan government received only some 7 percent of the total oil profits from 1919 to Gómez's death in 1935. Even so, the money had fallen from the skies as far as Venezuelans were concerned and – to a government accustomed to surviving on minimal local taxation – it seemed like a fortune. Roads, housing and port facilities were built, while the city of Caracas began the modernization that would wipe out its colonial past forever.

Local entrepreneurs jumped on the development bandwagon and made themselves rich, creating a Venezuelan middle class. The bolívar remained strong throughout the Great Depression, and Venezuelans began to appear in the salons of Paris and jewelry shops of New York.

Not surprisingly, everyone wanted a piece of the action. Rural peasants flocked to the burgeoning oil camps and suburbs of Caracas to pick up work. Landowners gave up their farms so they could indulge in the lucrative trade of brokering the sale of drilling rights from the State to US companies. Agriculture declined rapidly and there was no hope of starting up a manufacturing industry: Venezuela was importing everything from beans to refrigerators.

Autumn of the patriarch

Sealed up in his remote cattle ranch, overcome by illness and senility, Gómez began to suspect his closest allies of betrayal and a new rank of secret police thugs was brought to power in the struggle. The military watched the wretched spectacle of the president's last years, biding its time until it could gain more control.

When word finally leaked from Maracay in 1935 that the patriarch was dead, riots erupted around Venezuela. Thousands of *caraqueños* flocked into the streets to celebrate the autocrat's demise, sacking the houses of the most hated *gomecistas*, and, where possible, lynching them from telegraph poles. The military was too busy getting a new government ready

to protect the old figures – having regarded them with some contempt anyway – and tacit permission was given to purge the country.

The Gómez decades had transformed Venezuela, but they also left a curious void: the dictator's brutal repression had wiped out all previous political traditions and there was hardly anyone left capable of running the country. Thousands of exiles who had been living in Europe and the United States began returning to Caracas, to be greeted by avalanches of flowers and emotional reunions in the docks and airports.

The most famous and capable group were known as "the Generation of '28." As students,

they had led a great anti-Gómez riot in 1928 which resulted in their wholesale exile. Now they came back with a vision for Venezuela.

It was now that many Venezuelans accepted the idea that their country could and should take its place in the First World. Modernity became a national obsession, and the national model would be the United States.

Gómez's Minister of War, Eleazar López Contreras, assumed the presidency, proclaimed a new constitution and declared that he would lead the way to the democratic future. New institutions, including a central bank, were created along with laws giving Venezuela slightly more control of its oil wealth. Some indirect

LEFT: young bohemians in Caracas.
RIGHT: a chic matron promenading.

elections were allowed, and the Generation of '28 figures formed a political party called Acción Democrática (AD). López's successor, Isaías Medina Angarita, used the need for oil in World War II to guarantee Venezuela a 30 percent share of the oil company's profits.

Period of upheaval

This slow process of reform came to an abrupt end in 1945, when the Generation of '28 leaders in AD convinced a group of young military officers to stage a coup. Having seen the fall of fascism in Europe, intellectuals in Venezuela felt that the time had come for drastic action

than politician. Too many changes were pushed through, without popular support. Reformers misjudged the traditional sectors of Venezuelan society, and failed to notice that the military officers who had led the coup of 1945 had no intention of being left out of power.

In 1948, a military junta seized power in a bloodless coup, sent the novelist-president into exile and set about undoing most of the reforms of the previous 13 years.

Chief among the young bloods now in power was General Marcos Pérez Jiménez. This ruthless manipulator took over as president in 1952 after holding an election and

against the autocrats of the south. Some 2,500 people died in bitter fighting during the coup, mostly in the streets of Caracas, but Medina Angarita stepped down. To this day, the AD decision stirs heated debate in Venezuela: the coup eventually ushered in a moment of democratic rule, but was followed by a right-wing backlash that brought on the harshest dictatorships the country has ever known.

A junta now forced through the reforms needed to change Venezuelan society to an ideal image. Free elections were held, and the famous novelist Rómulo Gallegos became president. Unfortunately, the author of *La Rebelión* and *Doña Bárbara* proved a better writer

declaring it void when it looked as if he might lose. In a throwback to the Gómez days, secret police once again patrolled the streets of Caracas in search of the regime's opponents – only this time they could use modern phone taps, radio surveillance and electric cattle prods in the pursuit of their goals. Any union action or student demonstration was immediately crushed. AD leaders went into exile, and the party survived in hiding despite torture, assassinations and jailings.

Strikes by oil workers were now a thing of the past, and US companies such as Standard Oil were pleased in 1954 to receive tax cuts of US$300 million. Despite his brutality, Pérez

Jiménez became a staunch ally of the United States: in the same year as the tax cuts, he was the first to recognize a CIA overthrow of the elected government of Guatemala. The regime had become the most feared and hated in Venezuelan history when US President Eisenhower awarded Pérez Jiménez the Legion of Honor.

Still, the oil money was flowing more freely than ever and Pérez Jiménez began a program with the 1984-style title "New National Ideal" for the "conquest of the physical environment." Huge public works, including six-lane highways in Caracas, the giant Humboldt Hotel, high-rise office buildings and sumptuous clubs for military officers began to spread across the Venezuelan landscape. Corruption went hand in hand with the construction.

The regime seemed increasingly clumsy and capricious. When Pérez Jiménez finally held a plebiscite in 1958 – and again rigged the result – Venezuelans had had enough. Riots and a general strike led to the general packing his bags full of US dollars and boarding his private jet to Miami.

The new era

Venezuelans now had a second chance of forming a democracy, and this time the older, more moderate political leaders opted for slow reform. One of the Generation of '28, Rómulo Betancourt, became president in 1959 at the head of an AD government, starting a democratic era that has survived to the present.

During the 1960s, a succession of governments guided the country through threats by right-wing military officers and a left-wing guerrilla operation, but at the end of the decade stability was assured. As a major oil producer, Venezuela began taking its role on the world stage: in 1960, it took the lead in forming the international oil cartel, OPEC. Venezuela joined the Andean pact and formed a regional common market with its neighbors – although a long-standing border conflict with Guyana took the country to the brink of war.

Oil money poured in throughout the 1970s in ever greater sums. Taxes were raised so that Venezuela received nearly 70 percent of foreign oil revenues, and the Arab oil embargo of 1973 brought Venezuela a US$50 billion windfall.

Much of the money was used by President Carlos Andrés Pérez to nationalize industries from natural gas to iron, until finally oil production was taken over. Compensation was provided and the transition went smoothly. Soon a "Venezuelization" of oil company jobs would ensure that some nine tenths of the employees were locally born. Yet even at this time of surplus, things were going awry. The middle class was drunk on oil money; everyone else intoxicated by the thought of one day getting some. Few pondered what would happen when the hangover hit. ❑

LEFT: a petrol refinery built in the 1970s, at the height of the boom.
RIGHT: drumming up business: oil products at Paraguaná Peninsula.

A NATION ON THE BRINK

Uruguayan writer Eduardo Galeano observed in the mid-1970s: "Caracas chews gum and loves synthetic products and canned foods; it never walks and poisons the clean air... with the fumes of its motorization; its fever to buy, consume, obtain, spend, use, get hold of everything leaves no time for sleep. From surrounding hillside hovels made of garbage, half a million forgotten people observe the sybaritic scene. The gilded city's avenues glitter with hundreds of thousands of late-model cars, but in the consuming society, not everyone consumes. According to the census, half of Venezuela's children and youngsters do not go to school."

AFTER THE BOOM

The dramatic fluctuations in the country's economic fortunes over the past 30 years have left it still seeking to fulfil its potential

Since the 1970s, Venezuela has gone from being South America's richest nation to a nouveau-poor society in search of a new identity. Once known as the Saudis of the West, Venezuelans have seen their economic fortunes decline in exact proportion to the general fall in world oil prices. Even so, Venezuela's many problems were hidden from view until relatively recently, when austerity measures heralded the sort of economic crisis so painfully familiar to other Latin American countries. Runaway inflation, currency devaluations and violent riots have marked this new phase in Venezuelan history to which the country is still trying hard to adjust.

"Saudi Venezuela"

Venezuelans still live with the memories of the oil boom years, which began in earnest with the nationalization of the petroleum industry in 1976 and ended with a crash in 1983. The government coffers overflowed with revenues. Although a good deal was spirited away by corrupt politicians, some trickled down in the form of scholarships to study abroad, loans for small businesses, or jobs created by an expanding government bureaucracy, which would itself become a major factor in the impending fiscal crisis.

These were the days when middle-class Venezuelans grew accustomed to regular shopping trips to Miami, leaving Caracas with empty suitcases that returned packed with designer clothes, home appliances, gourmet foods and even titles to property in south Florida. Venezuelans became known as big spenders, their slogan the refrain, *Es barato, dáme dos* ("It's cheap, I'll take two").

Where consumer goods had been concerned, the word "imported" became synonymous with "quality" and "national" (domestic) with "inferior quality". One of the richest agricultural

LEFT: unionists march to protest against austerity measures in Caracas.

RIGHT: skyscrapers and sculpture in modern Caracas.

producers during colonial times, Venezuela was importing more than 70 percent of its food by 1983. National productivity at all levels was practically nil.

World oil prices began to slide in 1982, but Venezuelans did not feel the effect until February 18, 1983, a date now recalled as "Black

Friday." Alarmed by a capital flight which had reached almost $200 million a week, the government of President Luis Herrera Campins imposed exchange controls and devalued the mighty bolívar, which had remained stable for more than a decade and was widely regarded as the blue-chip Latin currency.

The devaluation more than doubled the price of the US dollar. For most Venezuelans, this meant no more shopping trips to Miami and a general restriction of the opulent lifestyle which many had come to accept as their birthright. Not surprisingly, Venezuelans decided to "kill the messenger" and determinedly threw the government out in the next elections.

The more populist Acción Democrática (AD) party won the election that followed despite the lackluster presidential campaign of Jaime Lusinchi, a physician by training. He maneuvered his way through the deepening crisis with measures designed to maintain social peace and bolster his rating in the polls. Inflation was kept in check by controlled consumer prices.

Industry enjoyed a preferential exchange rate (which boosted corruption with everyone seeking cheap dollars) for raw materials and spare parts, keeping factories going and the unemployment rate down – but at the cost of burning up the country's foreign reserves.

A VENEZUELAN EVITA

The affair of president Jamie Lusinchi with his secretary is considered by many to be the most shameful scandal in the country's history. Blanca Ibáñez came from an impoverished family in the Andes, and sought to create an influential place for herself in Venezuela, comparable to that of Eva Perón in Argentina. With none of Evita's charisma or media appeal, Ibáñez could only emulate her role as official distributor of government largesse to the poor. "Blanquita" often played the role of first lady at presidential functions, ruffling the feathers of diplomats and protocol officials. Inspite of her efforts, her popularity was practically nil, except among those who admired her audacity.

Lusinchi's administration was sullied by the scandal arising from his much-publicized affair with his personal secretary, Blanca Ibáñez. This affair also caused a rift within Acción Democrática when the president unsuccessfully tried to muscle a place for Ibáñez on the party's 1988 election slates, an action which subjected him and the country to ridicule.

Further fueling the scandal, Lusinchi's wife applied for a divorce despite the pleas of image-conscious party leaders to at least wait until her husband's term of office was over.

With soap opera flair, Lusinchi and Ibáñez got married when his term in office ended and, when charges of massive misuse of government power and funds were filed against them, skipped to Florida.

The rise and fall of "El Gocho"

Lusinchi's successor proved to be somewhat in the same mold: Carlos Andrés Pérez swept into office on a wave of popularity, with a long-time lover on the side (although with a smidge more discretion), and exited under a cloud of accusations of corruption.

Pérez has been an undeniable headline-maker in Venezuela's modern democratic history. He was born on a coffee hacienda in Táchira state, which has produced a regular crop of Venezuela's leaders. Known as "El Gocho", a nickname for natives of the Andes, he was the mastermind behind Venezuela's oil and iron nationalization during his first term of presidency 1974–79. In 1988, he won the mandate again – and immediately set about undoing reforms achieved during his first term in office.

Pérez drew up a privatization plan for state companies, followed by a harsh adjustment program to win approval and much needed credits from the International Monetary Fund. Price controls were removed from most consumer goods, causing the inflation rate to soar. Subsidies were cut from state-produced goods and services, including gasoline, electricity, and water. A floating exchange rate was introduced for the bolívar, which drove the dollar price and cost of imports to new highs.

The economic shock treatment provoked a popular uprising unlike anything in Venezuela's modern history. On February 27, 1989, triggered by an increase of public transport prices (more a last straw than the sole cause) a wave of wholesale looting and burning of property in key cities swept across the country. The uprising was brought brutally to an end as the government suspended constitutional guarantees, clamped on a curfew, and sent in the army. Order was restored but not before hundreds had been senselessly killed, as soldiers fired without asking questions.

Even with the trauma of the February 27 riots, Pérez reaffirmed his commitment to the economic plan. The country fell into a deep recession and he ran into problems with his own party, but he stood firm and, as the program progressed, signs of economic recovery appeared. Public finances were put in order, and the deficit was reduced. A 53 percent growth in non-oil exports took place in 1989 as the government weaned the country away from its oil habit.

In 1990, Venezuela got an unexpected boost from the Persian Gulf Crisis with an extra US$4 billion in oil income. Instead of easing off, Pérez kept up the push towards a free-market economy – difficult to swallow for people who had lived under protectionist regimes for decades.

Hoping to play on continuing public unrest over Pérez's economic measures, military insurgents mounted two coup attempts in 1992. The first was on February 4, with the most visible leader, Commandant Hugo Chávez Frías; the other, on November 27, by a disorganized group of Air Force rebels. Neither mustered the anticipated support from the masses, who were still licking their wounds from the 1989 riots which had not brought change, but loss of property and lives.

However, rather than another overthrow attempt, it was a different problem that brought Pérez down. On May 20, 1993 he was indicted by the Supreme Court for alleged embezzlement and/or misuse of 250 million bolívars (then worth around US$7 million). On May 21, the Senate suspended him from office pending the outcome of his trial and, in June, elected Ramón José Velásquez as interim president until Pérez's term ended in February 1994. Pérez was convicted, and served two years confined to his house (instead of prison, due to his

age – 70). Yet another president involved in extramarital liaisons, Pérez subsequently left his wife to take up with his mistress, Cecila Matos. New charges were later pressed against the two for having secret accounts where the absconded funds were supposedly funneled.

From one crisis to another

On January 13, 1994, focus shifted from political to financial woes when Banco Latino, Venezuela's second largest bank, closed. On January 17, the government took it over. Despite huge injections of funds to shore up other banks on shaky ground and assure cus-

tomers there was no cause to worry, all was for naught. When the dust finally settled at the end of 1995, the number of financial institutions in the country had been reduced by one third. Commercial banks that failed represented 46 percent of total deposits. By May 1994 alone, estimates were that it had already cost Fogade (the national deposit guarantee fund) the equivalent of 132 percent of Venezuela's oil income for that year – yet many depositors would never see their money again.

Rafael Caldera, president from 1969 to 1974, won re-election, taking office in February 1994 aged 78. Despite initial optimism, the country was sent reeling and investor confidence

---

LEFT: the Paseo de los Próceres, a monument to Venezuela's heroes, in Caracas.
RIGHT: modern politician: Irene Sáez went from being Miss Universe to 1998 presidential candidate.

plummeted with his policies: suspension of economic guarantees, 66 percent devaluation of the bolívar, exchange controls, return of price controls, a 1,000 percent increase overnight in gasoline prices, causing chaos for budgets and predictable downstream inflationary effects.

A brief respite and renewed enthusiasm came with the "Petroleum Opening", initiated with the formation of strategic associations in 1994 and, in 1996, with the genuine opening through the public auction of marginal fields which brought some US$245 million in additional revenue to the nation's depleted coffers as companies around the world clamored at the

opportunity. This marked the first time since nationalization two decades earlier that foreign companies were allowed to search for Venezuelan oil.

On April 22, 1996, control measures were lifted. Prices soared. Coupled with continuing monstrous internal debt and minimal reduction of bloated government payrolls, inflation hit 103 percent in 1996. Meanwhile, the value of the bolívar (and Venezuelans' purchasing power) continued on a downhill slide.

Although a new economic plan, privatizations, and the sale of many properties inherited during the banking crisis, were initially viewed as steps in the right direction, Caldera's eco-

nomic plan did not achieve desired effects. A budget based on unrealistically high projections for oil prices (that never materialized but instead hit in fact, historic lows), coupled with failure to reduce the bureaucracy and its associated costs were major factors leading to a grave economic crisis.

By 1997, the middle class had all but disappeared, with an incredible 90.5 percent of the population living below the poverty level (67.8 percent considered at a level of extreme poverty) according to official statistics. Frustrations of professionals unable to purchase basic items (much less reach their dream of owning a home or car) led to a wave of strikes by public sector staff, including doctors, teachers and administrators, who demanded a living wage.

A hint of dictatorship

This situation, in turn, unleashed political uncertainty. Recognizing that a major part of the population was fed up with the deteriorating economic situation and negative effects of budget cutbacks on basic services under recent traditional political regimes, former coup leader Hugo Chávez Frías threw his red beret into the ring for the 1998 presidential elections, promising revolutionary changes. His proposal met with a degree of enthusiasm that surprised and frightened national and international investors.

Without a doubt, Chávez gained a great deal of support simply because of events which were occurring as he was promising to make sweeping changes: public hospital physicians were on an extended strike across the nation, demanding a living wage (with the average monthly salary for a surgeon only a miserable US$500) and adequately supplied hospitals. Meanwhile, military doctors and fire department paramedics were attending emergencies in campaign tents. Most state schools did not re-open for the new school year because classrooms were in ruins. And the government was announcing that yet another sweeping budget cut was to be made.

Not only were major projects put on hold, but capital flight became monumental as speeches by Chávez alluding to dictatorial power became more frequent. Chávez went on to win the presidency, nevertheless, although his party, the Movimiento de la 5a República, did not gain an overall majority. ❑

LEFT: LA gear in Caracas.

Politics of Patronage

One of Venezuela's greatest achievements has been to maintain a functioning democracy for more than three decades. It has survived a serious leftist guerrilla threat in the 1960s and the nationwide popular uprising of February 1989, two coup attempts and the ousting of a president on charges of corruption. Venezuelans are, quite rightly, proud of their democracy. But democracy has also turned Venezuela into a highly politicized society in which the principal parties have an extraordinary influence on people's lives.

A Venezuelan's party loyalty affects everything from the awarding of government contracts or promotions in business to entry into a private club or professorships at the university. A card identifying a citizen as a member of the ruling party can even help him or her to negotiate a traffic violation or jump to the front of the line at a government office.

The asphyxiating influence of the parties is due to a certain extent to the tremendous power of the central government in doling out patronage. Until recently, the president appointed all state governors and was empowered to dictate economic policy by decree, without consulting Congress. Meanwhile, congressional figures can act as patrons themselves.

And, since the electoral system still requires the voter to select all the congressional candidates on one party's slate, without being able to pick and choose each one, everyone down to the most minor official ends up being an apparatchik from the ruling party – with little or no sense of responsibility to the voters.

The National Institute Ports of (INP), recently privatized, was a perfect example of patronage and the influence of parties on public sector employment. In 1979, at the end of the first administration of President Carlos Andrés Pérez, the INP had 3,000 workers, almost all of them from the governing Acción Democrática party. After COPEI presidential candidate Luis Herrera Campins took office, the INP's workforce was doubled with the addition of 3,000 workers, all *Copeyanos*.

This procedure continued during the next two presidential terms. By the time the government finally got around to privatizing the ports, the INP had 14,000 workers, and it was forced to admit that some 60 percent of them were unnecessary.

With the change, in Puerto Cabello, for example, which handles 77 percent of Venezuela's commercial cargo, in the first year after privatization, payrolls were slashed from 5,300 workers to 170, and efficiency and income soared. Privatization has helped to reduce bloated payrolls in these few entities, but where it is really needed – namely, in the public sector – no politician worried about future votes wants to be associated with unemployment.

Venezuelans have begun to rebel against this system and the injustices it provokes. The first direct elections for state governors and municipal offices were held in December 1989; a year and a half later, President Pérez relinquished absolute

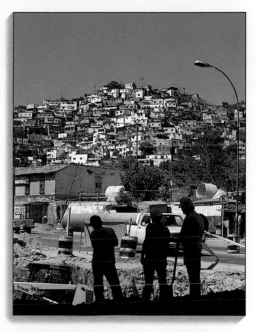

presidential power over economic policy. An electoral reform movement is now seeking to abolish the system of party slates and replace it with voting for each individual candidate.

Another encouraging feature has been the emergence of neighborhood civic associations (*asociaciones de vecinos*) which try to do for their communities what corrupt and inefficient government entities do not: fix potholes, guard against crime, and prevent new construction in areas where it is not legal. The neighborhood associations are taken seriously by the government and are seen as a way to circumvent local politics – getting basic services performed no matter what party card the neighborhood might be carrying. ❑

RIGHT: building for prosperity.

THE VENEZUELANS

The country's people are predominantly young and urban. Can they preserve their traditions against the pervasive culture of the United States?

To casual visitors, Venezuelans seem to import culture wholesale from the United States. There is little evidence of Venezuelan history in the public buildings; few signs of the indigenous cultures so prominent elsewhere in Latin America. Instead, Venezuelan radios blare a steady output of rock and reggae. Young people sport designer jeans and T-shirts with slogans in English. The impression is of a place trying hard to be like southern Florida but which has managed only to approximate the climate.

This attraction to the United States is even reflected in sport, as Venezuela is the only country on the South American continent where baseball is more popular than soccer.

All this may lead one to ask – where is the real Venezuela? The answer is, this is it: an overwhelmingly young, urbanized society, with a dwindling middle class, whose eyes are constantly fixed northward; a country in permanent, frantic motion, eating fast food and drinking its coffee from disposable plastic cups; a country that has lived through a debauch of fabulous wealth which it can't quite believe is over, despite the cold shower of austerity doled out in recent years.

City folks, country ways

Yet this Americanization of Venezuelan society is a relatively recent occurrence. Indeed, few of the world's countries have changed so much in such a short time as Venezuela, thanks to the discovery of oil. From a poor, isolated, agricultural nation that was the fiefdom of successive dictators, it was transformed within the space of a few decades into the consumerist, high-tech society that visitors see now: one with a democratic government and the trappings – if not always the benefits – of development.

PRECEDING PAGES: folk musicians in the Andes; vendors at the Caracas bus terminal.
LEFT: a face in the country.
RIGHT: a businessman wearing the *liqui-liqui* – traditional Venezuelan dress.

It has all happened so quickly that Venezuelan society is still endeavoring to keep up with the changes – leading to an often bewildering array of traditional and modern traits.

Venezuela today is the most urbanized nation in Latin America, with 83 percent of its 23.2 million people living in a handful of big cities.

Yet Venezuelans persist in a surprisingly rural lifestyle. They rise early, often before dawn, and are usually required to be at their jobs by 8am. Workers take two hours off at midday, during which time they are likely to return home for lunch. This routine may be logical for rural workers avoiding the noonday sun, but in a city the size of Caracas or Maracaibo it creates four traffic jams a day instead of two.

And while Venezuelans are surrounded by skyscrapers and high technology, they often display a surprising lack of sophistication. Even the telephone, which has been in use in Venezuela for decades, is an instrument to which many people seem unaccustomed. Telephone callers are regarded with suspicion unless they are known personally.

Facing up to change

Obviously, Venezuela hasn't quite shaken off its long history as a poor farming country largely isolated from the outside world. Only a few generations ago, it was a nation with a small population, few roads and little overall national coherence.

This meant that Venezuela developed as a fragmented rural country with strong regional

TRAVEL BY MULE

As recently as 1945, the journey from Caracas to the German immigrant town of Colonia Tovar (a distance of only 38 km/23 miles) had to be made on muleback.

tile roofs" had all but vanished. The city's shape reflected the new Venezuelan society: a high-tech heart of glass skyscrapers; luxury apartments of the burgeoning suburbs; and a ring of slums for the growing number of Venezuelans unable to get a slice of the country's wealth.

Adolescent nation

Meanwhile, Venezuela is a young country. Some 67 percent of Venezuelans are under 30 years old and 39 percent under 14. Only 6 percent are over the age of

identities. Everything was upset when oil wealth hit in the 1920s. Agriculture was no longer important, and there was massive migration from the country to the cities. During the period from 1936 to 1971, the rural-to-urban population ratio turned around completely: a quarter of Venezuela's people lived in cities during the 1930s, but by the 1970s that proportion had changed to three-quarters.

The velocity of change was nowhere more evident than in the capital city, Caracas. In 1945, Caracas had a quarter of a million inhabitants and only a few buildings more than two stories tall. Three decades later, the population had increased sevenfold, and the "city of red

60. As a result, Venezuelan culture is decidedly youth-orientated, as reflected in advertising and in the national passions for sport, beauty contests and other youthful pursuits.

At the same time, Venezuela has become a much more cosmopolitan nation. The vast majority of Venezuelans are *mestizos* – people whose descent mingles the blood of Spanish settlers with the indigenous peoples or African slaves. But after World War II, a wave of immigrants arrived from Europe and other parts of Latin America; Venezuela's last military dictatorships encouraged them to come in search of opportunities. Between 1948 and 1959, an estimated 412,500 immigrants entered

Venezuela, an almost indigestible number for a country that had fewer than 5 million inhabitants in the early 1950s.

The large number of first-generation Venezuelans has given rise to ethnic stereotypes: the Spanish taxi driver, usually a Galician (*Gallego*); the Portuguese grocery store or bakery owner; and the Italian car mechanic.

As well as Europeans, a large number of Chinese, and people from Middle Eastern countries, there are recent immigrants from nearby Latin American countries – especially Colombia, Ecuador and Peru. They came during the oil boom to work as laborers and domestics.

to one) but their influence is great. A small group of North American families have settled in Venezuela and founded successful businesses or industrial conglomerates. One case in point is the Phelps family, which owns Radio Caracas Televisión station and Aereotuy airlines.

The Americans who have come to Venezuela have, on the whole, been technocrats – oil industry engineers or executives with the multinationals. All have come to further their own interests but have nonetheless made contributions in terms of technology, science and culture. (For instance, the late patriarch of the Phelps family, William Phelps, was an

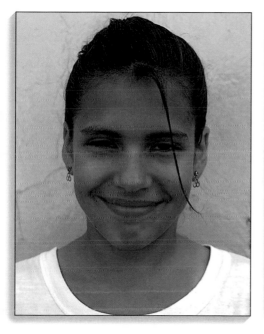

Blacks from Trinidad, Guyana, and other Caribbean countries also arrived at that time. Many of the poorer immigrants have returned home since the recent economic crisis hit, but a large number have stayed to raise families and take on Venezuelan citizenship.

Yankees, stay here!

As for North Americans, their numbers are few (European immigrants outnumber them by 50

ornithologist who wrote the definitive guide to Venezuelan birds. His widow, Kathy Deery Phelps, is an author, philanthropist and ardent environmentalist.)

Perhaps as a result, there is little in the way of resentment towards foreigners. The word *musiu*, a corruption of the French *monsieur*, which refers to a light-skinned foreigner, is not an insult. Similarly, Venezuela is racially tolerant, with marriage between *mestizos*, blacks and whites commonplace.

The only exception to this open-mindedness is the attitude towards the Colombians, Venezuela's poorer neighbors to the west, who have entered the country in large numbers, often

FAR LEFT: farmer in the Andean region of Mérida
LEFT: Guajira indian woman in Maracaibo.
ABOVE: a big grin on Isla Margarita.
RIGHT: Caracas vice.

illegally, since the oil boom days. Because the Colombians are generally acknowledged as hard workers and even their poor have usually benefitted from formal education, they are viewed with suspicion by poor Venezuelans, who see them as people who steal their jobs.

Defining "Venezuelan"

So, after all this, what are Venezuelans really like? Today's citizen might still be anyone from a barefoot cowboy in the *llanos* or a shop-owner in Caracas recently immigrated from Portugal; a high-powered oil industry executive in Maracaibo or a Yanomami indian

in the Amazon basin whose lifestyle has not changed a great deal from that of his forebears living thousands of years ago.

In general, Venezuelan society is unusually open, friendly and informal. Spanish speakers are sometimes surprised to note how quickly – often immediately – Venezuelans discard the polite *Usted* form of address and use the more familiar *tú*. To some, this is an excess of familiarity, behavior that borders on disrespect – especially when carried a step further, with men and women alike being addressed by people they have never even met before as "*mi amor*" (my love) – or some other equally affectionate greeting.

Venezuelans may seem exceedingly polite and unfailingly generous or hopelessly frivolous and maddeningly inconsistent. Friendships are struck up quickly but rarely last; people seem unwilling to take any relationship beyond the superficial level. On the other hand, someone with whom you have only a fleeting acquaintance will greet you effusively, as if you were a long-lost friend. Even among young Venezuelans who have been educated abroad or foreigners who have married into local families, deep-rooted cultural distinctions can be difficult to understand or overcome.

Superficial lifestyles

Unlike their southern neighbors the Argentines, who tend to psychoanalyze every conceivable issue, Venezuelans are little given to self-examination – a fact that may explain the surprising lack of literature about the country itself. Conversations often remain on the anecdotal level and people seem more comfortable with humor than serious topics.

Some Latin Americans regard Venezuela as a *nouveau riche* society where the prevailing norm is money without good taste. Others admire it for having maintained a democratic government during a period when almost every other South American nation was ruled by a military dictator.

Perhaps the dominant aspect of the Venezuelan mindset is its transitory view of life. Marriage, business, career, family, are all regarded as short-term concerns which could be here today, gone tomorrow. Venezuelans who invest in a business, for example, usually do so with the intention of making a quick profit and then selling out – something akin to buying a lottery ticket.

Women's role

Although Venezuela shares the cult of machismo with other Latin American countries, Venezuelan women have managed to achieve a place in society that would be the envy of their sisters in many developed nations. The first woman cabinet minister was named in 1968; the first female presidential candidate, Ismenia Villalba of the Unión Republicana Democrática, stood for election in 1988; and, in 1996, Cecilia Sosa Gómez became the first female elected to the position of chief magistrate of Venezuela's Supreme Court.

Women business executives, medical doctors, judges, engineers and architects abound; in some professions, such as law, women actually outnumber men in the current graduating classes. The push for sexual equality has been accomplished without the help of any nationwide women's organization or any cohesive feminist movement. Some writers believe their success in a male-dominated society has been due to their non-confrontational – and therefore non-threatening – approach.

Foreign feminists find it bizarre that this apparent success sits alongside such traits as a national obsession with traditional beauty

street crime. She was re-elected to a second term with a landslide victory of more than 90 percent of the vote, and was a presidential candidate in the 1998 elections.

At least part of the progress of Venezuelan women has been due to necessity. In Venezuelan society, infidelity is widepread and men often have entire second families. Many women have learned not to count on their husbands as a steady source of income.

Because of the high incidence of promiscuity, infrequent use of birth control, absence of legal abortions, and men who refuse to take any responsibility for paternity outside of

contests and cosmetics (*see Pop Culture Paradise, pages 71–75*). Venezuela's professional women maintain a high sense of glamor, playing up their femininity much more than their North American or European counterparts.

Proving that glamor and brains can mix, former Miss Universe, Irene Sáez, was elected mayor of the Caracas municipality of Chacao. Her winning looks surely didn't hurt in gaining a few votes. However, she quickly demonstrated an ability for fast, effective, and creative ways of handling everything from traffic to

LEFT: Piaroa elders in Amazonas.
ABOVE: *llaneros* (cowboys) strut their stuff.

EXTENDED FAMILY LIFE

Divorce, which was legalized in Venezuela in 1909, has become a fixture of family life. Most people approaching their forties are on their second marriage; men often refer to "my first marriage" as if that were a normal phase in life. All this has given rise to a disjointed family structure in which half-brothers, step-parents and in-laws co-exist (at times even under the same roof) in a manner that is often baffling to outsiders. Even so, family life is considered sacrosanct, and Venezuelans view the home as a refuge not open to outsiders. Unlike other Latin Americans, they do not often invite friends to their homes, which are generally reserved for the family.

marriage, single women – very often girls under 16 – with one or more children to support alone make up a huge portion of the poorer sectors of society.

Problem case for the Pope

On the whole, Venezuelans are not a religious people, with the exception of the western Andean region, where the Catholic faith has strong roots. In general, the church is regarded as a traditional but somewhat irrelevant institution, its role largely ceremonial. Church attendance is so low that, before the visit of Pope John Paul II in 1985, the Venezuelan Catholic

Remnants of traditional culture

The US cultural invasion of recent years doesn't mean that the centuries-old Venezuelan culture has been completely wiped out. You just have to look a little harder for it.

Music is a good place to start. Venezuela is an eminently musical country, in which singing comes as naturally as breathing, and everyone seems to be able to carry a tune. On trips to the beach or at parties, someone will inevitably produce a *cuatro* (the traditional four-stringed instrument, similar to a ukelele) and the singing will begin. Aided by a few good rums, even the shyest Venezuelan will begin to improvise

Bishops' Conference began a public relations campaign with the slogan: "The Pope wants to be your friend."

Statistics released by the conference showed that while more than 90 percent of the population claims to be Catholic, only 20 percent attend church regularly. There is, however, fervent devotion by many to figures such as Dr José Gregorio Hernández, a turn-of-the-century physician who dedicated his life to helping the poor and who has been postulated for sainthood. There are also numerous bizarre cults: perhaps the most popular of these is dedicated to María Lionza and combines elements of Catholicism with witchcraft.

lyrics in the *contrapunto* style which has its origins in the *llanos*.

Among the best traditional artists are the singing group Un Solo Pueblo (One Single People), who have become something of an institution during the past three decades and have even incorporated their children into the group. More than "folk singers," they are serious students of the different trends in Venezuelan traditional music and go to some length to explain it at concerts, detailing the names of the villages where the songs were collected and their particular significance.

Un Solo Pueblo presents the wide variety of Venezuela's traditional music: the plaintive country music of the *llanos*, with its nasal vocals and whimsical lyrics; the complex rhythms and exuberant dances of the *tambores* or drums of the Afro-Venezuelans in Barlovento and along the rest of the Caribbean coast; the gentle, nostalgic waltzes of the Andes; and the English-lyric calypsos of the Guayana Region, the legacy of the Caribbean blacks who worked in Venezuela's gold rush during the 19th century.

Venezuelans also excel in classical music. One of the country's most accomplished instrumentalists is guitarist Alirio Díaz, who has also served as Venezuela's ambassador to Italy. Caracas alone has four symphony orchestras, and cities throughout the interior have municipal orchestras and youth symphony programs.

Contemporary artists

In the plastic arts, Venezuela has produced some outstanding modern painters and sculptors. Jesús Soto, of Ciudad Bolívar, is responsible for much of the monumental art that graces the new buildings in Caracas, including the entrance to the Teresa Carreño Theater and the Chacaíto metro station. Other noted painters include Jacobo Borges and Héctor Poleo.

Venezuela's greatest living man of letters is Arturo Uslar Pietri, a towering figure who has been both a chronicler of contemporary Venezuelan events and an active participant in them. The winner of international literary awards, Uslar Pietri has been a novelist, a historian, a cabinet minister and a television commentator, among other things. Now in his eighties, he is remembered for urging Venezuelan governments, in the 1930s, to "sow the petroleum" – that is, to invest the tremendous income from the country's principal export in productive enterprises. Uslar Pietri is held in great esteem for his literary output, which includes *La Visita en El Tiempo* ("The Visit in Time"), winner of Spain's Prince of Asturias literary prize in 1991.

Looking to the future

The idea of Venezuela as a country bursting with natural wealth but lacking in human resources is common, particularly in other Latin American nations. The reality, however, is changing, as a generation of Venezuelans edu-

cated abroad take the helm of government, the private sector and the professions. They have returned with professional skills and a new style of management which is helping business and industry to modernize. Many were beneficiaries of a government scholarship program which, during the 1970s and early 1980s, sent some 40,000 Venezuelans abroad to study (the program still continues on a smaller scale). Others who did not benefit from such scholarships also had the opportunity to travel and study abroad during the "boom years."

Yet although many Venezuelans have lived or studied abroad, few have emigrated perma-

nently and, unlike other Latin Americans, few express the desire to do so. Shortly after the February 1989 riots, there was a move among first generation Venezuelans – sons and daughters of Spaniards, Portuguese and Italians – to obtain the passports of their parents' countries in preparation for a return to their land of origin. However, only a small number actually went through with emigration.

Despite their frustrations with corrupt politicians and inefficient public services, Venezuelans love their country and recognize its potential. Although their gaze may be distracted by the latest North American cultural totems, their feet remain firmly fixed on home soil. ❑

LEFT: dominoes for the boys, by Sinamaica Lagoon, near Maracaibo.
RIGHT: rooster and shades.

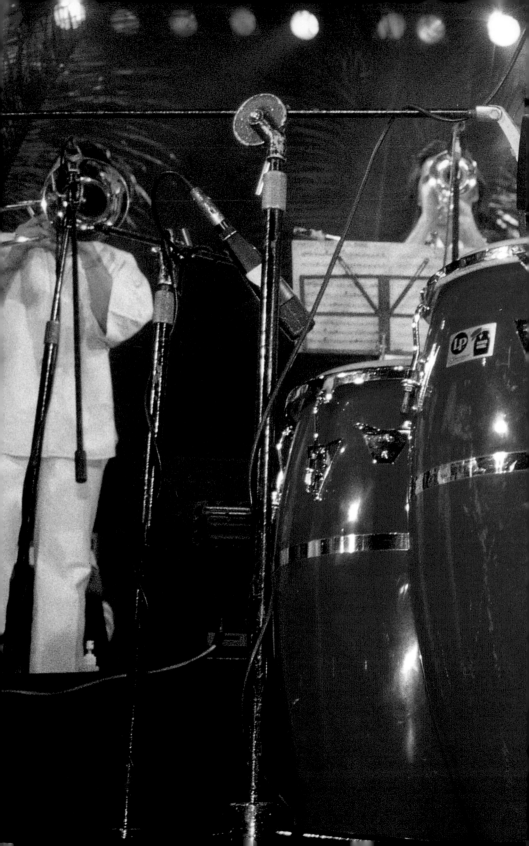

Reina
de
Corazones

POP CULTURE PARADISE

Pop entertainment is big business in Venezuela, launching many top performers onto the world stage

Take a disproportionately young audience fascinated with looks, music, and TV, and mix it with the world of pop culture (which, incidentally, grew up in an oil-rich environment that provided the disposable income to indulge in these fascinations) and you have Venezuela, where life becomes a show, and the show becomes an integral part of most of the population's lifestyle.

Pop culture paradise

Venezuela has produced a great number of well-known pop singers, and its television soap operas (*telenovelas*) are breaking records in Europe and the United States. Actress María Conchita Alonso appeared in a number of American movies, including *Moscow on the Hudson*, but she got her start as a beauty queen in Venezuela. The Caribbean's unchallenged "Devil of Salsa" is Venezuelan Oscar d'León, who has been shaking it up on stage for several decades.

South America's single most successful soap opera (*telenovela*) so far has been *Cristal*, a Venezuelan production that interrupted work and social schedules in half a dozen neighboring countries. *Farándula*, as the world of pop entertainment is called here, is serious business.

But those who claim Venezuela leads the continent in pop culture shortchange the nation. The sphere of influence extends far beyond South America. When the soap opera *Cristal* aired in Spain, it was one of the most popular TV series ever shown there; another 7 million Spaniards saw Venezuela's second most successful soap opera, *La Dama de Rosa*. Both soap operas broke ratings records in Italy.

Several Venezuelan singers, including José Luis Rodríguez, sell records in the United States

where they record in both English and Spanish and are wildly popular, especially with North America's burgeoning Hispanic population.

Geographically, Venezuela has everything needed to be a *farándula* heaven. Its proximity to Caribbean islands and countries long known as music spots has transformed it into

the gathering place for performers from the whole region. They find larger audiences in Caracas and it costs far less for a Dominican singer to travel to Venezuela in search of fame and fortune than it does to head straight for Miami, the world's undeclared capital of Spanish-language pop music.

Afro-Caribbean roots

The wild salsa, merengue, rumba, reggae, and calypso beats that find their way into Venezuela's infectious melodies and rhythms are pure Caribbean; much of this hip-gyrating music and dancing betrays African roots – intrinsic in Venezuelan music.

PRECEDING PAGES: belting out the rhythm in a Caracas night spot.
LEFT: Venezuela's soap operas have a following far beyond South America.
RIGHT: Eileen Abad, one of the country's many reigning soap queens.

Pop singer Yordano and the band Adrenalina Caribe claim they were influenced by Cuban *Nueva Trova* performers such as Silvio Rodríguez and Pablo Milanés, whose dark jazzy ballads with political themes talk of social inequality, the Latin American identity and regional integration.

A nation of addicts

But Venezuela's success may have less to do with its location on the globe than with its fascination with "the tube." When it comes to television, at least 83 percent of Venezuelans own a set, and those who don't generally live in the jungle or outback areas where transmissions won't reach. Even the humblest shacks in slum developments have television antennas popping up on their roofs; upscale neighborhoods are easily identified by a plethora of satellite dishes; and even places as remote as Santa Elena de Uarién – by the Brazilian border in Bolívar state – have DirecTV delivering steady transmission of channels from around the world. Some 98 percent of families in Caracas have access to at least one TV set. One is likewise hard-pressed to find any but the most luxurious restaurants or bars that don't have numerous televisions mounted to assure customers a

VENEZUELAN CINEMA ON SHOW TO THE WORLD

In December 1994, "Venezuela: Forty Years of Cinema, 1950–90" débuted in The Museum of Modern Art of New York, the first exhibition in the US to present the rich achievement of Venezuelan cinema. A subsequent tour of the exhibit included bookings at The Carnegie Museum of Art (Pittsburgh), Cinemathèque Quebequoise (Montreal), The Cleveland Museum of Art, Museum of Fine Arts (Boston), Pacific Cinema (Vancouver), and the National Gallery (Washington DC), among others. Highlighted were works by three of Venezuela's best-known film makers, including the internationally acclaimed documentaries of Margot Benacerraf (*Araya* stands among the first major social documentaries in Latin America, twice awarded at Cannes); the dramas of Román Chalbaud; and the visually expressive, experimental films of Diego Risquez. At the domestic box office, smash hits such as *Macú, The Policeman's Wife* (Solveig Hoogesteijn, 1987) outsold even some Hollywood "blockbusters." The film remained 83 weeks in Caracas theaters and 228 weeks in national exhibition, with the second-highest attendance ever. Domestically, 1985 was the best year for Venezuelan cinema. Of the top 10 most successful films of the year, including national and foreign films, six were Venezuelan, capturing 59 percent of the market.

steady fix, and providing a wonderland for television advertisers and a dream come true for performers in need of exposure.

Publications are also able to cash in on the craze. Any newsstand has magazines dedicated to the pop entertainment industry, aimed at satisfying the eager craving of gossip-hungry readers with the latest scandals, alleged loves, sexual preferences, and infidelities of Venezuelan music, movie, and television stars. Keeping abreast with entertainment developments is not a pastime, it is an addiction.

People on the street discuss the latest adventures of current soap stars such as Eileen Abad,

other aspects of everyday life that Venezuelans face have been dominant themes in commercial films. However, commercial success has still been limited to the domestic market and the economic recession beginning in the 1980s and the financial crisis and political uncertainty of the 1990s greatly slowed the momentum.

Farándula financial empire

If a performer makes it in Venezuela, his or her success is almost guaranteed and a ticket to Miami isn't far off. Some may argue that Venezuelans are not necessarily more talented than their counterparts in nearby nations but

Rosalinda Serfaty or Miguel de León as if they were intimate friends; and the goings-on in the latest episode of *Kaina*, *Contra Viento y Marea*, or *Todo Por Tu Amor* as if they were real life.

The big screen

Although their movie industry is fledgling, Venezuelan directors already have a number of documentaries and feature films which have garnered critical acclaim outside the country. Passion, struggles of life in the barrios, and

they receive an invaluable amount of promotion thanks to bountiful coffers in Caracas and the local record company's US links. Part of this promotion stems from the incestuous relationship which the recording monopoly, Sonorodven, has with the music video firm Video Rodven and TV station Venevisión. The trio is owned by the Cisneros Group, which also has a major chunk of the Galaxy consortium and DirecTV Internacional.

Sonorodven artists are advertised extensively on TV, and *telenovela* songs (guaranteed hits) are performed by Sonorodven musicians. Rudy Escala's recording of *Cristal*'s theme song was hummed in homes on three continents, and Jorge

LEFT: glued to the box.

ABOVE: *Aunque me Cueste La Vida* ("Though It May Cost Me My Life"), a top-rating soap opera.

Rigó's *telenovela* songs have overshadowed his other music to such an extent that he has become irreversibly identified as a soap singer.

Although actors can make it without singing, singers are obliged to take a role or two in local soap operas; *telenovela* work is detailed in recording contracts. Sometimes the TV fame supersedes the music and aspiring singers such as Guillermo Dávila became better known as leading men than musicians. "El Puma", Jose Luis Rodríguez, began his now stellar singing career as a soap opera leading man; it was his role in the historical soap opera *Estefanía*, not his tropical music, that pushed him to fame.

and exposed, dangling rhinestone earrings, and spike heels, and you can be sure she's on her way to work – as a bank teller or perhaps a legal secretary.

Fashion is likewise a matter of great national pride in Venezuela, with a number of designers attaining international fame. These include Carolina Herrera (with both *haute couture* and fragrances), Angel Sánchez (whose gowns traditionally grace Miss Venezuela winners), Mayela Camacho (whose streamlined *prêt-à-porter* outfits line the most fashionable outlets), and Dorita Vera (with show-stopping bathing suits), among others.

It is rare that a musician makes it big unless signed to the Sonorodven label. Conversely, artists may sign with the label then be pushed into the wings, blocked from performing or recording by iron-clad contracts like those of movie stars during the Golden Age of Hollywood in the 1930s and 1940s.

Dressing for success

In Venezuela, looks count. Although female executives are likely to be in an elegantly cut designer suit, for the majority of working women, dressing for success means the tighter the better. You see a woman slinking down the street in a skin-tight mini, plenty of cleavage

The business of beauty

Women have an additional path to fame and fortune in Venezuela: by means of winning a beauty contest. Annually, Miss Venezuela is virtually guaranteed an acting and/or singing career if she shows even the remotest amount of talent. Those who don't make it into feature films often make it into the advertisements that precede the movie.

Enterprising Venezuelans have made a business out of beauty. A Caracas "Miss" Academy has groomed three Miss Universes, four Miss Worlds and lots of runners-up. *Venezolanos* are among the highest per capita consumers of cosmetics and personal-care products.

A recent phenomenon has been beauty as a stepping stone to politics. Irene Sáez, a former Miss Universe (1981), entered the political ring in 1992, vying for mayorship of the prestigious and very populous Chacao municipality in Caracas – and won. Although looks and a familiar face probably didn't hurt in vote getting, the true test was in action. She founded a police force lauded for efficiency, friendliness, helpfulness, and honesty. For the first time in years, municipal taxes were not only collected, but put to work for the community. Abandoned parks were rescued, streets repaired, sidewalk vendors evicted, community events organized.

The startling difference earned Sáez re-election in 1995 with an astonishing 96 percent of the vote. In answer to public pressure, she ran for the presidency of Venezuela in 1998. Not a lone example, during the same period, Yvonne Attas changed roles from a popular soap opera star of the 1970s to that of mayor of Baruta – another huge Caracas municipality. With the same strategy, no sooner had the votes been counted than she set about effectively attacking problems and implementing improvements – and has won as dedicated a following in real life as she had on the TV screen.

A feminist's nightmare

In many countries, beauty contests are being downplayed as women's rights advance. Not in Venezuela. The Miss pageant has weathered feminism with barely a scratch. Here, beauty opens doors. Every aspiring model knows that entering the Miss Venezuela pageant can do much to boost her career. At his star-making Miss Academy, Osmel Souza has produced four Miss Universes; and five Miss Worlds.

How do women become Miss Venezuela contestants? It's not something they simply sign up for. First of all, they must be "discovered." Chances improve dramatically if a woman is from a prominent family and enrolled in a top Caracas modeling agency. While the candidates are officially representatives for districts or states throughout the country, in truth, recruiting in the interior is almost non-existent. Most are "discovered" in Caracas and are simply assigned to represent a given area after having passed muster. For example, the winner of the

1998 Miss Venezuela title, Lucbel Carolina Indriago Pinto, won as the representative of Delta Amacuro, but is a Valencia (Carabobo state) native and resident. This has caused problems at times in local interviews when the candidate for a certain zone clearly knows nothing about the place she is representing.

Once past the first hurdle of selection, she must then survive Osmel Souza's Miss Academy (which is not cheap, and she has to foot the bill – but they all willingly pay for tuition and brace themselves for the strict regimen with the glitter of a Miss crown in their eyes). Souza's goal is turning out not just another pretty face,

but a woman with that certain something that guarantees winning. He plays the roles of talent scout, agent, trainer, image-maker, fund-raiser, producer and, when necessary, whip-cracker.

As the song goes, you're never fully dressed without a smile. Teeth a little crooked? Nose not exactly like a button? It's no secret that cosmetic orthodontia and plastic surgery are all part of the beauty game. One Venezuelan magazine noted that "before smelling the sweet aroma of success, the majority of the participants have breathed the ether of anesthesia."

Clearly – regardless of gender – vanity and Venezuela have rather more in common than just the letter V. ❑

LEFT: backstage at the Miss Venezuela pageant.
RIGHT: a happy winner.

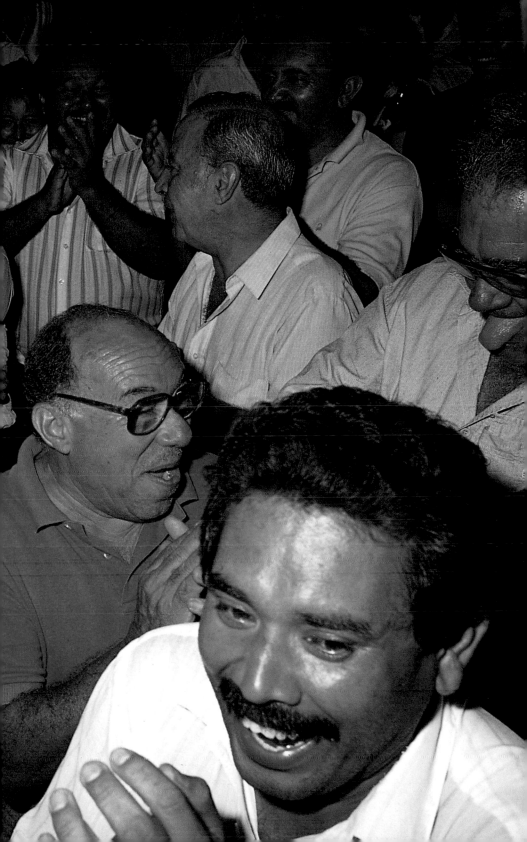

FIESTAS

The true character of the Venezuelan people is revealed at fiesta time.
Even religious festivals show how this nation loves to party

The least mentioned, but most unmissable events to be enjoyed by those exploring the distinct regions of the Venezuelan countryside, are the great number of colorful and varied folkloric and religious festivals taking place throughout the year. With the nation's rich ancestry, blending indigenous, European, African, and Caribbean cultures, its fiestas likewise have been spiced by diverse elements.

Most celebrations are linked with Catholic saints or other dates of religious significance, but the acts often seem more like pagan rites than anything remotely related to the church. Lively music, free-flowing liquor, sensual dancing, devils, and men dressed as women are common components.

Despite appearances, most participants are involved in the rituals as payment for solemn religious promises with a self-imposed commitment for years or even their lifetime. Whether observers get into the significance or not doesn't matter: the fiestas are entertaining, providing yet another view of Venezuela's multi-faceted personality.

Time to be merry

The Christmas season has the greatest number and diversity of festivals.

The Fiesta de los Pastores began in the village of Aguas Calientes in Carabobo state at least a century ago, and the tradition soon spread to the nearby town of San Joaquín and to El Limón in Aragua state. Each community has added its own touches to the celebration, which is based on the re-enactment of the *pastores* (shepherds) bringing news of the birth of Christ, their search for Him, and their jubilant dancing after finding Him.

Half of the main participants – all paying religious promises and all male – are the *pastores*, with skirts of long colored streamers worn over slacks, hats decorated with flowers, bows and more streamers, and a "musical instrument" – a long pole with loosely attached bottle caps to jingle when pounded on the ground as they sing and dance. The other half are *pastorcillas* (dressed as shepherdesses, complete with well-padded frilly blouses and full make-up). The complex series of dance patterns is performed before the crèche from dusk until the wee hours

of the morning led by the *cachero*, who is adorned with streamers and bows, and a set of horns in hand to keep his people in line.

Events start at dusk in Aguas Calientes. The most serious of the three fiestas (usually on the first Saturday in December), it includes an impressive candlelit procession prior to the dancing, with many people inching forward painfully on their knees before the image of baby Jesus. At El Limón (second Saturday of December), women are allowed to dance and it has the least traditional fiesta; and midnight mass on December 24 starts events in San Joaquín (the most elaborate, complete with a theatrical performance in the church).

PRECEDING PAGES: applauding fireworks at a fiesta.
LEFT AND RIGHT: Jesters and high camp at *Carnaval*.

The commemoration on December 28 of the *santos inocentes*, the innocent children killed by Herod, is celebrated throughout the country, with children donning old clothes and masks and generally having free rein. The event is also known as the Fiesta de Locos.

Formal celebrations take place in Aguas Blancas (Portuguesa) with *locos* and *locaínas* carrying out a military-type ceremony and dancing with small children to bless them. In Sanare (Lara), along with acts of buffoonery, *Zaragozas* dancers with distinctive masks and colorful costumes perform with children in their arms before a painting of the historic massacre. With

its own character, but the same motive, is the Fiesta del Mono in Caicara de Maturín. This dance has indigenous roots adapted to honor the *Santos Inocentes*. Most celebrants wear monkey masks and everyone joins in the dancing.

The black saint

In the Andes, acts for the *Santos Inocentes* are often combined with those for San Benito (a black saint, whose following is concentrated in the area circling Lake Maracaibo). On December 29, in Mucuchíes (Mérida), men and boys with blackened faces and bright-colored satin costumes dance before the saint, then they fire

PARTY TIME

Keep in mind that Venezuelans are as "relaxed" about starting hours for their fiestas as they are for every other aspect of life. Sometimes more so. After all, in the small villages, what else is there to do? Thus, elements of the celebrations often occur in different stages spread over a whole day with long breaks in between to eat, drink, socialize – and make the party last longer. Most of the celebrations tend to start at about 10am, usually by the main church and/or in the plaza.

In remote communities, the festivals are the social highlight of the year. Ice cream and snow cone vendors turn out en masse and there's always a beer stand.

black powder rifles and homemade shotguns with wild abandon! Just up the road, in Timotes, the *negros*, *indios* and *vasallos de San Benito* all dance in the street at once, the *negros* with blackened skin and grass skirts; *indios* with bronzed skin, war paint and feather headdresses; and the *vasallos* vassals in elegant white outfits adorned with long ribbon streamers and wearing glittering crowns, do their maypole-type dance – very colorful!

Paraujano indians in Zulia's Sinamaica Lagoon dedicate their fiesta to San Benito alone. They parade around the lagoon on December 27, dancing on the prows of their launches and carring images of the saint. Communities with predominately African roots, from El Moján down to Borbures and Gibraltar on the eastern shore of the lake, bring out their traditional drums to honor the San Benito with processions with his image, dancing and the beating of drums from December 27–31.

A day or two before New Year's Eve, effigies of the *año viejo* (old year) are seen along rural roads and city streets in many parts of the country. Representing the ills of the past year, on the night of the 31st they are ceremoniously set aflame. On Easter Sunday, similar effigies, these labeled Judas (though lately used to represent unpopular politicians with stinging

lights, painted decorations and music, turning the neighborhood into a spectacular scene.

Pesebres also take part in the Paradura del Niño (January 1 to February 2), "stealing" baby Jesus from the *pesebre*, searching for Him, then celebrating when He is found.

In the big cities, these holiday customs have mostly been replaced with more hedonistic fiestas. The main event is Christmas Eve – *Noche Buena*, with a huge family feast (*see Food, pages 89–95*), and ever-present music and dancing. Christmas Day is primarily for going to the beach or visiting friends. New Year's Eve celebrations depend more on per-

epitaphs read as they burn), are given the same treatment, with the *Quema de Judas*.

Christmas festivities

All through the Christmas season, many families set up elaborate *pesebres* (nativity scenes) in their homes – or outside for all to enjoy. Residents of the Táchira town of San Pedro del Río set them up all through the streets. In Carora (Lara) one neighborhood near Calle Torrellas pulls out all the stops with *pesebres*, colored

sonal taste than tradition – some spend the evening at home with family and friends, while others head for the big hotels which always host an all-out party with champagne toasts at midnight. On Christmas Eve and New Year's Eve fireworks light up the skyline for hours.

At the Romería de los Pastores ("shepherds' pilgrimage"), on January 6 in San Miguel de Boconó (Trujillo), you will see more folkloric and religious events in one day than anywhere else in the country: including *pastores*, devotees of San Benito, dancing to African-style drums (in a different style to the *pastores* of Carabobo and Aragua states); religious processions, *mama-rochos* (boys dressed as women), devils,

LEFT: dancing during the Romería de los Pastores.
ABOVE: drummers at San Benito celebration, Timotes.
RIGHT: dancers honoring San Benito in Mucuchíes.

the Three Kings on horseback, and more masks than you can imagine: and that's just for starters.

Every year, on February 2, Nuestra Señora de la Candelaria is honored in La Parroquia, just south of Mérida in Mérida state, with a colorful ceremony and dance with indigenous roots, by costumed males dancing to pay promises.

Carnival and calypso

Carnival, the last fling before Lent – and known here as *Carnaval* – is celebrated with tremen-

> **TOP FESTIVAL**
>
> If you see only one festival in Venezuela, the Romería de los Pastores in San Miguel de Boconó (in Trujillo state) on January 6 should be it.

Guanare, in the western state of Portuguesa, is known for its fertile crops, but in recent years its *Carnaval* has grown to outstrip those in any other part of the country, with spectacular floats and costumes, numerous *banda-shows*, and some 100,000 visitors converging on this otherwise sleepy farm town for the fiesta.

Common throughout eastern Venezuela at this time are folkloric celebrations such as the dance of La Bur and El Pájaro Guarandol (a person representing a large bird) acting out a popular legend.)

dous enthusiasm in some of the most unlikely places. Carúpano (Sucre), which is frankly dead at any other time of year, springs to life with people flooding in from all over the country for the big party by the beach. El Callao, a tiny gold town in Bolívar state, is another surprising venue for a big party – especially when the main part of the celebration involves calypso music and devil masks.

Calypso arrived with gold miners from Trinidad and the French and British Antilles who came during the mid 19th-century gold rush and stayed. The tradition of devil masks has resulted in intense competition for the most original creations.

Holy Week

At Catholic churches in every corner of the country, there are processions with images representing the Passion of Christ during Semana Santa – Holy Week – mainly from the Wednesday to Good Friday. In Caracas, one of the most awesome acts of faith is on Wednesday, when tens of thousands turn out to honor the 400-year-old image El Nazareno de San Pablo, the most venerated holy image in the city. People wearing purple robes, with offerings of orchids, form immense lines from 3am–9pm to pay homage in the Basilica of Santa Teresa.

Processions of Nazarenes, garbed in purple robes, and live Passion plays are seen in many parts of the Andes between Wednesday and Friday. In Ureña (Táchira) on Good Friday, dozens of groups, each with a person carrying a heavy wooden cross, make their way up Avenida 1º de Mayo to "Calvary", stopping at adorned stations of the cross along the way to pray. Same town, but different location, at about 9.30am at the church of the Sagrada Familia, costumed participants re-enact Christ's sentencing and also march to Calvary.

However, there are three places which outshine the rest for their superb, ambitious, well done *Pasión Viviente* – live Passion plays. One is La Parroquia (Mérida), with a week-long presentation, mostly taking place in or in front of the church (main days Thursday and Friday) about 7.30pm. Caripito (Monagas) has become the focal point for a week-long Passion play, one of the most ambitious in Venezuela, with hundreds taking part. The scene for most of the presentations is a hillside on the edge of town which makes for a perfect natural amphitheater. Tostos (Trujillo) is the third place, with a Good Friday drama which attracts hundreds of visitors to the picturesque mountain village.

Corpus Christi – the ninth Thursday after Maundy Thursday – is the day for devil dancers or *diablos danzantes* (*see pages 84–85*).

Flowers and feasts

Traditional celebrations for Cruz de Mayo are held every Saturday in May in private homes, with special altars set up for the cross, and decorated with candles and flowers, and such like. Friends are invited to join in the singing of the rosary, dancing to the rhythm of *tambores* (African-style drums made from hollow logs) and more social aspects with everyone bringing food to share.

On the *Fiesta de San Isidro* (May 15 in Tostos, Trujillo, and the Sunday closest to the date in Tabay, Mérida) farmers bring oxen, their yokes adorned with flowers and produce, to the church for blessing. In Tabay, there's a procession with a figure dressed as the saint.

The main annual event for communities with African roots, all along the central coast (with Curiepe in Miranda of special note), is the Fiesta de San Juan Bautista, June 23–4. A particular friend of the blacks, he is "baptized"

in the sea or river and fêted with sensual dancing to the *tambores* (drums) and abundant *aguardiente* (potent sugar cane liquor) or rum.

The Parranda de San Pedro, June 29 in Guatire and Guarenas (Miranda), relates to the legend of a slave, María Ignacia, who promised the saint she would dance throughout his feast day if he cured her daughter, Rosa, who was near death. The girl was cured and María Ignacia kept her promise. A man plays the part of María, carrying a doll representing Rosa, accompanied by black-faced fellow slaves.

Feasts of patron saints are celebrated across the country, in Valle del Espíritu Santo,

Margarita (the Virgen del Valle, September 8); Maracaibo (La Chinita, November 18); and San Cristóbal, Táchira (San Sebastián, January 20). Nuestra Señora de Coromoto, the patron of Venezuela, is fêted on September 11 in Chachopo (Mérida) with the Indios Cospes depicting the Virgin's appearance to their chief and his subsequent acceptance of the faith.

The night-long dance of the *turas* on September 23–4 in Mapararí (Falcón) is a celebration with indigenous-agrarian roots for the Virgen de Mercedes, while the Negros de San Jerónimo, men with blackened faces who dance for the saint every September 30, are found only in Santo Domingo (Mérida). ❑

LEFT: high times with the batmobile.
RIGHT: dancing to the *tambores* at Choroní.

DANCING WITH THE DEVILS

The pounding of drums, rattle of maracas, jangling of bells, and dancing men in masks paint a vivid scene of the diablos danzantes

On Corpus Christi, *diablos danzantes* (devil dancers) don grotesque masks, colorful costumes, and take to the streets of several towns along the coast. Hardly a frivolity, the event's participants are members of confraternities dedicated to the Eucharist, who dance to pay solemn religious promises (such as petitions for divine intervention or gratitude for cures), made for life or a specific period.

Active dance groups are concentrated on the Venezuela's central coast. Since participants are principally black, many people assume the tradition has African roots. In fact, the rites have been practised in Europe since the Middle Ages (antecedents date back to the feast of Natalis Calicis, recorded since the 5th century), and were brought to this continent by the conquistadores as a means of spreading Christianity. The Spanish ritual adopted elements from indigenous peoples, and later from African slaves, but it has retained the same common thread for five centuries: use of the Eucharist and symbolic figures representing acts of submission of evil or heresy to Christian doctrine.

Performances by *diablos danzantes*, each group with distinct costumes but enacting basically the same rites, can be seen in San Francisco de Yare, Naiguatá, Patanemo, Turiamo, Cata, Cuyagua, Chuao and Ocumare de la Costa.

▷ **INITIATION RITES**
As an act of submission, inititates into Turiamo's confraternity advance to the church on their knees to whisper their promise into the priest's ear.

△ **HANGING LOOSE**
Rather than face masks, many groups of devils wear their masks hanging loosely on the end of transparent fabric covering the head.

◁ **FEARSOME BEASTS**
The masks of Naiguatá's devils usually represent fantastic animals, based on the belief that the devil often appears in the form of an animal.

△ **SHE DEVIL**
Confraternities are usually male only, but in Yare, one woman, *La Capataz*, is annually elected by the brotherhood and permitted to wear a devil mask.

DEVIL MASKS HIT THE MARKET

In 1948, when Manuel Sanoja was just 10 years old, he joined the rank of the *diablos danzantes* of San Francisco de Yare. Even then, when he made his first mask to participate in the dancing, Sanoja's exceptional artistic talent was evident, with a very particular style making his creations immediately identifiable. Many other devil dancers, fascinated by his masks, contracted him to make theirs too.

The impressive quality of his work won the admiration both of the general public as well as of the savvy merchants of original Venezuelan crafts, who recognized the masks' commercial potential. As a result, the masks have provided Sanoja's livelihood for half a century, and nowadays family members help out in his workshop (tel: 58 39-29 191) to keep up with the enormous demand both at home and abroad. Sanoja even had the unlikely distinction of making the mask worn by Carolina Herrera as her "typical Venezuelan dress" when she won the Miss Universe title in 1984!

△ **EARLY COMMITMENT**
Very often, a father will commit his sons to the confraternity, with the promise to dance from an early age to protect them from possible future harm.

◁ **COLORFUL COSTUMES**
In Naiguatá, the devil dancers are distinguished by their very large masks, their colorful, hand-painted clothing, and by the wearing of many bells.

VENEZUELAN CUISINE

If deep-fried ants don't take your fancy, then don't worry – the variety of Venezuelan cuisine ensures that there's something for everyone

One word describes the Venezuelan palate: eclectic. Due to the country's fertile farm land and warm tropical waters it enjoys an abundance of beef and a great variety of seafood, freshwater fish, fruits and vegetables. Its distinctive regional specialties reflect a mix of foreign influences and local tradition. One can savor anything from a delicate mango *mousse* or exotic Thai delicacies in the capital, to stewed capybara, and cheese made from water buffalo milk in the *llanos*, or piranha and deep-fried ants in Amazonas.

Not by bread alone

For most Venezuelans, the staff of life is not bread but a flattened, fist-sized ball of fried or baked corn or wheat flour dough called an *arepa*. As pervasive as the *tortilla* in Mexico, the cheap and filling *arepas* are eaten in great quantities by the country's poor, but they also turn up in smaller, daintier versions in the bread baskets of fine restaurants, where diners slice them in halves and slather them with *natilla*, a cross between sour cream and butter.

Seldom are *arepas* eaten plain. Usually they are slit and part of the inside is scooped out to form a pocket that's stuffed with virtually anything imaginable. Favorite fillings include *reina pepiada* (chicken salad with sliced avocado), *carne mechada* (shredded beef), *ensalada de atún* (tuna salad), *diablitos* (canned deviled ham), or simply grated *queso amarillo* (yellow cheese). At breakfast, a popular filling is *perico*, eggs scrambled with tomato and onion.

The *arepa* accompanies Venezuela's national dish, *pabellón criollo*. This large, tasty dish comprises shredded beef spiced with onions, green pepper, tomato, *cilantro* (coriander) and garlic, a mound of white rice, a scoop of *caraotas negras* (black beans) and strips of fried plantain. With demand frequently outstripping national supply, black beans are often imported,

mainly from Chile. It has been suggested that this is the reason Venezuelan politicians traditionally maintain such good relations with this southern neighbor. *Pabellón* is not eaten on any particular occasion; rather it is part of the daily diet of many working-class Venezuelans and a standard on many restaurant menus.

On Isla Margarita, *pabellón* has a distinct local flavor, with flaked fish flavored with onion, peppers, and tomato taking the place of shredded beef.

Arepas, as with *pabellón,* vary from region to region. For example, in the Andes, particularly in Mérida, the standard variety is made with wheat flour rather than corn meal, and looks more like a stiff pancake.

The most traditional "bread" of all, however, is *casabe* (with a taste like shredded wheat cereal squares). Eaten by indigenous residents since long before colonists arrived, it not only continues as their staple, but is made throughout the interior. *Casabe* is made of grated bitter yucca

---

PRECEDING PAGES: fresh fruits of the sea.
LEFT: chef at the Avila Hotel, Caracas.
RIGHT: hard at work in a country kitchen.

root which has had its toxic juice squeezed out, before being toasted, then moistened and formed into large rounds – *tortas* (cakes) some 60 cm/24 inches in diameter – and "baked" on a hot griddle until dry and crispy. There is a thick version (about 1 cm/¾-inch) and a thin one – *galleta* (cracker). A sweet variation is *naiboa*, a thick round, about a quarter of the usual size, and with raw brown sugar pressed into the surface.

A flavorful tidbit is the *tequeño*, white cheese wrapped in thin pastry dough and deep fried. *Tequeños* may be served as *pasapalos* (hors d'oeuvres) or eaten as a snack. *Hallaquitas* are common accompaniments to grilled meat.

grated sweet corn. *Cachapas* are usually folded in half with a slab of local cheese such as *queso guayanés* or *queso de mano* inside.

Empanadas are deep-fried cornmeal turnovers filled with cheese, meat, fish or black beans. Meanwhile, the Andean version (like their style of *arepas*, relying on wheat flour rather than cornmeal) is the *pastelito* – usually round, with a delicate pastry stuffed with anything available, from cheese to smoked trout.

Surf and turf

For main courses, the country produces fine meats, fish and shellfish. Beef is mainly pro-

Made with a dough of white cornmeal, they are like a mini-*tamal* (another cornmeal snack popular in other Andean countries) – but without stuffing. The most common form is with cornmeal only, but sometimes bits of sweet pepper, *chicharrón* (fried pork rind), or cheese are mixed in the dough. They are wrapped in corn husks and boiled. The firm, hot mush inside is subsequently sliced and doused with *guasacaca*, a typical sauce used in many dishes, with a base of a variety of ingredients, including fresh coriander and parsley leaves, avocado, onion, oil, vinegar and garlic.

Another Venezuelan standard is the *cachapa*, a thick, slightly sweet pancake made with

duced in the *llanos* (central plains) and southern Zulia state. Menus feature cuts such as *punta trasera* (rump steak), *solomo* (chuck) and *lomito* (tenderloin). The *parrilla criolla* (mixed grill with beef and sausage) or *parrilla argentina* (with intestines also added) are regular favorites among serious meat eaters.

Andean lakes and streams are abundantly stocked with *trucha* (trout), which is farmed for export, too. Fishermen along the 2,500-km (1,500-mile) coast of Venezuela haul in *pargo* (red snapper), *dorado* and shellfish such as clams and oysters. Shrimp is also plentiful in many coastal areas. You may be disappointed though, at the scarcity of lobster and conch –

Venezuelan fishermen spirit this bounty away to the resorts of Aruba where they fetch a higher price.

Fruit paradise

Tropical Venezuela offers a cornucopia of fresh and natural foods that remain key parts of the diet despite the increasing presence of multinational processed-food companies. Widely available exotic fruits make succulent treats for visitors from cold climes. Street vendors sell amazing watermelon-sized *lechosa* (papaya), mangos, *guayaba* (guava), *guanábana* (custard apple), *zapote* (sapodilla plum), *níspero* (the crabapple-like fruit of the medlar tree), oranges, melons, pineapples, and strawberries.

You might also see vendors with carts full of what look like green ping-pong balls. They are *mamones*. Venezuelans buy them by the bagful, peel off the skin and suck on the pale pink flesh that clings to the pit. Some fruits go by names unfamiliar in other Spanish-speaking lands: passion fruit is called *parchita* rather than *maracuyá*, watermelon is *patilla* rather than *sandía*, and limes are *limones* (literally, lemons). Avocado is *aguacate* instead of *palta*.

Fresh juices are a thirst-quenching alternative to soft drinks. On a hot day, sip a tart, refreshing *limonada frappe* (limeade with crushed ice) or a *papelón con limón*, raw brown sugar dissolved in water with a squeeze of lime. Street vendors do big business with *jugo de caña*, pale green sugar cane juice and also coconut juice drunk straight from the shell (*coco frío*). Just about any fruit can be whipped into a *jugo* (juice), *batido* (frothed with ice) or *merengada* (with milk).

You'll find every kind of banana – from the stubby sweet *cambur*, ready for eating, to the large, starchy *plátano* (plantain) for frying. A favorite snack is crisply fried, lightly salted plantain chips called *tostones*.

Holiday dining

Food takes on a special significance during the Christmas season, when bosses throw parties for employees featuring *pan de jamón* (ham rolls) and families gather for home-cooked feasts. The most cherished holiday food is the *hallaca*.

This packet of cornmeal dough is bursting with a filling of chicken, pork and beef flavored with the following ingredients green: pepper, onion, garlic, tomatoes, capers, sugar, cumin, black pepper, parsley, pork fat, olive oil, almonds, raisins and green olives. Each *hallaca* is lovingly wrapped in banana leaves and steamed (the leaves are not eaten). Needless to say, the preparation takes hours, even days.

This festive dish reputedly has humble origins; supposedly, it was created by servants recycling the jumble of scraps from the master's table. Yet *hallaca* has grown so dear to Venezuelans that exceptions were made during

LEFT: lobster and wine tempt customers into a seaside café on Margarita.
RIGHT: tropical spread.

the era of import restrictions for such key ingredients as olives; and when supplies ran short or grew too pricey, people took to the streets and staged protests.

Local tastes

Because Venezuela is a large country, with many varied zones, distinctive regional cuisines have evolved. In coastal areas and on Margarita Island, you'll find various *hervidos de pescado* (fish soups). A favorite is *sancocho* (fish stew), a steaming brew with large chunks of fish, pumpkin, root vegetables, and tomatoes. *Consomé de chipi chipi* is a thin broth laced with

although this trout is intimately associated with Mérida, it is not in fact native to the Andes. The Venezuelan government imported the fish from Europe and the United States between 1938 and 1941, and now several trout hatcheries outside Mérida enjoy a thriving export business.

The *llanos* and southern Zulia are beef country. Since grass-fed tropical beef has little fat, it is often larded by making small knife-cuts which are filled with bacon or pork fat. One recipe calls for filling a tough roast with large whole carrots and onions, plus bacon or pork and cloves of garlic. As the piece cooks, it may swell to double its size and when carved, is a sur-

tiny clams that is reputed to be an aphrodisiac. *La tortuga marina* (sea turtle) is a delicacy, but the species is endangered. Conservationists also advise steering clear of *pastel de morrocoy*, a pie made from land turtle.

In Lara and Falcón states, *chivo en coco* (goat in coconut milk) is a specialty.

Home cooking is popular in the Andean region. The small white potatoes are remarkably sweet, and the home-made cheese fried in cubes is not to be missed. Sausages and Cured meats are sold by the roadside in many villages.

When the Pope visited Mérida, the Andean capital, in 1985, he was treated to *comida típica* ("typical food"), a dinner of rainbow trout. But

prisingly tender mesh of meat and vegetables.

In the Amazon region, indigenous groups fish, catch turtles and hunt tapirs, monkeys and birds – but not parrots, whose meat is considered too tough. Markets in Amazonian towns may offer unusual meat such as peccary (wild pig) and venison from tropical deer. Deep-fried ants are considered a delicacy – especially the large winged ones known as *culonas* (big bottoms). At the market in Puerto Ayacucho, you can buy bottles of an indigenous sauce, *katara*, made from the liquid of yucca, hot peppers and the heads of *bachacos* (a large, leaf-cutter ant with massive mandibles), said to have aphrodisiac powers.

Locally harvested cashews are sold along the roadsides between Puerto La Cruz and Ciudad Bolívar. *Palmito* (hearts of palm) is a mainstream delicacy from Delta Amacuro, but conservationists advise against eating *palmito* since harvesting the crop kills the trees.

Foreign influences

Although fried ants have not exactly caught on in Caracas, the impact of foreign cultures is obvious in restaurants of the capital. A sizeable Italian community ensures that pasta is a standard and well-prepared dish. If you see *pasticho* on the menu, that's lasagne. The Italian fruit bread *panettone* is all the rage at Christmas.

The Spanish influence shows up in the prevalence of *paella*, *tortilla española* (omelet with potatoes) and other Iberian specialties. Venezuelans prefer *paella a la valenciana* over other Spanish variations. French pastries, Swiss chocolates and Dutch cheeses are sold at delicatessens, and North America's pizzas, burgers and fries are becoming all too prominent.

While chains such as Tropiburger, Burger King, McDonald's, and Wendy's dish up standard American-style fast food, the multitude of curbside mobile hamburger and hot dog (*hamburguesa* and *perro caliente*) stands have a style of their own. *De rigueur* toppings for hot dogs are grated cabbage, crushed potato chips, and chopped onions – all slathered with ketchup, mayonnaise, pink sauce and mustard. Hamburgers may have microscopic beef patties, but they make up for this by adding a fried egg, slice of cheese and ham or bacon, avocado, tomato, lettuce, plus the toppings and sauces used on hot dogs.

Creole restaurants, *areperas*, hamburger chains and the ubiquitous *pollo en brasas* (spit-roasted chicken) stands are interspersed with eateries devoted to virtually every international cuisine. And although the present economy dictates that big splurges at restaurants are less frequent, 30 percent of the population still eats outside the home at least once a day.

After lunch there's a siesta, so *caraqueños* can enjoy a hearty noontime meal with a few hours to sleep it off before returning to work. Many restaurants close after lunch, and do not reopen for dinner until 8pm, but then carry on serving until midnight.

Coffee worshipers

More than just a drink, coffee is an integral part of the lifestyle in Venezuela. Rich, aromatic and always fresh, each *café* is brewed to order – Venezuelans would never dream of letting a pot languish on a heater. They enjoy coffee throughout the day: big milky cups at breakfast, small heavily

> **RESTAURANT HEAVEN**
>
> According to the National Restaurant Owners' Association, Caracas has more restaurants per capita than any other city in Latin America.

sugared shots from stand-up counters for breaks, glasses of cappuccino smothered in whipped cream late at night. Coffee comes in a dozen ways, and if you simply ask for *café*, the waiter won't know what you want. You must specify the size and exact degree of strength you desire.

Here's how you do it. Size is easy: *pequeño* (small) or *grande* (large). On the street, coffee is served in plastic cups without handles. A *pequeño* is the size of a large thimble; a *grande* is close to a *demitasse*. Venezuelans usually drink their coffee well-sugared – with a large cup you'll get at least two packets of sugar. It is specifying the coffee strength that takes a

LEFT: a colonial-style restaurant near Mérida.
RIGHT: warming up *arepas*.

little savvy. A black coffee is a *negro* – a small one, using the Spanish diminutive suffix, a *negrito*. A watered-down black coffee, about the closest thing to North American coffee, is a *guayoyo*. Coffee that's half milk, which Venezuelans often drink at breakfast but almost never after a meal, is a *café con leche*. Order by asking for a *con leche grande* or *con leche pequeño*. It's not necessary to say "*café*."

Coffee with only a spot of milk is called a *marrón* (brown): you would order a *marrón grande* or a *marróncito*. Coffee that's somewhere in between a *con leche* and a *marrón* is a *marrón claro* (light brown).

A taste for alcohol

In contrast to coffee, there are few choices when it comes to brands of beer. Venezuela's best-selling *cerveza* (by a wide margin) is Polar, which for several years has been exported with the gimmick of using refrigerated containers to ensure freshness. Other beers are *Nacional*; Regional, produced in Zulia with primarily local distribution; Polar Negra and Nacional Stout – dark, malty beers; Solera, a light beer (not in calories, just taste); and Brahma Chopp, which was introduced from Brazil and is produced at a local brewery.

On a hot day, ask for a *cerveza bien fría*, meaning you want it just short of frozen.

Throughout Venezuela's heady oil-boom days, the country is said to have consumed the highest per capita quantity of fine Scotch whisky in the world. Waiters at society parties would carry trays of nothing but premium Scotch and guests would choose their favorite brand. At restaurants, hosts would order bottles placed at the center of the table with mixers and diners would help themselves.

During the import restrictions of the 1980s, the best restaurants managed to smuggle it in – at a price. Although the exorbitant cost (then, as now, imports averaged $25–$50 a bottle) prompted many to switch to rum, this was only temporary. With taste buds attuned to Scotch, either something else in the budget had to give, or people condescended to drink cheaper brands of whisky, nationally produced under license, many of which are quite good.

Venezuelans drink rum with cola, almost any fruit juice (a favorite, and delicious, is *ron con parchita*, rum with passion fruit), *aguaquina* (tonic water), or with Angostura bitters (which were invented in the Orinoco port city of Angostura, now known as Ciudad Bolívar), on ice with fresh lime slices.

Rarely do Venezuelans choose clear drinks such as vodka and gin, nor are they noted wine connoisseurs, although, through an agreement with Chile to eliminate duty, wines from that country are reasonably priced. Venezuela's beer giant, Polar, has even entered wine making, with amazing results, earning top awards in European competitions for its whites and brut, under the Viñas de Altagracia and Pomar trademarks, respectively.

As with food, there are different regional spirits. *Llaneros* are known to swill the potent, clear *aguardiente*, made from sugar cane, until they slide out of their saddles. To brace them against the chilly air, *andinos* whip up *calentado*, hot brown sugar water spiked with the anise-flavored liquor, *miche*.

After a hard night, when Venezuelans groan "*Tengo un ratón*" (slang for "I have a hangover"), they don't take aspirin. There is only one cure – a steaming bowl of *mondongo* (tripe soup). If you're up early on a weekend morning, you'll probably detect its unmistakable aroma mingling with the scent of coffee. ❑

LEFT: a hearty buffet lunch at Hato Doña Bárbara in the *llanos*.

Cacao – Brown Gold

Long before the early European explorers arrived in Latin America, indigenous inhabitants were putting cacao to many uses: as a basic element in their diet, as a cosmetic, in their religious practices, as a medicine, and even as currency. The first known cultivation of cacao in Venezuela took place in the land south of Lake Maracaibo and in the western foothills of the Andes. Dominican priests introduced it to the northeast coast in 1580.

In 1600, the Province of Venezuela began exporting small quantities of cacao to Spain, making this country the first to export the product to Europe. By 1683, exportation had increased dramatically, with its price reaching the all-time high achieved during the colonial period. From that date, however, production decreased, mainly because of the wars of the Spanish Empire against other European powers which reduced inter-colonial navigation. Nevertheless, topping the list of Venezuela's riches in the 17th century, cacao boosted the country's foreign commerce and brought in a quantity of gold, prompting the development of a monetary economy. This in turn led to the strengthening of a criollo social class caustically dubbed by the lower classes as "*Los Grandes Cacaos.*"

By the mid-1700s, Venezuela was the world's largest cacao producer, a supremacy it maintained for more than 70 years, until its wars of independence, which left agriculture in ruins. By 1831, coffee had taken over as the country's top export, and even leather surpassed cacao in export importance.

In 1901, cacao moved back into second spot in export volume (after coffee) and, by 1915, production surpassed 20,000 tons annually. Ten years later, annual output reached 23,000 tons, the highest figure ever up until that date. Just when it looked as though the industry was on a steady climb, the rapid and surprising development of African cacao destabilized the international market from 1930–45, with a dramatic drop in prices; and in 1933 a cyclone devastated the cacao plantations in the eastern part of the country, reducing production by 90 percent. Many plantations were abandoned.

Today, a major effort is being mounted to improve productivity since Venezuela's cacao is still

regarded as the most aromatic and flavorful in the world. One company leading Venezuela's comeback is Chocolates El Rey, founded in 1929. Although principally a supplier of chocolate (made wholly from Venezuelan cacao) to the food industry domestically and abroad, it has also enjoyed success in the mass consumption market.

El Rey reports that while Venezuela's northeast and central zones have long been traditional sources for cacao, production in these areas is beginning to decline. Emerging as new prime sources are Barinas (where El Rey has installed its own plantation) and southern Zulia – the original growing areas in pre-Hispanic times.

One of El Rey's customers is Chocolatier La Praline. Belgian born and trained, Ludo Gillis set up shop in Caracas to be near the best cacao in the world. Although La Praline's premium bonbons are sold through its factory outlet and several select shops, it principally supplies customers such as the Hotel Tamanaco Inter-Continental, Caracas Hilton, and Marriott. A further testimony to their quality, in Chantal Coady's *The Chocolate Companion: A Connoisseur's Guide to the World's Finest Chocolates*, La Praline is the only maker from Latin America included and its bonbons are even rated above those of Godiva and Mary, the chocolate supplier for the Belgian Royal Household. ❑

RIGHT: chocolate delight – cacao beans recently extracted from the pods.

SPECTATOR SPORTS

Even when it comes to "spectator" sports, Venezuelans are lively participants, cheering, dancing and having a great time as they watch

The principal spectator sports favored by Venezuelans could be labeled "The Four Bs": baseball, basketball, bullfighting, and betting. Some might argue that the fourth is technically horse racing, but in reality it is not so much the horses or the challenge, but the fever for trying to win "The Big One" that appeals to 99 percent of Venezuelan fans.

Baseball is king

No question about it, baseball is the king of spectator sports in Venezuela. While soccer holds this honor in other South American countries, baseball firmly took root here as a favorite decades ago.

Unlikely as it sounds, this development was related to petroleum. When US oil companies came to Venezuela in the early 1900s, their personnel brought the game with them. Initially played only in the oil camps, baseball's popularity slowly took off, especially in the 1940s when the professional winter leagues were started in Venezuela.

Eventually, teams were built up throughout the country with North American support. As the level of play started to improve each year, major league teams began regularly scouting here and started giving opportunities to promising Venezuelans to compete for positions in *Las Grandes Ligas* ("The Big Leagues").

Extensive coverage in local newspapers of games in the US season and the performance of Venezuelans playing for these teams, has further contributed to enthusiasm for the sport.

The first great Venezuelan player in the majors, Alfonso "Chico" Carrasquel, earned the starting shortstop position for the Chicago White Sox in 1950. His success was the inspiration for thousands of Venezuelan kids to spend hours on dusty diamonds throughout the country, dreaming of the day they too would wear a major league uniform.

An idol with whom Venezuelan kids can even more easily identify than adult stars is Kenji García Sonofuku. In 1998, this 16-year-old infielder from Caracas signed a one-year deal with the New York Mets for a tidy $1.64 million to initiate in the minors… and see what the future brings.

The most remarkable Venezuelan player to date has been Hall-of-Famer Luis Aparicio, with an 18-year career. Some of his records as shortstop are still in place. More recently, the home-run tally of Andrés *El Gato* ("the cat") Galarraga (Atlanta Braves), with a major-league career which started in 1984, and the fielding of Omar Vizquel (Cleveland Indians), winner of multiple "Golden Glove" awards, have been principal subjects of headlines in the Venezuelan national media.

The local professional league season runs from October to February. Being the off-season for US baseball, Venezuelan teams hire several US players from AA or AAA teams (many go

PRECEDING PAGES: thumping a home run.
LEFT: Omar Vizquel, star of the US Cleveland Indians.
RIGHT: fan and mascot.

on to stardom after honing their skills here). Well-known players such as Dave Parker and Darryl Strawberry have played in the Venezuelan league; as did Pat Borobers, named "Most Valuable Player" in the 1992 World Series.

This "winter league" consists of eight teams organized in two divisions: the *Leones* of Caracas, the *Navegantes de Magallanes* from Valencia, *Tiburones* of La Guaira, *Cardenales* from Barquisimeto, *Tigres* of Maracay, *Aguilas* of Maracaibo, *Petroleros* from Cabimas, and *Caribes* of Puerto La Cruz.

The games draw huge crowds of loyal and raucous fans, who dance to their own bands and wave home-made banners. Even those who do not make it to the ballpark follow their favorites via television, radio and the newspapers.

Perennial rivals

Although each team has its *fanáticos* (fans), nothing compares with the passion evoked by the traditional rivalry between the *Magallanes* and *Leones*. Precisely how this started is not clear. However, in most people's opinion, the *Navegantes de Magallanes* have the largest and most rabid following of any team in the country. One reason might be that the team has moved around over the past half century, picking up

GAME FOR SOME BALL?

If you would like to combine some beach time with a little Latin American winter ball, make the trip to Puerto La Cruz – about four hours by car from Caracas – which boasts some of the country's liveliest resorts and a busy baseball season. There is also plenty of action in the capital, where the atmosphere is terrific for baseball – the lights are good, the fields are in solid shape and the fans are lively. For people passing through Caracas during the winter season, which begins in mid-October and finishes at the end of January, it is relatively easy to secure game tickets to see the Caracas or La Guaira teams in action. Just check the *Daily Journal* for the baseball schedule.

fans in each location. It started in Caracas. With a change of name, the team was sold and sent to the eastern part of the country, playing "home games" in three or four different cities. It then got the name *Magallanes* back and was sold to the city of Valencia (quite literally being owned by the city government – in itself unique), where it has remained.

Lively games

Leones–Magallanes encounters are a sight to behold. In Caracas, the experience begins with jostling crowds lined up hours ahead of game time to obtain the precious tickets for the 20,000-seat stadium of Universidad Central.

The first couple of innings are relatively tranquil. But "relatively tranquil" in Venezuela would translate to "rowdy" in most other places, with yelling, screaming, and dancing. By the third inning, the countless numbers of cold beer which have been downed start taking effect and anything can happen – from fights to hecklers being sent flying.

For this reason, security is tight throughout the stadium in both Caracas and Valencia. Attack dogs are placed on the field together with armed guards near the end of the games to prevent fans from entering the field. If you hadn't already heard about the passion sur-

around and recognition if a new record is set. To add a bit of flair, when hands go up, the plastic cups of beer they were holding usually go sailing into the air with them.

Summer basketball

Like baseball, the season for basketball is opposite to that of the US professional league, in this case, starting in early March and ending with the play-off finals in early July. And, in the same manner, during their off-season many pros from up north join Venezuelan teams.

The professional basketball league is composed of eight teams: two in Caracas (*Coco-*

rounding the *Leones-Magallanes* games, you'd think the president was expected.

Another distinct diversion at these contests is "the wave". This consists of fans in one vertical section of the stands simultaneously rising to their feet, lifting their arms to the sky, then lowering them and sitting down. This may not sound so difficult, but the motion has to be passed on to those in the adjacent seats, until "the wave" has gone completely around the stadium; then it circulates again and again. The scoreboard indicates the old record for time

drilos and *Panteras*), and one team each in Maracaibo (*Gaiteros*), Valencia (*Trotamundos*), Barquisimeto (*Bravos*), Maracay (*Toros*), Puerto La Cruz (*Marinos*), and Porlamar (*Guaiqueries*). Most games are televised.

La fiesta brava: bullfighting

All major Venezuelan cities have bull rings. Valencia's Plaza Monumental is the second largest in the Americas, surpassed only by the ring in Mexico City; and, in San Cristóbal, the capital of Táchira, top international bullfighters perform during the very popular annual festival in February in honor of the city's patron saint, San Sebastián.

LEFT: the "wave" makes the round.
ABOVE: a bullfight in Maracay.

Maracay is considered the real cradle and capital of bullfighting in Venezuela, having produced the country's biggest stars. Its beautiful Moorish-style ring, La Maestranza, is also called the Plaza de Toros César Girón, named after one of the city's and nation's greatest bullfighters. The most important contests take place during the annual fair for the city's patron saint, San José, in March.

Bullfights in Caracas are held in the Plaza de Toros Nuevo Circo on Sunday afternoons dur-

SIT IN THE SHADE

Seats for bullfights are sold as "*sol*" (sun) and "*sombra*" (shade). Since fights take place in the hottest part of the day it's worth paying extra for *sombra* seats, which are a lot more comfortable.

alternatives to man versus beast (with no weapons or killing of animals involved), which are enormously popular in rural areas.

The contest consists of a massive bull being set free down a long, narrow chute (the *manga* or "sleeve"), with about half-a-dozen contestants (called *coleadores*) on horseback racing behind him. Each contestant tries to earn points by grabbing the bull's tail, single-handedly throwing him down, and then keeping him on the ground for a given period, for which points

ing the November to March season. Local newspapers have exact dates and times. The bull ring is on Avenida Lecuna, one block east of Avenida Fuerzas Armadas. Because of the huge crowds and non-existent parking at Caracas' bull ring, the best way to get there is by the metro, with the La Hoyada station just a block to the west.

Tweaking the tail

While conventional bullfights tend to draw many elite fans and are replete with pageantry and spectators outfitted in elegant "typical" Spanish-style dress meant to be noticed, the *toros coleados* are totally unpretentious, macho

are earned: bullfighting is definitely not a sport for the faint-hearted.

Some of the fancier *mangas* actually have stands but, generally, one simply climbs up on the bordering rails, beer in hand, to cheer on the fearless contenders.

The sport of kings

Caracas has an excellent racetrack, La Rinconada, located at the south end of Autopista del Valle. (There is a Metrobus connection between El Valle and La Rinconada, which costs about US$0.50 each way.) On Saturdays and Sundays, there are 12 races (1–6pm). Along with the regular grand stands, there is the more select

"Section B", which offers a view of both paddocks and where men are required to wear jacket and tie (ladies must also be suitably dressed). In the upper tiers, there is an elegant restaurant for members only.

This scenario is repeated at the tracks in Valencia (located near the bull ring, with races on Fridays and Saturdays) and Maracaibo (races on Wednesdays). It should be noted that "Maracaibo's" track was moved some years ago to a much more spacious site on the other side of Lake Maracaibo, in Santa Rita, a short distance east of the pay station for the Rafael Urdaneta Bridge crossing the lake.

Betting on the ponies

There are undoubtedly some people who attend, or otherwise follow the races, because of their interest in a particular horse or simply the joy of watching the sleek animals run. But for 99 percent of the Venezuelan public, the weekly races mean one thing: a chance to pick a winning ticket and strike it rich.

Venezuelans are enthusiastic gamblers (not only on horses, but lotteries, and every other game of chance) and visitors will find it hard not to catch the fever. In addition to a wide variety of bets made at the track windows, there is the popular off-track system called "5 y 6". This consists of attempting to pick at least five winners of Sunday's last six races. Official "5 y 6" betting locations are found not only all over Caracas, but across the country, usually identified by a sign out front: "Sellado de 5 y 6", indicating their agents are authorized to officially stamp – *sellar* – them for validity.

Although Sunday mornings are usually rather lazy times, these places are jammed with people intensely reviewing the various weekly horse racing publications (available at newsstands), pull-outs from the newspapers, and last-minute scratch sheets, as they fill out their *cuadros* (official betting forms) to have them validated before the 11am deadline.

Soccer second

Although there are certain sectors (the strongly Portuguese, Italian, and Spanish communities) and areas (above all the Andean state of Táchira whose influence comes from Colombia) where soccer has a large following, *fútbol*, as it is known in Spanish, is universally acknowledged to be greatly overshadowed by baseball in popularity. However, this would have to be qualified with… "except during World Cup."

Venezuelans who at any other time are completely indifferent to the sport, inexplicably become rabid soccer fans – painting their faces in team colors, waving banners for their favorite team from car windows, and taking part in horn-honking caravans each time "their team" wins a game (particularly if, against the odds, they defeat or even score a goal against rival neighbours, Colombia or Brazil).

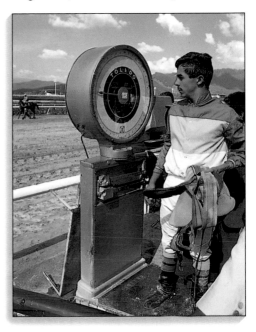

Every soda pop and beer producer puts out special cans allusive to the World Cup. Banks and stores offer promotions with the chance to win all-inclusive packages to final matches, and so forth. For all except the most elegant specialty restaurants and bars, it would be unheard of (or commercial suicide) not to install large-screen TVs and offer "World Cup Specials" to coincide with the games.

However, in typical Venezuelan fashion, when the final match is played, those who were adamantly rooting for the losing team, join in celebrating for the victor – with just as much fervor. After all, why would someone miss out on a party over a silly game? ❑

LEFT: La Rinconada race track in Caracas.
RIGHT: a jockey weighs in.

PARTICIPANT SPORTS

Blame it on the sun. In Venezuela, active participation in sports – and outdoor activities in general – is a national passion

When enjoying a climate that offers almost permanent "shorts" weather, one can dive, sail, run, climb, bike, or take part in just about any other sort of outdoor sport on any day of the year . And in Venezuela people enthusiastically do just that.

Going up?

In Caracas, ascending "El Avila", the capital's impressive mountainous backdrop, has assumed the character of a sacred rite. Particularly on weekends, thousands of *caraqueños* – young and old, male and female, pictures of fitness or frankly flabby – make their pilgrimage.

Although referred to as "El Avila", this is not just one mountain, but part of an 88-km (53-mile) long section of the coastal range in Parque Nacional El Avila, with trails of every degree of difficulty.

As much a social experience as a form of exercise, the young don their best gym outfits and there is lively interchange among participants. A popular route for casual hikers begins in Altamira just beyond Tarzilandia Restaurant (near the end of Avenida San Juan Bosco, on the 10th Transversal), and leads to Sabas Nieves, a park-like grassy area about 40 minutes up the trail.

Weekend crowds converging on this departure point have become so large that parked cars line every street for many blocks around the area; police have been assigned to keep traffic moving, and neighborhood associations regularly mount protests over the huge influx of hiking fanatics who jam their otherwise tranquil residential zones.

An excellent three-volume pocket-sized compendium (*Los Caminos del Avila*, written by Paul and Jocelyne Rouche in Spanish, published by Oscar Todtmann Editors) is available in local bookstores. This is a detailed step-by-step guide to 34 trails, with corresponding maps, and photographs of local flora, fauna, and notable landmarks.

On the run

Joggers, on the other hand, flock to Parque del Este (with a metro station at its entrance and a

measured 2,500-meter/2,750-yd loop around the park) every day of the week. Answering the sizeable demand, the park opens daily at 5am (even on Mondays when it is open until 8pm) and provides a safe, pleasant place for early morning workouts.

Every Sunday, three principal Caracas roads are closed to vehicular traffic from 6am–1pm so they can be used for runners, walkers, bikes, skateboarding and roller-blading. These are: the Cota Mil, between the exits for Avenida Baralt and El Marqués; Paseo Colam from just west of Plaza Venezuela to the Teatro Teresa Carreño; and Avenida Río de Janeiro, between Calle Veracruz and Avenida Jalisco, in Las Mercedes.

LEFT: landing a huge *dorado* fish, off the coast of La Guaira, takes skill and not a little strength.
RIGHT: a gentle stroll in the Parque Nacional El Avila, overlooking Caracas.

In the interior, Mérida is the prime target for hikers and climbers, offering a full range of options. In Parque Nacional Sierra Nevada experienced guides are available for anything from trekking from Los Pueblos del Sur to the plains state of Barinas, to scaling the glaciers of the country's highest peaks.

The gathering spot in Mérida for climbers and hikers is Calle 24, in front of the cable car station. Here, half a dozen or more businesses focus on organizing climbs, providing registered guides, and renting and selling equipment. Talking to fellow travelers is a good way to get recommendations.

Take to the skies

Many mountainous areas with easy access are ideal for para-sailing and hang-gliding, locally referred to as *parapente* and *ícaro*. Avid Venezuelan followers are estimated in the thousands and every year more and more aficionados from abroad come to try the best sites, with the year-round warm climate a definite plus.

Among the most popular sites are: in the Caracas area, Oripoto and Picacho de Galipán; in Aragua, El Jarillo, Loma Lisa (by La Victoria), and Placivel (30 minutes from La Victoria via Colonia Tovar); El Morro (in the Puerto La Cruz-Barcelona area); Anzoátegui and Humocaro in Lara; and, near the city of

Mérida, La Trampa, Cerro Negro, Las González, and Loma Redonda.

Surfing and windsurfing

Along the Central Litoral, the favorite spot for surfers is Playa Los Angeles (east of Naiguatá). Farther east, Chirimena (east of Higuerote in Miranda state) is another popular destination.

In Aragua, after the beautiful drive through Henri Pittier National Park to Cata, continue east to Cuyagua – considered Venezuela's best surfing beach. Meanwhile, surfers visiting Margarita head directly for Playa Parguita.

Rated among the top places in the world for windsurfing is Playa El Yaque, near Margarita Island's airport. (Waters off the neighboring island of Coche are also gaining popularity.)

Although not as widely publicized, windsurfing fanatics consider Adícora, on the west coast of Falcón's Paraguaná Peninsula, a prime location on a par with El Yaque. Also offering excellent conditions in Sucre state is Araya, at the tip of the peninsula of the same name (ferry service available from Cumaná; road access from Cariaco).

All of the principal windsurfing destinations have lodging directed specifically at windsurfers, including places for board and sail storage. They also offer lessons, and (except for Araya) rent equipment.

Those looking more for easy riding than for challenges enjoy windsurfing in Morrocoy National Park (Falcón), gliding between Chichiriviche shore and nearby keys.

Gone fishing

Although sport fishing is rarely promoted internally, outside of Venezuela, particularly among US fanatics, the quality and diversity of fishing in this country is renowned. Indeed, it has been known as a paradise for billfish alone for more than 30 years in international circles. And fishing for delicious yellowfin tuna on the La Guaira Bank (less than an hour off the East Coast from Caraballeda) is rated first choice in the world; from January to March catches of up to 20 a day are common.

After the tuna, the most sought-after species are: Atlantic blue marlin, white marlin, Atlantic sailfish, and swordfish. From February to April, grand slams (catching a blue and a white marlin, and a sailfish all in the same day) are more frequent than at any other time of the year.

Average white marlin on the La Guaira Bank are 45–68 kg (100–150 lbs), sailfish 27–68 kg (60–100 lbs), and blue marlin 55–159 kg (120–350 lbs), but catches can be much bigger: a recent record was a 545-kg (1,200-pound) blue.

Smaller but equally feisty game fish (all year) include wahoo, barracuda, bonito, and the colorful (chartreuse with blue dots) dolphin (locally known as *dorado* and not to be confused with porpoises, which frequently put on a ringside show, along with occasional whales).

Standard policy for sport fishing is catch-and-release (although a few *dorado*, tuna, peacock bass, and certain others can be kept).

all year round, but best in May, followed by June–September. Aereotuy airlines is the main operator, offering assorted packages through travel agencies.

Another option is La Tortuga island, northwest of Barcelona, a distinct virgin fishing destination where barracuda is the star.

Laguna de Tacarigua (at Río Chico) is the main location for tarpon, although the Gulf of Paria is another good spot. The *Salt Water Sportsman* magazine rates Venezuela as Number One for the period from July to August (though locals say that the biggest fish are more active from December–May), while the remaining months

Bonefishing in the flats of Los Roques Archipelago (a 35-minute flight from Maiquetía) has international fame. Fly fishing and light tackle are standard methods while wading the miles of firm, shallow flats is favored by the lightning-fast fighters. Their "discovery" in Los Roques has been relatively recent (since the late 1980s), but word spread rapidly of schools of thousands being common, most averaging about 1.8 kg (4 lbs) which is considered exceptional anywhere, and some more than 4.5 kg (10 lbs). Fishing is good here

TOP SPOT FOR FISHING

In a report in the magazine *Salt Water Sportsman* on the world's best fishing grounds, just for one period alone, in its February–March summary, Venezuela is listed as the first choice anywhere for Atlantic blue marlin, white marlin, yellowfin tuna, bonefish, swordfish; it was given second place for Atlantic sailfish and tarpon.

Especially convenient for foreign anglers flying in to Maiquetía, Venezuela's principal deep-sea fishing grounds are just northeast of there on the La Guaira Bank, less than an hour off the coast from Caraballeda (30 minutes east of the airport), where great quantities of billfish cruise the waters feeding on migrating tuna.

LEFT: windsurfing in Morrocoy National Park.
ABOVE: keeping dry – landsurfing on Isla de Coche.

carry a recommendation of Number Two on the globe. Tarpon here average 3–5 kg (8–10 lbs), although catches of 13–27 kg (30–60 lbs) are frequent, with even the occasional 70-kg (150-lb) whopper. Snook is another popular game fish, the best of which are bagged from February to April; this fish averages 1–3 kg (3–5 lbs), but up to 14 kg (30 lbs) is also possible.

The Andes is the top place for trout fishing, principally in glacial lakes of the *páramo* (roughly the area between Santo Domingo and Tabay) of Mérida.

TICKLE A TROUT

The trout season in Venezuela is from March 15 to September 30. Travel agencies can handle getting the required permit.

Payara, a fierce fighting fish with two huge razor-sharp lower teeth, is usually found in the same areas as *pavón*. Nevertheless, the biggest catches tend to come from fast-moving rapids.

Clubs and racquets

Participation in golf and racquet sports in Venezuela is rather limited because of the lack of public facilities in the country.

Public golf courses are non-existent. There are some excellent courses, but these are all within expensive country clubs. Although

Places throughout Venezuela provide great fishing for peacock bass (locally known as *pavón*), with its notoriously explosive strike and, pound for pound, considered the toughest-fighting freshwater game fish anywhere. Among favorite sites are Camatagua reservoir (Aragua), Guri reservoir (Bolívar), the Alto Ventuari and Casiquiare watersheds (Amazonas), and Cinaruco and Capanaparo Rivers in the heart of Apure's plains.

Reservoirs are usually easier to get to. But, along the Cinaruco River (best fished in January and February) 100 strikes a day are not uncommon, whereas in Amazonas there are fewer strikes but record sizes are much more likely.

access is sometimes available for guests at five-star hotels, this of course results in their use being restricted from the outset to the minority of travelers spending big bucks for lodging.

There are a few public tennis courts – which are normally in deplorable condition – but any worth using by serious players are found exclusively in private clubs or at certain 5-star hotels; the same circumstances apply for racquetball or squash.

Most of the top hotels have "Sports Clubs" which allow non-guests to use tennis courts, pool, gym, sauna, lockers, and other such facilities (depending on the hotel) with payment of a membership fee.

On two wheels

Perhaps because most of the population is carless, in rural areas in particular, bicycles are considered "the people's transportation" and cycling is very popular as a sport. Competitions are frequent throughout the country for all age and fitness levels and two major annual events draw international participants: La Vuelta de Táchira (a killer competition in this Andean state held in February) and the Vuelta de Venezuela (a cross-country contest held in late August or early September).

The combination of friendly climate and wide variety of landscapes has also begun

Soccer likewise has its company and community teams. Basketball tends to be limited more to pick-up games.

Bowling

Traditional bowling has never really caught on. Being an indoor sport and very disciplined it doesn't seem to fit in with most Venezuelans' idea of fun. But *bolas criollas* – similar to bowls but usually played on a bare dirt surface (not necessarily smooth and in a space of any chosen size) – is very popular, especially in the interior of the country. Rather than a sport, *bolas criollas* is perhaps better considered more

attracting great numbers of mountain bikers from around the globe seeking challenging, yet beautiful destinations.

Ball games

As with their followings as pro-team spectator sports, out of baseball, basketball and soccer, baseball is the most popular participant ball game, with nearly every company having its own team, along with a proliferation of community teams, and even Venezuela's equivalent to Little League: Los Criollitos.

LEFT: mountain biking in Mérida state.
ABOVE: *bolas criollas* on a sunny afternoon.

as an excuse for men to get out of the house and to have some beers with their buddies.

Two teams of four are formed, one using red, grapefruit-sized wooden balls, the other green ones. A small target ball, known as the *mingo*, is tossed out a short distance, and then players take turns trying to lob their ball as close as they can to it. To liven things up, if the opposition's balls are blocking the target, a player can always decide to blast the offending balls out of the way with a mighty direct hit. Add this to the usual cheering and heckling over close measurements, and what you have is a lot more fun than sedately rolling a ball down an alley over and over again. ❑

BENEATH THE WAVES

The great number and diversity of dive sites along the coast and around hundreds of offshore islands provide options for beginners and pros alike

On land, there's no denying that Venezuela offers it all to the tourist and explorer, from pristine beaches to the Andes mountain range and Amazon jungle. But for the adventurous snorkeler or scuba diver, there is a whole new world of life and breathtaking beauty to explore underwater.

Several of Venezuela's diving sites rate right up there among the top forms of marine viewing available in the Caribbean. *Aficionados* are beginning to discover that parts of the Venezuelan coastline can hold their own with Bonaire and the Cayman islands – considered two of the top diving sites in the world. The news hasn't caught on, and Venezuelan diving remains a diamond in the rough, with few tourists taking the time to discover its virgin offerings.

Anyone with a pair of goggles and a snorkel can enjoy the underwater life in Venezuela, but it should be noted that scuba diving can be dangerous if the right precautions aren't taken. There are only two compression chambers in Venezuela – one in Maracaibo and the other in La Guaira. Since quick transportation to the chambers may not always be possible, divers should already be fairly experienced before they come to Venezuela, or else take lessons in the country with qualified instructors.

Choosing a site

Unlike many other Caribbean destinations, Venezuela's long coastline offers a whole range of diving areas, giving divers the opportunity to explore new and different marine life each time in the water. In addition to the underwater flora and fauna, divers can also explore the remnants of sunken ships, some of which have been lying on the seabed since the 17th century.

There are three marine-based national parks in Venezuela, all ideal for different types of diving: Los Roques National Park covers a group of more than 350 tiny islands just off the northern Venezuelan coast; Morrocoy National Park

is located in the state of Falcón, on the country's western coast; and Mochima National Park is in the Puerto La Cruz/Barcelona area.

As well as marine-based National Parks, there are literally hundreds of potential sites scattered along Venezuela's coasts. Although it's possible to dive directly from the shoreline,

the best underwater life is found around the plethora of islands nearby. That means that divers must make arrangements to get to the islands by boat – and back to shore again!

The following is a run-down of what are currently considered the most exciting dive spots in Venezuela.

Chichiriviche de la Costa

The bay at Chichiriviche de la Costa, which also has a pleasant beach for non-diving companions, is a 90-minute drive via the Caracas–El Junquito–Colonia Tovar road, taking the turn-off to the north for El Límon-Chichiriviche de la Costa just before the entrance to Colonia

---

LEFT: among the coral on the Caribbean coast.
RIGHT: ready to take the plunge.

Tovar. Unfortunately, the road has deteriorated greatly in recent years, making access to Chichiriviche, as well as to the departure point for diving, possible only in a four-wheel-drive vehicle.

In Chichiriviche, a coral wall along the sides of the bay drops to a depth of 45 meters (145 ft), then a sand slope continues down to 90 meters (290 ft). The somewhat rocky bottom gives divers the opportunity to glimpse rock and crevice-dwelling marine life such as lobsters and moray eels, while the shallow bay offers a

> **CLOSE TO CARACAS**
>
> One of the closest dive sites to Caracas, Chichiriviche de la Costa is a perfect place for divers to spot large groupers, angelfish and an occasional sea turtle.

beautiful collection of brilliantly colorful small fish, octopus and sea horses.

Although good diving and decent snorkeling can normally be expected, visibility is sometimes limited here by the sediment deposited into the ocean by the river.

Easier access

With a focus on facilitating access to sites west of the central coast, a new service is being offered by Abismo Azul, based in the five-star Hotel Puerto Viejo (about 15 minutes west of Caracas's Maiquetía airport).

Its owner, Luis Fonseca, offers access by fast boats directly from the hotel's marina to many destinations that would normally require far more lengthy drives to reach departure points. Chichiriviche de la Costa or Oricao in Distrito Federal, for example, would otherwise require a drive of at least 90 minutes via the progressively deteriorating coastal road; or Cepe and Chuao, in Aragua state, normally first call for the drive of Caracas-Maracay-Choroní-Puerto Colombia (some 2–3 hours from Caracas), then a boat transfer from the port there of about $60.

Puerto Cabello

Farther to the west of Caracas, and about a 25-minute ride from the city of Valencia, is Puerto Cabello. Although this town is mainly known as an industrial port and a stopping-off point for container ships, it's possible to find some good diving on outlying islands. Isla Larga and Isla del Faro are the major diving sites here, although the latter is more suited for snorkelers since the maximum depth around the island is only about 15 meters (50 ft).

The waters off Isla Larga are also home to two ships sunk off Venezuela's coast – both World War II cargo ships. The rear of one boat sticks out of the water just off the island, while the prow is on the bottom at a depth of about 20 meters (65 ft). A coral wall has formed around the hull, giving an added dimension to the dive. In addition to the sting rays that can be seen roaming the sandy ocean bottom, many sponges, barracuda, lobsters, crabs and coral have taken over the hull of the 50-meter (165-ft) boat.

Another favorite dive spot, Islas Las Aves, is accessible by boat from either Puerto Cabello or Tucacas. Las Aves features some of the greatest variety of sea anemones that can be found in Venezuela. Another sunken boat – this one from a 17th-century fishing fleet – is located here. Exploring the wreck should be limited to experienced divers: the currents here are notoriously treacherous.

Morrocoy National Park

A three-and-a-half hour drive west from Caracas, Morrocoy is considered the best area for beginners. The water is especially clear and divers can only go down to around 30 meters (100 ft). The sandy sea bottom is comfortable and less intimidating than the rocky bottoms found at places such as Chichiriviche de la Costa and at islands in the Puerto La Cruz area. In addition, the water temperatures off Morrocoy are almost always warm so that a full wetsuit is not necessary.

Diving facilities in Morrocoy are provided by the long-time union of boatmen operating from both Tucacas and Chichiriviche. They offer a very reliable and regular shuttle service to all the islands (with posted prices for the round trip and pick-up at the hour you designate, even if you camp there overnight). Alternatively, you can contract them for full-day exclusive use.

creatures and colorful coral, which emerge to feed just when the sun goes down.

Higuerote

To the east of Caracas and about a 90-minute boat ride from the town of Higuerote (covering approximately 50 km/30 miles) lies Farallón Centinela. It and its partner, Faralloncito ("Little Farallón"), are nothing more than a couple of big rocks sticking up out of the ocean. But upon entering the adjacent waters, divers can only marvel at the variety of underwater flora and fauna on display. Farallón is actually the tip of an underwater mountain and

The sandy sea bottom is home to many species of coral, sea fans and sponges, all of which are growing out of the ocean bed. Because of the clarity of the water, excellent snorkeling can generally be found within a short swim of these islands' shores. It's easy to spot brightly colored angel fish, trumpet fish, needlefish and an occasional barracuda – all in water as shallow as 3 meters (10 ft).

Night diving is a special attraction at Morrocoy. A swoop with an underwater flashlight can often reveal otherwise unseen nocturnal

is equipped with a lighthouse at its peak, 30 meters (100 ft) above the surface. The area is located on the continental shelf, where the ocean bottom begins a gradual drop off to a depth of more than 400 meters (1,300 ft). Among other attractions, an 8-meter (26-ft) long underwater tunnel approximately 27 meters (80 ft) below the surface of Faralloncito is home to sharks, big groupers, large schools of barracuda and many queen angelfish.

At Farallón, divers rarely have a clue as to what interesting creature might float up from the ocean depths. Divers have even reported seeing whale sharks in the area. According to Marvi Cilli, a diving instructor for Subma Tur

LEFT: tube sponges.
ABOVE: pink anemones.

in Tucacas, "If you don't see a shark in Farallón Centinela, you'll never see one in your life."

The boat ride to Farallón can be a rather hair-raising experience. But the incredible diving at the other end makes it all worthwhile. However, it's worth noting that since strong currents are the norm, only experienced divers should try it.

Puerto La Cruz

Farther east – about five hours' drive from Caracas – lie the islands off Puerto La Cruz and

FAVORED WATERS

La Tortuga, about 80 km/48 miles off the coast northwest of Puerto La Cruz, is favored for its under-water wall and clear water, with a great abundance and variety of corals, crustaceans and fish.

More distant isles

Although they are more difficult to reach, for those underwater enthusiasts wanting an experience of a lifetime – one that rivals diving in Bonaire and the Cayman Islands – Los Roques archipelago and La Orchila are not to be missed.

Divers who have visited Los Roques come back raving about the strikingly beautiful marine life at Gran Roque, including sharks, barracuda, jacks, spotted rays, black margates and the soft coral that inhabit the arch-

Barcelona, included within Mochima National Park, where there is some excellent deep-water diving. Unlike Morrocoy, divers in this area can reach depths as great as 45 meters (150 ft). The currents are strong, and the water can be cold, so full-body wet-suits are mandatory.

Divers who make the effort will be enthralled to see the greatest variety of anemones anywhere in the world. Anemones are prevalent in the Puerto La Cruz area because they thrive in the rocky terrain that exists here. Divers have also reported seeing dolphins and an occasional whale. It's advisable to go to this area between July and November, when underwater visibility is at its very best.

ipelago. There are also several caves at depths around 25–30 meters (80–100 ft), which are guaranteed to leave any underwater photographer spellbound.

Although commercial airlines generally don't allow divers to bring full tanks aboard, with the recent development of the tourist industry on Los Roques there are now compressors available there. Moreover, most of the boats furnishing tourist services have their own compressors as well.

Isla La Orchila is even more difficult to get to, since it is a Venezuelan military and government retreat. Although civilians are rarely allowed to visit, diving groups are sometimes invited for long weekends – which turn out to be unforgettable experiences. Since relatively few divers visit the virgin waters of La Orchila, they are teeming with fish, crustaceans and underwater plantlife. Divers have reported spotting huge lobsters, moray eels, manta rays, large groupers and schools of hundreds of different fish species.

Preserving the underwater world

It's safe to say that the environment has hardly come to the political forefront yet in this developing country. Nevertheless, some Venezuelans in the diving community are working assidu-

technically speaking the waters of Morrocoy, Los Roques and Mochima are off-limits to spear fishermen. Unfortunately, a large number of poaching spear fishermen have put them on their itineraries, not thinking twice about obtaining fish illegally at the expense of the underwater habitat. On rare occasions, a spear fisherman gets caught in the act and is reported to the authorities (the National Guard). However, it's highly unusual for a violator to be severely punished, so the financial incentives outweigh the risks.

Part of the problem is that there are simply not enough National Guardsmen to patrol ade-

ously to make sure its pristine marine areas stay that way. It's not an easy job. "The Venezuelan people are going to ruin all that they have before they realize how lucky they were to have it," laments Marvi Cilli of Subma Tur.

One of the most long-standing environmental controversies in Venezuela has been the killing of dolphins by tuna fishermen who use the archaic purse seine nets, which led to a boycott of the industry by the United States.

Other issues have received less publicity. Because they are classified as national parks,

quately the vast areas that make up the marine national parks. And once people are nailed in the act of breaking the law, they can quite often avoid criminal prosecution by giving the underpaid guardsmen a bribe.

Environmental damage is also done by boat owners who decide to dock on the coral reef itself. Many boaters drop their huge anchors overboard without any forethought, possibly killing entire colonies of coral. Scuba divers and snorkelers in Venezuela must be certain not to touch coral because even the slightest contact can kill the vegetation.

"We teach our students never to touch anything when diving," says Marvi Cilli. ❑

LEFT: a school of fish in Morrocoy National Park.
ABOVE: coral in the Aves de Sotavento archipelago .

PLACES

A detailed guide to the entire country, with principal sites clearly cross-referenced by number to the maps

To the delight of visitors and residents alike, Venezuela is an easy country to explore. The road system is considered the best in South America, and scheduled commercial airlines service every part of the country. Moreover, since most of the population doesn't own private vehicles, there is plentiful and inexpensive public transportation in every part of the country.

Caracas is the "first encounter" for most travelers, being the capital and just across the coastal mountains from the country's principal international and national airport of Maiquetía. Spread out in a narrow, high valley, with year-round spring-like climate and a beautiful backdrop of the mountains of El Avila National Park, it offers a wide range of cultural attractions, restaurants, shopping, top-class hotels, parks, and an excellent subway system. However, like any large city, it also suffers from traffic congestion and areas of obvious poverty.

But it is the Venezuela outside Caracas that most travelers come to see. A key attraction is its 3,000 km (1,800 miles) of Caribbean coastline with beaches and water sports to suit every taste. The most luxurious resorts are found east of Caracas, including Venezuela's most popular tourist destination, Isla Margarita. Another "hot spot" is Los Roques Archipelago National Park, a 45-minute flight north from Maiquetía. Less developed is the coastline to the west, where the most popular beach areas are those of Playa Colombia (near Choroní) and the islands and cays of Morrocoy National Park.

Second in popularity is the Andean region, with the state and city of Mérida being the principal targets. The city is proud of having the world's longest and highest cable car, providing a close-up view of the country's tallest peaks. Picturesque mountain villages seem like scenes from past centuries and proudly conserve age-old traditions.

The arid northwest offers everything from the internationally acclaimed colonial architecture in Falcón's capital of Coro to adjacent sand dunes, and the oil-rich state of Zulia.

Venezuela's richest farmlands are in the midwestern plains; while the central plains of Apure and Barinas, referred to simply as the *llanos*, are Venezuela's Wild West, with sprawling cattle ranches, fiercely independent cowboys, and fame for great bird-watching.

The "last frontiers" of the Guayana Region comprise nearly half of the national territory. Here, the sparce population is primarily indigenous and the richly endowed geography is among the most spectacular in the world, including the huge and fascinating delta of the Orinoco River; and magnificent *tepuyes* (mesas of rock billions of years old) topped by unique life forms and inspiration for works such as Sir Arthur Conan Doyle's *The Lost World*. ❏

PRECEDING PAGES: a holiday weekend in Choroní; siesta hour in the *llanos*; a young mule train leader in the Sierra Nevada de Mérida.
LEFT: Checkpoint Carlos in Los Aleros, the reproduction of a typical pre-1950s Mérida village.

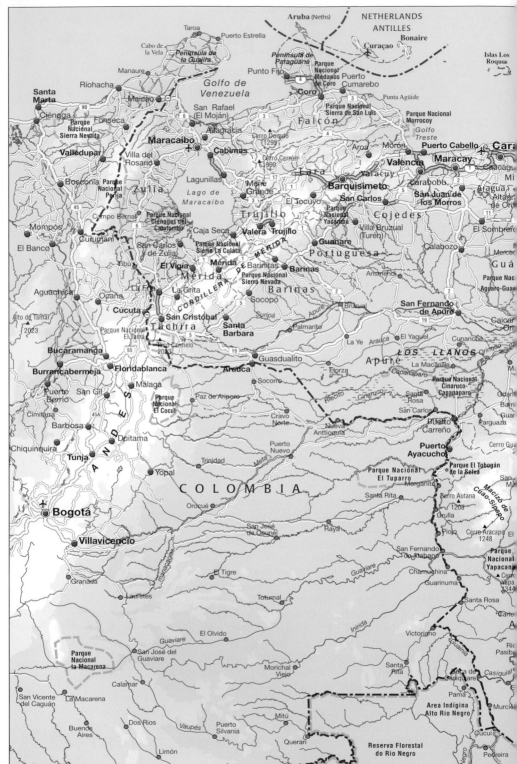

Venezuela

CARIBBEAN SEA

ST VINCENT AND
THE GRENADINES

St George's GRENADA

0   100 km
0   100 miles

N

Isla La
Blanquilla

Isla de
Margarita

Islas Los
Testigos

Tobago

Isla La
Tortuga

Nueva Esparta
Punta de
Piedras   Porlamar
Carúpano

Parque Nacional
Península de Paría

TRINIDAD
AND
TOBAGO

Toco

Port of
Spain

Sangre Grande

Cumaná

Sucre

Güiria
Golfo de Paría
Punta Campana

Trinidad

San Fernando

Puerto La Cruz

Parque Nacional
Mochima

Parque
Nacional
Turuépano

Clarines

Barcelona

Carúpito

Onoto

El Caribe

Maturín

Pedernales

ATLANTIC

Zaraza

Anaco

Monagas

Guamal

Parque
Nacional
Mariusa

Misión San
de Guavo

OCEAN

San José
de Guanipa

Temblador

Tucupita

El Tigre

Chaguaramas

Delta
Amacuro

San José de
Amacuro

Zuata

Anzoátegui

(Puerto
Ordaz)

(San Félix)
Ciudad Guayana

La Ceiba

Morawhanna

Requeña

Soledad

Upata

Campamento
Río Grande

Mapire

La Carolina

Ciudad
Bolívar

La Ceiba

Villa Lola

El Cogollar

El Miamo

El Callao

Reniquea

Bochinche

Port Kaituma

Cerro Mato
1063

La Esperanza

Embalse
de Guri

El Manteco

Tumeremo

Purgatori

Arakaka

Marlborough

Las Trincheras

Hato
Bucaral

La Quina

La Paragua

Maipuru

Cuyuni

Fairfield

La Vergareña

Sabanita

El Dorado

La Reforma

Aurora

Peters
Mine

Georgetown

San José
de Nicharo

Bolívar

Caño Negro

Irlana

Las Claritas

Dartica

Meseta
de Icutú

Entre Ríos

Paraguá

Wareipa

Parque

Sierra de Lema

Llepa

Kamarang

GUYANA

Paranaquire

Gualquinima-
tepui

Cerro Pigma
1703

Panipa

Auyán-
tepui

Nacional

Iboribo

LA GRAN SABANA

Opadai

Oma

Cerro Daku
1790

Tanimiña

Campatoy

Caroni

Urimán

Canaima

Monte Roraima
2810

Orinduik

Mahdia

Ituni

Parque Nacional
Jaua-Sarisariñama

Ganacoco-
jidi

Wonkén

Arinichi

Santa Elena
de Uairén

Kurupukari

SURINAM

Junglaven

Sarisariñama-jidi
2500

Meseta
de Ichún

Mahigia

Area
Indígena
Raposa
Serra do Sul

Annai

Apoteri

Kumaka

Mowichiña
macare

Culpigima

Cerro Kirikiri
1312

Içabarú

Milagre

SERRA PACARAIMA

Pirara

Lucie

rque Nacional
ida Marahuaca

erro Duira
232

Esmeralda

Tepequém

Santa Cruz

Uraricoera

174

Lethem

Dadanawa

Aishalton

Parque
Nacional

Parque

Indígena

Boa Vista

Mucajaí

Isherton

Parima-
Tapirapecó

Cerro Delgado
Chalbaud
2997

Mayajan-teri

Jaya-teri

Yanomami

Caracaraí

Bilaku

Sierra de Unturán

Aratabi-teri

Akave-teri

BRAZIL

Vista Alegre

Novo
Paraíso

Serranía Tapirapecó

San José
de Ahua

Moderna

174

a de
ina

Denati

CARACAS

Glass-walled office buildings tower over the few remaining colonial structures in central Caracas, while makeshift slums form an ever-expanding ring around the nation's capital

Map on page 130

Caracas

When conquistador Diego de Losada founded Caracas on July 25, 1567, he thought he had found an ideal location. The city would lie in a narrow valley with refreshing breezes, few mosquitos and days that were sunny and warm – but never too hot – all year round. Naturally, de Losada did not dream of the explosive growth the city has seen in recent decades. He certainly did not foresee that more than four million people would one day squeeze into the farming hamlet named for the fierce Caracas indians.

Today, Caracas is a city with growing pains, some spectacular. Shanty towns spread up the slopes of the mountains boxing in this glitzy, glittering city. But, for the most part, the solution to overcrowding has been to build vertically, making Caracas the high rise capital of South America that city architects love and hate. Except for the crumbling streets of the La Pastora neighborhood and historic buildings surrounding Plaza Bolívar, visible signs of the past are gone.

Backwater to a chaotic capital

Caracas was never an important Spanish viceroyalty and Venezuela did not have the gold, the sophisticated indian civilizations or even the strategic importance of some other South American countries. Because of this rather pale history, *caraqueños* (as the city's inhabitants are called) worship the modern. In the boom years of the 1970s and early 1980s their petroleum wealth gave them enough money to follow the philosophy of buying new rather than repairing or restoring the old.

Colonial Caracas is difficult to imagine, looking at the Caracas of today. The Guaire River is still there, now murky and controlled within concrete-lined channels, but you'd have to strip away highways, flatten the skyscrapers and insert farm fields and palm trees before you come close to picturing the original city. If the task requires too much imagination, you can always head downtown to the Concejo Municipal, the town hall, and take a look at the 18th-century painting of *Nuestra Señora de Caracas* (Our Lady of Caracas) hanging there. Much of the canvas is occupied by the white-clad virgin, but tucked into the center bottom of the painting is the city of Santiago de León de Caracas as it was known in the 18th century: nothing more than a collection of adobe houses with red tile roofs and courtyards. While Lima was filled with mansions for Spanish viceroys, Quito was graced by more than 50 colonial churches and Potosí basked in the wealth of its silver mines, Caracas was a small malaria-ridden outpost where nothing happened except for the occasional earthquake or pirate raid.

As recently as a century ago Caracas was still a plain dotted with trees, farmers' fields and one-story

PRECEDING PAGES: a panoramic view of central Caracas. **LEFT:** music to *caraqueños'* ears. **BELOW:** jammed traffic gives way to a mobile market.

Central Caracas

↑ Barcelona

500 m
500 yds

whitewashed houses. The tallest structure was the Cathedral spire. In 1955 the population of Caracas hit one million, although it wasn't until 1958 that the first building of more than six stories was completed, the Centro Simón Bolívar. Now, skyscrapers fill the valley and the population is four times greater, explaining why Caracas' reservoirs are inadequate and water is rationed in the dry season, why its highways are bumper-to-bumper and parking – let alone walking – is a definite challenge.

Superb subway

One exception to flagging public services is the Caracas Metro, the best friend of tourists wishing to explore the city. The Metro opened in 1983 following a year of public education advertisements aimed at teaching normally unrestrained *caraqueños* that graffiti, pushing, yelling, eating and a long list of other infractions would not be permitted. Against all expectations, the campaign was a success. The Metro is clean, quiet and efficient – astonishingly different from the above-ground scene of undisciplined commuters who shove through lines to enter buses, or the sometimes uncooperative drivers.

Since its inauguration, the French-built subway has extended its original east-west line and added two north-south lines, as well as complementary Metrobus feeder lines which service areas well beyond subway coverage, connecting with given Metro stations, and with tickets good for both a bus and Metro ride.

Although a raging success, the Metro could never accommodate the city's entire demand for public transportation. That is why, above ground, Caracas is complete chaos. Streets are jammed with slow, fume-spewing buses, honking mini-buses (known as *por puestos*) and tens of thousands of taxi cabs, along

Map on page 130

BELOW: an example of the Caracas Metro's impressive art collection.

ART IN THE METRO

Almost everyone visiting Caracas has noticed some of the artwork situated under or above ground at the stations of the capital's subway, but normally without realizing the extent of the Metro's "collection".

More than three dozen major works decorate the stations, with the list of their creators a virtual "Who's Who in Venezuelan Artists": Héctor Poleo, Harry Abend, Marisol Escobar, Carlos Cruz Diez, Jesús Soto, Lya Bermúdez, Rafael Barrios, Gego, Mercedes Pardo, Francisco Narváez, Alejandro Otero, Enrico Armas, Max Pedemonte, Beatriz Blanco, and many others.

Most of the art inside the stations is beyond the turnstiles. This means that you have to buy a maximum-price one-ride ticket to see it, but also that one ticket will let you observe the great majority, getting off the train to view the art at each station and re-boarding without leaving the station and having to pay again. If you want to see the outdoor art, you will have to pay to re-enter the system.

You can also save time and money with multi-ride Metro tickets (just for subway, or *Ida y Vuelta* – round-trip destination ticket. They can be purchased at many newsstands and shops bearing a large "M" sign near Metro stops as well as in each station.

with the private vehicles of any *caraqueño* with the need to drive in the city. And, like Los Angeles in the US – another car-loving city built in a basin – air pollution is a problem, especially with the lack of any emissions controls and the use of leaded gasoline.

According to statistics, more than 40 percent of Caracas residents spend at least two hours in cars and buses every day, not because they travel long distances to work, but because of traffic congestion. Another 37 percent commute for at least an hour.

Unplanned expansion

There are no easy solutions to the city's problems. Already overtaxed, Caracas is still growing. Immigration to the city continues, fuelled by poor Peruvians, Ecuadorians, Colombians and other South Americans who find it easier to buy visas or forged papers into Venezuela than to continue north to the United States. The homeless and the mentally ill sleep on cardboard in shop doorways. And Caracas' sidewalks are clogged by street vendors offering everything from strawberries to shoulder pads.

Studies show that there are more than one million vehicles in Caracas.

Even so, experienced South American travelers will find the Venezuelan capital empty of the abject poverty rampant in other countries. There are fewer beggars and panhandlers. The shanty towns of the poor are not built of discarded cardboard and tin sheets but of cement and clay blocks; some squatter neighborhoods (*barrios*) even have running water, electricity and sewage systems. Still, millions of *caraqueños* live in poverty and are surrounded by crime.

BELOW: herbs and traditional medicines for sale on the roadside.

The Caracas workday begins long before dawn. For the poor, this is due to the long lines and time-consuming transfers for public transportation. However, even residents of exclusive suburban apartments and houses with private vehicles start filling the freeways as the sun is just appearing to drop the kids off at school and join the *cola* – the daily traffic jams at peak hours – from 6–9.30am, 11.30–2.30pm, 4.30–8.30pm and most hours in between.

Trying to keep their heads above water in the face of continually rising costs and decreasing real income, lower and middle class *caraqueños* now inevitably have something going on the side to bring in extra money, with secretaries often selling cosmetics or jewelry to colleagues, executives doing some freelance consulting, or technicians offering repair services at evenings and weekends.

Colonial Caracas

Although Caracas prides itself on being a modern metropolis, if one looks hard, there are still some historic corners. The best place to begin exploring the city is at the colonial center, **Plaza Bolívar ❶**. In a country where nearly every city and town has a plaza named after independence leader Simón Bolívar, it is some honor to be the original Plaza Bolívar – which this Caracas square is.

Towering centenary trees shade the equestrian statue of the Liberator at the plaza's center. Children chase pigeons around its edges, the disabled hawk lottery tickets and camera-wielding tourists snap photos.

Map on page 130

Aged *caraqueños* sit on shady benches and reminisce about the days when Caracas was a smaller and considerably quieter capital.

Just as Plaza Bolívar is a hub of activity now, it was the scene of spy rendezvous, political forums, concerts, public executions, markets, and even bullfights in past centuries. The plaza is flanked by Venezuela's symbols of power: the Catedral, Palacio Arzobispal, Concejo Municipal, Capitolio Nacional where the Congress meets, and the so-called Casa Amarilla which houses the Foreign Ministry.

The **Casa Amarilla** ❷ is one of the oldest buildings in the city, reconstructed in 1689 on the foundation of an earthquake-damaged structure dating from 1610. It formerly served as presidential palace and residence, and even as the Royal Prison. Among various stories relating to the origin of its name is that when Gen. Guzmán Blanco became president, he had it painted the color of his political party, yellow (*amarillo* in Spanish).

It is a curious *caraqueño* custom, a holdover from colonial days, to identify addresses not by street or number but by their location between corners which each bear a nickname. Many corners have logical names – having been named for a long-standing building or activity there, but others are frivolous or linked to now-forgotten anecdotes. "Hospital", self-explanatory, was the name of the corner where medical treatment was dispensed; "Pelota" (Ball) is the corner where ball games were once played; "Pele el Ojo" (Keep Your Eye Peeled) was once a seedy part of town; but few remember how names such as "Cola de Pato" (Duck Tail) or "Aguacatico" (Little Avocado) made their way onto the Caracas scene.

The **Catedral** ❸, at the corner, is known as La Torre ("the tower") in recognition of the church spire's former lofty status. Although rebuilt after earthquakes, and modified to accommodate new architectural styles over the

BELOW: pigeons and polaroids in the Plaza Bolívar.

centuries, the Cathedral is modest by Latin American standards. But its collection of religious art is outstanding. The painting of Christ's Resurrection is said to be a Rubens donated by a French admiral who escaped harm during a storm which blew off the coast of Venezuela. The unfinished *Last Supper* is a work by beloved Venezuelan painter Arturo Michelena, and *Purgatorio* by Cristóbal Rojas is a haunting canvas. The crucifix in the church is a model of the cross Columbus took to the Dominican Republic in 1514; the copy was given to Venezuelan Cardinal José Alí Lebrún during a visit by Pope John Paul II.

A side chapel in the Cathedral is dedicated to the Bolívar family. Here, under a Moorish ceiling painted to represent the Holy Trinity, lie the remains of the Liberator's wife and parents. Twelve years after his death, Simón Bolívar's remains were brought from Colombia and interred in the chapel. They were moved to the Panteón Nacional in 1876.

At the south side of the Cathedral is the **Museo Sacro** ❹ (closed Mon; token admission fee), the former convent, which has been restored to highlight its vintage architecture and to provide a space for rotating art exhibits and even a popular café.

The **Palacio Arzobispal** ❺, more than 350 years old and remodeled yet again in recent years, is one of the few structures in the plaza to have survived earthquake damage. From 1637 to 1803 it was the bishop's residence before it was upgraded to its present status as the home of the archbishop. Next door is the **Concejo Municipal** ❻, a structure that may have had more functions than any other building in the downtown area. The original building, a seminary dedicated to Santa Rosa of Lima, was the only higher education facility for young men in the whole of Caracas. Severely damaged in the earthquake of

Plaza Bolívar is home to Edificio La Fancia, a gold lover's paradise that houses floor after floor of tiny jewelry shops. Some of their designs incorporate the now hard-to-find Margarita pearls and Venezuelan gemstones.

BELOW: a friendly disagreement.

1641, it was formally reinaugurated, after major reconstruction, in 1696. In 1725, the Spanish King Felipe V ordered it to be renamed the Royal University, a center for learning open only to young men with the proper lineage and Christian morals. In the structure's chapel, a holdover from the building's religious origins, Venezuela's Declaration of Independence was written. It was not until 1870 that the complex became the seat of the city government. Rebuilt and modified, much of the present building dates only from the turn of the century.

The little-known **Museo de Caracas** (open Tue–Fri 9am–noon, 2–4.30pm; Sat, Sun, hols 10.30am–3pm; free), hidden away in the Concejo Municipal (facing Plaza Bolívar), houses some half-dozen scale-models of central Caracas created by architect Ruth Neumann depicting how it looked in different periods of its history – not only the buildings, but figures showing dress, transportation, wares of street merchants, and such like. The museum also contains a marvelous collection of miniatures created by Raúl Santana depicting every aspect of early life in Venezuela. Between these two lovingly made displays, one can clearly visualize Caracas (and Venezuela) of the past. As a bonus, there is also an ample representation of the works of Venezuelan painter Emilio Boggio (1857–1920).

Gobernación, the headquarters of the Distrito Federal government, has an art gallery on the ground floor with frequent exhibits, but no fixed hours.

Convent turned Capitol

The gold-domed building by the southwest corner of Plaza Bolívar is the **Capitolio Nacional ❼**, or Congress building. When the rabidly anti-Catholic Antonio Guzmán Blanco, one of Venezuela's string of 19th-century dictators, outlawed all convents – declaring they were incompatible with the ideals of a

Map on page 130

LEFT: golden dome: Capitolio Nacional.
BELOW: tropical gothic at Santa Capilla.

liberal and advanced society, the exiled included the nuns from the Concepción convent which was once located on this spot. The building was leveled and the new Legislative Palace, built in an amazing 114 days of construction, opened in 1874. The main building of the Federal Palace was completed four years later, but the gold dome was not added until 1890.

The walls and ceilings of this Federal Palace (closed Mon and 12.30–3pm; free) are covered with patriotic works by Venezuelan artists, including *Tovar y Tovar*, whose scene of the Independence War's decisive Battle of Carabobo was painted in sections in Paris then shipped to Venezuela to be fitted into the building's cupola. Here, too, is Peruvian artist Gil de Castro's famous painting of Bolívar standing on an orange and black checked floor.

The black marble box displayed in the Capitolio holds the gold key to the urn containing the Liberator's remains in the **Panteón Nacional** 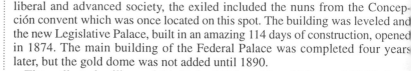 (open Tue–Fri 10am–noon, 2.30–4.30pm, opening an hour later on weekends, hols; free), the national monument half a dozen blocks directly north of the Cathedral. Guarded around the clock, the Panteón is the mausoleum for Venezuela's most venerated heroes. An ideal time to visit the Panteón is just before it closes, when guards parade through the building.

The **Biblioteca Nacional** or National Library (open Tue–Sun; free) faces the Panteón. Along with expected books, it has an exposition salon with rotating in-depth shows, such as one on the science, art, and culture related to the Orinoco River, and another hall used as the **Centro de Fotografía de Conac** (open Tues–Sat; free).

Although he died alone and penniless, shunned by fellow Venezuelans, Simón Bolívar today is one of the continent's most revered heroes. Two blocks east

TIP

Visitors are welcome to enter the Capitolio Nacional to admire its art, however no photography is permitted.

BELOW: inside the Bolívar museum.

om the Capitolio, between the corners of San Jacinto and Traposos, are the **Museo Bolivariano 9** (with a permanent display of memorabilia relating to Bolívar himself and to the most important Venezuelan families of the Bolivarian era) and the neighboring **Casa Natal 10** (both open Tue–Fri 9am–noon, 2–5pm, Sat–Sun 10am–1pm, 2–5pm; free). The latter is the reconstructed house (now museum) where the Liberator was born to María Concepción Palacios y Blanco and Don Juan Vicente de Bolívar, a wealthy businessman 32 years her senior. When Don Juan Vicente died at 70, he left a young widow with four children, Simón being the youngest.

The house remained in the Bolívar family until 1806. Sold by heirs, it passed through numerous hands and fell into disrepair. In 1911 it was purchased through private donations and ceded to the nation to create a museum honoring Bolívar. In the patio of the Casa Natal is the stone font where he was baptized.

Fighting talk

It was not far from the Casa Natal that the Liberator met one of the biggest challenges to his campaign to free Venezuela from Spanish rule. Painter Tito Salas has captured in oil the moment when Bolívar, on the plaza at the corner of San Jacinto, addressed the priests and people who had claimed that an 1812 earthquake that destroyed the plaza was God's message to him to stop his seditious talk. "If Nature opposes us, we will fight against her and we will make her obey us,"Bolívar exclaimed. The famous quote is recorded here in huge letters on one side of the building.

Several blocks to the south is the **Teatro Nacional 11** (Avenida Lecuna, at the corner of Cipreses), inaugurated in 1905, and whose restoration after years of neglect was finally completed in 1998. However, despite looking much smarter now, from a security point of view its location is far from ideal for attracting culture fans.

On the corner El Chorro stands the headquarters of the H.L. Boulton Company, as it has since 1870. A modern high-rise has replaced the original one-story building. However, neither its history nor that of the country has been forgotten. On the 11th floor, one can visit the **Museo Fundación John Boulton 12** (open Mon–Fri 8.30–11.30am, 1.30–4.30pm; free), with an outstanding collection, built up by the family over a period of more than 150 years. It includes colonial furnishing and art, china and pottery, paintings by renowned artists, the largest collection of memorabilia relating to Simón Bolívar in the world, original books from the Boulton Company since its foundation in the early 1820s, and an extensive microfilm and document library on economic and historical themes.

Although some way from other principal tourist attractions, if you have a vehicle at your disposal, you might take a quick detour to visit **Los Próceres** (Vivienda Los Próceres, Autopista El Valle, exit: Los Próceres). These formal gardens were built in the '50s by dictator Marcos Pérez Jiménez as part of one of the most opulent officers' clubs in the world. At their southern extreme are two towering marble pillars with the names of Venezuela's *próceres* – heroes –

Map on page 130

The Panteón Nacional: the resting place for Venezuela's great Liberator.

BELOW: the Casa Natal, Bolívar's birthplace, overshadowed by the modern city.

carved into them. A guard of honor in colonial-style uniforms keeps vigilance On July 5 (Independence Day) there is a colorful parade with attendance by the president and an immense Venezuelan flag is hung between the two pillars.

Slum renovation

A few blocks west of the Casa Natal is the city's most misnamed neighborhood, **El Silencio**. Even the oldest *caraqueños* don't remember a time when the title was appropriate for the traffic-clogged area, noisy with sidewalk vendors.

Venezuela was the first colony to proclaim independence from Spain on July 5 1811. The annual parade on this day along the Paseo de Los Próceres is a colorful event.

BELOW: Bolívar's words after the 1812 earthquake.

Years ago, this neighborhood, which had degenerated into miserable slums, was designated as the guinea pig in the city's boldest experiment in urban planning. Buildings were razed and replaced with Venezuela's first urban renewal project. Completed in 1943, the El Silencio *bloques* are low-rise apartment buildings, designed by architect Carlos Raúl Villanueva. Although the overall excellent design and handsome details such as the distinct stone doorways are still evident, unfortunately, lack of maintenance and the low socio-economic make-up of the area have contributed to its increasingly seedy appearance.

Far away from the eastside neighborhoods of the rich, here is the **Palacio de Miraflores** , once the most opulent home in the country, constructed by former president General Joaquín Crespo in the 1880s. Unfortunately, in the eight years it took to build the mansion, Crespo died in battle. The man whose name is most associated with Miraflores never had the chance to live there.

Since the early 20th century, when the government purchased the building, Miraflores has been used by every president as a work-place. It is decorated with European tapestries, damasks and French and Italian furniture.

Atop a steep hill to the west of El Silencio is Caracas' oldest park, El

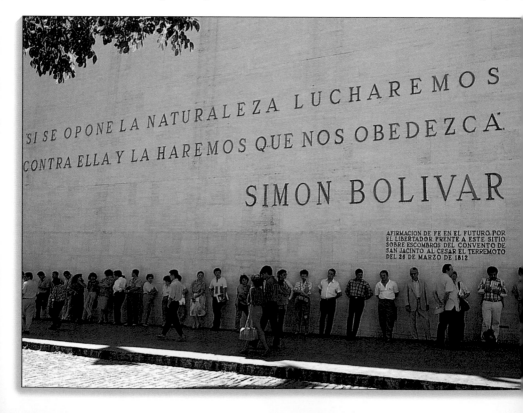

SI SE OPONE LA NATURALEZA LUCHAREMOS CONTRA ELLA Y LA HAREMOS QUE NOS OBEDEZCA

SIMON BOLIVAR

AFIRMACION DE FE EN EL FUTURO POR EL LIBERTADOR FRENTE A ESTE SITIO SOBRE ESCOMBROS DEL CONVENTO DE SAN JACINTO AL CESAR EL TERREMOTO DEL 26 DE MARZO DE 1812

Calvario ⓐ, built in the 1870s. Named for the Stations of the Cross once found at its summit, this was once a gathering spot for pilgrims who, with lighted candles in hand, followed paths up the hill past the crosses that marked each station. The one cross that survives is in a museum. Although it appears in many guidebooks, the park is not safe to enjoy any more, singly or in groups, by day or night, because of the dangerous *barrio*, 23 de Enero, immediately behind it.

Museum mecca

Most museums, galleries, and parks (which have entrance gates) are closed Mondays and at the few which charge admission, the entry fee is usually less than US$1, used more as a means of controlling entry than for income.

One of the city's most outstanding museums is the **Quinta de Anauco Museo de Arte Colonial** ⓑ, a restored coffee hacienda converted into a showpiece of colonial art and furniture (open Tue–Fri 9–11.30am, 2–4.30pm; Sat, Sun, hols 10am–5pm; closed Carnival Tues, Thu, Fri of Holy Week, 1 May, 20 Dec–10 Jan; token admission fee). On Avenida Panteón in San Bernardino, this house, with Andalusian and Moorish touches, was built in 1797 by a well-connected military official. The owner fled to Curaçao with others loyal to the Spanish Crown during the revolution, and the house was confiscated and rented to the Marqués del Toro, a friend and collaborator of Simón Bolívar. A bust of del Toro sits amid the orchids and citrus trees in the tropical garden. Bolívar was a frequent guest at the house, which he loved for its view, and he spent his last night in Caracas here before heading to Colombia, where he died.

Within several blocks to the south and east of the Bellas Artes Metro station, is the largest concentration of museums and cultural centers in Venezuela.

Map on page 130

BELOW: Caracas has a wide-ranging cultural scene.

Tickets for the *Museo de los Niños* can be purchased in advance and are good for either the morning or the afternoon. Visitors can go with guides or explore independently.

To the south is the mega-complex urban renewal project of **Parque Central**. It was designed to solve the deficit of downtown housing, office space, moder shops, and is a city in itself, complete with school, its own Catholic parish, an all other services. It has seven 44-story apartment towers; two 225-meter (740 ft)-high office towers (offices of the Tourism Ministry – Corpoturismo – are i the west tower); more than 40,000 sq. meters (47,850 sq. yards) of commercia space; and three museums:

◆ **Museo de los Niños** ⑯ (at the west end; open Wed–Sun 9am–noon 2–5pm; admission fee; very crowded with families at weekends). This is a outstanding, privately operated, hands-on children's museum with participa tive displays over five levels on all aspects of the physical sciences, biology communications, and ecology. There is also a huge new center which focuse on science and technology, complete with rocket simulators.

◆ **Museo de Arte Contemporáneo de Caracas Sofía Imber** ⑰ (open Tue– Sun; free). In the eastern extreme of Parque Central, this internationall acclaimed museum has changing exhibitions and a permanent collection tha features Venezuela's finest contemporary artists, including Marisol, Carlos Cru Diez, Alejandro Otero and Jesús Soto, and many others. It also has one of th finest collections of the works of Pablo Picasso in Latin America; and works b Chagall, Matisse, Braque, Leger, Fernando Botero and Henry Moore, amongs other famous names. There is a café, which serves salads in its sculpture garde and an extensive library.

◆ **Museo del Teclado**, or Keyboard Museum (open Wed–Sun 9am–noon 2–4pm; token admission fee). This has exhibits (mostly of antique musical instru ments) and also puts on weekend concerts.

BELOW: trips to the theater are popular with *caraqueños*.

A short distance to the west of Parque Central on Avenida Bolívar is the new **Museo de la Estampa y del Diseño Carlos Cruz Diez** (open daily; free), with exhibits of works of its renowned namesake plus other design themes.

Map
on page
130

ine Arts district

iagonally from Parque Central, in front of the Caracas Hilton, is the *Bellas rtes* (Fine Arts) area. Its focal point is the **Teatro Teresa Carreño** ⑱, a vast omplex with two main halls, including the national theater, national symphony rchestra and the contemporary dance troupe, Danzahoy. Guided tours, lasting n hour, are given several times a day, for a small fee.

Next to the TTC is the home of the avant-garde Rajatabla theater troupe, and ne **Ateneo de Caracas** ⑲, venue for stage presentations, film festivals, and oncerts, as well as two art galleries, a restaurant, and a huge bookstore. Behind ese you'll find the **Museo de Ciencias Naturales** (closed Mon), a science useum with free admission to the general exhibition halls but special hours and e for *"Tierra Increíble,"* featuring a robotic dinosaur: 9am–noon, 2–4.30pm hu; 9am–1pm Fri; 10am–5pm Sat, Sun, hols.

Facing the science museum is the classical-style **Galería de Arte Nacional** ⑳ losed Mon; free), which features exclusively works of Venezuelan artists, and so houses the Cinemateca Nacional – the national film library, with an ample rogram of classic, art, and foreign films (for programming, call 02 576 1491). ehind is the ultra-modern **Museo de Bellas Artes** (closed Mon; free), which ffers changing displays of art from around the world. Both of these museums ere the work of the same architect, Carlos Raúl Villanueva, who also directed l Silencio's rebirth.

BELOW: guitar lesson on the Sabana Grande Boulevard.

The **Universidad Central de Venezuela** ㉑, or simply UCV (three bloc
south of Plaza Venezuela, with the Jardín Botánico providing a buffer from t
Francisco Fajardo freeway), is another master work of Villanueva, who manag
to incorporate into the design four large colored-glass windows, four frescos,
major sculptures and 49 murals, among other works of art. Its construction to
from 1945–57. While maintenance has not been perfect, the integration of a
and function in the campus presents an interesting documentary of what, in
time, made headlines on the international level. It is still considered one of t
most important architectural complexes in Venezuela.

Open-air "mall"

*Many of the poor in
Caracas live in small
hillside shanties
called ranchos.*

Except for the wealthy who live in large homes (*quintas*) surrounded by walle
in grounds with exuberant flowers, mango trees and bougainvillea, and the po
who live in hillside shanties, most *caraqueños* live in skyscrapers. Yet, despi
being high above ground, *caraqueños* haven't lost their farming roots. Vines tra
down the sides of buildings, bright flowers spring from window planters an
inside apartments, potted plants thrive in the tropical climate.

But Caracas is not all high-rise concrete jungle. The biggest outdoor gathe
ing place for pedestrian fun is **Sabana Grande** ㉒, a car-free boulevard th
stretches 2 km (1 mile) from **Plaza Venezuela** ㉓ to the Chacaíto subwa
station, the latter unmistakably marked by a giant yellow kinetic sculpture
acclaimed Venezuelan artist Jesús Soto. Clothing and shoe boutiques, perfun
shops, bookstores and outdoor cafés line one side of the sidewalk while stre
vendors lay out their goods on tables and plastic sheets on the other.

There may be discount clothing and tacky home decorations, but there are als

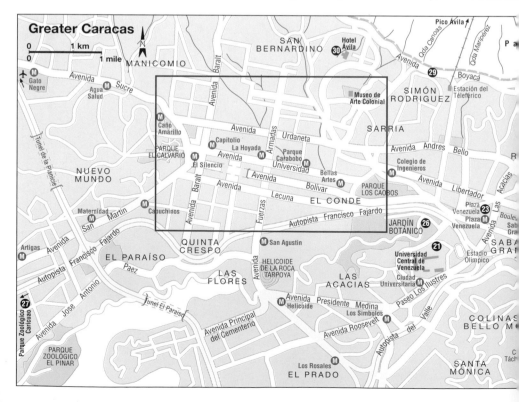

urdy hammocks, finely crafted avant-garde jewelry and fashionable shoes ixed among the untaxed sales items. Buyers are young couples strolling hand--hand; families out for ice cream, businessmen who stop at Sabana Grande's rs for a cold Polar beer or shot of Pampero rum after work, and fashion-con-ious women in mini-skirts and stiletto heels, who come here to be seen.

A favorite among the many sidewalk cafés grouped at the west end of the ulevard is the **Gran Café**. Cappuccinos compete with the more traditional nge of coffees and elaborate ice cream concoctions, while guitarists and ndean flute players vie for attention and tips. This is also the haunt of betting thusiasts seeking updates on the popular *"5 y 6"* horse-racing cards. Some trons of the open-air cafés lounge for hours, discussing politics or the eco-mic situation, or simply watch the passing parade of people; while other bles are occupied by chess aficionados, oblivious to the stares and comments passers-by.

With a bit of everything, Sabana Grande also has abundant upscale lodging, ch as Hotel Lincoln Suites, Hotel President, and the enormous Gran Melia aracas Hotel, Suites and Conference Center – just blocks from the "hot sheets" tels, as they are known by gringos in the city, with rooms at hourly rates ed for on-the-sly romantic encounters and as the workplace of prostitutes ho fill the zone by night.

For handicrafts, you should check out **Artesanía Venezolana**, across from the aza Venezuela fountain at the western edge of the pedestrian mall. If you visit re at night, note that despite being very pretty with its multi-colored lights, the ne undergoes a distinct change of atmosphere after dark – when it is best ewed while driving by.

Map
on pages
142–3

BELOW: playing chess on the Sabana Grande.

While pedestrian traffic in the Sabana Grande mall runs all day and most [of] the night, there is nearly as much activity underground. The Metro line ru[ns] directly below the boulevard, with stops at Plaza Venezuela, the mall's end [at] Chacaíto – and an intermediate station, Sabana Grande.

Shopping paradise

If your preferences lean more toward enclosed shopping malls, you won't be di[s]appointed. A few blocks east of Chacaíto is the sophisticated new **Centro Lid[o]** with shops, offices, and the five-star Hotel Centro Lido. The newest on t[he] scene is the **Centro Comercial Sambil**, on Avenida Libertador in Chaca[o] which opened in mid-1998. Said to be the largest in Latin America, it has 5[5] shops and opening hours that have proved very popular: 10am–9pm Monday [to] Saturday, and 1–7pm on Sunday and holidays. This is exceptional in Venezue[la], where even in malls, shops usually close at 7pm, and always on Sundays a[nd] holidays – the only times most working people can shop.

Not far off is the **Centro Plaza**  (on Avenida Francisco de Miranda), tw[o] blocks east of the Altamira Metro. En route from the subway, take time to st[op] at **Centro de Arte La Estancia** (closed Sun pm, Mon), in the restored 18t[h]-century La Floresta coffee *hacienda*. The focus here is on three-dimensional a[nd] graphic design, photography, and artistic alternatives to objects in common us[e]. You can also go on a guided tour of the *hacienda*'s beautiful gardens.

Along with its shopping and cultural activities, the district of Altamira-L[a] Castellana-Los Palos Grandes has some of the city's best restaurants, and, wi[th] the opening in 1999 of the **Hotel Four Seasons Caracas** (next to the Altami[ra] Metro and Plaza Francia), it is also a key site for lodging.

BELOW: La Hoyada Market: one of many to be found in Caracas.

Crossing over to the south side of the Francisc[o] Fajardo freeway, shopping areas include **Centr[o] Comercial Ciudad Tamanaco** – better known a[s] CCCT, which is one of the capital's most exclusi[ve] collections of boutiques. Mixed in with the design[er] stores and hair salons are ice cream shops, movi[e] theaters, bistros, and the Best Western CCCT Hote[l].

A few blocks away from CCCT and the highratin[g] Eurobuilding Hotel and Suites is **Las Mercedes** an upscale district known for its huge selection [of] excellent restaurants and night spots, as well as f[or] its shops. It also has the largest concentration [of] private art galleries in Caracas. Sunday, when gallerie[s] open 11am–2pm, is a good day to visit, with man[y] artists and art circle personalities present.

At the eastern extreme of this sector, facing th[e] grand dame of Caracas lodging, the five-star **Hote[l] Tamanaco Inter-Continental**, another popular shop[ping option among moneyed *caraqueños* is the **Centr[o] Comercial Paseo Las Mercedes**, an older but sti[ll] elegant shopping mall (which also houses the four[-]star Hotel Paseo Las Mercedes). Among its stores an[d] restaurants, hidden back in the La Cuadra section b[y] the exit to the car park, is a shop run by the **Audubo[n] Society**, which sells books specializing in birds an[d] natural history, as well as native crafts. You can sig[n] up here for the society's own ecotourism excursion[s] (which do not feature only birds).

The trendiest spot for exploring on foot is **El Hatillo** (with Metrobus connection from the Altamira station), on the southern outskirts of Caracas. The streets surrounding its tree-filled plaza (complete with a pair of resident sloths) and the colonial church are filled with the shops of local artists and craftsmen; unusual clothing boutiques; antique and art galleries; Hannsi – the most comprehensive shop for Venezuelan crafts in the country; and some of the best restaurants and coffee shops in the metropolitan area, from traditional *criollo* to Japanese, Swiss and American fare.

Saturday night fever

Although there are many good places for music and dancing scattered throughout eastern Caracas, the most popular area – for the great number of choices and its upscale clientele (which flocks there in droves to see and be seen) – is Las Mercedes. This is also one of the safest parts of town for night action.

Caraqueños unwind in a big way, especially on weekends when all kinds of live music are available, from *mariachis* to Latin jazz, salsa, and rock. Pitch-black discos don't start to fill until nearly midnight (and don't slow down until near dawn). Here, energetic couples take control of the dance floor while illicit trysts take place in the shadows. These clubs are so dark that doormen literally lead patrons to their seats with flashlights. Some only allow couples; others allow groups regardless of gender, but single women may be refused entry.

However, if you have never seen Caribbean dancing, don't miss this golden opportunity to dress up (at many, men must wear jacket and tie). Venezuelans take their music seriously and their dancing is amazing, although the sound volume may make you wish you had brought ear plugs. Alternatively, if you

Map
on pages
142–3

TIP

Take plenty of money if you go to a disco in Caracas. On weekends, in particular, clubs often require *consumo mínimo* ("minimum consumption"), which means that single drinks, soft drinks, and wine by the glass are not available.

BELOW: late nights at L'Attico bar and restaurant.

want a quiet evening the city abounds with cozy jazz bars and excellent restaurants, serving food from around the world, to suit all tastes and budgets.

The great outdoors

Despite the capital's growth, numerous beautiful green spaces have been reserved to give harried *caraqueños* oases of calm and contact with nature. **Parque Los Caobos**, planted with mahogany, or *caobo*, trees that inspired its name, is a huge park located behind the Museo de Bellas Artes. Sundays are the biggest day with families out in force, joggers, kids on bikes and roller blades, games of softball and soccer, clusters of chums practising karate or dance moves.

Across the highway from the south side of Parque Los Caobos, prefacing the entrance to the Universidad Central de Venezuela, is the **Jardín Botánico**  (no picnicking allowed) – magnificent botanical gardens with more than 150,000 examples of over 2,200 species, a herbarium, and orchid greenhouses.

For a more cozy setting, try the tiny park called **Los Chorros** (Final Avenida Cachimbo,closed Mon; token entrance fee; no pets) tucked against Caracas' northern hillside with a cascade and stream running through its wooded setting (swimming allowed). Although pretty all year round, Los Chorros breeds ferocious mosquitos during the rainy season, so be prepared with repellent.

The city's biggest and best zoo is the **Parque Zoológico Caricuao** ㉗ (closed Mon; token admission fee; Zoológico Metro stop is a block from the entrance). Opened in 1977, the Caricuao Zoo has hundreds of animals displayed in natural uncaged habitats, as well as a petting zoo which allows children to get close to domestic animals. You may also read about the El Pinar Zoo, but neither its maintenance nor its neighborhood can compete with Caricuao.

There is also a zoo in the huge **Parque del Este** ㉘ (open Tue–Sun; closed Mon except for joggers, 5–8am; token admission fee; no bicycles or roller skates allowed), which was designed by Brazilian landscape architect Robert Burle Marx, with a Metro stop of the same name at the north entrance. Delights here include grassy areas for picnics and games, paths for strolling or jogging, a lagoon with pedal boats for rent and a replica of Christopher Columbus' ship the *Santa María*. There is also the Planetario Humboldt (open Sat, Sun, hols; half-hour programs shown hourly 1–4pm; token admission fee), and a bandstand where free concerts and other performances are offered on weekends.

An overhead walkway at the park's eastern edge joins this park with the grounds of the **Museo de Transporte** (open Sat, Sun; token admission fee).

Lofty landmark

Parque Nacional El Avila, comprising some 88 km (55 miles) of the coastal mountain range separating Caracas from the Caribbean Sea, forms the city's impressive northern backdrop. On sunny days, fluffy clouds cap the peaks. Dark clouds gathering above them signal the inevitability of the drenching rain that floods city streets in minutes, mercilessly pounding the pavement and pedestrians until, just as quickly, it stops and the sun returns.

TIP

Since Sunday is the traditional day for Venezuelan families to go out together to visit museums, parks, and restaurants, all of these – even the eateries – tend to offer special programmes, including clowns, live music and lots, lots more (usually free).

BELOW: children fooling around in a fountain in Parque Los Caobos.

In the foothills of El Avila is **Avenida Boyacá** , which runs along the 1,000-meter (3,280-ft) mark – or the "Cota Mil," as the avenue is also known in Spanish – above which no houses may be built. Special viewing areas, or *miradores*, where motorists can pull off the road, offer a panoramic view over the city. On Sundays, the avenue is completely closed to traffic between 6am and 1pm to allow joggers, bikers, and roller skaters to use its full expanse. Numerous marked trails can also be followed to explore its upper reaches (*see Participant Sports, pages 105–109*).

You can see the lines and stations of the *teleférico* (cable car) leading from the Maripérez section of town to the mountain-top **Hotel Humboldt**, but it has been inoperative for most of the past two decades – as has the other line, which runs between the coast and hotel. As a result, the Humboldt Hotel, built at the summit of Mount Avila by dictator Marcos Pérez Jiménez in the 1950s and virtually inaccessible without the cable car, has been turned into a giant and highly visible white elephant. However, things may change in the future since the cable cars are due to be auctioned off as part of the government's privatization program, which should herald a resumption of services.

Hotel Avila , despite being at the base rather than in the park itself, is a well-loved landmark. Built with the riches of the Rockefeller family from North America half a century ago, the hotel has been well-maintained. While nowadays it is overshadowed in popularity by the five-star hotels in the heart of the city's shopping and restaurant districts, it is still sought out by many for its cool, tranquil atmosphere in a residential setting, with fair prices as an added bonus. Furthermore, there is no more romantic outdoor swimming pool in the city than that of the Avila, surrounded by cool, tropical foliage. ❏

Map on pages 142–3

Epiphytic bromeliads cling to the trees in Parque Nacional El Avila.

BELOW: the open spaces of the Parque del Este.

Colonia Tovar

Acool mountain breeze wafts into the restaurant where blond, blue-eyed, German-speaking waiters serve sauerkraut and *wienerschnitzel*. After a meal washed down with a stein of beer, diners might stroll along the steep streets before returning to their mountain cabins. But this is not Bavaria but Colonia Tovar, a mountain village near Caracas, first settled by German immigrants, which has maintained many of its traditions during years of total isolation.

Venezuela's 19th-century War of Independence stripped the countryside of its slave workers and farmers. To ease the labor shortage, immigration laws were rewritten to entice European farmers. In 1843, 145 men, 96 women and 117 children from the Black Forest community of Kaiserstuhl made the ocean crossing to Venezuela where they had agreed to farm virgin land owned by a wealthy creole named Martín Tovar. Smallpox aboard ship claimed 70 lives and put the vessel in

quarantine when it finally reached Venezuela. After 40 days of isolation, the confused colonists were allowed on shore near Choroní, down the coast west of La Guaira.

But news of the disease had spread and there was no welcoming committee, no fanfare, not even transportation. Accompanied by their own priest, tailor, teacher, druggist, carpenter, printer and blacksmith, the colonists trudged 30 km (20 miles) up the mountains to Tovar's lands, burdened by their farm implements, fruit trees, seeds and the barley that would make their beer.

A second boatload of Germans arrived soon after but Venezuela's cold reception of the first immigrants was never forgotten. The ill-will was further fueled when the Germans were told they would need signed permission from the government bureaucrats each time they wanted to leave the town. In response to this demand, the colonists set up the most closed community the country had ever seen.

Isolated, Colonia Tovar residents recreated the Black Forest community they had left. They ate German-style sausages, drank home-produced beer, kept traditional customs and married their blond-haired children off to one another. Venezuela's many 19th-century conflicts passed them by and for more than a century they survived, excluded and excluding, in the cool, sunny clime of their highland home.

But with the end of World War II came the fad for outdoor treks, which lured Venezuelans to the peaceful town. Robust walkers made 9-hour weekend trips from Caracas, 30 km (18 miles) away, while those with less stamina mounted mules to explore the hills surrounding the Humboldt Valley. Many stayed in the Hotel Selva Negra (Black Forest Hotel), which dates from 1937. They drank coffee grown by the colonists, ate barley bread and bought bouquets of flowers grown in fields around the town. Gradually, Colonia Tovar's walls of isolation crumbled.

With the arrival of a paved road in 1963 came regular visitors who bought baskets of strawberries and blackberries, handcrafted cuckoo clocks and local beer. With the - outside contact, the German language began to disappear. There is still a majority of fair-skinned, light-haired residents but their grandchildren have dark hair and Spanish names, and the once typical Black Forest costumes are now worn mostly to please tourists.

Seen from a distance, Tovar buildings look as if they have been culled from the pages of a European magazine. But, although nearly all appear to have traditional *frachwerk* construction, on closer inspection one sees that while some of the older structures, (such as the beautiful Muhstall Café and general store), are indeed made with massive numbered beams and freshly whitewashed plaster, most of the newer buildings have plain, smooth walls with "beams" painted on the surface. Somehow, even when we know this, we can forgive the trick, because the *trompe l'oeil* was done to create a harmonious visual aspect to maintain the Germanic image.

The summary of development glosses over the details of the progress of "La Colonia" from 1843 to the present, with residents not given due credit for their tenacity. Aside from problems caused by an outbreak of smallpox when they arrived, the settlers quickly discovered that promises of basic shelter, some animals and cleared farmland awaiting them when they arrived were falsehoods. Thus, the struggle for survival began from day one.

Even once they had established farms to provide for their own needs and as a source of income, the extremely difficult journey to markets and the negligible ability to communicate in Spanish proved to be great obstacles for commerce. They persisted, but until the paved road was built, daily life was hard.

It took 120 years, but that single factor, the new road, opened the way for easy, two-way traffic, and marked the turning point for the village. Marketing of its products rose dramatically and tourism boomed, to the extent that today Colonia Tovar enjoys the highest per capita income in Venezuela.

The village – inspiration for the fictional town in Isabel Allende's contemporary bestseller, *Eva Luna* – is a curious and anachronistic escape from Caracas. Travelers winding their way up from the smoggy capital see palm trees and pines side by side. By day, the air is brisk but at night it gets downright cold. The streets are steep but good for strolling. At the main plaza is the L-shaped Catholic church, drawn from the plans of a chapel in Germany. The interior is simple, its most valuable possession an organ made by a local craftsman. On the bell tower you can see inscriptions in German.

Behind the church is one of the three mills (two for corn, one for coffee) of the original six still in existence in the colony. Walk downhill on the main roadway from the church to see the cemetery, hidden among pine trees at the side of the road. The graves of the first German immigrants are marked by checkerboard patterns of ceramic tiles. Burials continue in the old-style, with lines of black-clad mourners following the pallbearers – all on foot – down the hill from the church and into the graveyard.

Fine local potters and woodworkers display their goods in shops around the town. Hot breads, bowls of fruit or glasses of strawberry juice sold at outdoor cafés and kiosks sustain visitors until they work up an appetite for German sausage and *strudel* – always washed down with a beer. ❑

LEFT AND RIGHT: descendants of the original German immigrants still live in their village in the Andes.

EL LITORAL

From popular resorts thronging with thousands of sun-seekers to private clubs and hotels or solitary, idyllic spots, El Litoral offers the closest Caribbean beaches to the capital

Map on pages 152–3

Caracas

L ike lemmings going to the sea, every weekend and holiday *caraqueños* don swimsuits, fill their coolers and, whether in public buses or private cars, flock to the beaches of El Litoral Central – known more popularly simply as El Litoral. They may face monumental *colas* (traffic queues) on the route across the mountains between the capital and the Caribbean coast that put Caracas rush-hour traffic to shame, but there are no complaints because now they are on their way to play, not work.

Western beaches

On reaching the coast, on the road to the west of Caracas, you almost immediately pass the terminals of **Aeropuerto Simón Bolívar** in **Maiquetía ❶**, the principal airport serving Caracas and Venezuela. Although there are beaches in this direction, their popularity doesn't come close to that of those to the east. Unfortunately, facilities of the *balneario* (bathing beach development) installed many years ago at **Catia La Mar ❷** have been virtually abandoned, and the area is plagued by problems of pollution and personal security.

The principal destination for beach-goers heading in this direction are the various private clubs and tourism developments, such as **Marina Grande**, **Oricao** and **Shangri-la**, which have blocked off sections of the beach, limiting access to members or to those paying entry fee for day use (a practice theoretically prohibited in any area of the coast).

Aside from the private nature of these places, access to them by road is not easy either. Thus the grand majority of people going to El Litoral follow the coastal road eastbound from Maiquetía.

Historic port

The first town encountered on this route is **La Guaira ❸**. Founded in 1589, it was chosen as the site of the country's principal port because of its closeness to Caracas (20 km/12 miles), despite the fact that its geography was not the best for this purpose. The installation of breakwaters and constant dredging have made this a safer haven now than in the early days, but its current importance is far overshadowed by Puerto Cabello (in Carabobo state) which handles 77 percent of Venezuela's commercial traffic.

La Guaira has many buildings dating back to the 18th and 19th centuries which have maintained their original architectural details, the most outstanding being the **Casa Guipuzcoana ❹**, facing the coastal highway. It was erected in 1734 by the Basque Guipuzcoana Company which, through an agreement with Felipe V of Spain, enjoyed a commercial monopoly for half a century in exchange for protect-

LEFT:
Todasana beach.
BELOW:
Los Caracas beach.

ing the coast and developing agriculture and trade. Because of outrageou abuses, the company came to be hated by locals. Its demise eventually cam because of commercial liberty conceded by Carlos III. Its privileges were abo ished in 1781 and the company ceased to exist in 1785. During the 1970s, th building was restored for use as the Ateneo de La Guaira and to house variou public offices. It subsequently served as the mayor's office. Although hanc some overall, one notes certain deterioration inside due to lack of maintenanco

Some of the other buildings along the road have had their façades restored, a have the former 19th-century headquarters of the **Boulton Company** and th 19th-century **Catedral de La Guaira** and **Ermita de Carmen** (both of whic have undergone restoration numerous times, only to be allowed to decay fron neglect after the work was completed). However, the majority of residentia buildings, still bearing their original façades, are desperately in need of som loving care and attention.

Standing as silent sentinals above the town are **La Pólvora** (a 17th-centur fort used to store munitions), **El Vigía** (with a 19th-century construction atop th foundations of another fort), and the **Castillo de San Carlos** (a classic sta design fort built in 1610).

Macuto: resort of presidents

Refreshing jungle juice for sale on the beach.

During the late 19th and early 20th centuries, **Macuto** ❺ was the "in" beac resort of the coast. President Guzmán Blanco even had a rail line built betwee Caracas and La Guaira-Macuto, inaugurated in 1883, and had a seaside hom erected – **La Guzmanía** (facing Plaza de las Palomas) – which is still used b Venezuela's presidents today. In the early 1900s, Juan Vicente Gómez ordere construction of the **Hotel Miramar**, further boosting the resort's popularit

Today, the landmark hotel is closed, but the beach extending westward fron it is as lively as ever. Numerous outdoor restaurants and modest hostels line th pedestrian boulevard shaded by sea grapes, and breakwaters assure calm water

Exploring Macuto is complicated by the fact that the main eastbound roa skirts the upper edge, so you must double back on the one-way westbound roa to follow the shoreline and see the old district. Worth a visit is the **Muse**

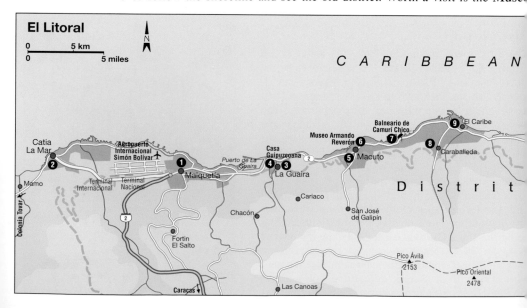

Armando Reverón ❻ (open daily; token admission), in the former home of one of Venezuela's most famous (and eccentric) impressionist painters (1889–1954). Westbound from the museum are numerous inviting seafood restaurants.

The large *balneario* of **Camurí Chico** ❼ lies a short distance east of Macuto, offering three swimming areas, changing facilities and bathrooms, ample parking, and countless vendors offering everything from seafood platters and cold beer to bathing suits and beach balls.

Map below

Tourist center

Caraballeda ❽ (inland) and **El Caribe** ❾ (closer to the beach), with no visible separation between the two, offer the most upscale facilities along this section of coast, with two five-star hotels (Macuto Sheraton Resort and the recently privatized Gran Caribe, formerly the Meliá Caribe), and a large marina filled with yachts and sailboats. A handful of three-star hotels, along with many restaurants, line the main avenue passing through here.

Naiguatá ❿, 13 km (8 miles) farther east, is better known for its *tambores* and devil dancers *(see Fiestas, pages 79–85)* than its beach; but its neighbor, **Playa Los Angeles**, is a magnet for surfers and the young and beautiful who congregate there to see and be seen.

The unpaved coastal road

Los Caracas ⓫, at the end of the paved road, has a surprisingly large (although somewhat decaying) resort area operated by INCRET (Institute for the Training and Recreation of Workers), complete with a huge swimming pool, beach area, many types of lodging, and other services.

The unpaved coastal road between Los Caracas and **Chirimena** is a favorite destination for those with 4x4 vehicles looking for more solitary beaches. Those with at least some nearby services (including various lodgings, ranging from small *posadas* to a spa) are located by the villages of Osma, Oritapo, Todasana, La Sabana, and Caruao. **Playa Chirire** (near Chirimena) is popular with surfers. If returning to the capital, the easiest route (all paved) is via Higuerote–Caucagua–Guarenas–Caracas, a drive of about 90 minutes. ❏

La Sabana beach, along the eastbound unpaved coastal road, is accessible only to those with 4x4 vehicles.

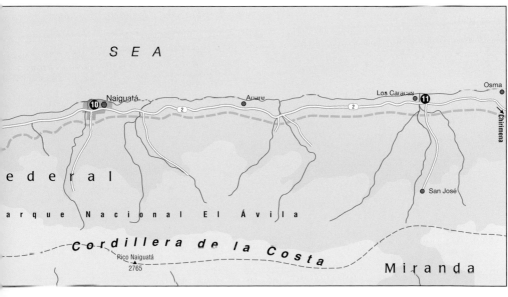

LOS ROQUES

*Take warm, shallow waters and beautiful reefs, then add mangroves
and the blue Caribbean Sea. The result: an idyllic setting
in this conveniently situated archipelago*

Map
on page
156

Caracas

A corner of paradise is how most visitors describe the **Archipelago of Los Roques**, lying approximately 128 km (80 miles) north of Maiquetía. With some 40 islands and cays (*cayos*) large enough to bear names, and more than 300 others emerging during low tide, pristine white sand beaches, and crystalline waters, it is rapidly becoming one of the country's most popular tourist destinations.

Although the steady flow of visitors has predictably had an effect on the former image as a haven for a small population of humble fishermen, the archipelago remains relatively tranquil and unspoiled. This is partly due to access for tourists being possible only by small planes or private yachts and sailboats, and partly because Los Roques has been protected as a national park since 1972. The archipelago covers an area of more than 225,000 hectares (556,000 acres), making it one of the Caribbean's largest marine preserves.

Wildlife sanctuary

While the archipelago bakes under a blazing sun all day, at night it is caressed by cooling trade winds that keep annoying insects at bay. Most of the *cayos* are low, their pure white sands barely rising above the surface of the turquoise and emerald waters. A few have rocky outcroppings. Clumps of mangrove trees, cactus and seagrass add splotches of green to the arid landscape that is home to iguanas and lizards. Marine turtles lumber ashore to lay their eggs.

Over the years, many names in the archipelago have changed due to fishermen writing phonetic spellings in their charts. North East Cay is now **Nordisquí ❶**, Sailors Cay is **Selesquí ❷**, Domus Cay is Dos Mosquises – now **Cayo Estación Sur ❸**.

Seabirds are abundant, both nesting and migratory species, including frigate birds, boobies, terns, pelicans and herons. The tiny western island, **Selesquí**, has the largest bird population, earning it the nickname "Cayo Bobo Negro" (Black Booby Cay). Flocks of gulls nest on **Francisquí ❹** (Cayo Francés).

Snorkelers and divers will be delighted by schools of rainbow-colored parrot fish, royal blue angelfish, puffy porcupine fish and slender trumpet fish. There are molluscs, sponges, sea urchins and many varieties of coral including gorgonia, brain and fire. Occasionally you will see a barracuda or moray eel.

The islands of Los Roques have been known for centuries, but because they have no fresh water, they have not supported permanent settlement until recently.

Long ago, the archipelago may have held some mystical significance. Prehispanic ceramics, possibly used in sacred or magical ceremonies, have been

LEFT: despite a steady flow of visitors, the islands are still unspoiled.
BELOW: pelican patrol.

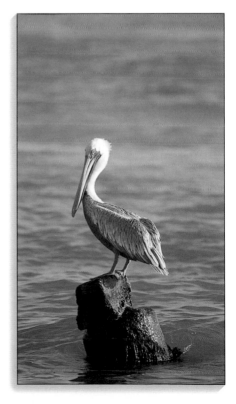

found on four islands. Cayo Estación Sur has yielded a number of squat human figurines, including a man with "doughnut" eyes, and women with tiny arms and hands and large rectangular heads that have been pricked or incised. More recently, Los Roques have been a secret haven for Venezuelan sun-worshipers who flew in by private plane for a day's amusement or sailed their yachts over for a long weekend.

In the 1980s, when the Venezuelan currency crashed and the country imposed import restrictions, *contrabandistas* (contraband runners) found Los Roques to be a convenient stopping-off place. Restaurateurs in Caracas had a secret pipeline from the Caribbean for obtaining duty-free liquor, crystal and fine china.

A prize catch: lobsters are usually spirited away to top restaurants on nearby Aruba, where they command a high price.

Foreign invasion

Today, Los Roques are being discovered by sailors and sport fishermen from abroad. The islands are reputed to offer some of the world's best bonefishing (*see Participant Sports, pages 105–109*). Aeroejecutivos, Aereotuy, Amazonair, and Roque's Air, Land & Sea are among local companies now offering regular flights, usually sold as all-inclusive packages. But take note, even the "all-inclusive" packages do not usually include the 16.5 percent sales tax or the National Parks Institute entrance fee for Los Roques that everyone has to pay: the equivalent of about US$5 per person for residents and Venezuelans, US$10 for non-residents.

The only permanent settlement is on **Gran Roque ❺**, the biggest island. At 3 km (2 miles) long and scarcely more than 1 km (½-mile) wide, that is none too big. It has the only paved airstrip in Los Roques. All of the more than 40 *posadas*, which have flourished to accommodate tourists are located here.

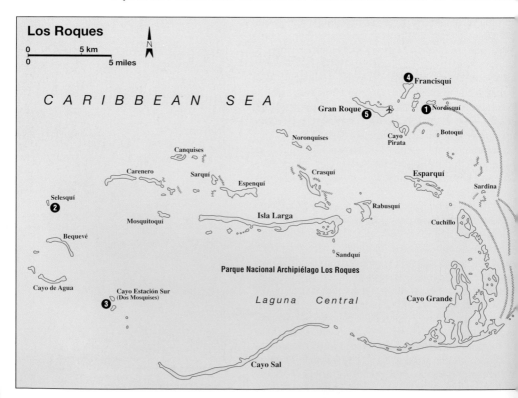

Unfortunately, because of the new-found popularity, prices have soared. However, unless you plan to do extensive diving, fishing, or sun-worshiping, day tours are a viable and less costly alternative (averaging about $100 per person). The economy of *Roqueños* is based on fishing, with wooden boats beached on the sand and nearby hungry pelicans dive-bombing fish in the shallows. Everything except fish is imported from the mainland. There's a desalinization plant, but the navy sometimes has to supply fresh water.

Fishermen haul in *pargo* (red snapper), *mero* (grouper), lobster and shellfish. For fish their main market is La Guaira, but most catches of lobster, crab, and queen conch have been spirited away to restaurants in Aruba, where they command a higher price. From time to time, moratoriums on the harvest of queen conch have been instituted to preserve their waning numbers, but as visitors can testify, the piles of empty pink conch shells on the beaches continue to grow.

On Gran Roque, the favored dish is *sancocho de pescado* (fish soup). *Consomé de chipi-chipi* is also popular; the little clams that go into this pot are said to be an aphrodisiac. They're found mainly around the island of Crasqui.

Biological research

Researchers at the marine biological station run by the **Fundación Científica Los Roques** on **Cayo Estación Sur** have been trying to farm lobster and crab, which are being dangerously overfished. So far the lobster experiment has failed, but the crab shows promise. The foundation also studies marine turtles and investigates other ecological issues, supported by grants from government and industry. Courses in marine ecology are open to small numbers of qualified students. The navy helped build the laboratory, and there's a dirt landing strip. ❑

TIP

The beaches of Los Roques are shadeless. This, combined with the high degree of reflected sun from the water and white sand make the wearing of sun block, a hat, and sunglasses imperative.

BELOW: Gran Roque Pueblo – the only permanent settlement on the archipelago.

EL ORIENTE

The entire northeastern sector of the country, referred to simply as "El Oriente", spells beach resorts to Venezuelans but also offers historic sites and ecotourism

Map on pages 162–3

For *caraqueños* with just a day free, "going to the beach" means heading for El Litoral. But, given a full weekend or *puente* (long weekend, literally "bridge") – it goes without saying that the destination for most of Caracas' sun worshipers is El Oriente – the east coast.

Tambores and cacao

Barlovento, meaning windward, applies to the eastern third of Miranda state, from Cabo Codera to Boca de Uchire. Fed by many rivers and receiving steady moisture-carrying trade winds, it is one of the few areas along Venezuela's coast to be lush and green all year long.

When the Spaniards first came to Venezuela they imported cacao plants and large numbers of African slaves to work the huge haciendas. The crop would be a principal source of the country's wealth for nearly three centuries. But, during the long War of Independence, plantations were abandoned as men took to the battlefield. After the war, with the abolition of slavery, working the huge plantations was impossible. The *gran cacaos* ("big cacaos"), as the rich plantation owners were called, disappeared. But the former slaves remained and, in their isolated setting, maintained the purity of their race, conserved their cultural traditions, and tended the cacao.

Along with cacao trees, one of the most distinctive plants seen growing among the lush tropical foliage along this route, between **Caucagua** and **El Guapo**, is the heliconia, a member of the bird-of-paradise plant family with beautiful, brilliant red flowers edged in pale green. These flowers (cut), as well as rooted orchids and bromeliads, are sold along the roadside.

Not much has changed since slavery was abolished. The population is largely black. Cacao trees with their pink, orange, and deep red pods growing directly out of the trunks flourish in the luxuriant environment. All along the pavement and on concrete patios, nuts from the cacao pods are spread out in the sun to dry.

The African-style drums of Barlovento – called *tambores*, and made from hollow logs – and the sensual dance performed to their beat, are well known, particularly for their role in the Fiesta of San Juan Bautista; St John the Baptist is especially revered by people with African roots, and his festival (June 23–24) is a great occasion.

Curiepe ❶ is famous for its all-out celebration in honor of San Juan Bautista, which attracts a great numbers of visitors. The saint's effigy is baptized in the river. Then, to the sound of the drums, and with celebrants downing copious amounts of rum and *aguardiente*, everyone dances to the *tambores* throughout the night.

PRECEDING PAGES: Playa Colorada, between Puerto La Cruz and Cumaná. **LEFT:** a leap in the deep. **BELOW:** jewelry for sale at Puerto La Cruz.

Not far away from Curiepe is the tiny mountain village of **Birongo** , considered the "magic capital of Venezuela" and renowned for having the most powerful *brujos* (witches) in the country. They can cast and remove spells, make predictions, and perform other "works" for those who come to ask for their help – and a surprising number do come, from every social and economic group, and from far and wide.

Parque Nacional Laguna de Tacarigua is a breeding ground for crocodiles.

Barlovento's beaches

The main towns in Barlovento are **Higuerote** ❸ and **Río Chico** ❹, both about 90 minutes by road from Caracas. The towns themselves have virtually nothing to offer in the way of "attractions", but no matter. What people come for are the beaches. Those in Higuerote are characterized by murky water, owing to sediment from a nearby river, which local bathers don't seem to mind and *guacucos* (small clams) obviously adore, because they are plentiful. Gathering *guacucos* to cook up in a rich broth on the beach is a ritual among visitors to these shores.

If you are more interested in crystal-clear water than you are in clam-gathering, then you should make your way farther north to the beaches of **Buche Island** (to which there is shuttle boat service), **Puerto Francés**, or **Chirimena**; the latter is favored by surfers because of its powerful waves.

The best beaches at Río Chico border Los Canales (natural canals connecting with the sea, a key place for the development of vacation property), such as Playa Cocada. To the east is **Tacarigua de la Laguna** ❺, the entry point for **Parque Nacional Laguna de Tacarigua**.

This national park has two distinct parts: a 30-km (18-mile) long lagoon bordered by mangroves, rich in birds, fish (attracting sport fishermen for tarpon and

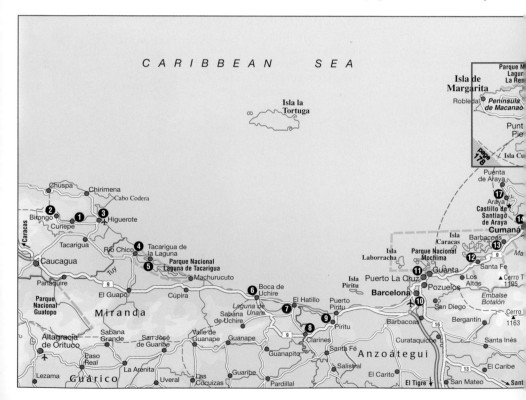

snook), and a breeding ground for crocodiles; and 30 km (18 miles) of pristine sandy, palm-lined Caribbean beach on the outer banks. In the channel between the sea and lagoon, fishermen toss out their circular nets. Close by, taking no notice of them at all, roseate spoonbills, scarlet ibis, and herons feed.

Thousands of these colorful birds put on a show every day at dusk as they come home to roost, completely covering one of the large clusters of mangroves inside the lagoon. Arrangements can be made with fishermen at the mouth of Laguna de Tacarigua, by the park ranger's station, to watch the return of these huge flocks of birds to a single spot in the late afternoon. Unfortunately, because of the descending darkness, it is almost impossible to photograph this "show."

Since the area's designation as a national park in 1974, no building has been allowed within its borders. However, **Club Miami** at the west end and the **Club Managua Caribe** at the east end, which were both there before park status was declared, were allowed to remain. Staying at either of them is by reservation only, since both operate on the basis of all-inclusive packages. Club Miami is accessible only by boat (this service is included in the package), while the Managua Caribe can be reached by land. Both are in excellent locations, but have suffered from a certain amount of deterioration.

No vehicular traffic at all is allowed on the beach since it is an egg-laying area for marine turtles. Boatmen in Tacarigua can be hired to take visitors to the beach or the lagoon.

Boca de Uchire ⑥, at the western extreme of **Laguna de Unare**, has a lovely beach. Driving east along the outer bank, after passing a string of beach houses, there are wide bands of solitary beaches. The road now runs all the way between

One of many coastal shrines decorated with shells.

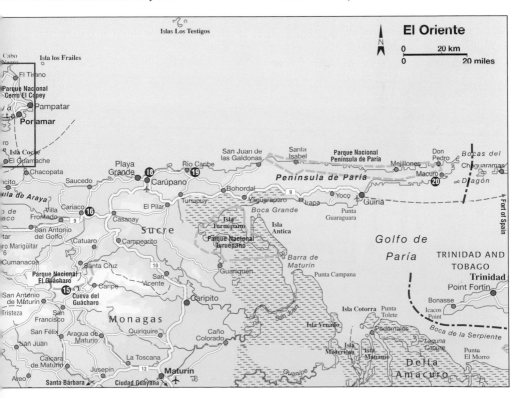

Boca de Uchire and **El Hatillo** ❼, making it possible to explore the beaches little fishing villages, and lodges which stretch along the full length of the sandbar; however, the condition of the road is deplorable.

Colonial temples

Clarines ❽ is worth a quick detour to see its 18th-century church and the surrounding streets, where the town's colonial heritage is eminently visible.

Píritu ❾ and its seaside neighbor, **Puerto Píritu**, lie 16 km (10 miles) farther east. The focal point of Píritu is its church, in a commanding hilltop location. Dating from the mid-1700s, the exterior is plain and fortress-like. But inside, it harbors ornate colonial altar-piece. The port town has some simple old buildings along the waterfront, but the focus is the beach, which is one of the prettiest of the shadeless, sandy beaches in El Oriente; it is bordered by seafood restaurants. From a dock at the west end, boatmen will take you on the 40-minute ride to **Las Isletas**, two small islands with sandy beaches.

All along the highway by Píritu, there are roadside stands where artisans sell local crafts: hand-carved wooden platters and rustic, bent-wood furniture.

Petroleum port and tourist mecca

The main destinations in El Oriente are Barcelona and Puerto La Cruz in Anzoátegui, which are less than four hours' driving from Caracas under normal conditions. The state is a major source of petroleum; after Zulia, it is the largest producer of oil in the country, and has three huge refineries, two of them in Puerto La Cruz; the giant José Complejo Criogénico de Oriente, with an important orimulsion fossil fuel energy project, is just west of Barcelona.

One of the main harvests from the Laguna de Unare is shrimp, available simply prepared in the modest restaurants at the eastern extreme of the outer banks, or in the multitude of dining spots along the old highway by the south shore.

BELOW: colonial mannequins in the Museo de Anzoátegui.

These areas are also major magnets for tourists. **Barcelona ⑩** is the capital of the state, and the site of the airport which services the two towns. As well as having a handsome colonial zone, it is the location of the mega tourism project, Complejo Turístico El Morro.

The two areas of historic interest in the capital center on the three main plazas: Bolívar, Miranda, and Boyacá. The first two, on Avenida 5 de Julio, are actually adjacent, and facing them is **Casa Fuerte**, the ruins of the former Convent of San Francisco – outfitted with cannons and used by Republican troops during the War of Independence as a fort to defend Barcelona. In a fierce battle on April 7, 1817, Casa Fuerte was destroyed by the Royalists, who massacred everyone there. It has been preserved as it was, a memorial of the disaster.

Plaza Boyacá, the original square of Barcelona when it was founded in 1671, is surrounded by colonial buildings, many dating from the 1600s. The **cathedral** was built between 1748 and 1773, but work was set back in 1766 by a major earthquake, which destroyed part of the building. This is a surprisingly picturesque zone, and a strong contrast with the newer – and frankly unattractive – downtown area that you have to pass through to reach it.

The **Museo de Anzoátegui** (open daily 8am–noon, 3–6pm, except in Dec when it is open 8am–4pm; free), in the oldest existing house in the city, built in 1671 and handsomely restored, now serves as Barcelona's historical museum.

El Morro tourist project

Between Barcelona and Puerto La Cruz, a turn-off leads to the huge **El Morro** tourism complex and beaches. One of the first places you see when you make this turn is the large new **Centro Comercial Plaza Mayor**, striking for its

Map on pages 162–3

BELOW: fishermen set out.

design based on the colorful architecture typical of the historic waterfront area of Willemstad, capital of the former Dutch Caribbean colony of Curaçao.

Avenida Principal of Lecherías is another commercial zone where the entire avenue is lined with small shopping centers and many restaurants.

The El Morro project was initiated in 1971 to accommodate 60,000 tourists in single-family homes, condos and hotels. It is constructed on a maze of canals which provide boat access to the sea from every building. Among the most ambitious projects in the complex is the **Golden Rainbow Maremares Resort and Spa** (a huge five-star complex with various lagoon-sized pools, a golf course, and so on). Several projects, including a shopping center directly in front of Maremares, which were paralyzed for some time in the aftermath of the banking crisis of 1994–95, have been acquired by new investors and are nearing completion.

Continuing past the tourist complex, the main coastal beach area of Puerto La Cruz and Barcelona – consisting of Playa Cangrejo, Playa de Lecherías, and Playa Mansa – is on the isthmus to El Morro. Restaurants, such as **La Churuata del Morro**, do a brisk trade, serving meals to hungry sun worshipers.

Paseo Colón: action around the clock

Although **Puerto La Cruz** ⓫ came into being in the late 17th century, just 10 years after Barcelona, you will find no trace of the old town. Shiny new and geared toward tourism, the focal point is **Paseo Colón**, a waterfront boulevard jammed with hotels, restaurants, bars, nightclubs, and shops on the south side; and a beach bordered by a wide pedestrian walkway lined with seafood restaurants, outdoor cafés, and local artisans selling their wares on the other.

BELOW:
Caribbean sunset.

Even though the long, palm-lined beach bordering Paseo Colón looks appealing and offers great opportunities for shelling (murex, long-tailed spindles, cone shells, turret and augers are so plentiful they are practically regarded as "garbage" shells), the water is too polluted for safe swimming. But don't be disheartened: lying off shore are the island beaches of **Parque Nacional Mochima**. Explosub, operating out of the Maremares resort, is one of the companies which offers a variety of packages on yachts with visits to several islands.

The "anchors" on Paseo Colón are the **Meliá Puerto La Cruz** (still the only five-star hotel on this strip and the only hotel right on the beach), the **Hotel Rasil Puerto La Cruz** and the ferry terminal (for trips to Margarita) on the west end. With only 12 blocks between these two hotels, and the great concentration of dining, drinking, sleeping, and shopping places, it is hardly surprising that the boulevard is busy with visitors and residents by day and night. Directions for finding recommended spots are not really necessary, and neither are maps, because everything you want can be found right here.

Island fun: shelling and diving

From Puerto La Cruz, the best option for transfers to the beaches of **Parque Nacional Mochima** is with the well-organized and reliable boatmen's union, Transtupaco, located at the east end of Paseo Colón. It runs shuttle services to **Playa El Faro** on Isla Chimana del Sur, and to **Playas Puinare** (good diving) and **El Saco** (good shelling) on Chimana Grande; there are departures all morning to Chimana Grande, with return trips from 4–5pm, as well as special boats for deep-sea fishing and diving trips. Just east of town, at Pamatacualito, shuttle boats go to **Isla de Plata** and **Isla de Monos**, also good for diving.

Map on pages 162–3

 TIP

Some of the best *empanadas* (cornmeal turnovers) you will find in Venezuela are made fresh and sold at a string of stands at the west end of the ferry terminal at Puerto La Cruz. With the local style of thin dough, they are light, crispy and not at all greasy.

BELOW: luxury boats at Puerto La Cruz.

From **Playa Arapito**, *peñeros* (the traditional wooden fishing boats) are available to take you to La Piscina and Isla Arapo, a popular diving site. From **Mochima** (about 45 km/30 miles east of Puerto La Cruz), shuttle boats go to Playas Careñero, Tacuarumo, and Coral (all of which are good for shelling); to the Playas La Cruz, La Playuela, and Las Cuicas (all on the Península de Manaure); and to Playas Blanca, Cautaro, and Cautarito, on the coast, with access only by sea.

"Route of the Sun"

Beyond its insular part, the Mochima national park also includes a continental stretch between Puerto La Cruz and Cumaná, aptly referred to as the "**Route of the Sun**", one of the most scenic coastal roads in the country. The steep, winding highway is cut into the sides and along the base of steep mountains that plunge dramatically into the sea. Rounding each curve, you are presented with yet another beautiful vista of rugged coast with pounding waves, or coves harboring beaches rimmed with palm trees. The arid, rocky hills covered largely with cactus form a stark contrast to the lush seaside valleys snuggled between them.

Although there are appealing beaches along the full length of the route, two of the most famous – and most photographed – are **Playa Arapito** and **Playa Colorada**; the latter is on a small protected crescent bay known for its reddish-colored sand (hence the name).

Making a detour from the highway into **Santa Fe** ⓬ is well worth the effort. It has one of the most spotless beaches in Venezuela (the residents clean it daily) and it has benefitted from a successful grass-roots effort to establish a network of family-style tourist lodging, all right on the beach.

Playa Arapito: a long white sweep of sand, edged with palms, and mountains forming the backdrop.

BELOW: Spanish ramparts at San Antonio Fortress, Cumaná.

As you approach the turn-off for the fishing village of **Mochima**, the road climbs Cerro Aceite Castillo and you get a spectacular view of the islands of Mochima National Park. Take the clearly marked side road down into the village for access to the docks where boatmen will pounce on you to offer transfers to the islands. There are also more than a dozen modest *posadas*. For dining, **El Mochimero** is tops with a view over the water, excellent food, and a great collection of jazz recordings being played for background music.

There are numerous places all along this route where local *artesanía* (handicrafts) can be purchased directly from the creators at stands by the road. Near **Barbacoas** ⓭, you can buy traditional black-faced rag dolls, beautiful delicate bird cages made with thin reeds, and hand-carved replica sailboats. If you are interested in boat building, watch for craftsmen at work using age-old techniques.

Map on pages 162–3

Cumaná: South America's oldest city

The first view on approaching **Cumaná** ⓮ via Avenida Universidad is the long public beach, Balneario Los Uveros, with a number of small, basic beachside hotels plus several large four-star offers at its west end. Situated near the eastern end of the avenue, opposite the Sucre campus of Universidad de Oriente, is the **Museo del Mar** (open daily; 8.30–11.30am, 2.30–5.30pm; token entry fee). Displays range from typical boats to old-time diving equipment, shells, and a preserved example of a coelacanth, the "fossil fish", which was believed long extinct. It also has a modest-sized aquarium.

Cumaná, nicknamed "First-born of the Continent," was the first Spanish settlement on the continent of South America, established by Franciscan friars in 1515. After destruction through indigenous attacks, it was founded again by

BELOW: handmade dolls at Barbacoas.

Gonzalo de Ocampo in 1521. However, faced with continual assaults b
Cumanagoto indians, the fledgling city would fall several more times until,
1569, Diego Fernández de Serpa founded the city that survives today.

Fortifications have been of primary importance in the history of Cumaná. Fir
they protected against attacking Caribe and Cumanagoto indians; and subs
quently against assaults by English, Dutch, and French pirates and slave trader

The most visible landmark today, as in the past, is the imposing **Castillo d
San Antonio de la Eminencia**, majestically overlooking the city and coast
waters from Cumaná's highest point (open daily 9am–noon, 3–5pm; free). Th
first fort on this site was erected in 1660. An earthquake in 1684 destroyed it an
most of Cumaná, but by 1686 a new fort had been built. In 1853, another eart
quake left the fort in ruins. Dictator General Cipriano Castro had it rebuilt in th
early 1900s, but once again nature prevailed and, in 1929, yet another eart
quake, this time joined by a tidal wave, left the fort (and many other building
in ruins. It has since been restored and is now open to the public.

Down the hill is the **Castillo de Santa María de la Cabeza**, a fortress co
structed from 1669–73 to give residents a closer refuge than La Eminenc
when pirates attacked. Entrance is through the **Iglesia de Santa Inés**. First co
structed in 1637, this church, like most of Cumaná, was destroyed and rebui
five times between 1637 and 1929.

Several blocks south is the former **Convento de San Francisco**, location of th
first school on the continent. It is due to human neglect rather than the forces
nature, however, that this historic landmark now stands abandoned. In the stree
surrounding the nearby **Plaza Bolívar** are the state's tourism office (ope
Mon–Fri 8am–noon, 2–4pm); the **Casa Andrés Eloy Blanco** (open Mon–F

BELOW: colonial
splendor, Cumaná.

am–noon, 2–4pm, Sat 8am–noon; free), birthplace of the revered, early 20th-
century Venezuelan poet, now a museum; and the **Ateneo de Cumaná**, where
art shows and musical presentations take place (open Mon–Fri 8am–noon,
2–5pm; free).

In the center of town, an inviting park borders the Manzanares River and is
the site of the **Museo Gran Marisical de Ayacucho**, with a mix of historical
exhibits and artifacts (open Mon–Fri 8am–noon, 2–4pm, Sat 8am–noon; free).
To get a better feel for the people and soul of the city, visit the **market** by the
fishing port on Avenida Los Manglares. From 5am to noon, the place hums
with activity as shoppers come to buy fresh produce and handicrafts such as
Cumaná's famous *cuatros*, the four-stringed instrument most closely associated with Venezuelan folk music, and, of course, to stop at the rows of tables
where cheerful women prepare fried fish, *arepas*, and other tasty delights.

From the nearby marine terminal, you can catch ferries to Isla Margarita and
to the Araya Peninsula, just across the Gulf of Cariaco (which provides most of
the sardines consumed in Venezuela).

*The mouth of Cueva
del Guácharo: the
path inside is often
muddy because of an
internal stream, so
wear old shoes.*

Venezuela's largest cave

Many visitors to Cumaná fit in a side trip to the **Cueva del Guácharo** ⓑ (tours
8am–3pm; entrance fee); it lies about 90 minutes to the south in Monagas state
near **Caripe**. The cavern is home to the nocturnal, fruit-eating *guácharo* – or oil
bird – and is renowned for being Venezuela's largest and best cave, with an
extension of more than 10 km (6 miles). Information about the cave first
emerged on a widespread basis in the writings of German naturalist Alexander
von Humboldt (*see page 173*) after his visit there in 1799. You can enter the cave
only on guided tours with park guards. Nothing may
be taken in – no flashlights, cameras or purses. Guides
lead you using only a kerosene lamp. You will not be
able to see the birds, only hear them. Incidentally, the
town of Caripe has many excellent *posadas* and cabins,
including options on working coffee and fruit farms.

BELOW: a fisherman
monument at
Cumaná.

From hot springs to a colonial fort

Continuing eastward, distinct among the usual
balnearios are swimming areas with hot springs.
These include the **Núcleo Integral Turístico Recreacional Cachamaure**, along the coastal highway near
San Antonio del Golfo, the **Balneario Los Cocoteros**
and **Poza Cristal**. The last two are reached via
Cariaco-Casanay (about 8 km/5 miles from the turn).
Cariaco ⓰, the second oldest town on the continent, is the point of departure for the road along the
Península de Araya. The route, with startlingly beautiful desert landscapes, solitary beaches, and excellent shelling, leads to **Araya** ⓱, at the western tip of
the peninsula (where the Cumaná–Isla Margarita ferry
also stops). After passing the eerie-looking salt-evap-
oration lagoons with brilliant lilac-colored water and
bordered with a ring of glistening salt crystals, you
will find a gorgeous expanse of beach (with outstanding windsurfing off shore), the giant Ensal plant
(the source of most of the country's salt), and the
imposing ruins of the **Castillo de Santiago de Araya**.

Map
on pages
162–3

Map on pages 162–3

The fort, begun in 1618, was the most important and costliest construction of the colonial era. There were tremendous difficulties in building it, due to the lack of drinking water or land suitable for growing crops, meaning all supplies had to be shipped from the mainland. In addition, the salt ate through the workers' shoes, and the sun was so brutal that work could be done only at night.

A hurricane in 1726 turned the salt lake into a gulf, ruining the beds. With the tremendously expensive upkeep, especially when the salt was no longer a factor, the Spanish abandoned the fort in 1762, after blowing it up so it wouldn't fall into enemy hands. The haunting ruins beg to be explored and photographed.

The far east

Carúpano ⑱ has little to draw tourists – except during **Carnival** when visitors flock to the town for its lively celebration (*see Fiestas, pages 79–83*) – but is important as a commercial center for agriculture and fishing. Its port houses large tuna fleets, which supply several onshore canneries.

Continuing eastward along the coast, it is evident that fishing is the core of the economy: with the waters filled with fishing fleet launches; yards with boats of all sizes being constructed of wood and steel; and the strange sight of gutted fish "hung out to dry" in the sun along the roadsides.

Although principally a fishing village, **Río Caribe** ⑲ has a pretty beach, various pleasant lodgings, and attractive tree-shaded streets lined with old houses. This is also the exit point for **Playa Medina**, one of the most beautiful beaches in Venezuela. En route, you pass through the village of **San Francisco de Chacaracual**, with houses and fences painted every color of the rainbow.

Densely forested mountains form the lush green backdrop for the spectacular Playa Medina. Lined with a thick grove of palm trees nearly to the water's edge (providing welcome shade), it has an outstanding tourism infrastructure. There is an immaculate beach, controlled parking, and inviting food stands; the latter are operated on a concession basis under strict controls, despite their quaint appearance in open-sided thatch-roofed huts (*bohios*). Fried fish, *arepas*, *orejones* (sweet, deep-fried pastries) are all prepared fresh as you wait. There is also a group of cottages, built with earthen walls painted in rich earth tones, offered for tourists in packages with lodging, meals, open bar, excursions, beach service, and transfer to and from Carúpano airport.

You can also continue from here to other pristine beaches farther east: **Playa Puipuy** and those in the village of **San Juan de los Galdonas**, some 80 km (50 miles) from Carúpano.

Although the route along the Península de Paria to Güiria doesn't offer any specific "tourist attractions" it is a pretty drive, with the verdant mountains of the **Parque Nacional Península de Paria** to the north and glimpses of the Gulf of Paria to the south.

Of great historical importance for Venezuela but not really worth the effort of getting there, is **Macuro** ⑳, near the tip of the peninsula. The village is famous because, as far as anyone knows, this was the only place where Christopher Columbus ever set foot on the mainland of South America.

Von Humboldt

Simón Bolívar described Humboldt as "the true discoverer of America because his work has produced more benefit to our people than that of all the conquistadores". Praise indeed from the Liberator of the Americas. But how did this wealthy Prussian minerologist come to play such a vital role in the history of the continent?

Alexander Von Humboldt was born in Berlin in 1769. As a young man he studied botany, chemistry, astronomy, and mineralogy. At the age of 27, he received a legacy large enough to finance a scientific expedition. With his companion Aimé Bonpland, Humboldt set off for Venezuela, the first non-Spanish scientists to be permitted to visit South America since Charles de la Condamine in 1735.

After passing through the valleys of Caracas and Lake Valencia, he proceeded through the *llanos* to Amazonas in 1800. His goal there was to prove that the Brazo Casiquiare was the natural canal which united the hydrographic basins of the Amazon and Orinoco rivers. The route from the present-day Puerto Ayacucho followed the Orinoco, Atabapo, Guiania, and Negro rivers as far as the junction with Brazil and Colombia; returning via San Carlos de Río Negro, Brazo Casiquiare; then to Tamatama and La Esmeralda. From there, he headed east via the Orinoco to its delta, then north toward Cumaná.

En route, Humboldt explored Venezuela's largest cave, which would later bear his name: "Monumento Natural Alejandro de Humboldt" (more popularly known as "Cueva del Guácharo" for the colony of *guácharo* – oil birds – inhabiting one of the chambers. He was the first to classify the *guácharo*, indicating this word in old Castillian means one who sobs or laments continually. Although the cave was known by early Spanish explorers, and by indigenous residents long before, it wasn't until Humboldt's writings were published in Paris in 1814 that information about the cave became widely known.

More than just an adventurer, Humboldt was an astute observer. His detailed accounts painted a vivid picture of the countryside, and of the lives of indigenous peoples encountered in the Amazonas region.

Humboldts contributions seem endless. His *Essays on the Geography of Plants* were pioneering studies of the relationship between a region's geography and its flora and fauna. He claimed another first by listing many of the indigenous species: vanilla, avocado, yucca, maize and manioc, among others.

Off the west coast of the continent, he studied the oceanic current, which was subsequently named after him; his work on isotherms and isobars laid the foundation for the science of climatology.

Humboldt's admirers were many: Goethe, a close friend, found him "exceedingly interesting and stimulating", a man who "overwhelms one with intellectual treasure"; and Charles Darwin, who was inspired by the Prussian scientist's earlier journey to Tenerife in the Canary Islands, knew whole passages of Humboldt's *Relation Historique* by heart, and described him as "the parent of a grand progeny of scientific travelers". ❑

ISLA MARGARITA

North of the Venezuelan mainland, this sun-kissed island where pearls the size of eggs were once found is now a beach resort drawing tourists from all over the world

Map on page 178

Caracas

Venezuelans – inveterate shoppers – have long flocked to Isla Margarita on weekends and vacations because its duty-free status makes it an inexpensive spot to buy imported cheeses, perfumes, liquors, electronic goods and clothes. Foreigners may dish out bolívars for beautiful hammocks, baskets and pottery but their main bargain is the beach, miles and miles of it. Since the mid-1980s, it has become the Caribbean's budget destination for Europeans and North Americans who want to enjoy sun and surf without seriously denting their wallets. But Margarita and its sister islands offer a great many other delights besides sun, sand, and shopping.

Indians and pirates challenge settlers

Margarita, as well as the tinier islands of Coche and Cubagua off its coast, had strong ties with the fierce Caribe indians and the peaceful Arawaks and Guaiquerís before the Spanish conquest. The Caribes were relentless warriors who gave their name to the hurricane-besieged Caribbean.

Despite the Caribes' conquering ways, they too fell victim to an even more ruthless foe: the Europeans. Reports by Christopher Columbus of the pearls worn by indians of the Paria Peninsula immediately aroused interest. Less than a year after his provocative find, Cristóbal de la Guerra and Pedro Alfonso Niño discovered the source: the pearl beds off the island of Cubagua. The "Pearl Rush" was on as word spread. Before the end of the year 1500, some 50 fortune hunters had arrived, and it wasn't long before pirates began raiding the island – prompting the construction of the forts, which still stand today. Because of great decline of the beds, no pearl fishing has been allowed since 1962.

In 1529, Coche produced 373 kg (820 lbs) of pearls a month. They were to influence European fashion and, in 1589, Caracas town council authorized their use as money, a practice which continued into the 1700s.

First stop: Porlamar

Visitors reach the island by ferries departing from Puerto La Cruz and Cumaná to the town of **Punta de Piedras**, or they fly into the General Santiago Mariño Airport. Either way, one of the first landmarks spotted are the two rounded mountain peaks officially named the Tetas de María Guevara (María Guevara's breasts). Some say María Guevara was a 19th-century independence movement heroine, others that she was a local madame well known to sailors who docked here.

The first destination for most visitors is usually **Porlamar ❶**. Founded on March 25, 1536, this once quiet fishing town is now a dynamic city with 150,000 residents, wide boulevards of shops, plenty of fine

PRECEDING PAGES: fishing boats at Puerto Fermín. **LEFT:** Playa La Galera, near Juangriego. **BELOW:** colonial clock tower in La Asunción.

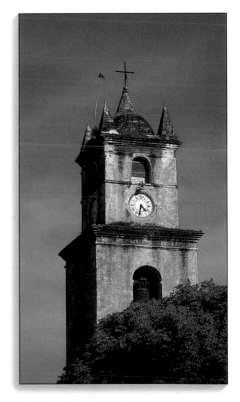

restaurants and hotels in every price range, and an active night life. The city's orig inal name was Puerto de la Mar but, in true Venezuelan style, the words were run together and shortened.

Porlamar lives on tourism and commerce, and streets such as Avenida Santiago Mariño and Avenida 4 de Mayo, are filled with stores that sell every thing from French perfume to locally produced T-shirts – along with a great concentration of restaurants, bars, and downtown hotels.

A pleasant departure from the relentlessly commercial nature of downtown Porlamar is the **Museo de Arte Contemporáneo Francisco Narváez** on Calle Díaz (open daily; free). Named for the Margarita-born sculptor, its main exhibit hall contains a permanent collection of his works, while additional rooms have rotating shows by other Venezuelan artists. Elsewhere on the island, his creations can be seen next to the Cathedral in La Asunción and around the fountain at the **Hotel Bella Vista** – the first of the big hotels to open on the island and now a Margarita landmark.

Colonial treasures

Northeast of Porlamar is the town of **Pampatar ❷** with its Castillo de San Carlos Borromeo, which was the island's most important pirate defense. The present fort, constructed in 1664–84, was built on the site of the original one which was destroyed in 1662 when the city was burned by the Dutch. During the War of Independence, Spanish soldiers fleeing the fort tried to blow it up but revolutionary troops discovered the 635 kg (1,400 lbs) of explosive powder hidden in the complex. The fort has been restored and is open to the public (open Mon–Sat, 8am–noon, 3–5pm; free).

TIP

Although none of the duty-free liquor outlets post the information, it is prohibited to take more than one case per person of any one type of liquor, such as whisky, rum or champagne, out of the island. Custom officers will confiscate any excess they find.

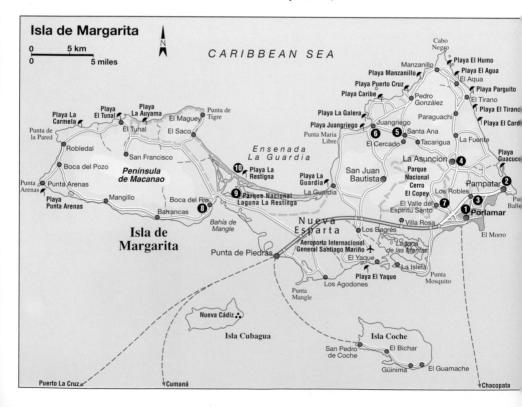

Isla de Margarita

Facing the fort is the **Iglesia del Santísimo Cristo del Buen Viaje** (Church of the Holiest Christ of the Good Voyage). The external stairway to the bell tower is a distinctive feature seen in most of Margarita's churches, but in only one or two in the rest of Venezuela. Sailors claim that the crucifix over the altar of this church was brought on a passing ship which found itself unable to lift anchor until this religious article was left behind. At **Playa Pampatar**, the local beach, visitors can watch the grizzled fishermen take out their boats. These same fishermen can point out the way to **Cueva El Bufón**, an underwater cave that is popular with divers. Locals say this is where pirates hid their loot.

Near the church is the former Casa de la Aduana (Pampatar's customs house), which now serves as the headquarters for FONDENE (Fund for the Development of Nueva Esparta State). Constructed in 1863, it has been restored and houses a permanent exhibition of art (open Mon–Fri). Overlooking Playa Pampatar is another 17th-century defense, Fortín Santiago de La Caranta.

Between Porlamar and Pampatar is **Los Robles ❸** (also known as El Pilar). Inside the town's colonial church is the solid gold statue of the Virgin of Pilar, sent to the colony in 1504 by Spanish Queen Juana La Loca, Isabella's daughter. The state's tourism office is inside the Centro Artesanal Gilberto Menchini, Calle Jóvito Villalba, as you enter Los Robles (open Mon–Fri, 8.30am–12.30pm, 2–5pm; tel: 09 562 4194).

Vintage capital

Since its foundation in 1565, **La Asunción ❹** has been Isla Margarita's strategic center. It was placed just far enough inland to make it both inaccessible to pirates and harder for the rebellious Caribe indians to attack. Today, it is the

Map on page 178

Warding off pirates: the Castillo de San Carlos Borromeo, Pampatar.

BELOW: colonial defenses at Pampatar fortress.

political seat of Nueva Esparta state, consisting of Margarita and the islands of Coche and Cubagua.

Little more than a century after Captain Pedro González Cervantes de Alborno founded La Asunción, the **Castillo de Santa Rosa** was built to guard the town (open Mon–Sat 8am–noon, 3–5pm; donation). The scene of important battles, it was here that the pregnant 16-year-old wife of Juan Bautista Arismendi, a well known hero of the War of Independence, was held hostage. A plaque marks the cell where she gave birth to a daughter who died in the fortress. Luisa Cáceres de Arismendi survived and was later reunited with her husband.

In front of La Asunción's Plaza Bolívar is the **Catedral de Nuestra Señora de la Asunción**, the oldest church in Venezuela. Construction began in 1571 but it wasn't until 46 years later that it was completed. Diagonally across from the church is the **Museo y Biblioteca Nueva Cádiz**, the seat of government in colonial times, now housing exhibits ranging from pre-Columbian artifacts to model ships (open Tue–Sun; free).

On the main road northwest of La Asunción lies **Santa Ana ❺**. The simple church on the main plaza is where, on May 6, 1816, Simón Bolívar signed the decree abandoning the war and proclaimed the formation of the Third Republic. The so-called Assembly of Notables met at the church and formally recognized Bolívar as Supreme Chief of Venezuela and its armies.

Sunsets, skiffs and seafood

If a piña colada at a seaside café at sunset sounds appealing, then **Juangriego ❻** should not be missed. On the north coast, on one of the island's prettiest bays with clean waters, brightly colored fishing skiffs and explosive sunsets, this

The bell tower of La Asunción's Cathedral is the only one still standing in Venezuela which was built in the 16th century.

BELOW: Margarita Hilton on Playa Moreno, between Porlamar and Pampatar.

Map on page 178

fishing village also has various restaurants along the waterfront, predictably specializing in seafood. Perhaps the best place for sunset viewing is from the hilltop landmark, **Fortín de La Galera**. Spanish General Pablo Morillo slaughtered the patriot forces here when he retook Juangriego from the independence army in 1817. Behind the fort is the **Laguna de Los Mártires** (Martyrs' Lagoon) where the waters are said to have turned red with the blood of 200 political prisoners executed by Morillo.

At the **cemetery** is the headstone of James Towers English, an Irish Legion commander who died far from his homeland while helping Venezuelan independence forces in 1819. English was contracted by Bolívar to organize an expeditionary force to fight in the war against Spain. During a battle in Margarita, the young officer died of a cerebral hemorrhage but his troops went on to fight in the Battle of Carabobo in 1821, the decisive victory in the Venezuelan revolution (*see History section, page 37*).

Beloved virgin

The island's most renowned religious spot is in **El Valle del Espíritu Santo** ⑦, home of the **Santuario de la Virgen del Valle**, the chapel guarding the image of the patron saint of Margarita and all of eastern Venezuela. According to the legend a Guaiquerí indian found the beautiful image of the virgin in the Piache Cave located in a hillside above the town.

An ornate pink and white neo-Gothic chapel was built by the town's main plaza to house the revered image. There is always a steady stream of admirers visiting the chapel, but during the week surrounding her feast day, September 8, thousands of pilgrims come from all parts of the country to pay homage to the

Pelican on board. Margarita's fishing boats traditionally have "eyes" painted on their brows to guide them safely home.

BELOW: Margarita is famous for its handicrafts.

HANDICRAFT HEAVEN

For anyone interested in traditional crafts, Margarita is ripe for exploration. Not to be missed is a visit to Taller de Artesanía Así con las Manos, Tierra, Agua y Fuego (open daily; small fee) just a short distance west of Juangriego on the coastal highway.

Clearly visible on the left side of the road, it is a combination museum, artisan community and craft shop in one, unlike anything else in Venezuela. A large shop, jammed to the rafters with every kind of local craft, is closest to the highway, but the truly fascinating part is behind it: something of an artisan's vision of a vintage Venezuelan village, including shops and a church, in a dozen or so hand-built *bahareque* (mud-walled) structures joined by paths in a desert garden setting. Some contain only memorabilia to create the spirit of the place, others also sell crafts (largely produced by local artists working on the premises).

Other handicraft areas include El Cercado, just outside La Asunción, famous for its ceramics; to the southeast of Juangriego, Los Millanes is known for its hand-rolled cigars; Tacarigua for its *chinohorros* (lacy, openwork hammocks); Pedrogonzález, for its *mapires* (handwoven pocket-style bags in every size); and Atamo, east of La Asunción, for its sturdy *mara* baskets.

virgin. On this occasion, she is usually dressed in an elegant gown covered with daisies – *margaritas* in Spanish – and a gold crown.

It is traditional to leave gifts for the virgin, either when asking favors, or in thanks for those granted. Sometimes these are things of great worth, at others they are simply a symbolic representation associated with the favor. For this reason, you see license plates (to protect the driver), graduation diplomas and trophies (thanks for help in attaining these goals), and wedding bouquets (for a successful marriage). In matters of health, *milagros* (charms in the shape of an arm, leg, and so on, which make reference to the part of the body affected) of gold or silver are the usual offering. The degree of devotion to this virgin is obvious in the **Museo Diocesano** adjacent to the chapel, created to hold the incredible volume of offerings that have been left over the years (open Tues–Sat 9am–noon, 2–5pm; Sun, 9am–1pm; free). The display has to be seen to be believed. Nearby is the **Casa Natal Santiago Mariño**, recently restored birth-place of one of the most important heroes of the independence (open daily; free).

Arid peninsula

Travelers who have exhausted the island's eastern attractions can cross the 18-km (11-mile) isthmus to the western **Península de Macanao**, the largely uninhab-ited arid terrain that locals call "the other island." As would be expected, cactus dominates the landscape, but to soften its harshness puts on seasonal shows of color as the low-lying prickly pear variety bursts into bloom with large yellow flowers, and bright red fruit adorns the tall spiked columns of the *cardón* cactus.

BELOW: the dry Macanao Peninsula.

Linked to the rest of Margarita by a bridge at the mouth of Bahía de Mangle, residents of **Boca del Río ❽** – the peninsula's largest town – live from commercial fishing. Here and in some of the smaller towns, there are shipyards where you can watch construction of the small boats called *peñeros*.

The main attraction for visitors to Boca del Río is the **Museo Marino de Margarita** (open Tue–Sun, 9am–5pm; free), a project of the Universidad de Ori-ente. The museum has seven salons focusing on the sea in general, on corals, sea turtles, marine mam-mals, boats and ships, traditional fishing methods and a marine inventory of the area. Guided tours are avail-able in English and Spanish. In large tanks outside, the university is experimentally raising shrimp, marine turtles, and various species of fish.

Boca del Río is close to one of Margarita's main tourist attractions, the **Parque Nacional Laguna La Restinga ❾** (open daily; fee). A boatmen's union, operating from the dock behind the park guards' office, has the concession to carry visitors on tours through the 100 sq. km (38 sq. miles) of lagoon, and canals cut through the dense growth of mangroves which ring it. Price is based on a flat fee per round trip per boat.

Depending on the season and time of day, you can see a wide variety of water birds, including flamin-goes, herons, scarlet ibis, gulls, pelicans, cormorants, and magnificent frigatebirds. While passing through the canals, watch for colonies of oysters clinging to the aerial roots of mangroves.

The park is about 40 km (25 miles) from Porlamar, but tourists without transport are warned that although getting there is easy, getting back can be tough. It's best to hire a taxi and agree a time for the driver to return and pick you up; or else to go with an organized tour.

Playa La Restinga , on a 23-km (14-miles) long barrier reef bordering the lagoon, is covered with finely crushed fossils over its full length. This magnificent Caribbean beach, rather than the lagoon, is the target of most local visitors. Near the docking area informal restaurants serve freshly fried fish and other simple fare.

Sandy shores

Although Margarita is a treasure chest of history, most visitors are more interested in the sun. To satisfy them there are dozens of beaches, each with its own character. The planting of palm trees has helped to increase the amount of shade.

The beach closest to the airport is **Playa El Yaque**, which has acquired international fame for its outstanding conditions for windsurfing, with a steady breeze in the afternoons and safe shallow waters. This is where Margarita's windsurfing competitions are held. Shops offering equipment rental and lessons abound.

The most popular east coast beaches, reached from the route indicated for Pampatar-Manzanillo, from south to north, are: Guacuco, El Tirano, Parguito, and El Agua.

Development projects have marred the appeal of **Playa Guacuco**, which these days seems to be more popular with locals than with tourists; still, it has a fine sandy, if narrow, beach. When the surf comes in during the late afternoon, the water rises to the line of the palm trees that shade the beach. **Playa Tirano** (in Puerto Fermín), the least frequented of this group, has a southern backdrop of

TIP

Watch for the endemic Margarita yellow-headed parrot (*cotorra margariteña*), often seen feeding in bushes on side roads penetrating the center of the Macanao Peninsula from its western beach road.

BELOW: touring the mangrove swamps of La Restinga.

Map on page 178

Windsurfing at Playa El Yaque: most local lodgings have space for board and sail storage.

picturesque peaks. The village offers several pretty *posadas*, and pleasant restaurants dot the waterfront drive.

The most popular beach is **Playa El Agua**, with soft waves (but a powerful undertow), and everything from walk-in sushi bars to informal seafood restaurants, which often put on live Caribbean music to entertain diners. Although palms shade the eateries, natural shade is at a minimum close to the water. But beach-chairs and awnings (*toldos*) can be rented.

Just as windsurfers have their beach, so do surfing fanatics. **Playa Parguito** has the island's highest breakers thanks to an offshore shelf of rocks. This is a pretty beach next to Playa El Agua, with a handful of food kiosks and palm and sea grape trees. Bring sandals because pebbles, not sand, dominate the beach. Because of its location, furthest from the road, it is never too crowded.

North shore beaches

A number of new hotels and vacation properties have recently been built on or near key beaches. One example is a huge luxury hotel, Isla Bonita, which has appeared on **Playa Puerto Cruz**, a long, curving white sand beach. Some of the hotels have tried closing off parts of these public beaches for their private use.

RIGHT: the Caribbean beckons. **BELOW:** even the pirates like Spanish *tascas* (bars).

At the base of the mountain pass that joins the towns of Pedro González and Manzanillo, is **Playa Puerto Viejo**. The beach can be reached on foot by walking to the far northeastern end of Playa Puerto Cruz, scaling a small rocky hill and descending. Although this is a narrow strip of sand, the surf is calm and the water is shallow – heightening its appeal for swimmers and children. It's best to pack a picnic and plenty to drink because all that's guaranteed here is soft sand, clear Caribbean water and shady coconut trees.

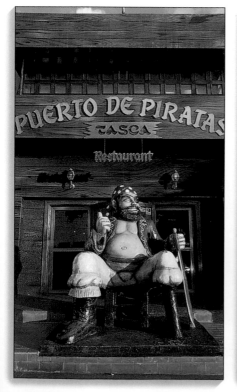

Playa Pedro González is picturesque with its well-preserved traditional-
:yle beachfront homes and wide sandy beach. With the buildings facing a wide
romenade (and the sea) shaded by sea grapes and dotted with several small
dewalk cafés, it is more geared toward those looking for relaxation than action.
[owever, if it is action you are looking for, the newest "in" spot is nearby **Playa
'aribe** – as crowded by night as by day thanks to a string of lively bars and
:staurants with live music.

he pearl islands

.t the beginning of the 16th century, it was not Margarita but the tiny islands
f **Cubagua** and **Coche** which were the focus of attention thanks to their rich
ffshore beds of pearl-bearing oysters.The settlement established on Cubagua
a 1500 was destroyed by an earthquake and tidal wave in 1541. Except for a few
shermen's shacks and a research station, there has been no redevelopment of
ae island. Coche was not as affected by the 1541 quake and has several small
illages along with a pair of small hotels. With its new free-port status, more
:owth here is sure to come. Many Margarita travel agencies offer day tours by
»at (with lunch, bar and snorkeling) to Coche and Cubagua. There is also a
ar/passenger ferry service between Punta de Piedras and San Pedro de Coche.

ar-flung day tours

:veral companies offer day tours from Margarita, to capture tourists who fly
rectly into the island with charters. Among these are trips to La Blanquilla
land (off the eastern shore of Margarita); Canaima, Kavac and Uruyén in Par-
ae Nacional Canaima in Bolívar; and to Delta Amacuro.   ❑

*Because of the
scarcity of natural
water sources on
Margarita, a pipeline
was installed from
the mainland that
carries fresh water to
the thirsty island. But
there is not enough
water, and shortages
are often a problem.*

BELOW: islanders
strumming up
a storm.

EXPLORE VENEZUELA'S COASTLINE

With attractions such as coral cays and mangrove swamps, the country's beaches are much more than places for lying around and soaking up the sun

With its 3,000 km (1,800 miles) of Caribbean coast, an island state where tourism based on sun and surf is the principal livelihood, three superb marine parks, and year-around summer climate, it is little wonder that Venezuela is still thought of primarily as a beach holiday destination, both for its own citizens and for visitors from around the world.

NATURAL ATTRACTIONS

Unlike most Caribbean neighbors, whose beaches are essentially the same, the great variety of Venezuela's beaches is a bonus. Those of the east, near the Paria Peninsula, enjoy a backdrop of mountains blanketed with tropical forest and shorelines bordered by swaying palm trees. Waters off Margarita Island's southern shore and the east coast of the Paraguaná Peninsula offer world-class windsurfing. Los Roques Archipelago presents a menu of incredible diving, pristine beaches, and bonefishing rated tops in the world. The dramatic, twisted rock islands of Mochima National Park and the sandy cays of Morrocoy National Park beyond intricate, mangrove-lined canals have both dramatic landscapes and fascinating wildlife. Beyond that, nearly a dozen colonial forts can be visited, installed along the coast to ward off pirates. Likewise many areas, such as Cuare Wildlife Refuge and Laguna de Tacarigua National Park harbor a wealth of species to delight bird watchers. And, to satisfy those who may just want a relaxing holiday, a full range of lodging is available, from small cozy inns to five-star mega-resorts with all the trimmings.

△ **SWEEPING BAY**
After a drive through the Henri Pittier National Park, plunge into the clear waters off Puerto Colombia's beautiful Playa Grande.

▽ **GIFTS GALORE**
The booming tourist industry on Margarita Island has opened the doors of opportunity for entrepreneurs, large and small.

△ **NET PROFITS**
Worrying where their ne: meal is coming from is r a problem for fishermen the central coast.

▷ **CRYSTALLINE SEA**
There is no natural shad Los Roques, so most visitors explore the beac from the comfort of a bo

EASTERN FISHING FOCUS

△ **WAVING THE FLAG**
Cayo Sombrero is the most popular of over a dozen inviting cays in Morrocoy National Park.

▽ **STRESS RELIEF**
A hammock swinging gently between the palms provides total relaxation to even the most hyperactive types.

Most visitors may have more leisurely pursuits in mind, but Venezuela's warm Caribbean waters also support a large fishing industry. The principal commercial fishing areas are in the east, especially in Sucre. The Gulf of Cariaco produces most of the sardines consumed in Venezuela, with processing plants in Cumaná and Marigüitar. This zone is also abundant with mollusks and crustaceans, including shrimps, crabs, mussels and various types of small clams. Large-scale fishing fleets based in Cumaná take advantage of the quantity of tuna in the open sea, and several large tuna canneries have set up in the area around Carupano. Fishermen on the Gulf of Paria find shrimp, marine catfish, mullet and weakfish to be the most viable commercially, while many lobster and conch are caught off Los Roques Archipelago.

▷ **ROCKY PERCH**
Pelicans, boobies, herons, cormorants, flamingos, frigate birds and scarlet ibis are just some of the many bird species that can be seen all along the country's coast.

WEST COAST STATES

*The West's natural areas – from cloud forests to island beaches
and sand dunes – are superb, and colonial history lives
on in fascinating cities such as Puerto Cabello and Coro*

f you want to get to know the northwestern states properly, set aside at least a week. Leave Caracas via the *Autopista Central*, a modern super-highway which winds south then west to the agro-industrial city of Maracay. From Maracay you can head north across the mountains, through the magnificent cloud forest of Parque Nacional Henri Pittier, to glorious palm-fringed beaches.

Alternatively, you can go via the Lago de Valencia, on to the important industrial center of Valencia. North from that city is the thriving port town of Puerto Cabello, with its two colonial forts. To the northwest are the islands and cays of Parque Nacional Morrocoy, home of many water birds and a paradise for snorkelers and divers.

From there, you can continue northwest to Coro, with its renowned colonial zone, and, just outside the town, sand dunes. The Península de Paraguaná is dry and dotted with cactus and windswept beaches. The Sierra de San Luis offers everything from quaint mountain villages where age-old indigenous rites are maintained to beautiful caves.

Westbound on the Autopista Central

If your destination is Maracay, Valencia or points farther west, you can whiz there quickly on the *autopista*, which is now a toll road. However, taking a detour at the La Victoria exit can lead you to various interesting attractions.

A little past the toll booth, turning left on the old Carretera Panamericana – Pan American highway – takes you to **La Victoria ❶**. Although not a major tourist center, there are still things to see here. These include: the town's **colonial church**, on Calle Candelaria facing Plaza Riba; a gigantic, handsome castle-like military fort, the **Cuartel Marinao Montilla** (open to the public at weekends); the pretty tree-filled **Parque La Victoria** (closed Mon), with the restored station for the long-gone train line which ran between La Guaira-Caracas-Valencia; and the colonial chapel, **Capilla de Nuestra Señora de la Candelaria** facing Plaza Bolívar.

Continuing westward on the main avenue, watch for the highway sign indicating the turn for **Colonia Tovar ❷** (*see pages 148–9*). *Caraqueños* usually go here via El Junquito, being a shorter drive from the capital, but this route is infinitely more picturesque, climbing up the mountains on a steep twisting route offering magnificent views.

Staying on the Pan American highway, you will pass **San Mateo ❸**. Nearby is the former hacienda of Simón Bolívar's family – a sugar, coffee, and cacao plantation founded in 1593. Bolívar was born in Caracas, but spent much of his childhood here. The former

PRECEDING PAGES:
the beach at Golfo
Triste.
LEFT: colonial
charm at Choroní.
BELOW: strutting
flamingos at the
Cuare Wildlife
Refuge.

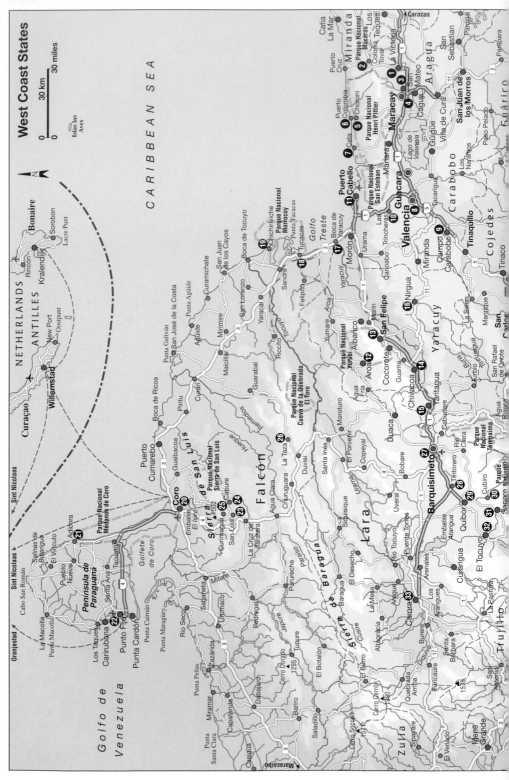

West Coast States

0   30 km
0   30 miles

Islas las
Aves

Bolívar family home is now a historical military museum (labeled **Ingenio Bolívar** outside). The hacienda's sugar mill, across the road, has been restored, housing the **Museo de Caña de Azúcar** (Sugar Cane Museum). (Both museums are open Tue–Sun 9am–noon, 2–5pm; token admission fee.)

Map on page 192

The Garden City

Maracay ❹ is the modern capital of Aragua state. The fortunes of this region have always been made from agriculture: coffee, cacao, indigo, cotton and tobacco. It earned its nickname, however, from its abundance of green spaces.

Dictator Juan Vicente Gómez (in power 1908–35) governed the country from here from 1912 until his death. Gómez is largely responsible for making Maracay what it is today, leaving a legacy of beautiful architecture and parks. Most are concentrated along Avenida Las Delicias (whose continuation leads to Choroní/Puerto Colombia) and Avenida 19 de Abril, both of which are also where most of Maracay's best restaurants and hotels are found. At the far end is the compact but complete **Zoológico Las Delicias** (closed Mon; token admission fee), originally Gómez's country house and personal zoo.

Gómez began Venezuela's first commercial air service – to Maracay, Maracaibo and Ciudad Bolívar. In honor of Maracay being the birthplace of Venezuela's military aviation in 1936, the country's only **Museo Aeronáutico** (irregular hours, usually open weekends; free) is found here, by the intersection of the two avenues. Opposite it is the Complejo Cultural Santos Michelena with the excellent **Museo de Arte Contemporáneo de Maracay Mario Abreu** and the **Casa de la Cultura** (open Tue–Sun; free), along with schools of music and art, and a public library.

Within a few blocks, down Avenida 19 de Abril, is the beautiful Moorish-style **bull ring** (known both as La Maestranza and Plaza de Toros César Girón), designed by Carlos Raúl Villanueva, who designed several landmark buildings in Caracas (*see page 141*). Nearby is the Ateneo de Maracay, with a schedule of events posted outside.

Other main attractions surround the main squares along Avenida Bolívar. Around Plaza Girardot (with a monument in honor of American volunteer soldiers in the War of Independence) are: the colonial **Cathedral**, the **Museo de Historia**; **Museo de Arqueología**, with an extensive collection of indigenous artifacts and skeletons in burial urns from local digs; and the **Instituto de Antropología e Historia del Estado de Aragua** – the three museums all under the same roof (open Tue–Sun; 8–11.30am, 2–5pm; free).

The **Plaza Bolívar** is the largest and perhaps most beautiful squares of this name in Venezuela. Behind it is the art deco Teatro de la Opera, one of the best theaters in the country.

Natural wonderland

Two routes from Maracay cross the mountains to the coast, both with continual, sometimes hair-raising, hairpin turns. Because of this, while the distance is short (about 50 km/30 miles), it takes at least 90 minutes – but the gorgeous scenery compensates.

TIP

Be sure to check out the Centro Cultural Higuaraya Capanaparo in the base of Maracay's bull ring. Run by Maruja Da Silva for some two decades, it has a shop jammed with native crafts, classes in the arts, cultural presentations and a reference library.

BELOW: Henri Pittier National Park.

The 107,800-hectare (266,400-acre) site was set aside in 1937 as Venezuela's first national park. Initially named for its Rancho Grande cloud forest, it was renamed **Parque Nacional Henri Pittier** in 1953 to honor the Swiss botanist who classified 30,000 Venezuelan plants and promoted the national park system.

The abundance and variety of fauna and flora is awesome in its life zones which range from dry forest and xerophytic lands to cloud forests. The highest mountains in the park rise to about 1,280 meters (4,200 ft). Portachuelo Pass, a V-shaped dip in the terrain, is a migratory route for insects and birds. Mammals, reptiles, and amphibians abound, but the stars of fauna, with more than 500 species found here, are birds.

From Maracay, heading north on Avenida Las Delicias past the zoo takes you past the city's fanciest lodging, Hotel Pipo Internacional, with the park entrance just beyond. Almost immediately is **Las Cocuizas Recreational Area** (with river swimming and picnic areas; closed Mon; token admission fee).

Endemic birds in the Parque Nacional Henri Pittier include the handsome fruit-eater, the blood-eared parakeet and the helmeted curassow. You might also see a harpy eagle, a white tipped quetzal and flocks of lilac-tailed parrotlets.

Protection from pirates

A few kilometers before the coast is a pretty village of traditional colonial houses. This is **Choroní** ❺, once at the heart of a rich cacao-growing region, with its great haciendas worked by slave labor. In colonial times, Dutch and Spanish merchant ships plied the coast. The journey was fraught with danger as pirates stalked these waters and sometimes ventured ashore. That is why Choroní, like Cata and many other towns, was built well back from the sea, to afford some protection from the marauders.

Puerto Colombia ❻, the port for Choroní, is right on the water, with its fleet of brightly painted wooden boats moored in a little river flowing into the sea. A string of small bars and informal restaurants lines the waterfront.

BELOW: Choroní fisherman.

The swimming beach, **Playa Grande**, is just east of Puerto Colombia, wrapped around a bay lined with coconut trees and a few open-air snack bars. Several local beaches are reached only from the sea, by fishing boat from Puerto Colombia. Fishermen offer transfers from the port.

The only way to progress further west overland is to return by the same route to Maracay and take the Cata road back across the cloud forest, passing the Rancho Grande research station in the Henri Pittier National Park. But, for beach, continue to **Cata** ❼. Except for two ugly apartment towers at the near end (which can be easily blocked out of photos taken from the ridge above), it is one of the most picturesque beaches in the country. The village of Cata lies a short distance inland. Cata is a swimmer's beach, while **Cuyagua**, 13 km (8 miles) to the east is considered the best in Venezuela for surfing.

The populations of these coastal villages are predominantly composed of descendants of African slaves who were brought here to work the cacao plantations. They have maintained three important traditions which combine Catholicism, folklore, and paganism: devil dancers (in Cata, Ocumare de la Costa, and Chuao) who perform on the feast of Corpus Christi; celebrations of Cruz de Mayo; and *tambores* (African-style drums made from hollow tree trunks) and the sensual dancing to them (*see Fies-tas and Devil Dancers, pages 79–85*).

If planning a trip to the beaches near Choroní, with access only by sea, pre-pare yourself for inflation. The transfer that used to cost a few dollars (before the popularity surge of Puerto Colombia) now starts at about US$50–60.

Map on page 192

Early indigenous presence

Back in Maracay, if you head west, skirting Lago de Valencia, you'll arrive at Carabobo's capital, **Valencia ❽**. Beginning some 4,000 years ago, the area was settled by various indigenous groups. Archeologists have unearthed ceram-ics and other evidence of early indian cultures, along with fossils of mastodons and other animals. Many are in the anthropological museums of Valencia and Maracay. But, for a look at evidence of ancient indigenous presence *in situ*, visit **Parque Piedras Pintadas**, between Guacara and Vigirima, where scores of petroglyphs cover the hillside. Do not explore the park alone – there have been many hold-ups of lone visitors recently.

Manufacturing capital

Valencia has grown into Venezuela's third largest city, despite its troubled history. Less than a decade after its founding in 1555, it was nearly destroyed by the invading forces of Lope de Aguirre, the barbaric conquistador on a quest to find El Dorado (*see page 30*). The city was later attacked by Caribe indians, sacked by French pirates, and devastated in the earthquake of 1812.

Although the decisive Battle of Carabobo took place near Valencia, in 1826 it became the first city to resist Simón Bolívar's Gran Colombia. An assembly

If you want a coconut in Choroní all you have to do is learn to climb a palm tree.

BELOW: a hacienda near Maracay.

TIP

Every Friday, Valencia's *El Carabobeño* newspaper publishes a page on art and culture, reporting a weekly schedule of events for the city's theaters, museums, galleries, concert halls, parks, etc, as well as including a list of principal restaurants.

BELOW: the arch guarding the eternal flame of the unknown soldier at Campo Carabobo.

held here declared Venezuela a sovereign state and, for a brief time, Valencia was its captial city.

Now, Valencia is principally known as Venezuela's manufacturing capital. In 1948, when the government declared no further industry could be installed in Caracas (and existing factories were moved), Carabobo's leaders took advantage of the opportunity (and the city's excellent location) to launch development of an industrial zone which now has more than 900 companies, ranging from vehicle assembly plants to food manufacturers.

History and culture in Valencia

Valencia has a great deal of historical interest. In the **El Viñedo** neighborhood there are several important private art galleries, including the Galería de Arte Ascaso (open Mon–Fri 8am–noon, 2–6pm; Sat–Sun 10am–2pm; free). Opposite is the open-air Parque de Escultura Andrés Pérez Mujica, with dozens of sculptures by top Venezuelan artists. Continuing the artistic theme, there are two sites dedicated to one of Valencia's most imortant modern artists – the Centro Cultural Braulio Salazar (Paseo Cabriales; irregular hours) and the Sala de Exposiciones Braulio Salazar (Avenida Andrés Eloy Blanco; open daily; free).

Avenida Bolívar Norte (to the north of the center, between Avenida Cedeño and the Guaparo Redoma) is best known for its concentration of restaurants, but here you also find the **Ateneo de Valencia Ⓐ**, home of the prestigious annual Salón Michelena, as well as exhibitions and stage productions (Mon–Fri 8am–noon, 2–6pm; Sat–Sun, 11am–5pm; free).

Historic attractions are concentrated near the **Plaza Bolívar**. These include the colonial **Cathedral Ⓑ**, home to a statue of the Virgen del Socorro in a bejeweled

gown. In 1910, this became the first statue in Venezuela to be crowned – with the Pope's permission – in recognition of the many favors granted by the Virgin.

General José Antonio Páez, who forged a formidable army of *llaneros* (plainsmen) and served as Venezuela's first president, lived in Valencia for a time. His former home, **Casa Páez** ⊙, has a patio with murals depicting nine battles in which he fought, restored rooms, and a former subterranean prison used during Gómez's dictatorship (Mon–Fri 9am–noon, 3–6pm; Sat–Sun 9am–noon; free).

Another area of focus is around Plaza Sucre. On one side, the **Capitolio** ⊙, a former convent (built in 1722) and the current headquarters of Carabobo's state government, has enjoyed recent restoration (open Sat, Sun, hols 10am–2pm; free). Facing it are the **Templo de San Francisco** ⊙ (site of the call in 1826 for Venezuela's separation from Bolívar's Gran Colombia) and the restored **Teatro Municipal** ⊙, built in 1892 and apparently designed to emulate the Paris Opera House; it has now been declared a national monument. On Avenida Soublette, the **Casa de la Estrella** ⊙ is of interest only for its historical significance: this is where the sovereignty of Venezuela was declared in 1830. Two blocks south is the colonial Casa de los Celis, the beautiful former home of the Celis family, and now a history and art museum (open Tue–Fri 8am–2pm; Sat, Sun 9am–noon; free).

To visit the city's **aquarium** (closed Mon; small admission fee), head west of the center along Avenida Cedeño, follow it to the end, and then turn right.

Valencia's bull ring, the **Plaza de Toros Monumental**, has a capacity of 27,000 and is the second largest in the Americas after Mexico City's. Adjacent to it is the Parque Recreacional Sur, site of the **Museo Antropológico** (closed Mon; token fee).

Map on page 196

BELOW: petroglyph at the Parque Piedras Pintadas

PIEDRAS PINTADAS PARK

Petroglyphs (*piedras pintadas* – literally "painted rocks," although designs are incised) are found in many parts of Venezuela, but there is a great concentration in Carabobo state around Lake Valencia (which was sacred to early indigenous inhabitants); the most easily reached are found just east of Valencia, on the Guacara-Vigírima route. Enter Guacara then double back toward the freeway via the Plaza Bolívar. Your turn will be 6.6 km (4 miles) north of the point the road passes under the freeway. Here, turn left toward Tronconero then, after a little over 1 km (0.6 miles), to the right at the school. Continue to the end and park at the former museum at the base of the hill of Parque Piedras Pintadas, covered with scores of etched rocks (take chalk to highlight the designs if you plan to take photos).

Some have easily identifiable human or animal forms, but the significance of abstract shapes remains a secret. Some may be maps, and abstract forms are possibly magical or religious symbols – but their significance, age, and even who created them is unknown. Faces, outlines of feet, spirals and holes bored in the rocks are among the most common themes. There are more on the hill, including a line of upright stones, one with "points" bored in it, which is seemingly a trail marker.

Hot baths at Las Trincheras.

BELOW: the fortress at Puerto Cabello.

Battle memorial

Some 26 km (16 miles) southwest of Valencia lies **Campo Carabobo ❾** memorial to the Battle of Carabobo (1821) which virtually secured Venezuela's independence from Spain. There are two dramatic monuments: the first is a large arch marking the Tomb of the Unknown Soldier; and the second, commemorating the battle itself, is topped by an equestrian statue of Bolívar. Honor guards in red colonial-style uniforms stand at rigid attention, except during the impressive changing of the guard ceremony every two hours from 6am–6pm. A road to the west leads to the Mirador (shaped like a massive inverted pyramid) overlooking the battle site. Inside, there is an audiovisual presentation (with an English version) detailing the historic confrontation.

Gateway to the sea

Heading north from Valencia toward Puerto Cabello, you will pass the exit for **Las Trincheras ❿**, site of the second-hottest thermal springs in the world 98°C (208.4°F) after Urijimo, Japan. It now has a 120-room hotel, giant pools fed by the springs, saunas, steam baths, and naturally heated mud.

Once through **Taborda**, with its shoulder-to-shoulder stands selling shark turnovers, *arepitas dulces* (puffy fried circles of sweetened white cornmeal dough with aniseed), fresh fried fish, iced coconuts, and other such snacks, you reach the coast road, with the giant state-owned oil refinery to the west, and the large natural port of Puerto Cabello to the east.

Following the road toward the port city, at the western edge of Puerto Cabello is a large hill topped by **Fortín Solano**. Financed by the Guipuzcoana Company and finished in 1770, it was the last colonial fort to be built in Venezuela. Take

the San Esteban exit, then stick to the street closest to the hill. A large portal on the right marks the entrance via a steep winding road.

Seven km (4 miles) farther south – via part of what used to be the route of the colonial Camino Real between Valencia and the coast – you come to **San Esteban**. In the early days, this was a favorite spot for German merchants of the port to live because of its cooler, healthier climate; explaining the surprising number of large (although some now a bit neglected) 19th-century mansions constructed by them.

From the parking area at the end of the road, continue on foot on the old trail, which passes a large petroglyph with the only known example in Venezuela showing a person in a boat, as well as a colonial era Spanish bridge at Paso Hondo.

Map on page 192

Port with a past

Puerto Cabello ⑪ has been an important harbor since its foundation in the mid-1500s; it now handles 77 percent of Venezuela's commercial traffic.

Almost from the start, the port was plagued by pirates who tried to intercept Spanish galleons loaded with gold and other riches. After a time, Dutch merchants gained a foothold. Cacao, coffee, indigo and cotton crops moved from Venezuela to the nearby Dutch islands via Puerto Cabello. The Spanish government made a pact with a group of powerful Basque merchants, promising them a virtual monopoly if they squelched the Dutch competition. The group formed the Guipuzcoana Company in 1728, and erected **Castillo Libertador** (aka Fortín San Felipe) at the harbor entrance. They also set up offices and warehouses, stimulating the local economy, but were despised by the local people. After nearly six decades, the company met its demise and the headquarters

BELOW: Iglesia El Rosario at Puerto Cabello.

BELOW: works of
art in Minas de
Aroa Park.

became the customs house: known as the **Casa Guipuzcoana**, this now holds
a library, cultural center, and offices. It overlooks the Plaza Monumento El
Aguila, with a statue dedicated to ten North Americans who were executed by
royalists in 1806, while fighting in Venezuela's War of Independence.

Fortín San Felipe was the only independent defense unit in Venezuela country
never taken by force. Following defeat at the Battle of Carabobo, Spanish troops
retreated here and managed to hold out for two years. In the 1900s, the fort
was put to grim use by the dictator Gómez, who had his political enemies
chained in the dungeons.

The entire historic section of town, facing the fort and **Paseo Malecón**, the
waterfront boulevard, recently underwent complete restoration. This not only
rescued dozens of fading architectural gems, but has given impulse to a number
of pleasant new restaurants and shops; artists once again set up their easels, and
families take strolls along the streets to admire the distinctive architecture.

Calle de los Lanceros is named for the victory ride of General Antonio Páez
and his lancers down it after retaking Puerto Cabello from the Spaniards in
1823. The second-story walkway over this street extends from the rear of the
Museo de Historia Colonial. Above its entrance on the next street to the south
is the most beautiful of the "flying" balconies which characterize the port's
vintage buildings. At the end of this street is the **Iglesia El Rosario**, dating
from 1780, with the only existing wooden bell tower of the era in Venezuela.

Eastern beaches

Puerto Cabello is hot throughout the year, which makes the seashore especially
enticing. Beaches east of town include **Quizandal**, which has a snack bar and
is jammed on weekends. More beautiful and less hec-
tic is **Isla Larga**, an island reached by a ride of 15
minutes in shuttle boats departing from Quizandal.
There are two underwater wrecks for divers and
snorkelers, and you can camp on the white sand. Vendors sell snacks but there are no bathrooms or other
facilities. **Patanemo Bay**, about 12 km (7 miles) from
Puerto Cabello, is a wide half-moon, fringed by
coconut palms.

Heading inland

The main attractions of Yaracuy state are located
along four distinct routes:

◆ **Route 1**: From the Caribbean coastal highway, via
Morón-Marín-Aroa-Duaca.

The highlight of this first route is **Aroa ⑫**, or,
more specifically, the **Parque Bolivariano Minas
de Aroa**. This features buildings associated with a
now-defunct copper mine, dozens of sculptures by
Venezuelan artists, various recreational areas, and an
English cemetery. The area was purchased by the
Venezuelan government in 1957, and then passed on
to Yaracuy in 1972, when it was developed as a park.
Because English settlers in Aroa were Protestant, burial in the Catholic cemetery was forbidden, thus, an
English Cemetery was established. Here, you can
admire gravestones from past centuries with the
inscriptions written in English.

Map on page 192

Route 2: From Marín, take the low road to San Felipe, continuing via Guama-Yaritagua-Barquisimeto.

San Felipe ⓭, the state capital, is the first stop. For an insight into times past, visit **San Felipe "El Fuerte,"** a historic archeological park and museum (open Tue–Sun; token admission fee). As well as more than 100 species of trees, the 10-hectare (25-acre) park includes ruins of the formerly glorious city leveled by an earthquake in 1812. Museum exhibits relate the historic, social, and economic evolution of the city.

You should also stop at the striking modern **Cathedral** on Plaza Bolívar; then head for the north edge of town where you'll find the Parque Nacional Nurubí and Parque Leonor Bernabó, with swimming pools, picnic shelters, playgrounds (closed Mon; token admission fee). On the outskirts of San Felipe are the **Parque de la Exótica Flora Tropical**, which claims to be the largest garden of exotic tropical flowers in Latin America, with hundreds of showy species protected by trees (open Tue–Sun, 10am–5pm for tours; admission fee). The adjacent **Misión Nuestra Señora del Carmen** was reconstructed in the original style on ruins of an 18th-century Capuchin mission and houses a chapel, museum and restaurants (open until 11pm).

Next, **Chivacoa ⓮** is the entry point for the **Monumento Natural María Lionza**, whose mountains are the birthplace of important rivers as well as of the mystical cult of María Lionza (*see below*).

In **Yaritagua ⓯**, a beautiful stone neo-classical building (dating from 1861) has been converted into the **Centro Turístico Los Carrascosa** (Carrera 8 at Calle 19; open daily, 7am–7pm; free), which includes a museum, a conference center, and a *posada* with top-quality rooms, piano bar and restaurant. Along the

BELOW: a typical handmade country house, using only natural materials.

CULT OF MARIA LIONZA

Based on the legend of an indian princess who became the Goddess of Nature, María Lionza (popularly referred to as *La Reina* – the queen) is the central figure of a cult combining elements of Catholicism, nature worship, and paganism, followed by hundreds of thousands of Venezuelans of all walks of life.

María Lionza is the central figure, with Negro Felipe and the indian chief Guaicaipuro always by her side (this group is known as "Las Tres Potencias" – the three powers). They are served by many "courts" which seemingly exclude no one – from Catholic saints and African tribal gods to Hitler, Cleopatra, Queen Isabel, Simón Bolívar, John F. Kennedy, and the Pope, to name a few.

At two principal sites at the natural monument by Chivacoa, Sorte and Quivallo, (Monumento Natural María Lionza) followers begin pilgrimages up the hill, stopping at "altars" along the way to perform their rites. They allow non-believers to discretely observe, but discourage them from passing beyond a certain point on the mountain (the higher, the more sacred).

On holidays and long weekends, thousands of followers flock to this site – definitely *not* a recommended time for the casual visitor).

highway are attractive *Aldeas Artesanales* (craft villages) created by the state tourism board: Guama (features basketry), Camunare Blanco (ceramics), Pase Artesanal José Antonio Páez (naïf art sculptures), La Casona (varied crafts

◆ **Route 3**: This circuit enters Yaracuy via Valencia-La Encrucijada-Montalbá in Carabobo, continuing via Nirgua-Chivacoa-Yaritagua.

Near **Nirgua** ⓰, about 10 km/6 miles south of town, you can explore th ruins of the San Vicente fortress. This was built in 1577 to protect gold (said be the first found in this part of the New World) extracted from the Buría Min prior to its shipment to Spain. Parque Embalse Cumaripa, just before the Chiv coa interchange, is a 14-hectare (35-acre) park along the reservoir's easter shore (closed Mon; token admission fee).

◆ **Route 4**: The most impressive way to penetrate the state is on the Yaracu River, via the Caribbean coast at **Boca de Yaracuy** ⓱ (from where boat excu sions are run). Minutes from the highway, you enter another magical worl traversing narrow channels lined with mangroves and tall trees where silence broken only by the sounds of animals. Eventually, the river widens to form se eral huge lagoons, teeming with fish and where abundant wildlife is seen.

Parque Nacional Morrocoy

A little more than three hours' drive from Caracas, via Valencia then west on th coast road, is **Parque Nacional Morrocoy** in Falcón state; it was created 1974 to protect its mangroves, sea-bird rookeries, and coral reefs. Once line with nothing but coconut plantations and seaside shacks, the approach road now bordered by waterfront condos and resort developments. The park itself a paradise for snorkelers, divers, and bird watchers. There are about 30 *cayo*

BELOW: enjoying the mangrove islands in Morrocoy National Park.

cays, or reef-formed islands), some quite large with palm trees and mangroves, others low-lying with pure white sand. The mangroves are nesting grounds for frigate birds. The two main points of access to the park are Tucacas and Chichiriviche. (There is also an entrance between them with marinas, a coast guard station, and several *posadas*, but this is mainly used by people with boats.)

The town of Tucacas ⑱ guards the eastern edge of the park. In the early 1700s, it was a thriving port for Dutch merchants who traded with nearby islands. It later fell on bad times, but the tourist boom has once again revived it.

Local boatmen have a well-organized, dependable union, both here and at Chichiriviche, offering a shuttle service to the islands and cays for a fixed fee. When they drop you off, agree a specific pick-up time. The tariff per round trip boat ride depends on distance, with a higher fee if you plan to camp overnight.

Camping is allowed in Morrocoy National Park, but is strictly controlled to reduce environmental impact. It is allowed on just four cays. You must first call the National Parks Institute, Inparques, at their toll-free number (tel: 800-4 847) to request a permit and make a reservation. No fires are allowed (cooking must be done with gas units). The park entrance fee is about $2 per car.

At home in the mangrove swamps: the magnificent frigate bird.

Gateway to the northern cays

It is 37 km (22 miles) north from Tucacas to **Chichiriviche** ⑲, gateway to Morrocoy's northern cays. A bonus en route is that the 12-kilometer (7-miles) causeway into town passes through **Refugio de Fauna Silvestre de Cuare** (the Cuare Wildlife Refuge), abutting the national park. Its protected, mangrove-lined, shallow salt flats serve as a major feeding ground for brilliant scarlet ibis, roseate spoonbills, numerous species of herons, cormorants, and a population of

BELOW: loading up bananas at Tucacas.

some 20,000 southern Caribbean flamingoes who come from Bonaire to dine
Chichiriviche is also developing, with resort property rising out of the mud flats.

Distinct options

There are many caves in the park and wildlife refuge in the large coral sandstone
promontory, **Cerro Chichiriviche**, between Tucacas and Chichiriviche. Bu
two popular options to visit, despite their names, are not caves at all.

Efforts are now being made to conserve the glyphs on the wall at Cueva del Indio, Morrocoy National Park.

   Cueva del Indio (Cave of the Indian) is a high stone wall completely cov
ered with petroglyphs created by indians who inhabited the area long ago
Thanks to the efforts of the conservationist group FUDEA, in cooperation with
Inparques, a pier and rail-lined boardwalk have been installed to facilitat
access (boatmen offer a shuttle service from Chichiriviche), protect the man
groves from trampling and assure that damage is not inflicted on the glyphs
Cueva de la Virgen, a cove with rock walls, viewed from the water, has par
ticular significance to local fishermen who place religious statues and offer
ings here to protect them while at sea.

Key to the northern cays

There are seven main cays in the northern part of Morrocoy National Park
Cayo Muerto, just offshore, has an outpost of the Environment Ministry. A
short distance to the north is **Cayo Sal**, with its salt lagoon in the center. The far
thest is coral-ringed **Cayo Borracho** to the north, a favorite for campers and
scuba divers. **Cayo Peraza** is another coral-ringed beauty. The tiniest, **Cayo
Pelón** (Bald Cay), is a treeless desert island only about 50 meters (162 ft) long
Cayo Pescadores, as the name implies, is favored by fishermen.

BELOW:
untouched cays
near Chichiriviche.

One of the most distant – and the most popular for sun-worshipers – is **Cayo Sombrero**. The central lagoon attracts a family crowd, with parents and children splashing in the shallow, calm water and brightly colored tents pitched among the palms. Vendors sell drinks and food on Sombrero, but you should take plenty of provisions, including mosquito repellant, when you visit any of the cays.

Map on page 192

Colonial elegance

The next stop on this West Coast route is the colonial city of **Coro 20**, the first capital of the Province of Venezuela. Santa Ana de Coro, one of the earliest settlements in South America, was founded by Juan de Ampiés in 1527. In a rare event for the conquest era, he was welcomed by the local chief, Manaure. Ampiés maintained peace with the indians by dealing fairly with them and shielding them from the slave raids that were common on the coast at that time. Sadly, this unusual harmony was short lived. In succeeding years, a series of German governors, interested only in finding gold, used Coro as a base for their expeditions. They ruled by exploitation, and the indians fled.

Coro began to flourish in the 18th century, becoming the supplier for the islands of Bonaire and Curaçao, some 104 km (65 miles) away. Agricultural produce and animals were shipped from La Vela de Coro, east of the capital. The Venezuelan flag was planted for the first time on August 3, 1806, at La Vela, by Francisco de Miranda. The tricolor flew over the San Pedro Fort, now gone, but a monument remains. By the shore here is the former customs house (*Aduana*), now holding a marine research center with interesting displays of collected samples. In front is a statue of a girl in typical Dutch dress, recalling the important trade links of the 1700s with the Dutch islands.

Between La Vela and Coro, along the Intercomunal, is the Jardín Xerofítico. This garden contains a large collection of xerophytic plants from all over the world. Even when it is open, the gates are kept closed to prevent goats from wandering in and munching on the plants.

BELOW: the sand dunes of Coro.

Worthwhile is a stop at the little village of **Taratara**, a short distance befo
Coro (exit to the north). Most of its houses are colorfully painted with creati
designs and at its small museum you can usually arrange for one of the loc
children to lead you on a walk of about 40 minutes to the sea, passing throug
a dry gorge whose walls are embedded with fossilized seashells. A great var
ety of birds and lizards can be observed on this walk, and at the beach there
an unusual grouping of petroglyphs.

*The early 18th-
century chapel on
Plaza San Clemente
in Coro.*

Coro's colonial treasures

Careful conservation of the streetscapes of Coro's colonial zone in a near
pristine state earned Falcón's capital designation by UNESCO as a Wor
Patrimony City. A short stroll down Calle Zamora, starting from several block
west of Avenida Manaure, will make it clear that this honor is well-deserve
Beautifully maintained buildings line the cobblestone streets extending we
and south from the hub, **Plaza San Clemente**, with its early 18th-century chap
and wooden cross which was supposedly carved from the tree under whic
Ampiés met Chief Manaure.

Just east of the plaza is the 19th-century **Iglesia de San Francisco**. But it
the former convent (built in 1620) next door which is of principal interest to vi
itors, now it houses the **Museo Diocesano Lucas Guillermo Castillo**, with
marvelous and handsomely displayed collection of religious, colonial, and de
orative art (closed 12–3pm daily and Sun pm; free).

The **Casa del Sol** (House of the Sun), on the street across from San Clemen
chapel, got its name from a sun design above its door. Built in the 17th centur
the house has served as a private residence, a monastery, a college, and toda
it holds public offices.

BELOW: a colonial
façade at Coro.

On the corner beside the chapel, heading west o
Zamora, is **El Balcón de los Arcaya**, one of the fe
two-story buildings in Coro. It was built by a Spanis
nobleman in the late 17th century, and was boug
about 100 years later by Don Ignacio Luis Díaz o
Arcaya, remaining in his family's possession to th
day. The name comes from this and the distinctive ba
cony which runs along two sides of the house. Som
years back, the house was restored and converted int
the **Museo de Cerámica Histórica y Loza Popula**
(Museum of Historic Ceramics and China; ope
Tue–Sun 8am–3pm; free). Among the exhibits is
room which has pre-Hispanic ceramics found by th
anthropologist J.M.Cruxent, juxtaposed with piece
still being created by local potters.

Farther down Zamora is the **Casa de las Ventana
de Hierro** (House of the Iron Windows), most ac
mired for its beautiful baroque doorway, although th
name comes from its wrought-iron window grille
imported from Seville at a time when the locals use
only wood. Next door is the **Casa del Tesoro** (Trea
sure House) belonged to prominent Bishop Marian
Talavera y Garcés, a relative of the patriot Josef
Camejo. It was rumored to have a secret tunnel an
years of digging finally produced one 8 meters (2
ft) underground, but no treasure was ever recovere
Neither of these houses is open to the public.

Map on page 192

Coro's **Cathedral** (facing the Plaza Bolívar) was one of the first churches in 'enezuela, started in 1583. Built like a fortress, its tall tower has gun slits, and deed the Cathedral served many times as a fort during the pirate attacks of the 6th century. The citizens prepared for these frequent onslaughts as best they ould, and the wealthiest built secret caches or tunnels to hide their riches. Even day there are tales of secret tunnels with hidden treasure.

Two blocks from the Cathedral, on Paseo Talavera, is the **Museo de Arte ontemporáneo de Coro** (open Tues–Sun 9am–12.30pm, 3–7.30pm; free), the rmer home/store of the Senior family of Curaçao, well-known Jewish mer-ants. Through the impulse of the founder of Caracas' contemporary art museum (ACCSI), Sofía Imber, it reopened as the Cora art museum in 1988. Exceptional orks by Picasso, Botero, Bracque and others from the MACCSI's permanent ollection have traveled here for shows.

Coro has long had a significant Sephardic Jewish population. The Dutch lands were a haven for Jews fleeing the Inquisition in Spain and, when enezuela's War of Independence erupted, they offered support to the new public and were among the first to trade with the rebels. The Venezuelan overnment's guarantee of freedom of worship attracted many Jews to the Coro ea at the beginning of the 19th century. A Jewish cemetery (not open to the blic) is said to be the oldest still in use on the continent.

araguaná Peninsula

oro (meaning "wind" in Arawak), capital of the country's driest state, is at e base of the isthmus joining the **Península de Paraguaná** to the mainland. 's a fitting name, for the continual east winds have formed shifting *médanos*

BELOW:
an isolated farm
on the Paraguaná
Peninsula.

(dunes), the tallest reaching heights of more than 25 meters/82 feet. To protec the dunes, a strip 30 km (18 miles) long by 5 km (3 miles) wide, encompassin the entire isthmus plus a section of the continental coast, has been designate **Parque Nacional Los Médanos de Coro**.

The peninsula, originally an island, became linked over time to the mainlan by a long isthmus of sand. Pirates took refuge in this desolate landscape c cactus to plan their attacks. Today there are said to be more goats than peopl here. In the rural eastern part, goat herding is a common livelihood. The pec ple sell goat's milk cheese and *dulce de leche coriano* (goat's milk fudge *Chivo en coco* (goat in coconut sauce) is a specialty served in restaurant throughout the region. There are also cottage industries producing tradition. leather work, pottery and furniture carved from cactus wood. The 815-mete (2,670-ft) mountain and natural monument, **Cerro Santa Ana**, in the center c the peninsula, is its highest point.

Adícora ㉑ is at the edge of a protected bay on the east coast. While thi keeps the wave action down, the continual high winds make the waters excel lent for wind surfing. No longer a secret, fans of this sport come from aroun the world to test their skill. The colorful houses by the waterfront show earl Dutch influence in architectural details such as finials on gable ends, windov grilles with pedestals and decorated caps, and shutters painted in contrasting col ors. There are some half dozen *posadas* to accommodate visitors.

The northern extreme of the peninsula is a wilderness of cactus and salt bed: **Cabo San Ramón** is a cape where pelicans dive and fishermen cast their net beneath the rocky cliffs. In contrast to the rest of the peninsula, the wester side is modern and developed, thanks to the oil refineries that opened in 1947

The solitary, non-swimming beaches of the isthmus offer good shelling, especially for the abundant tiny winged scallops.

BELOW: the Posada El Duende, on the outskirts of Cabure.

Map on page 192

Today, **Punto Fijo** ㉒, having grown along with the refineries, has a population of 70,000 people, making it the largest city in Falcón state. Unlike the astern beaches, the ones on this side offer light breezes and calm waters. Those t **Villa Marina** and **Punta El Pico**, formerly contaminated, have been cleaned p, but be warned: there is no shade, and the sun can be fierce.

Mountain backdrop

The mountains south of Coro pertain to the **Sierra de San Luis**. Whether pproaching them from the north or south, en route you pass through desert andscapes where xerophytic species are the only plant life seen. But, as you limb the mountains, the vegetation changes progressively from cactus to ry forests to lush cloud forests. On clear days, from the road ascending the orth side, you have a dazzling view of the coast, and sometimes even as far s the island of Aruba.

The limestone mountains contain more than 1,000 caverns and sinkholes, plus umerous underground rivers which spew forth their waters along the north slope.

Because of its importance as a source of water for Falcón's arid coastal towns as well as filling **Embalse El Isiro**, a reservoir excellent for fishing), 20,000 ectares (49,500 acres) of this range were decreed a national park in 1987.

The area's many different habitats, along with its function as a corridor for igratory birds, contribute to this being a good area for birding. Of particular ote are three easily accessible areas: Cerro Galicia (the range's highest point, ,500 meters/4,900 ft), El Haitón, and La Uria. The land around Posada El uende, on the outskirts of Cabure, also shelters many species.

The important mountain towns and villages of **San Luis** ㉓, **Cabure** ㉔, and urimagua ㉕ are grouped roughly in a triangle, in an rea primarily involved with coffee growing.

In the villages of Mapararí and El Tural, descendants of early indigenous inhabitants maintain the traition of an ancient agrarian rite, the *Baile de Las uras*, celebrated 23–24 September, with dancing all ight around an altar decorated with sugar cane stalks nd ears of corn to give thanks for the harvest.

Guácharos and an underground river

a Taza ㉖ is the jumping-off place for the **Parque Nacional Cueva de la Quebrada El Toro**, best nown for its three caverns which are among the argest in the country. In the dry season, it is somemes possible to drive from La Taza to the park, but there has been any rain a four-wheel drive vehicle s essential. You can contract locals to drive you there you do not have a 4x4. The caves can be visited nly with the park's personnel. Flashlights and phography are permitted.

In the second is the most interesting cave, with ight-flying, fruit-eating *guácharos* (oil birds) and he largest subterranean river in Venezuela. This is arrow and shallow up to the part occupied by the irds, but then broadens to fill the entire width of the assageway at the end of this chamber. A small boat s necessary for further exploration. Deeper within he cave, the river forms two great reservoirs. ❑

BELOW: the breathtaking view across to the coast while ascending the north side of the Sierra de San Luis.

LARA

*Since pre-Hispanic times, Lara has been the
principal crossroads for travel and commerce in the
central western region of Venezuela*

Map
on page
192

Despite the barren look of its dominant desert landscapes, Lara grows most
of the nation's produce and has one of the largest wholesale markets in
South America, which supplies not only all of Venezuela, but also many
Caribbean destinations. Sold through this market are 85 percent of the grains,
75 percent of the rapidly perishable vegetables and 60 percent of all other produce consumed in Venezuela. Lara has 80 percent of the country's largest sugar
cane growers and has proved to be ideal for growing both table and wine grapes.

This market is located in **Barquisimeto** ㉗, the capital of Lara and one of the
oldest cities in Venezuela, founded in 1552. It is now the fourth largest city in
the country, within four to five hours by road from the main cities of Caracas,
Maracaibo, Valencia, and Maracay, and the hub for travel to the western plains
and Andean states.

Capital attractions

The principal attractions in Barquisimeto are focused around the **Plaza Bolívar**
between Carreras 16 & 17, and Calles 25 & 26). At its southwest corner is the
Iglesia de la Concepción. The original 16th-century church was destroyed,
along with most of the city, by an earthquake in 1812, but it was later rebuilt.
A block farther south is the Museo de Barquisimeto
(closed Mon; token admission), with exhibits ranging
from art to archeology. Two blocks north, the Teatro
Juarez puts on a variety of live presentations.

LEFT: the dramatic
landscape of the
Lara region.
BELOW: one of
the instrument
makers for which
the area is famous.

Two blocks east of Plaza Bolívar is **Plaza Lara**. On
the south side is the Iglesia de San Francisco, erected
in 1865 and Barquisimeto's cathedral until dedication
of the current modern one (Carrera 26, between Calles
30 & 29). The Centro de Historia Larense, on the
square's east side, is also worth a visit (open Mon–Fri
8am–noon, 3–6pm; Sat–Sun, hols 10am–5pm; free).
It has a large collection of antiques and miscellaneous
memorabilia. Also in the square is the Ateneo de
Barquisimeto, a popular venue for everything from
art shows to classic films.

The **Parque Zoológico y Botánico Miguel
Romero Antoni** (also known as **Parque Bararida**),
on Avenida Los Abogados at Calle 15, is a refreshing
oasis with many shade trees and a compact yet well-
stocked zoo (closed Mon; token admission fee). You
can also escape the city streets in **Parque del Este
José María Ochoa Pile** (closed Mon); you'll find this
just past Redoma Las Trinitarias, on Avenida Libertador Este, unmissable with its giant Carlos Cruz Diez
sculpture, *Homage to the Rising Sun*.

The principal restaurants and modern malls in
Barquisimeto are on or around Avenida Lara, between
Paseo Los Leones and Avenida Vargas.

*Reproductions of
indigenous-style
pottery from the
Quíbor area.*

Western attractions

The main attractions outside Barquisimeto lie within about an hour's drive to th
west, via the road from the Obelisco roundabout which is clearly marked fc
Carora/Quíbor. About 15 minutes out of town, the highway splits: one rout
heads towards Carora (an hour directly west of the capital), while the othe
runs southwest toward Quíbor, Sanare and El Tocuyo.

From either road, just past the split there is access to **Tintorero** 28, renowne
for its weavers. Many homes bear signs announcing the sale of hand-wove
goods. Before 2pm on weekdays or noon on Saturdays, visitors can also watc
the weavers at work. Several families there also specialize in ceramics.

Southwestern route

Long before explorers arrived, the **Quíbor** 29 area was settled by indigenou
tribes dedicated to farming and with a well-developed ceramics tradition.

Underscoring Quíbor's past, opposite the Iglesia de Nuestra Señora d
Altagracia (beside the Plaza Bolívar, at Calle Pedro León Torres and Avenida 8
is the site of an active dig in an indian cemetery. You can visit the Muse
Arqueológico de Quíbor, one block south of the church, to see some of the arti
facts and skeletons discovered at various local digs (open Tue–Fri 9am–noor
2.30–6pm; token admission). If time allows, walk nine blocks north to see th
ornate 17th-century chapel, La Ermita de Nuestra Señora de Altagracia.

On entering Quíbor, signs indicate a southern bypass (lined with crafts stands)
which will take you up winding roads away from the desert and into fertile, ver
dant hills dotted with farms. You come first to **Cubiro** 30, whose main attrac
tion is **Las Lomas**, above the town. With its summit usually in the clouds, it ca

BELOW: a weaver's
workshop in
Tintorero.

be quite cool, but visitors wrapped in sweaters flock there at weekends to rent horses or picnic in the velvety meadows.

Beyond Cubiro is **Sanare** ③. Things worth seeing here include El Cerrito, a small restored colonial zone at the southern edge of town, and, a short distance farther south, the **Parque Nacional Yacambú**, with lush cloud forests and abundant birds (attracting numerous bird watchers). Surrounded by mountains in the interior of the country, it is surprising to learn that **El Tocuyo** ㉜ is one of the oldest towns in South America, founded on December 7, 1545. Furthermore, from 1546 until 1577, it was capital of the Province.

El Tocuyo is also known as the "Cradle of Folklore." One of its best known celebrations (June 13) is the Tamunangue, a seven-part dance preceded by a mock battle with sturdy sticks called *garrotes,* initially a form of martial arts. In the earthquake of 1950, most of El Tocuyo's seven colonial temples and magnificent vintage homes were leveled. Its principal church, **Iglesia de Nuestra Señora de la Concepción**, was severely damaged, but was rebuilt by the government. Its colonial altar-pieces somehow went unharmed, and are gems.

Colonial Carora

The best-kept secret of **Carora** ㉝ is its marvelous colonial district. Following the principal westbound avenue, at the main intersection (signs indicate Maracaibo north, Trujillo south) continue straight for seven blocks. Turn right onto Calle San Juan, which is lined with handsomely restored homes and leads to the plaza and 17th-century **Iglesia San Juan Bautista**. In contrast to this church's restrained design is the handsome baroque **Capilla del Calvario**, built in 1787, at the end of the southbound street bordering the plaza. ❑

Map on page 192

TIP

Tours of Bodegas Pomar winery, Carora, whose wines and champagnes have gained international acclaim, are available for groups with advance reservations, tel: 05 221 2191.

BELOW: Carora's beautiful colonial zone.

NORTHERN ZULIA

*Thanks to the money and machismo generated by the oil industry,
Maracaibo dominates this region. Its inhabitants enjoy a
startling mixture of modern and traditional life styles*

Map
on page
218

Caracas

For newcomers, the strongest initial impressions of northern Zulia are the large presence of indigenous women in traditional native dress, the forest of oil derricks in Lake Maracaibo, and the perpetually hot, sunny climate. With an average year-round temperature of 28° C (82° F), it is nicknamed *La Tierra del Sol Amada* – "the land of the beloved sun." Those used to cooler climes may melt at first, unless they follow the lead of the locals. By dawn, residents are on their way to work and markets are a beehive of activity. But, being neither mad dogs nor Englishmen, they do not go out in the midday sun: instead they take a long break until around 3–4pm for a leisurely lunch at home or with friends in one of the many excellent restaurants, to enjoy a snooze, or to head for park. They then restart their activities once the heat of the day has passed.

Oil capital

To most of the world, mention of Venezuela conjures up one image: oil. And Maracaibo ❶, rather than being known just as the capital of Zulia state, is considered "capital" of the nation's petroleum industry.

Although Lake Maracaibo separates the capital from the oil fields along the eastern shore, the city of Maracaibo is the seat of power of the industry. Modern high-rise towers, filled with offices of the oil companies and those providing complementary goods or services, as well as plush urbanizations populated by oil company executives, each attest to the effect of petroleum wealth on the city.

In pre-oil days, Maracaibo's geographical position contributed to its development as a transit point for voyages across the Atlantic – with the lake also providing a shipping link between the Andean states and the coast for important products such as coffee. With silver, gold, and other riches from across the continent also loaded in Maracaibo, the city was a frequent target for pirates. In the 1800s, brisk trade between Venezuela and the nearby Dutch islands boosted Maracaibo's commerce. However, it was the announcement by the entrepreneurs at the well called Barrosos No. 2 on December 14, 1922 of the wealth that lay below its surface that changed the course of Venezuela's history.

Viewing the oil derricks

The huge deposits along the northwestern shores of Lake Maracaibo lie principally below the water's surface; thus you see only grasshopper pumps and an occasional derrick on land. To view those in the lake, there are access roads to the dike bordering the lakeshore from the oil towns such as **Tía Juana** ❷ and **Lagunillas** ❸. Your best bet is to enlist the ser-

PRECEDING PAGES:
fish for dinner.
LEFT: entering
the mouth that
feeds you.
BELOW: a Guajira
woman.

vices of local taxi drivers who know the best access routes. The visual impact of the forest of derricks covering the lake surface etches a graphic impression of the vast liquid wealth being extracted, that no words can equal. However, taking photos of the derricks is illegal for security reasons – so if you see a National Guardsman approaching, stash your camera.

Access to Maracaibo from the east is via the **Rafael Urdaneta Bridge**, the longest pre-stressed concrete span in the world, 8 km (5 miles) long and 50 meters (164 ft) above the water at its highest point to permit easy passage by giant oil tankers. It crosses **Lake Maracaibo ❹**, the largest lake in South America, at the neck of water between the lake and the Gulf of Venezuela in the Caribbean Sea. Just east of the bridge is the **Hipódromo de Santa Rita**, Maracaibo's horse-racing track (races Wed, from 5.30pm; free entry; *see pages 102-3*).

Feisty residents

The oil boom shaped the city and its people. Maybe it's the heat or the hard labor required to sweat out a living in the oil fields or on the region's cattle ranches, but something toughens the *maracuchos*, as local residents are known. Easily identifiable by a mile-a-minute way of speaking, a maracucho man would think nothing of walking into a Caracas bar wearing a hand-lettered T-shirt bearing a politically sensitive message. And nobody is likely to bother him too much either. *Maracucho* machismo is the stuff of legends.

Reshaped city

Government coffers loaded with oil money bank-rolled urban development based on the notion that "modern is best." In a controversial move, most of

Despite the presence of oil, fishing is still a source of income on Lake Maracaibo.

BELOW: Sunday service at Maracaibo Cathedral.

Maracaibo's oldest neighborhood, **El Saladillo**, was razed to make way for a seven-block-long park and pedestrian boulevard, **Paseo Las Ciencias**.

An attack on tradition provoked public ire over the move. The wrecking ball leveled a great concentration of the unusual Maracaibo-style houses characterized by marked Dutch influence, with tall windows and doors, elaborate designs applied to the façades, and vivid contrasting colors. But even more than the buildings themselves, was the loss of the heart of one of the two rival districts claiming to be birthplace of the *gaita*, the traditional music of the *maracuchos* (who maintain this destruction killed the city's "spirit").

Originally, the *gaita* had lyrics with a pious theme, dedicated to various saints, but the prevalent form now is a popular (some would say profane) adaptation which is political, humorous, and totally irreverent – no topic or person is sacred. Lively verses are sung to music typified by the use of the *furruco* and metal *charrasca*. The first makes a distinctive deep sound produced by rhythmically stroking a pole fastened to the head of a drum; and the latter is a rhythm instrument looking like a metal grater, played with a small rod.

Paseo de Las Ciencias, filled with trees, benches, and sculptures by Venezuelan artists, extends from the **Plaza Bolívar** Ⓐ to the church dedicated to Zulia's patron saint, the **Basílica de Nuestra Señora de Chiquinquirá** Ⓑ. This is where you will find the main historic sites of Maracaibo.

Beginning at Plaza Bolívar, unmistakable with its statue to The Liberator in the center, the restored colonial **Cathedral** Ⓒ is home to the highly venerated Black Christ of Maracaibo, a statue dating from the 16th century. Two blocks behind it stands the **Capilla de Santa Ana** Ⓓ, a colonial chapel with a fabulous *mudéjar* (moorish-style) ceiling and handsome vintage altar-piece. Diagonally

Maps:
Area 218
City 220

The season for gaitas is considered to be October 15 to February 2. But due to the increasing popularity of the music, it is now heard all year long in Zulia, and Caracas clubs and restaurants import the best known gaita groups during the Christmas season.

BELOW: colors of Maracaibo's Santa Lucía district.

across from the chapel is the **Mercado de los Guajiros ⓔ**. Next to the cathe dral are the **Casa de Gobierno ⓕ** (state government headquarters in an impres sive early 19th-century building with two-story arcade) and the **Casa de la Capitulación ⓖ** or Casa Morales. The last of these was the home of the last Spanish Captain General in the city, Francisco Tomás Morales. The Casa Morales is now the only remaining residential colonial building in Maracaibo. The Treaty of Capitulation was signed here by Spanish forces defeated in the 1823 battle of Lake Maracaibo. It is now a museum (open Mon–Fri; free). Its neighbor, the **Teatro Baralt ⓗ**, was reopened in 1998 after years of restoration.

Behind the theater is the **Calle de la Tradición**, a restoration of the few houses of the old Saladillo neighborhood that escaped demolition. Many have been turned into small shops. The focal point is **El Zaguán**, a restaurant-garden- café and often the site of live entertainment.

On the other side of the *paseo* in the Concejo Municipal (city hall) is the **Museo de Artes Gráficas ⓘ** (open Tue–Sat; free.) A block south, the Iglesia de San Francisco stands at the entrance to Plaza Baralt.

Markets past and present

At the far end of this shop-lined plaza is the **Centro de Arte de Maracaibo Lia Bermúdez ⓙ** (open daily; free). The huge structure entered into service in 1928 as the city's principal market. For the last 20 years it has been through hard times. Ambitious plans for restoration were initiated, and sometimes completed, but always lacked a clear vision of the ultimate purpose. Success finally came when a private group of artists and cultural activists petitioned the governor to convert it into an arts center honoring one of Maracaibo's most famous sculptors.

Although at street level many of the commercial buildings lining Plaza Baralt have been "modernized" (for the worse), if one looks hard, especially above the store fronts, there are many interesting architectural details, ranging from Herculean pillars to the head of the messenger Mercury.

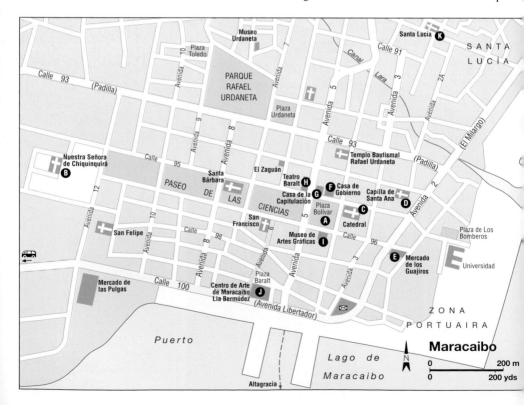

The result was the creation of a foundation with representatives from the private and public sector which undertook the rescue work. The beautiful center now houses galleries, a large theater, conference rooms, a museum, an art and book shop and a cafeteria; and dynamic programming, which makes it a magnet on Maracaibo's waterfront and one of the city's most important cultural centers.

Map on page 220

Opposite the art center is Maracaibo's **Mercado de las Pulgas**, or flea market. It is at once fascinating and a study in utter chaos: jammed together under the roof of a huge warehouse and outside are hundreds of stalls, tables, plastic sheets spread out on the ground – all piled high with every imaginable type of goods. Music blares, hawkers scream offers, bargain hunters push and shove through the narrow aisles. Most of the vendors are Guajira and Paraujana indian women in their traditional flowing *mantas* (a floor-length, loose caftan-like dress). The market operates daily, but Saturdays are busiest.

Back to the *paseo*, the basilica, at its western end, appears to have an ornatedly sculptured façade. Closer inspection reveals these are all painted-on. The same *rompe-l'oeil* technique is used in its elaborate interior. The focal point, however, is the tiny image of the Virgin of Chiquinquirá, affectionately known as *La Chinita*. Legend has it that the virgin's image miraculously appeared on a board that had floated to shore on the lake and was taken home by a local woman. *La Chinita*'s feast day, November 18, is celebrated with a week of processions, bullfights and music.

A local maracucho *fast-food treat is* patecones. *This is a sandwich, but one in which bread is replaced with fat slices of green (i.e. starchy, not sweet) plantain which have been pounded to pancake thickness and deep fried until crisp on the outside, tender on the inside.*

Other Maracaibo attractions

Some half dozen blocks north of the historic zone is the Santa Lucía district. Getting its name from the **Iglesia de Santa Lucia K** at its hub, this is the rival

BELOW: religious icons outside the Cathedral.

area of the old El Saladillo neighborhood, also claiming to be birthplace of the *gaita* and with the same Maracaibo-style architecture. Some houses by the church have been restored, but most need a dose of loving care to bring them back to their former glory. The principal commercial streets are Avenida 5 de Julio and Avenida Bella Vista, lined with modern shopping malls and the city's most popular restaurants. A popular venue for cultural events, the **Centro de Bellas Artes** (open Mon–Fri 9am–noon; Sat 8am–12.30pm; free), is nearby.

The colonial fort on Isla de San Carlos.

Northern side trips

Heading north toward the Guajira Peninsula via the road for El Moján (San Rafael on some maps), you encounter the ambitious **Complejo Científico, Cultural y Turístico Simón Bolívar** (closed Mon; token admission) which has a planetarium, anthropological museum, health museum, park with artificial lake and boats to rent and with huge playground areas, horse riding, picnic areas, and soda fountain with live music on weekends.

El Moján ❺ is the departure point for shuttle boats to **Isla de San Carlos** ❻ (with a stop at Isla Taos). A photogenic **colonial fort** on its southern point is the dominant feature of the island; with well-informed guides providing a tour. A long, wide stretch of sandy, shadeless beach extends northward.

Indigenous homeland

BELOW:
the *palafitos* of
Sinamaica Lagoon.

Continuing northward from El Moján, after crossing the El Limón bridge, at **Sinamaica** ❼ follow signs to the *muelle* (dock) at Puerto Cuervito, where Paraujano indians offer boat tours to the **Laguna de Sinamaica** ❽. The traditional construction of the Paraujanos (meaning the water or boat people) is a one-

Map on page 218

oom *palafito*, built independently on piles in the lagoon, with thatched roofs and walls made of *esteras* – reed mats lashed together. All movement between houses and to the shore is by boat. It was this same type of dwelling which prompted Amerigo Vespucci in 1499 to call the area *Venezuela* – "little Venice" – because it reminded him of his Italian hometown.

In Maracaibo, it is impossible for most people to differentiate between the Guajiro and the Paraujano indians since their most identifiable trademark is the *manta* worn by the women of both groups (the Paraujanos copied the style from the Guajiros). However, in their homelands, one knows immediately which is which. The Paraujanos are sedentary, living on the water, and depending primarily on fishing for their livelihood. The Guajiros, on the other hand, are nomadic, erecting temporary houses, and moving freely between the border lands of Venezuela and Colombia with their herds of goats and cattle.

Los Filudos ❾, just beyond Paraguaipoa, 32 km (20 miles) north of Sinamaica, is the site of the **Guajiro market** (Saturdays and Mondays are usually the busiest days). It's not geared toward tourists, so don't expect to find indigenous crafts here, although their finely woven hats and amulets are plentiful. This is where fresh produce and livestock, piles of animal hides, medicinal herbs, and kitchen equipment and other utilitarian items are sold. It is also one of the few places outside the wild upper Guajira Peninsula where you see Guajiro men in traditional *guayucos* (a cross between a diaper and short sarong) and hear practically nothing except their native language. Go early to the market, since it is active only in the cool morning hours.

The National Guard warns against going farther north than Paraguaipoa because of dangerous border problems and drug-trafficking. ❑

The Guajiros are fiercely independent. They simply ignore any governmental attempts to control their cross-border movements or make them get cédulas (national ID cards); they are Guajiros and they move about as they please.

BELOW:
the Guajiro market.

Map on page 228

THE ANDES

With its principal peaks soaring to heights far above the tallest in western Europe, the Venezuelan Andes present a dramatic surprise in a predominantly lowland, tropical country

L ogically, a visit to the Andes promises some distinct contrasts to Venezuela's sun-drenched beaches, Amazon rainforests, or the great central plains. And, even within the the Andes themselves, visitors will be surprised at the great variety in climate, landscapes, lifestyles, folkloric customs, and much more. However, just looking at the landscapes alone – from tropical forests and coffee plantations in the foothills to barren high moors, glacial, lakes, and snow-capped peaks – gives you a clue that a trip through these mountains is likely to be a highly rewarding experience.

Regular commercial flights go from Caracas and other major cities to key destinations including Valera, Mérida, Santo Domingo (servicing Táchira's capital of San Cristóbal) and San Antonio de Táchira; or you can take a bus. But you should go by car to fully savor this beautiful region, to be able to stop to inspect fragile orchids growing along the roadside, sample smoked trout at a roadside stand, and to walk through the cobblestone streets of a remote colonial village.

Take the scenic route

The most scenic route through the Venezuelan Andes can be enjoyed by taking the westbound exit for Biscucuy in Trujillo state from Guanare in Portuguesa.

The road almost immediately begins to climb, passing through a major coffee-growing region as it winds through the mountains toward **Boconó ❶**.

Slopes are covered with coffee plants shaded by towering "mother trees," nearly every house has a large patio for drying harvested beans in the sun, and the air is redolent with the aroma of toasting coffee.

Boconó was dubbed "The Garden of Venezuela" by Simón Bolívar for its variety of flora. Today, the name more fittingly applies because of the multitude of farms blanketing surrounding hills.

Worth seeking out downtown, half a block north of Plaza Bolívar, is **La Vieja Casa**, a delightful restaurant and museum (closed Tue and 3–7pm daily). Following the main downhill street, past the front of the church, you'll find the **Museo Trapiche de Los Clavos**. This restored 19th-century sugar mill contains three museums (coffee, brown sugar and botanic) as well as offering cultural events (open Tues–Sun; 8am–noon, 2–5pm; token entry fee.)

The best places for local crafts are the **Centro de Acopio Artesanal** within the farmer's market (open Tues–Sun, 8am–4pm; free), and the **Centro de Servicios Campesinos Tiscachic** (three blocks north on the last street before the bridge as you leave town). This artisan cooperative with reasonable prices sells some unusual stone-polished black pottery of the Briceño family, and particularly outstanding carved

PRECEDING PAGES: mule trains through the mist. **LEFT:** a roadside ice grinder. **BELOW:** the rooftops of Mérida.

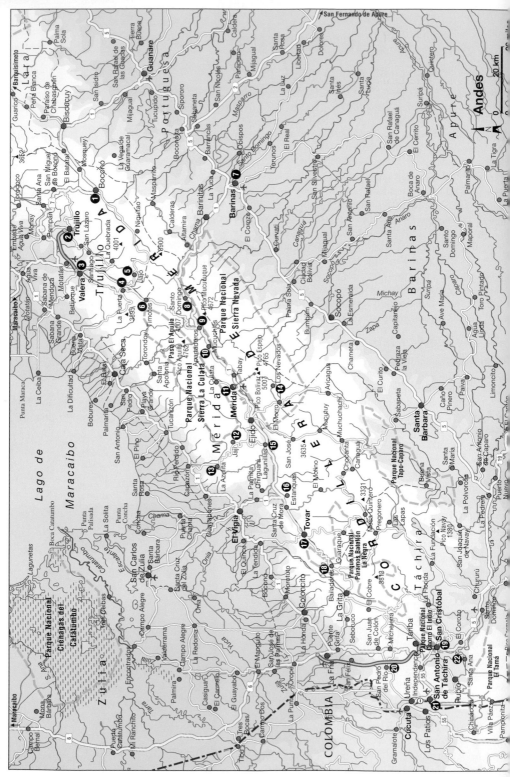

wood *arte popular* (naïf art) sculptures; Trujillo's most famous artist of this genre, Rafaela Baroni, lives in Boconó.

There are several interesting villages en route to Valera: **San Miguel de Boconó** is note here are the polychrome altar-piece in its colonial church and the singular annual festival on January 6, with more fascinating folkloric and religious ceremonies on one day than you will see elsewhere in Venezuela. It is also worth stopping off at **Santa Ana**, with pretty traditional streetscapes, and **Burbusay**, which has another outstanding altar-piece in its 18th-century church.

Heading south

Detouring to the south takes you to **Trujillo ❷**. Once, having passed through **Plazuela**, the state's capital and a restored colonial zone, then battled your way through Trujillo's shopping area to the Centro, exploring is easy with only two main streets: Independencia (one-way southbound) and Bolívar (one-way northbound). Various handsome colonial structures, including the 17th-century **Cathedral**, are by the Plaza Bolívar.

South of town, you can visit the 46-meter (150-ft) tall image of the Virgen de la Paz overlooking Trujillo (an internal elevator goes to the top). And farther south is the pristine 17th-century village of **San Lázaro**. You can continue on a good unpaved road along the mountain crests to Santiago, La Quebrada, and on to **Valera ❸**. This is the state's largest and most economically important city – although without tourist appeal. **Motatán**, 12 km (7 miles) north of Valera, has hot springs at Hotel Hidrotermal San Rafael. Detour west from Valera for **Isnotú**, best known as birthplace of Dr José Gregorio Hernández, founder of bacteriology in Venezuela and postulated for sainthood for his philanthropic labors attending the poor.

To take the alternate southbound "fast route" to the cities of Mérida or San Antonio del Táchira through the tropical lowlands and cattle country bordering Lake Maracaibo, continue west past Isnotú and Betijoque to join Highway 1 (taking the turn-off at El Vigía for Mérida).

Before **La Puerta ❹** (known as the "gateway to the Andes"), landscapes are pretty; beyond it, they are spectacular, as you pass through soaring mountains with terraced fields and ancient houses with pounded-earth walls, where farmers still work the land with wooden plows pulled by oxen. **Jajó ❺** (37 km/22 miles east of La Puerta) is a thoroughly picturesque colonial village.

Mérida

Mérida state is known as *el techo de Venezuela* – "the roof of Venezuela" – with the country's highest peaks permanently capped by snow.

The people of this often harsh Andean terrain are hardworking, resourceful and religious, and Mérida is an enclave of tradition. Peasant farmers eke out a living on steep terraced plots. Villages with indian names are strategically situated about a day's mule trek apart. Often these settlements are little more than clusters of crooked, red-roofed, single-story houses built flush against the narrow road.

Map on page 228

TIP

Comfortable daytime temperatures tend to prevail all year long in Trujillo. However, at night or if it is particularly rainy it can turn chilly.

BELOW: stall selling local produce.

As you continue toward the city of Mérida (the state's capital), the road is never boring – with views or hairpin turns, switchbacks and a few sheer drop-offs. The Transandean highway traces part of the trail Simón Bolívar braved on his campaign to liberate Nueva Granada (Colombia).

The first stop in Mérida state is **Timotes** ❻, legendary among trout fishermen. Casting for brown and rainbow trout is a popular sport in the streams and lagoons all over Mérida.

Some 45 km (28 miles) from Timotes, you'll reach the freezing **Paso El Aguila** (Eagle Pass), just below **Pico Aguila**. This is the highest point in the Venezuelan highway system, at an elevation of 4,007 meters (13,146 ft). Bolívar and his troops marched through the pass in 1813 on the Admirable Campaign that concluded with his triumphant entry into Caracas.

If you aren't prepared for the chill, you may want to stop at a roadside stand to purchase a *ruana*, the woollen poncho of the region. The most distinctive style is made of double-sided cloth – one side red, the other blue.

Barren beauty

The area above the treeline – from about 3,500 meters (11,500 ft) – is called the *páramo* (high moor). The Venezuelan expression "to end up in the *páramo*" is used to describe someone at death's door. Life is hard here, for the climate is cold, windy and wet. Little grows at these altitudes, but it is not all bleak. The poverty is not as widespread as in the Andean regions elsewhere in South America. And the terrain has its own eerie beauty. If you visit in October, you will see the *frailejón* at the height of its flowering period. This plant has fuzzy leaves and usually yellow flowers that grow on tall stems up to 2 meters (6 ft) high.

The trout season is mid-March to the end of September. Permits are available (weekdays only) from the Ministerio de Agricultura y Cría (Ministry of Agriculture) in Mérida or the Oficina Nacional de Pesca (National Fishing Office) of the MAC in Caracas.

BELOW: walking in the Andean foot hills in Merida state.

One particularly unusual type can be seen at the beginning of the road from Paso El Aguila, via the quaint farm village of **Piñango**. These look more like trees with thick trunks formed of layer after layer of dead leaves, some of which are up to 200 years old. Another, the *frailejón morado* (purple *frailejón*) is well known for its medicinal benefits.

Andinos have numerous ingenious uses for *frailejones*. They wrap home-churned butter in one type to impart a delicate flavor and stuff another type in mattresses. They fry the pith of the stems of yet a third kind for munching.

Bird watchers will find the *páramo* a rewarding challenge. Mérida harbors nearly 600 species of bird. In the rainy season, from May through to October, when the wildflowers bloom, the high plain positively buzzes with humming-birds; the *frailejones* attract the bearded helmetcrest.

Friar's delight

The Transandean highway winds through the *páramo* to Apartaderos. From there you can backtrack, along the road to **Barinas 🥈**, to visit the famous **Hotel Los Frailes** (The Friars). Probably the most attractive and popular resort in Mérida, the hotel is built on the site of a 17th-century monastery and offers comfortable rooms with wooden beams set around a cobblestone courtyard with fountain. If you ask in advance, you can hire horses to ride across the *páramo*. The hotel offers a fine, rather elegant restaurant. Even if you find no room at the inn (reservations must be made well in advance), be sure to visit the dark, cozy bar where a fire roars in the hearth. Try one of the local drinks, such as *calentado*, a toddy with the anise liqueur *miche*, brown sugar and hot water; or *ponche andino*, with warm milk, *miche*, brandy and cinnamon.

Map on page 228

The frailejón *is considered the symbol of the* páramo*. Some 45 varieties of these "tall friars" grow here.*

BELOW: mountain village near Mérida.

If you decide to go for a hike behind Los Frailes, be wary of the "killer llamas" kept in one of the fields. Many people have suffered aggressive attacks from these "cuddly" animals, apparently based on jealousy of the males of anyone entering their territory.

Returning northwest on the main highway again brings you to the town of **Santo Domingo** ❽, with its trout farm, Truchicultura El Baho. The rare Andean cock-of-the-rock bird can be found in the countryside around Santo Domingo.

Mountain park

The Parque Nacional Sierra Nevada, extending from Santo Domingo to well south of the city of Mérida, includes the Andean ranges of Serranía Nevada de Santo Domingo and Sierra Nevada de Mérida. Besides the mountains, the national park encompasses *páramo* dotted by *frailejones*, pine forests and some 170 glacial lagoons. The largest, Laguna Mucubají, seems bleak at first but offers a surprising abundance of birds, including the speckled teal, black-chested buzzard-eagle and the *páramo* pipit. Snows from Pico Mucuñuque, the highest mountain in the Santo Domingo range, melt into streams that feed the enchanting Laguna Negra, an hour's hike from the park entrance. Laguna Los Patos is a hard, 2.4-km (1½-mile) trek past Laguna Negra. Fishing, camping and horse riding are allowed in areas of the park.

Between Pico El Aguila and Apartaderos is the exit for the Observatorio Astronómico Nacional de Llano del Hato. Visitors may view the heavens from this observatory, at 3,600 meters (11,800 ft), with four giant telescopes (high season: open daily 10 am–10.30pm; low season: open Sat 10am–10.30pm, Sun 10am–4.30pm; entry fee).

Culinary treats

BELOW: highway through the Andes.

By the intersection of the Transandean and the Barinas highways lies **Apartaderos** ❾, famous for its cold, cured hams, which hang from the rafters

Map on page 228

f roadside *charcuterías* (delicatessens). The meat tastes like Italian prosciutto. ʼold, smoked sausages are another local specialty, and many Venezuelans vouldn't consider a visit to Mérida complete without bringing home the bacon, o to speak. *Charcuterías* also stock the local white cheese, *queso del páramo*, vhich is available smoked (*queso ahumado*).

Many people fry cheese as part of an Andean breakfast that also includes *repas* made of wheat, rather than cornmeal. Other *charcutería* staples are *man-ecada*, sweet bread made with a yellow cornmeal base, and bottles of *miche*.

ush valleys

s you descend from the *páramo*, you'll notice sweeping green valleys, fields f yellow mustard, bright carnations (destined for markets around the country), rchids, lilies and dahlias. Most farms are still small, labor-intensive opera-ons. Farmers grow potatoes, garlic, carrots, onions and all manner of vegeta-les. In the valleys you'll find every kind of fruit tree, including mango, orange nd avocado. Berries are gathered from bushes in the wild as well as cultivated.

Farmers in the area till their fields with wooden plows pulled by oxen, main-ining this is the most efficient, effective, and economical method to deal with nallholdings where the soil is full of rocks, and the fields are often steep and arrow, and each property small. You'll see that fields are divided by stone alls. All this rock was painstakingly pulled from the soil to make the land till-le. They serve to define property lines, fence in animals, and as a depository r rocks that at times seem to "grow" better than the crops. Some of the walls Apartaderos are said to date back to the Timoto-Cuica indians, and the fields e still called by their traditional indian name, *poyos*.

BELOW: harvesting by hand is still the norm in the Andes.

Here and there you will see a large, low circular wall in the midst of a field. These are primitive mills, still in use, where the walls keep animals harnessed to a long pole attached to a pair of central millstones in a circle, which they rotate to grind up the grain.

BELOW: chapel of San Rafael de Mucuchíes.

When the Spanish arrived in the area during the 17th century, they found civilization of skilled farmers. The indians were growing more than 30 crop including maize, potatoes, squash and beans. The conquistadores killed mar of the men and married the women, so today there are hardly any pure indian But the indigenous culture has survived in the foods, the folklore and to degree, the place names. Most celebrations honoring Catholic saints featur dancing to the beat of drums and *maracas* (typically indigenous) and dressir in costumes with masks. Nearing Mérida city, you'll notice several names wit the prefix *mucu*, an indian word meaning "place of."

Farther along the Transandean highway at **San Rafael de Mucuchíes** is curious little chapel made of thousands of stones. It was pieced together by th enigmatic Juan Félix Sánchez, an artist who was also revered locally as a my tic. He finished the project in 1984, when he was 84 years old. The chapel actually a small replica of the one Sánchez built at his isolated homestead in E Tisure, high in the mountains. Sánchez was honored with the National Prize f Art when he was 90 years old. While his chapels and carved wood scuptures ar best known, it was his beautiful weaving that first brought him fame. He die just short of reaching the century mark.

An Andean breed of dog

The next town, **Mucuchíes ⑩**, has a tidy plaza dominated by a blue and whi church and with a famous statue of an indian boy Tínjaca and his dog, Nevad (Snowy). The story goes that Bolívar stayed in the area in 1813 and that his ho gave the boy and the dog to El Libertador as a sign of allegiance. Supposed they both stayed faithfully by Bolívar's side until they were shot down ar

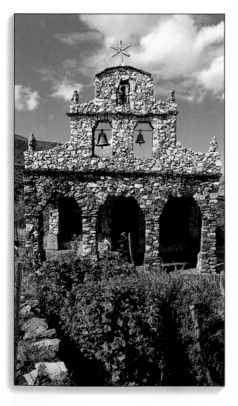

killed in battle. The dog Nevado was a Mucuchíe breed – seen usually only in the Andes and the close thing Venezuela has to a national canine. When full grown, the dog resembles a Saint Bernard and has white coat splotched with brown and black.

The Mucuchíes breed was developed in the ear 18th century, when Spanish monks established monastery in the Andes and began raising sheep. The imported Pyrenean Mountain dogs from Europe t guard their flocks; the dogs mixed with local mutts t eventually create the Mucuchíes. Although the Pyre nean Mountain dogs were prized for their loyalty, obe dience and strength, Mucuchíes have an adde characteristic: ferocity. They are often used as guar dogs on Andean farms. (A colorful local celebratic for San Benito is held in the town of Mucuchíes c December 29 . *See Fiestas, pages 79–83.*)

Stepping back in time

Along the highway, only about 20 minutes north c the city of Mérida (between Mucuchíes and Tabay), the popular Los Aleros, the re-creation of a typic Andean village of times past (open daily 8am–6pm admission fee). Visitors go up to the old hilltop se tlement in old-time buses to explore the building constructed using the traditional pounded eart method; demonstrators in vintage clothing go abo their chores just as they did in the past, baking brea

Map
on page
228

n a wood-fired oven, arranging type in the print shop and so on. Live music, daily wedding, and such like are also part of the fun. This was created by 100 ercent private initiative on the part of Alexi Montiel. Due to its success, he ubsequently opened another place with the same idea but broader scope, Alexi's Venezuela de Antier, via Jají. Although interesting, both charge expenive entrance fees.

Beside Los Aleros is **Catalina Delicattesses** (open daily 8am–6pm) which, n 1993, moved its principal location here from the original outlet on the El Valle-La Culata highway north from the city of Mérida (they now have a smaller hop there and another in the Mercado Principal). Since 1984, this operation of he Ramírez family has become famous for its some 100 flavors of homemade onserves, plus cakes, smoked trout and cheeses.

A tranquil place to live

An unexpected change in Mérida from the ubiquitous statues of Simón Bolívar.

Even the metropolitan state capital of **Mérida** ⓫, which shares the state's name, maintains a tranquil air. It is not a beautiful city, but its setting is spectacular. Sitated on a high plateau with the Chama River at its base, it is accented by trees raped with Spanish moss, and enjoys a dramatic backdrop of five of the highst peaks in theVenezuelan Andes. Locals call the mountains Las Cinco Aguilas Blancas ("The Five White Eagles"). They are La Corona, La Concha, La Columna, El Toro and El León. La Corona is actually two peaks, Humboldt nd Bonpland, and La Columna comprises Espejo and Bolívar. All are more than ,700 meters (15,420 ft); Bolívar, at 5,007 meters (16,427 ft), is the highest.

About 130,000 people live in Mérida, including more than 30,000 students of he **Universidad de Los Andes** (ULA). The community definitely has a uni-

BELOW:
Andean people.

versity flavor, making for lively intellectual and nightlife (as well as occasion, disruptive demonstrations).

A difficult beginning

Mérida may seem a tranquil place today, but its foundation involved scandal an bloodshed. Juan Rodríguez Suárez, an officer who was supposed to be explo ing the Sierra Nevada with a party of soldiers in 1558, decided to found a tow which he named after Mérida, Spain. In those days, towns were founded onl by royal proclamation, so Rodríguez Suárez found himself in serious trouble. H was branded a criminal, tried and sentenced to a gruesome death. But sympa thizers intervened and helped him flee to Trujillo, where he was granted th first political asylum in the New World.

Rodríguez Suárez had founded Mérida on the site of present-day Lagunilla Hostile indians forced the settlers to pack up and move some distance to the eas to a place now known as La Punta. Finally, Juan Maldonado y Ordóñez, the ma who had arrested Rodríguez Suárez, established Mérida once and for all at i present site, giving it the grand name, La Ciudad de Santiago de los Caballero de Mérida. *Caballeros* means gentlemen, and for many years Mérida was know simply as "the gentlemen's city." Even today, Mérida remains perhaps the mos polite metropolitan area in Venezuela. *Merideños* tend to be well-mannered but also reserved and conservative.

In Mérida there is great respect for the Church. When Pope John Paul II firs visited the country in 1985, he drew consistently large crowds here. There is als respect for Bolívar. Mérida was the first place to proclaim him *El Libertador* on May 23, 1813. As an indication of the degree of admiration, up until recentl

BELOW: handwoven rugs: an Andean specialty.

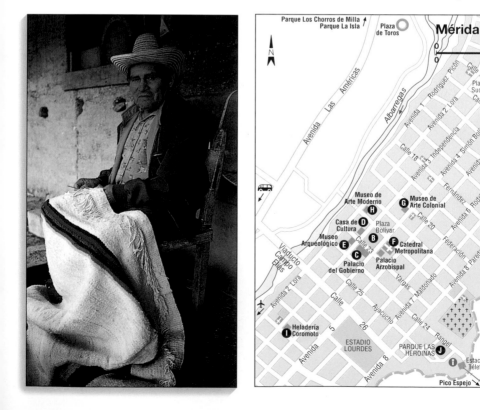

ne would have been subject to police reprimand for carrying a large bundle, uitcase, or even a backpack too close to Bolívar's statue in the plaza.

Not surprisingly,given the setting, *Merideños* appreciate nature and sports. Vithin the city alone they hav around 40 parks and gardens. The climate at this titude (1,645 meters/5,400 ft) is pleasant and moderate. It's usually warm in ae daylight hours – from 21–31°C (70–80°F), but at nightfall the mercury rops and it gets nippy – about 5°C (40°F).Siesta hour is a good time to head to ne of the city's many parks. **Parque La Isla** features hundreds of orchids, and arque Beethoven has two clocks – one made of flowers and one with wooden oldiers that march around a chalet to the tune of Beethoven compositions when ae hour strikes. The **Parque de las Cinco Repúblicas (Park of the Five epublics) Ⓐ** features a tall white column bearing a bust of Bolívar. When rected in 1842, this was the world's first monument dedicated to *El Libertador*. he park also has soil from each of the five countries that Bolívar emancipated.

Among Mérida's parks, perhaps the best loved is the **Parque Zoológico horros de Milla** with its beautiful cascades, pretty gardens, and a small zoo pen 8am–6pm; high season, Mon–Sun; low season, Tue–Sun; small admission e.) Local legend says that an indian princess whose lover was murdered by the onquistadores cried so hard that her tears turned into the falls. There's a statue f the tragic princess at the park entrance.

Beethoven Platz, in Parque Beethoven, Mérida.

ity center

a the heart of Mérida is the peaceful, green **Plaza Bolívar Ⓑ**. On its south de is the **Palacio del Gobierno Ⓒ** (state government headquarters), which has monumental triptych by painter Ivan Belsky representing the three zones of

Map on page 236

BELOW: view over Mérida.

Mérida state, from the steamy lowlands near Lake Maracaibo to the high plai
and the Andes. In the formal reception room upstairs is a painting by Jorg
Arteago of Bolívar's entrance into Mérida in the Admirable Campaign of 181.
The guards usually let you in to have a look at the triptych, at least if you pre
sent some kind of identification.

Along Calle 3, is the **Casa de Cultura Juan Félix Sánchez** **D**, named for on
of Mérida's most beloved naïf artists (at the close of this edition, out of servic
for remodeling.) About half a block off the plaza is the Universidad de Lo
Andes, one of the largest and oldest in Venezuela, founded in 1810 after fir
opening in 1785 as a seminary. A stained-glass window over the entrance bear
the biblical quotation (in Latin): "You cannot hide a city on a mountain." To han
dle ULA's great growth, its different schools are now scattered all over the city
with the largest part near Chorros de Milla. In the Rectorada (dean's office) c
the university is the **Museo Arqueológico** **E**, with only a small display of art
facts (high season: open Tue–Sun, 2–6pm; low season: open Tue–Fri, 8–11am
2–5.30pm; small admission fee)

On the plaza's Calle 4 side, is the long-suffering cathedral. Construction of th
massive **Catedral Metropolitana** **F** began in 1803, but damage from war an
several earthquakes required continuous rebuildings, and the cathedral wa
completed in its present form only in 1958. The result is an eclectic architectura
style. One of the paintings is supposedly of God. Beside the cathedral is the Pala
cio Arzobispal (Archbishop's Palace).

Nearby is the **Museo de Arte Colonial** **G** in the recently restored Casa Jua
Antonio Parra (Avenida 4, between Calles 20 & 21). It features religious paint
ings, furniture and ceramics (open Mon–Fri 8am–noon, 2–6pm; Sat–Su
9am–4.30pm; entrance fee, but children under 10 free

One block from here, within the Centro Cultura
Tulio Febres Cordero (between Avenida 2 & 3 an
Calles 21 & 22) is the **Museo de Arte Moderno** **H**
with a small but high quality collection of contempo
rary works by national artists (open Mon–Fri 9am
–noon, 3–7pm; Sat–Sun 10am–5pm; free entry.)

On the side streets near the plaza are a number c
colonial houses that have been converted into shop
and restaurants. National Monument plaques on thei
walls give information about the building's history

Food for thought

The many small, typical restaurants downtown serv
dishes such as *trucha andina* (trout caught fresh from
mountain streams), usually accompanied by the smal
sweet white potatoes grown in the area. The Mérid
version of *hallacas*, which are *tamal*-like packets o
stuffed cornmeal steamed in banana leaves, are als
popular. In the rest of Venezuela, *hallacas* are strictl
a Christmas food, but in Mérida they are eate
throughout the year and their filling is quite distinc
with potatoes and chickpeas (*garbanzos*) often mor
dominant than the usual meat base. Other local spe
cialties are *pisca andina*, a soup with potatoes an
eggs, and *mondongo* (tripe). Local drinks includ
chicha andina (the Andean beverage made from
corn), and hot punches such as *calentado*.

BELOW: statue of
the Liberator on
Pico Bolívar.

The large new **Mercado Principal**, the city's farm market on Avenida Las Américas, is a fascinating place to explore (open Mon, Wed–Sat; 7am–6pm; Tue, Sun morning only). Garden fresh fruits and vegetables are star attractions, but there is also a bit of everything. In season, look for baskets of sweet *fresas* (strawberries). There are always plenty of bags of *dulces abrillantados*, a chewy, taffy-like candy rolled into balls and coated with colored sugar, giving it the sparkling effect from which it gets its name; and many small restaurants serve more substantial fare.

Map on page 236

Ice cream with a difference

If you are an ice cream fan with a craving for something different, then head straight for **Heladería Coromoto ❶** (Avenida 3 at Calle 29; open Tue–Sun, 2–10pm) in front of Plaza El Llano. Owner Manuel Da Silva Oliveira was searching for a new taste sensation when he dreamed up his first exotic flavor, avocado. It took 50 kg (110 lbs) of experimenting to get it right. From there, things blossomed. In 1991, Oliveira's ice cream shop first entered the *Guinness Book of Records* as having more flavors of ice cream than anywhere else in the world – then with nearly 500. By the end of 1998, at the last count, the figure stood at 720!

The flavor list takes up the entire back wall. Along with more traditional combinations for the less adventurous, there are definitely unusual options such as pumpkin, ginger, garlic, beet, fried pork rind, fresh trout and beer. Among the most requested is *pabellón criollo*, a take-off of the national Venezuelan dish of shredded beef, black beans, rice and plantains. Each day Heladería Coromoto offers a rotating short list (simply for logistics) of 60 flavors.

BELOW: lookout on top of Pico Espejo.

Near the southern extreme of the city, via Avenida Andrés Bello, are tw other places worth visiting. **Parque Jardín Acuario**, along with its expecte tanks with many species of fish, also has interesting displays with life-size fi ures depicting various aspects of traditional Andean life of the past (ope 8am–6pm; daily in high season, Tue–Sun in low season; small entry fee.) Hig lights of the **Museo de Ciencia y Tecnología de Mérida** include the first rob model in the world of a giant prehistoric elasmosaurus, displays on the Andea cloud forests and optical phenomena (just off Andrés Bello, via Laguna L Rosa, Urb. Las Tapias with signs indicating the turn; open 10am–6pm, daily i high season, Tue–Sun in low season; admission fee).

After being closed for several years due to serious cable problems, the first three stages of Mérida's teleférico were finally reopened in 1996. As of October 1998, the final section is still waiting to be back in service.

Pico Espejo: high-wire adventure

Mérida's *teleférico* (cable car) is the highest and longest (12.5 km/7.5 miles) i the world. The cars climb in four stages to the top of **Pico Espejo** at 4,76 meters (15,630 ft), where a large statue of the Virgen de las Nieves (Virgin c the Snows), patron saint of mountaineers, stands with open arms amid th swirling mists. Departure is from **Parque Las Heroínas ❶**, at the end of Call 24 (ascents 7.30am–2pm; high season, Tue–Sun; low season, Wed–Sun; fee

The area in front of Parque Las Heroínas has also come to be *the* gatherin place for those wishing to hike in the mountains, scale the icy peaks, or g parasailing. All of the half dozen or so tour agencies and shops here offer mour taineering equipment for sale or rent, guides, and more.

No matter how warm it is in Mérida, there's always snow on Pico Espej Take winter clothes to beat the cold. Most people carry sweaters, ski jackets an gloves, layering them on as they ascend.

There are four stations along the ascent. The first pa of the ride swoops up and over the Río Chama gorg and soon the entire city of Mérida, on its long narro plateau, is in view. **La Montana station**, at 2,40 meters (8,000 ft), offers a view of nearly the entir Chama Valley. The station has a little restaurant-bar.

The second stop is **La Aguada**, at an elevation c 4,045 meters (13,272 ft). This is the starting point fo many easy treks on foot, horseback, or mountain bik – normally down to the base station, or (with a guide to La Vega and Chorros de las Nieves. Hang glider also take off from here.

En route to the third station, **Loma Redonda**, at a altitude of 3,400 meters (11,300 ft), you'll be flyin over treeless *páramo*. It's here that some people begi to feel a bit light-headed or experience a shortness o breath – symptoms of *soroche* (altitude sickness) There's oxygen at each station, and a doctor at th top. If you start to feel uncomfortable, take it slow Drinking or eating something may help. Don't hesitat to ask for oxygen if you're getting queasy.

Just a short walk from the Loma Redonda station past the shrine to the virgin, you can see the twi lagoons, **Los Anteojos** (The Eyeglasses), shimmer ing black in the valley. At this level there are usuall a number of guides with mules offering to take visi tors to **Los Nevados**, a 400-year-old indian villag that's about a six-hour hike or mule-ride away alon steep, narrow trail. Some 2,000 people live in this agricultural settlement, where potatoes, garlic, wheat and beans are farmed. Villagers haul their produce by mule to the *teleférico* station and whisk it down to Mérida in the cable cars. With the popularity of Los Nevados, there are now more than half a dozen *posadas* formally operating there, offering basic lodging plus optional meal service.

It's cold at the top, the fourth station, but there's a shop selling comforting cups of hot chocolate, big slices of cake and other snacks. The rocky summit of Pico Espejo rises beside the platform, and if the weather isn't too gray or snowy, you can see the glacier on neighboring Pico Bolívar. A fit hiker could reach Bolívar from here in three to five hours, but it's a tough journey.

Day tripping

There are several trout farms in the Mérida area that are open to visitors. A few decades ago the government introduced rainbow trout from North America. The industry has flourished. Besides Truchicultura El Baho near Santo Domingo (*see page 232*), you can visit El Paraíso at **Mucunután**, where big Mucuchíes dogs stand guard over the tanks fed by icy mountain spring water. If you're lucky, you may get to feed the fish from a large bag of nutrient-rich pellets called "trout wheat." When you see how they gobble the stuff up, you'll understand how it takes only a matter of months for the fish to grow to market weight.

Besides the trout farm via Mucunután, numerous local artisans – particularly wood carvers – live along this route and offer their creations at roadside stands or in small shops in their homes with signs identifying the locations.

Via El Valle-La Culata, northbound from Mérida, there are many small stands selling typical Andean snacks and crafts. Another attraction is the **Parque**

Map on page 236

BELOW: mists roll in on the mountain village of Jají.

Pueblito Sueños del Abuelo, a vintage village in miniature (open high seaso-only; 9am–5pm; entry fee). This drive climbs through pretty wooded hills, wit-the **Parque Nacional Páramo La Culata** at the end – a favorite for hikers.

Colonial restoration

A popular day trip from Mérida is to the restored colonial village of **Jají**
Buses leave from Mérida, and cab drivers will also negotiate a price to tak-you there. The 40-km (25-mile) ride northwest offers splendid views, followin-a winding mountain road washed by streams and waterfalls. The governmen-restoration of Jají was completed in 1971. Houses have traditional woode-grilles on the windows. Almost everything worth seeing is clustered around th-plaza with its typical church, souvenir shops, and places for tourists to grab-snack. It's all charming, but sometimes the place is almost overwhelmed b-tourists, mostly Venezuelans.

La Azulita ⓭ is a little village near Jají, located in the midst of mountain-covered with lush tropical forests, accented by crystalline streams and occa-sional cascades, and abounding with avifauna. The setting serves as a magnet fo-bird watchers and other nature lovers; as well as a large number of alternativ-religious and spiritual groups attracted by the consummate serenity of the setting

Remote villages

Deep in the mountains south of the city of Mérida, are a number of small villages **Los Pueblos del Sur**, which, because of their isolation appear untouched by time Access to most is only possible by 4x4, by mule, or on foot; except for Puebl-Nuevo, which is an easy drive by car. All have one or more basic *posadas*. Bes-known is **Los Nevados** ⓮. Insiders recommend goin-by road (4–5 hours) with one of the "*Toyoteros*" wh-gather in the early mornings at Mérida's Plaza La-Heroínas, staying overnight, then returning by mul-(4–5 hours) to the third the cable car station. You ca-then descend the rest of the way by that means.

Other routes thru the mountains include going from-Las González, via Tierra Negra (top spot for paraglid-ing), to San José, the Páramo de San José (wit-dozens of different species of *frailejones*), Mucutuy-Mucuchachí; from Estanques via El Molino, La-Mesas, Canaguá and Chacantá; and from Tovar vi-San Francisco and Guaraque to Mesa Quintero.

Changing landscapes

Once south of the city of Mérida, the mountain-change dramatically, with those bordering the high-way (which follows the Chama River) dry and scarre-with deeply eroded surfaces. You pass the entrance-marked for various villages to the north of the high-way: **Lagunillas** ⓯ is best known for its Laguna d-Urao, from which soda crystals have been "harvested"-since long before the arrival of colonizers; and **Chir-guará** has a central area with a very photogenic ol-look, and a surprising xerophytic garden near th-entrance to town.

From **Estanques** ⓰ southward the landscape-become very tropical. Sugar cane, coffee, and banana-

TIP

If exploring the El Valle-La Culata route, be sure to head back by mid afternoon since thick fog begins to roll in around 3pm making the steep, narrow winding road very dangerous.

BELOW: dumplings on a street stand.

re the important crops. Just beyond this village is the La Victoria *alcabala* (National Guard checkpoint). Right next to it is the beautiful Hacienda La Victoria, originally the focal point of the coffee plantation which commercially produced coffee bearing its name. Several years ago it was restored, with rooms surrounding the huge central patio (formerly used to dry coffee beans) now housing the **Museo de Café** and **Museo de la Inmigración** (open 9am–6pm; daily in high season, Wed–Sun in low season; entrance fee). The first demonstrates history, processes and implements associated with the cultivation of coffee. The second, with old photos, documents, and personal items, deals with the Europeans who came to this area to work the first coffee plantations.

The road to the right is the old way to the Highway 1 crossroads at **El Vigía** (now reached by a new toll freeway from Estanques); to the left the road continues south to Santa Cruz de Mora, **Tovar** ⓱ (second largest city in Mérida and heart of coffee and sugar-cane country), and **Bailadores** ⓲ (near the border of Táchira state; best known for its cultivation of strawberries and flowers.)

Map on page 228

Orchid by the roadside.

Táchira

Outside Bailadores, the highway rises steeply into the mountains and rolls on into Táchira, the home of many Venezuelan dictators. It produced at least five strongmen in the 19th and early 20th century, including perhaps the most notorious of them all, Juan Vicente Gómez. The portraits of various native sons displayed in the bars and homes of Táchira show that some locals are still proud of the mark these *andinos* made on the country.

It is interesting to conjecture why such an isolated region should yield such a surprising number of dictatorial rulers. One historian suggests that it may be

BELOW: Santo Domingo, in the *páramo* region.

because *tachirenses* possess "deep and unbending patriotism stimulated by the condition of being a frontier people." This may be true but other, perhaps more objective, observers have noted that the Andeans do tend to appoint their cronies to influential positions, thus ensuring a more or less inherited line of power.

Although it receives virtually no promotion, Táchira offers multiple attractions: landscapes ranging from tropical lowlands to *páramos* (high moorland), hot springs, a strong artisan tradition, colorful religious manifestations and fairs. There is easy road access via the western plains on Highway 5 (entering Táchira via Santo Domingo – site of the state's principal airport) and Highway 6 (through the tropical lowlands along the eastern edge of Lake Maracaibo, via La Fría and San Juan de Colón); or the more scenic approach is by Highway 7 passing through the mountains via La Grita.

Captivating capital

All routes lead to **San Cristóbal** , the capital, and an ideal base from which to explore. San Cristóbal's annual Feria Internacional de San Sebastián, celebrated at the end of January, attracts thousands of visitors who come to enjoy activities including its famous bullfights, the *Vuelta de Táchira* bicycle race (drawing competitors from around the world) and many other sporting events, agricultural exhibits, presentations by big-name entertainers, and more.

San Cristóbal's highlights include the Complejo Ferial (between Avenida España and Universidad), Plaza de Toros Monumental (bull ring), Olympic Stadium, Baseball Stadium, and the **Museo Antropológico de Táchira** (Tue–Fri, 9am–noon, 3–5.50pm; Sat–Sun, 10am–6pm; free). Its historic zone (Carrera 3, between Calles 3 and 6) has the requisite **Cathedral**, and colonial structures around Plaza Juan Maldonado Ordóñez and Villaquirán (honoring San Cristóbal's founder) and Plaza Rafael Urdaneta. The architecture of buildings surrounding **Plaza Bolívar** (Avenida 7 at Calle 9) present startling contrasts, with the elegantly ornate traditional design of the Salón de Lectura (cultural foundation, constructed 1907) on one side and modern Centro Cívico facing the other. Within the civic center is the **Museo de Artes Visuales y del Espacio** (1st floor, Torre B; Open Mon–Sat; 8am–noon, 2–7pm; Sun, 8am–1pm; free).

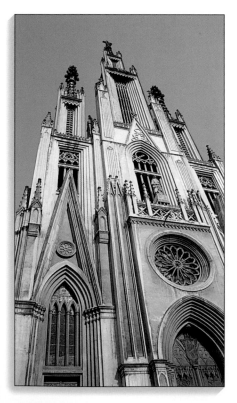

Fascinating architecture

Central San Cristóbal abounds with distinct architectural gems. Many such buildings, with a great variety of styles can be found along Carreras 9 and 10 between Calles 4 and 6: the epitome of the "wedding cake" and art nouveau styles are particularly evident in the elaborately decorated façades of the Universidad Abierto Nacional and its neighbor; a two-story private home with very traditional Spanish styling and whimsical owl sculptures incorporated in its window grilles. Another example worth a closer look is the colorful central doorway (the only part of the façade to have survived) of the former **Hospital Vargas** (Carrera 6, Calle Carabobo).

Three churches display particularly interesting designs: **El Angel**, on Carrera 23 at Pasaje Acueducto with the huge figure of an angel sculpted in its façade; the Gothic style **San José,** on Carrera 9 at Calle 8; and **El Santuario**, on Carrera 13 at Calle 13, built with stone blocks in shades of beige, ochre, and muted orange; the blocks of its interior space are painted pink, yellow, and blue).

Western loop

San Pedro del Río ⓴ is an obligatory stop. The beautifully restored colonial village is always delightful, but more so during the Christmas season when numerous *pesebres* (nativity scenes) are erected in the streets.

During Easter Week, live passion plays and processions take place throughout Ureña. Neighboring Aguas Calientes is sought out for its hot springs. **San Antonio de Táchira** ⓴ is the lively commercial border town marking the entry point to Colombia. Some nearby villages are of interest: Rubio is noted for its unusual brick church, while Independencia and Libertad (a.k.a. Capacho Viejo and Capacho Nuevo) are famous for ceramics.

North and south

Palmira and **Abejales** (above Táriba) are known for its split-cane baskets, while the main plaza in **Peribeca** is ringed by craft shops, cafés, and places selling local culinary specialties; there is also a distinctive Alpine-style church. Just above it is **El Topón**, a typical farm village which has been developed as a tourist attraction. Traveling between Páramo, La Negra, and Zumbador, you can enjoy beautiful mountain landscapes and traditional architecture.

The area around **Santa Ana** ⓴, to the south, is an important coffee-growing region, and nearby **La Alquitrana** was the site of Venezuela's first oil well. ❑

TIP

A drive on the road between Zumbador and Michelena should not be missed; it follows the crest of the mountains most of the way and offers spectacular views.

BELOW:
mule transport in Táchira.

OIL IN TACHIRA

Although most people assume that Zulia was the birthplace of Venezuela's petroleum industry, this is not the case. La Alquitrana (between Santa Ana and Rubio) holds that honor. Parque la Petrolia now marks the spot where, in 1875, oil began seeping out of the ground on the land of Manuel Antonio Pulido. He obtained mineral rights and formed La Compañía Nacional Minera Petrolia de Táchira. Initially, oil was extracted in buckets from hand-dug pits, but after a trip to Pennsylvania to check out the petroleum industry there, in 1880, Pedro Rincones (an associate of Pulido) shipped back a cable-tool drilling rig to be incorporated.

In 1882, a primitive distillation unit was installed and the company also sank its deepest well, 42 meters (138 ft). Most of the 15 barrels a day produced was sold in Táchira for lighting. Petrolia remained the nation's only petroleum producer until 1907 when the first important concessions were granted. Its wells were still producing a small amount when its concession ran out in 1934. Some of the ancient artifacts associated with the pioneering company, including the remains of the rudimentary "refinery", are displayed in the attractive 10-hectare (25-acre) park.

THE LLANOS

The savannah is beautiful and terrible at the same time; it easily accommodates both beautiful life and atrocious death. The llanos *are terrifying; but this fear does not chill one's heart; it is hot like the great wind of its sunburnt immensity, like the fever from its swamps*

– RÓMULO GALLEGOS, *Doña Bárbara*

Map on page 250

Caracas

The vast, blisteringly hot plains, referred to as *los llanos*, hold a special place in Venezuela's mythology, something akin to the Great Plains of the United States, the pampas in Argentina and the outback of Australia. Opened up as cattle country in the 19th century, the area became a wild frontier of cowboys and ranchers about which modern Venezuelans still become dewy-eyed.

Taking up fully a third of the country's land mass, the region contains only a minuscule fraction of its population. A single paved highway links the few, widely scattered towns in the southern *llanos*, and hard-bitten *llaneros* (as this Venezuelan breed of cowboy is known) still chase herds on horseback across the plains.

Along with this lingering "Wild West" feel, the *llanos* comprise one of the great wildlife-watching areas of South America. More bird species can be seen here than in the United States and Great Britain combined, and in such abundance that binoculars are hardly necessary. Crocodiles inhabit the lagoons; jaguars prowl its fields (though are rarely sighted by visitors) and, with luck, freshwater porpoises can be spotted in the rivers.

A macho past

Eleven Spanish families were the initial colonial settlers to move into the *llanos*, introducing the first cattle ranch near the modern town of Calabozo in 1548. The production of leather and salted meat were crucial in colonial Venezuela, and the march of hooves proved unstoppable: 200 years later, more than 130,000 head of cattle roamed the enormous ranches, *hatos,* of the *llanos* while local indian tribes had all but disappeared.

Despite the economic importance of the *llanos* and the contribution made to the independence struggle (*llanero* troops made up the backbone of Bolívar's army), the area has often aroused mixed emotions in the rest of the country. While its inhabitants were admired for their toughness, honesty and frontier spirit, they were at first feared as barbaric, then later mocked for their backwoods slowness and lack of sophistication. Their homeland was viewed as a hot and primitive backwater best avoided by civilized folk.

When oil was discovered in Zulia in the 1920s, the country began turning its back on the *llanos*. After all, if Venezuela needed beef, it could be imported just as cheaply from abroad. Suffering from attitudes such as this, the *llanos* stagnated for decades, and only after the oil crisis of the early 1980s did Venezuelans again think of developing the vast resources to the south.

PRECEDING PAGES: a line-up of Venezuelan cowboys, *llaneros*. **LEFT:** the man with the golden grin. **BELOW:** *llaneros* rope a steer on Hato Doña Bárbara.

Even so, every country needs the folk memory of a romantic past, and there is a lingering feeling that the *llanos* somehow embody the "real Venezuela." Photographs of the *llanos* still hang in many Venezuelan bars, dignitaries occasionally dress in the typical *llanero* collar of the *liqui-liqui* (traditional *llano* costume) and, most importantly, the *llanos* provided the setting for the most famous Venezuelan novel: *Doña Bárbara*.

Written by Rómulo Gallegos in 1929, it is a melodramatic and bleakly sexist work about a woman called Bárbara, who is gang-raped when young and learns to dominate and destroy men in revenge. By a mixture of seductiveness, malice and the threat of witchcraft, she becomes the virtual ruler of the otherwise male-dominated *llanos* – that is, until an upright man from Caracas awakens her long-repressed feminine instincts and finally destroys her.

The novel nicely sums up Venezuelans' ambivalence towards the *llanos*. The hero, Santos Luzardo, finally marries Doña Bárbara's abandoned daughter – thereby bringing the refined elements of the urban dweller together with the raw, natural spirit of the frontier, and ensuring a neat ending.

White-necked heron on the llanos.

Central flatlands

The stereotypical image of the *llanos* – and indeed the principal destination for tourists visiting this region – is that of the sparsely inhabited lands south of the Apure River in the state of the same name. However, the great plains of Venezuela actually include a wide band of land stretching for nearly 1,000 km (600 miles) through the entire mid-section of the country, extending from the base of the Andes all the way to the banks of the Orinoco River marking the western border of Delta Amacuro.

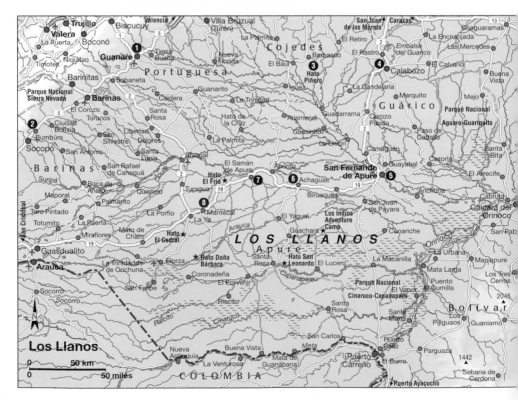

For geomorphological reasons, the *llanos* are divided into the "western plains" Portuguesa and Barinas), "central plains" (Guárico and Cojedes), "eastern lains" (Anzoátegui and Monagas), and "southern plains" (Apure).

Map on page 250

Dramatic climate changes

n the wet season (May to November), the lower *llanos* is so flooded that it ooks like an inland sea. Roughly 80 percent of the land of the southern and central *llanos* is under water. Many sections of even its elevated roads are covred, and cattle have to be driven to outcrops of higher ground to prevent their rowning. The dry season (December to April) is the best time of year to see vildlife, since animals congregate around receding watering holes. With the otal absence of rain for nearly six months, one can also see many animals, uch as the anaconda (one of the world's largest snakes), trapped to die in the hick mud that remains as the watering holes disappear.

All year round the heat of the *llanos* is intense – although "winter" (the wet eason) is, predictably, much more humid. In both seasons, the desolate plains re hauntingly beautiful.

Routes for visitors

ndependent travelers with their own transportation have several routes from vhich to choose. They can head almost directly south from Caracas via Somrero and Calabozo to San Fernando de Apure – the capital of Apure state, then vest to La Ye through lands which are the epitome of the *llanos* image. For the elatively flat but fertile western section, go west from Caracas via Valencia nen to San Carlos, Acarigua, Guanare and Barinas – the four main towns of the

BELOW: San Juan de Los Morros, gateway to the *llanos*.

The Llaneros

The *llaneros* of Venezuela stand alongside the gauchos of Argentina as the finest horsemen in the history of South America. The true *llaneros* have now all but died out, and their descendants are rapidly shedding *llanero* traditions and dress. But even so, small groups of these tropical cowboys can still be seen on ranches in the plains of Apure and Barinas, rounding up and branding cattle using traditional skills or listening to melancholy *llanero* ballads.

The *llaneros* come from a racial mix dating back some 400 years, combining the blood of Spanish frontiersmen, escaped black slaves and local indians. It was during the lawless colonial days that the *llaneros* developed the distinctive customs that can still, on occasion, be seen today: their own working style and a tropical variation on the classic cowboy dress – wooden stirrups, woollen ponchos (often worn in the rain, despite oppressive heat), and straw hats.

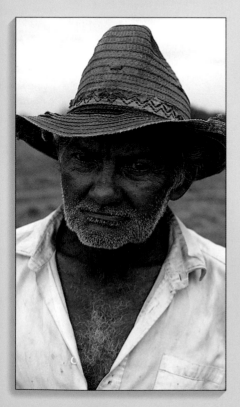

A haunting form of music began to accompany *llanero* ballads, usually about knife fights, sexual conquests or prowess in breaking horses. In this macho cult, leaders won respect for their skills in the field, and once proven, could demand total loyalty.

The German explorer Alexander von Humboldt was impressed by the *llaneros'* toughness, especially their diet of pure salted meat, but also noted their laziness. "Being always in the saddle, they fancy they cannot make the slightest excursion on foot," he recorded. Despite their abundance, cows were never milked, and during summer, *llaneros* preferred to drink fetid yellow water rather than dig a well.

Even so, the hard-living *llaneros* became a terrifying fighting force during the wars of independence, first on the side of the Spaniards and only later with Bolívar. They made up the backbone of the Liberator's army, fighting without food or pay – instead taking both from the towns and villages they brutally pillaged. *Llaneros* did not even need to be supplied with arms, since they took a fresh supply of lance points from every outcrop of palm trees they found.

In the end, the average *llanero* gained little from his contribution to Venezuela's independence. By law, every *llanero* was given some land as reward – but the small plots proved impossible to work profitably. Wealthy officers were easily able to buy up the smaller lots, and a new landowning class was born. Most families owning *hatos* today are descended from these purchasers.

The rest of the 19th century saw a boom in beef exported to Europe, along with the declining freedom of the *llanero*. However, just as the Venezuelan cowboy began to disappear as part of an identifiable group, writers and intellectuals began to romanticize him as embodying important traits of the "national character": independence, toughness, an egalitarian spirit born of living in the wild. It was a mish-mash of values similiar to those being praised in diminishing frontiers as far away as Argentina, Australia and the US, with the *llanero* standing in contrast to the sickly, Europeanized city-dwellers, cut off from the primal forces of nature. ❏

LEFT: *llanero* gaze.

western and central plains states. From Barinas, travelers can connect with La Ye. If you want to visit the other main town, apart from Calabozo and Sombrero, in the high *llanos*, detour south to El Baúl (extending this drive to Arismendi offers some great opportunities for wildlife watching).

The western and central plains

The country's richest farmlands are found in the "western plains", particularly in Portuguesa. The area also has its attractions for tourists. In **Guanare ❶**, capital of Portuguesa, for instance, there is the interesting **Museo de los Llanos** which includes in its grounds a *posada* with western theme (closed Mon; free); and, a short distance to the west of Guanare, the impressive **Templo Votivo Nacional a la Virgen de Coromoto**, the monumental national sanctuary and highly revered pilgrimage site honoring Venezuela's patron saint, which was formally dedicated by the Pope during his visit in 1995.

Barinas has various groupings of petroglyphs located near **Bumbúm ❷** and, recently, river rafting has also become popular here too – not just for the white-knuckle exhilaration of the activity, but because those taking part can also enjoy the observation of abundant wildlife in the calmer stretches.

One of the highlights for visitors to Cojedes is **Hato Piñero ❸**, east of El Baúl, the pioneer in Venezuela of the ranches installing tourist facilities. In fact, this was an outgrowth of the Branger family's 80,000-hectare (200,000-acre) cattle ranch which had functioned since 1953 as a private wildlife refuge for the recovery of endangered species and the conservation of those which abound on their land; in 1982 a biological station was set up to facilitate the work of researchers studying the flora and fauna of the zone.

Map on page 250

TIP

While in Guanare, be sure to stop at the Basilica dedicated to the Virgin of Coromoto (facing the Plaza Bolívar) to admire its beautiful 18th-century altar piece and silver tabernacle.

BELOW: round-up time.

TIP

For the best wildlife sightings, independent travelers through Apure should make their "crossing" from west to east, since the greatest concentration of animals is in the western portion and they are at their most active in the first hours of daylight.

The installation of tourism facilities came about in answer to the many requests for a place to stay by avid birders and researchers (the income now goes to support the biological station). With land that includes a variety of life zones more typical of this section of the "high plains" – ranging from hills covered with semi-evergreen forests to wetlands and savannah subject to annual flooding – the variety of fauna is tremendous.

San Juan de los Morros, capital of Guárico state, with its backdrop of a grouping of pink sandstone *morros*, or promontories, from which its name derives, is considered "the gateway to the *llanos*" from the central region. Just minutes from **Calabozo** ❹ is the closest of the "dude" or tourist ranches, in the *llanos*, Chinea Arriba.

Into the wilderness

The city of **San Fernando de Apure** ❺ (population 40,000), capital of Apure state, has little appeal. The streets are mostly lined by undistinguished buildings, although one, the old Palacio Barbarito (the old customs building), is worth a look. Hunters at the turn of the 20th century would bring here egret feathers they had collected, for export to Europe and the United States. The trade in these feathers was so valuable that it was the cause of ambushes, gun fights and blood feuds. Locals say that one particularly large shipment of egret feathers actually led to seven deaths.

Adjacent to this building is a *redoma* (traffic roundabout) with an unusual concrete fountain based on a crocodile motif. And in another nearby roundabout is a bronze statue of Pedro Camejo, on a rearing mount with spear in hand, one of the most famous *llanero* lancers who fought in the independence struggle, hero-

BELOW: a saddle sale in San Fernando de Apure.

cally dying at General Páez's feet at the Battle of Carabobo. Ringing the statue
are glass containers with samples of earth from various battlefields where he
fought around the country. Within sight of the plaza, craftsmen often set up
informal stalls from the backs of their pick-up trucks, selling a variety of leather
goods: new saddles, stirrups, bullwhips and leather boots. Other stores sell
small carvings made from *azabache*, a petrified wood that is like a smooth
black stone. Meanwhile, at the Apure River docks, motorboats and *bongos* (big
dugout canoes fitted with outboard motors) load up with goods for delivery as
far away as Ciudad Bolívar.

Map
on page
250

*Bracket fungi found
in the* llanos.

Making the drive between San Fernando de Apure and **La Ye**, small towns
such as **Achaguas ❻** and **El Samán ❼** begin to appear, each with a "Wild
West" atmosphere so strong that they feel like a Latino version of old Hollywood film sets.

In **Mantecal ❽**, the largest settlement en route, unshaven men stand on the
unpaved street corners, thumbs hooked in their jeans and cowboy hats cocked
at a Clint Eastwood angle. Occasionally a *llanero* will amble by on horseback,
or tie up his mount at a roadside post. The image continues in the bars, where
everyone is served standing up and although they would not refuse to serve a
woman, there is little doubt these are strictly male domains.

In these steaming rural outposts, people tend to work from 4am to around
noon, leaving the afternoon for a long siesta before returning to their labors
after the heat of the day. Even the truck drivers stop work then, hitching up
their hammocks in the shade beneath their rigs to take a snooze.

The heart of the *llanos*

Beyond Mantecal, the landscape changes from scrub
to the classic Venezuelan savannah. The grassy plains
stretch off to the horizon in every direction, and the
only trees are perched on occasional isolated hillocks
(*metas*), lost in the distance.

BELOW: a local
Arauco indian.

Driving through here, it is easy to sympathize with
the German scientist Alexander von Humboldt (*see
page 173*), who was aghast at the landscape during a
journey in the 18th century. "There is something
awful… about the uniform aspect of these steppes,"
he wrote. "All around us the plains seem to ascend to
the sky, and the vast and profound solitude appears
like an ocean covered with seaweed. Through the dry
mist… the trunks of palm trees are seen from afar,
stripped of their foliage and… looking like the masts
of ships descried upon the horizon."

The road here is elevated for the rainy months. In
the early 1970s the Venezuelan government started
building dikes (locally called *módulos*) to help control the devastation and to save water for the dry season. These, combined with *préstamos* (artificial
lagoons) that were privately installed on the sprawling ranches, provide areas of small, muddy "lakes"
adjacent to the highway, are utterly teeming with
wildlife during the dry season.

On this route, you'll be lucky to see a vehicle every
hour, so it is easy to pull over for some wildlife-
watching without animals being disturbed by passing

traffic. A great deal can be seen just from the road. White egrets pick among the reeds. Clouds of colorful birds erupt from the watering holes. Crocodiles – known as *babas* – and turtles sun themselves in the mud by the lagoons' shores, although they will disappear in a flash at any noise.

Tourist-friendly ranches

Although independent travel through the *llanos* is possible, most visitors opt to stay at one of the ranches offering tourist packages. Verify the specific dates for the change between high and low season prices before you commit yourself. And booking a week before or a week after can save you considerable cash.

While the ranches of the northern part of the plains previously mentioned are certainly enjoyable, the heart and soul of this region still remains in the *llanos adentro* – the interior of Apure state. Catering to visitors' fascination with the lifestyle of the ranches and the fabulous fauna, various ranches have followed the lead of Hato Piñero in actively working in the area of wildlife conservation. Many places now offfer similar packages with lodging, meals, and excursions to observe the flora and fauna (some also specialize in fishing for peacock bass, which abound in its rivers (*see Participant Sports, pages 105–9*).

The best known of these ranches are Hato El Cedral, Hato Doña Bárbara, Los Indios Adventure Camp, Cinaruco Bass Lodge, Campamento Sorocaima, and Aventura San Leonardo Reserva Ecológica. (The extremely popular and well-regarded **Hato El Frío** – which also has a biological station – unfortunately closed its tourist facilities in 1998.)

One of the attractions of the ranches is being able to see their everyday workings. Early in the morning *llaneros* can be seen rounding up the longhorn cattle

BELOW: the *hoatzin* is part of the exotic wildlife of the *llanos*.

Map on page 250

round the ranch, often chasing after them with lassoes. They also give demonstrations of their extraordinary riding skills, and how to swing cattle to the ground by their tails. Milking cows by hand is another dying tradition that is kept up.

Abundant wildlife

From all of the *hatos* in the area, excursions on horseback, by boat, and in trucks especially outfitted for photo safaris are made to observe the astounding variety and quantity of fauna. Birds are a dominant feature, and it is not unusual to ride over a ridge in the farm and see a lagoon full of roseate spoonbills sieving food through their beaks– and then to be able to watch them unmolested for several minutes before they disappear in a graceful cloud.

The *llanos* are also a habitat of the world's largest rodent, the web-footed capybara (known here as the *chigüire*), which is as much at home in the water as on land. The rivers may be infested with piranhas and electric eels, which deliver a nasty shock. So swimming here is not recommended, despite the heat.

Monkeys, such as the red howler and capuchin are frequently seen, as well deer. But don't count on seeing a wildcat. Although species including pumas, ocelots, and jaguars are found here, most visitors will be lucky even to see tracks in the mud of these human-wary animals.

A stay in the *llanos* turns out to be surprisingly affecting. Along with the heat and barrenness, the extremes of flooding and dryness, there is the serenity of being lulled to sleep by crickets or the distant haunting song of a ranch hand; or watching the activity of birds at dawn or with the background of a brilliant red sunset. Many people find that images from the *llanos* linger in their minds more clearly than recollections of yet another Caribbean beach. ❑

TIP

Although some ranches receive tourists all year long, the dry season (Dec–Apr) is the best time for wildlife observation.

BELOW: the capybara, whose numbers are multiplying thanks to their protection on the *hatos*.

THE *LLANOS* – A VENEZUELAN SAFARI

Protected on huge ranches, where protection of thecountryside is the norm, the abundance of wildlife on the llanos *is mind-boggling*

Covering nearly a third of Venezuela, from the base of the Andes in the west to the delta of the Orinoco River in the east, the vast, plains, or *llanos*, present a stunning vista: huge ranches (*hatos*) and enormous expanses of land, but scant human population. They include the richest farmlands in the country in the high northwestern plains, yet even dry grasses struggle to survive in the lowlands to the south where, during the May to November rainy season, they take on the appearance of a huge inland lake; while in the other half of the year, months pass with scarcely a drop of rain, turning the land rock-hard and scarred by deep cracks.

WILDLIFE HAVENS

Thanks to scarce human interference on the extensive ranches, wildlife abounds. Many of the *hatos*, realizing the importance of conserving this treasure, have become self-designated wildlife reserves, with strict "no hunting" policies.

Some half a dozen *hatos* have established ecotourism camps as an up-and-coming sideline, complete with organized excursions by boat, 4x4s, on horseback… geared specifically toward observation and photography of the wildlife. Many have also compiled checklists of fauna found on their spreads (on most, numbers of bird species alone exceed 300!).

Aside from the species diversity, the quantity of animals that gathers around shrinking water holes during the dry season is stunning, making it obvious why the Venezuelan *llanos* are a lure for nature lovers.

◁ **MATERNITY WARD**
During the rainy season, ibises (*shown here*) and other water birds gather in huge flocks in tree-top areas, called *garceros*, to build their nests.

△ **TURTLE TOTER**
Reptiles abound in *llanos* rivers and lagoons, including the *babas*, or spectacled caiman; the hu[...] Orinoco crocodile; as well as several species of turtle[...]

◁ **ROLLING PLAINS**
The concentration of huge ranches and lack of urban development on the *llanos* have meant that enormous areas of countryside have remained unspoilt and provided safe haven for rare plant and animal species.

△ **OLD WAYS KEEP GOING**
Many traditions and working practices on the ranches have changed little over the centuries, such as boiling down sugar cane juice to make a thick, honey-like syrup.

WHERE ALSO THE BUFFALO ROAM

For the *llaneros* – the tough, independent inhabitants of the *llanos* – the central plains have been synonymous with *hatos* and cattle-raising since colonial times. Some of the ranches have bred cattle that are very resistant to the local climate and environment. Among these ranches, Hato Piñero in Cojedes state has become one of the most prestigious in South America for its work with pure-breds and for crossing breeds as diverse as ones from India and Pakistan, Holstein and Swiss Brown from Europe, and Longhorns – descendants of herds brought over by Spanish colonizers.

In recent years, many *hatos* have even introduced water buffalo, found to be well adapted to the tropical climate and producing a higher yield of meat and milk than traditional cattle. A whole new side industry has been developed on many *hatos*: making world-class mozzarella cheese!

SWIMMERS BEWARE!
thers should check before nging into rivers and es here – they might be ested with piranhas, ngry caiman or the ormous anaconda.

▷ **FOR THE BIRDS**
Hundreds of bird species live here, including macaws, herons, ibis, storks, vultures, hawks, the highly eccentric hoatzin and white egrets (*shown here.*)

▽ **MEDLEY OF MONKEYS**
Various species of monkeys can be found on the *llanos*, including the highly vocal *araguato* – red howler, and the tiny capuchin monkey (*shown here.*)

GUAYANA REGION

This region has lured fortune-hunters, inspired great writers and left explorers and tourists with indelible memories

The entire area to the south and east of the Orinoco River – encompassing the states of Amazonas, Bolívar, and Delta Amacuro – comprises Venezuela's Guayana Region. Despite accounting for nearly 50 percent of the nation's territory, it shelters less than 6 percent of the population – many of whom are indigenous peoples. There are more than a dozen different groups, ranging from those who have had significant contact with *criollos* (people of mixed Spanish-American descent) to others who, because of the remoteness of their homelands, have changed little since the Stone Age.

The region's name comes from its geological base: the Guayana Shield of pre-Cambrian rock, nearly 3 billion years old, among the most ancient on earth. The oldest parts of this formation are concentrated in the entire Gran Sabana region of Bolívar state and in the *tepuyes* of Amazonas.

Without a doubt, the region's most distinctive features are its *tepuyes* – mesas of ancient rock formed through a process of erosion over millennia and towering majestically above the surrounding grasslands or jungle. Those who have explored their summits describe the environment as seeming to be from another place and time, incomparable with anywhere else. And, indeed it is. Isolated from the surrounding land for millions of years, a great percentage of the flora and fauna is endemic, having evolved to adapt to the extremes of temperatures and, in the past, having also faced glaciation. Constant wind and rain have likewise affected the plants and animals, along with creating other-worldly formations.

A great motivation for exploration here by the earliest adventurers and conquistadores was the lure of riches based on the legend of El Dorado: Prince Dorado, a descendant of the Incas fleeing from the Spanish, was believed to have founded a kingdom of great treasures in the city of Manoa, a golden capital located somewhere in this region.

While the Europeans fruitlessly searched for this city, they failed to realize that fabulous treasure was really there – below the ground on which they were walking. The region has proven to be among the world's richest in mineral resources, with enormous reserves of gold, iron, bauxite, diamonds, magnesium, and more. Now, it is valued not just for its minerals, but for its great wealth of biodiversity and the role of its vast expanses of virgin rainforests as a supplier of oxygen to the world. Moreover, tapping the power of its mighty rivers, without destroying the water resources, has permitted non-contaminating generation of electricity to assure the progress of a nation.

The Guayana Region's great natural beauty and its diverse attractions has also opened the doors for tourism, letting visitors in on some of the region's secrets. ❑

PRECEDING PAGES: the banks of the Orinoco; the Canaima Lagoon, Gran Sabana.
LEFT: more than a dozen groups of indigenous peoples live in the Guayana Region.

Map on page 270

DELTA AMACURO

With the opening of tourist camps in the interior of this water wonderland, visitors have a chance to observe its abundant fauna and learn about its principal inhabitants, the Warao indians

Caracas

Delta Amacuro state was first visited by Spanish explorers in 1532, it has thousands of kilometers of roads, and some 370 km (230 miles) of coastline along the Atlantic Ocean – yet few visitors have had contact with the natural beauties and indigenous inhabitants of this extraordinary environment. The principal reason for the delta's relative anonymity is the fact that except for roughly 100 km (60 miles) of routes which can be traveled by land vehicles round the capital, Tucupita, the delta's system of "roadways" is all fluvial: hundreds of fingers and arms of the Orinoco River, known as *caños,* which divide the delta into countless humid islands covered with dense foliage. The state's name comes from the Amacuro River, in its southern sector, which merges its delta with that of the Orinoco.

PRECEDING PAGES: Warao indian stilt houses on the delta. LEFT: view across one of the world's largest deltas. BELOW: adventurers take to the water.

great river

For millennia, the world's eighth-largest river, the 2,140-km (1,330-mile) long Orinoco has surged toward the Atlantic, creating some 44 meters (144 ft) of new land each year. There, the exceptionally strong Equatorial Current has forced the mighty river to deposit its load of sediment along the coast, creating one of the world's largest deltas and Venezuela's youngest state (since 1991). Seventy percent of the national territory and a portion of the Colombian Andes and plains are part of the Orinoco basin, with 2,000 rivers (including 196 of the largest in Venezuela, fed by 530 tributaries) emptying over 1.1 trillion cubic meters (31.4 trillion cubic ft) of water into the Atlantic Ocean each year.

The Warao

The geography has dictated that since the delta's original inhabitants, the Warao indians, settled here in prehistoric times, their entire lifestyle has revolved around the water, with the Orinoco considered "The Mother of our Land".

Warao means "the boat people" in their language, and from the earliest days of the discovery and conquest of Venezuela, the Warao became famous for their skill as dug-out canoe builders and navigators, being sought after as shipwrights and seamen by explorers from many nations.

The Warao are a fishing society, even though certain fish, such as catfish, are not eaten because of their supposed magical qualities. They have also hunted birds since mythological times, but marsupials, snakes, primates, and carnivores are never eaten. It is only recently that small animals such as agouti and small reptiles such as iguana have been considered acceptable for food. The traditional Warao aversion to hunting larger wild animals is because these are

considered "people of the forest," with blood like that of man. Eating the
would therefore be like cannibalism. These indians practised no agricultu
before 1860. Now, the root vegetables *ocumo* (taro) and yucca are staples.

The Warao usually live in small extended family groups, but apart from th
their social organization is very weak. According to sociologists, the Warao
not even consider they belong to a nation. However, all speak the same la
guage. There are currently about 14,000 Warao living in Guyana, Surinar
and principally in Delta Amacuro.

*The one curious
attraction of Tucupita
is its new Cathedral,
an amazingly huge
and imposing
structure considering
the small and
generally poor
population.*

Few settlements

Except for small settlements established by missionaries in the interior, only tv
main towns have developed: Pedernales (at the northeastern extreme) and tl
capital of Tucupita (along its midwestern border).

In the past, **Pedernales ❶** (accessible only by boat or small private plan
enjoyed a great economic boom when oil was exploited on nearby **Cotorr
Island ❷**. When the operating firm abandoned the well three decades ago, tl
economy tumbled and most of the population departed. However, with tl
Petroleum Opening initiated in 1994 and reactivation of the old fields ther
Pedernales is again enjoying a boom as preliminary work is taking place f
production anticipated to begin in the year 2000.

Tourist camps

Although **Tucupita ❸** is easily reached by road, it is hardly a tourist mecc
However, the genuine attraction in the ecotourism sector has been the estat
lishment of some ten tourist camps in the delta's interior.

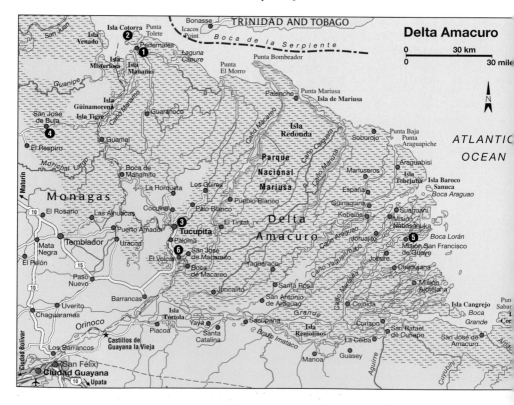

Most are concentrated roughly halfway between the capital and the coast along near Caño Manamo, the major channel defining the state's western border, ιich empties into the Atlantic at Pedernales. Previously, tourists were transrted by boat from Tucupita. But now, since Tucupita's airport has been out of tion for several years, most tourists arrive by plane to Monagas' Maturín airrt, from where they are transferred by land to **San José de Buja ④** for a fairly ort boat via the *caño,* taking them directly to the zone of the main camps. The ιer camps, mostly clustered around the **Misión San Francisco de Guayo ⑤** ιar the mid-eastern coast, require a day-long boat ride. The usual departure int is the port of **El Volcán ⑥** (near Tucupita).

Regardless of their location or degree of comfort, all the camps try hard to ve visitors a feel of life in the delta. They offer boat excursions to visit indigeus communities living in Warao-style *palafitos* dwellings (built on piles at ᵉ water's edge), and a chance to observe the abundant flora and fauna.

Spending several days and nights in this environment is an incomparable perience. Without artificial lighting to interrupt darkness, the night sky comes ve with stars. Without TV, radio or traffic, city dwellers may have their first counter with natural silence, broken only by the "night music" of crickets and ιgs. As dawn approaches, nature's alarm clocks – howler monkeys, toucans, ιcaws, and countless other birds – begin sounding their wake-up calls. On cursions, you will be able to observe the uncomplicated manner in which the ιrao live in harmony with nature, as well as watch the women weave their ιutiful baskets (surprisingly, not a traditional craft) and hammocks from ›riche palm fiber or artisans carving animals from the light, white wood of the ›agon's Blood tree; you can purchase crafts directly from them. ❏

Map on page 270

TIP

Freshly caught river fish, such as *lau-lau, morocoto,* and *sábalo,* feature in Tucupita's restaurants and at the tourist camps.

BELOW: a Warao indian house on the Orinoco delta.

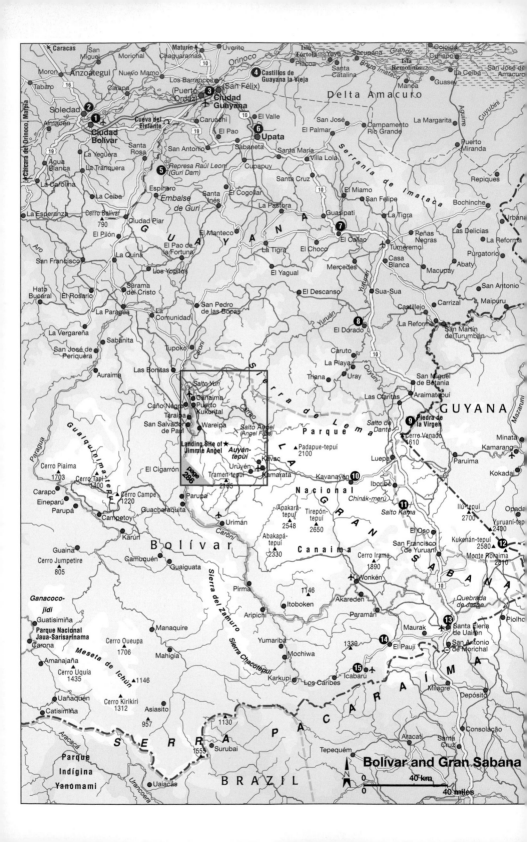

Bolívar and Gran Sabana

NORTHERN BOLIVAR

*The important cities of Ciudad Guayana and Ciudad Bolívar
are full of surprises for the visitor. But the gold-obsessed
El Dorado is no place for dreamers*

Map
on page
274

Caracas

The Guayana Region's two largest cities, as well as Venezuela's center for
heavy industry, are located in the northeast corner of Bolívar state on the
banks of the Orinoco River. Ciudad Guayana is the site of giant steel and
aluminum plants, while Ciudad Bolívar is of greater historical importance.

Historic capital

The capital of Bolívar state, **Ciudad Bolívar** ❶ is a relaxed colonial city. It was
founded in 1764 as Santo Tomás de la Guayana de Angostura – Angostura
(meaning "narrows") for short – because its site was chosen at a point where the
Orinoco River is less than a mile wide. During the independence struggle,
Simón Bolívar used Angostura as a base to regroup after his early defeats.

On February 15, 1819, the Liberator installed the Congress of Angostura and
gave his celebrated speech proposing the ideals of a free and united South
American federation. Twenty-seven years later, Congress renamed the city in his
honor. For the next century, Ciudad Bolívar was the key transhipment point for
goods from the interior to markets around the world.

Ciudad Bolívar developed in tandem with its sister city, **Soledad** ❷, across
the river, which could be reached by boat. It was only in 1967 that Soledad and
Ciudad Bolívar were linked by the Angostura sus-
pension bridge – still the only bridge to cross the
Orinoco over its 2,140 km (1,330 miles). It stretches
1,678 meters (5,505 ft), and is 57 meters (187 ft) above
the river at its highest point. Small motor launches
still ferry passengers between the two banks from
early morning to late at night.

A project is in the works – to be carried out on a
concession basis – for the construction of a second
bridge over the Orinoco, with the crossing point by
Puerto Ordaz. It will also include a rail and highway
link to a new deep-water port to be constructed on the
east coast near Cariaco in Sucre state.

Slow rhythm of life

Today, Ciudad Bolívar is a city of 100,000 people,
but it retains the feel of a small town. With an average
temperature of 28°C (82°F), the city's residents cher-
ish shade. Traditional homes face the Orinoco and
have floor-to-ceiling windows to take advantage of
the cool breezes (as well as the view). Commerce
grinds to a halt in the heat of the day while people
enjoy a siesta. In the evenings, families relax in the
shade of an open doorway or stroll by the river. The
waterfront remains a hive of activity, with many shops
located in the arcade on Paseo Orinoco. Here craftsmen work with precious gems and fashion gold into
distinctive brooches shaped like orchids.

PRECEDING PAGES:
the Angostura
bridge crosses the
Orinoco River.
BELOW: a room
with a view:
Ciudad Bolívar.

Across the street, overlooking the river and bridge, is the viewpoint, **Mirador Angostura** 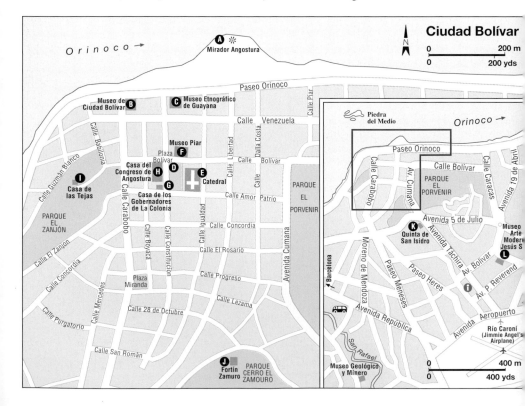. You can also see the calibrated rock, Piedra del Medio, which shows the depth of the river. Normally the Orinoco is highest in August and lowest in March, the end of the dry season.

On Paseo Orinoco, west of the Mirador, is the **Museo de Ciudad Bolívar** (closed Mon; free) where the *Correo del Orinoco* was formerly printed. It circulated from 1818 to 1822 as the government's official newspaper, established by Simón Bolívar and published in English as well as Spanish for the benefit of his British troops. Along with a display of the original printing press, are antiquities and a collection of works of art contributed to the museum.

One block east, the restored fortress-like former jail, now contains the **Museo Etnográfico de Guayana** (entrance on Calle Constitución), highlighting indigenous cultures of Bolívar state as well as housing historical archives.

Two blocks up from Paseo Orinoco takes you to the **Plaza Bolívar** , with statues representing the five countries Bolívar liberated – Venezuela, Colombia, Ecuador, Peru and Bolivia. Bordering the plaza is the **Cathedral** , dedicated to Nuestra Señora de las Nieves (Our Lady of the Snows) – a curious choice since snow is unknown here. The building was started in 1765, eventually completed in 1840, and restored in 1979.

Across the street is the **Museo Piar** (closed Mon; free), dedicated to General Manuel Piar, who was put to the firing squad against the side wall of the church on October 16, 1817 as a "conspirator and deserter." One of the leaders of the independence struggle, Piar had refused to be subordinate to Bolívar and was accused of encouraging Venezuela's *pardos* (people of mixed blood, as Piar was himself) and slaves to begin their own rebellion.

The **Casa de los Gobernadores de La Colonia** , on the west side of the plaza, was built for the Spanish governors and is now the state government's headquarters. The influential Don Manuel Centurión lived here from 1766–77, while settling the district, founding towns and opening the first secondary school.

Next door is the elegant **Casa del Congreso de Angostura** , built in 1766–77 to house the national school of Guayana. It was later the site of the Congress of Angostura, and now has historical exhibits, art shows and salons for cultural events (open Tue–Sat 9am–noon, 4–7pm; Sun 9am–noon; free).

Although Angostura is now known as Ciudad Bolívar, the old name lives on in the world-famous Angostura bitters. A key ingredient in the still-secret recipe is derived from the bark of a local tree. A mixture of this substance with honey is said to have saved the life of German scientist Alexander von Humboldt in 1800, stricken with a fever following an expedition to the Upper Orinoco.

Solid foundations

Enormous boulders, called *lajas*, are found throughout the city, particularly in the old part of town near the waterfront. Since moving them for construction was out of the question, residents have simply worked them into the plans. Thus, one sees entire houses built atop mammoth rocks with relatively flat tops, buildings using them as one wall, with them protruding into rooms of houses.

An ideal place to see this is in **Parque El Zanjón**, a few blocks west of the plaza via the street on its upper side. Here, all the houses incorporate the *lajas* and a path has been defined between them with little pocket gardens planted in their crevices. One such house is a brick one known as **Casa de las Tejas** which was recently restored and is the focal point of the area.

Map on page 276

TIP

Parque El Zanjón offers one of the most picturesque points in the city to take a representative photo, including the aspect of the *laja* and old-style houses, with a backdrop of the Orinoco River and the Angostura Bridge.

BELOW: traditional homes in Ciudad Bolívar, facing the Orinoco River.

The Museo de Arte Moderno Jesús Soto.

BELOW: the Quinta de San Isidro, believed to be the site of Bolívar's historic address to the Congress of Angostura.

Old and new

Some 10 blocks to the south, entered from Paseo Héroes, is **Fortín Zamuro ⓙ**, named after a vulture for it site, poised on a hiltop, watching over the city. In colonial times a battery occupied this spot. The present fort, erected in 1901, saw military action as late as 1903 when General Juan Vicente Gómez waged a victorious battle to end a civil war (closed Mon; free).

From 1818 to 1819, Bolívar stayed at the **Quinta de San Isidro ⓚ**, supposedly penning his address to the Congress of Angostura here. The handsomely restored house, another structure built on *laja*, is now a museum (open daily except Thu, 9am–noon, 2–5pm; free).

On a more contemporary note, the **Museo de Arte Moderno Jesús Soto ⓛ** (open daily; free) features works by the world-famous kinetic artist. Soto was born here in 1923 and can occasionally be seen around town.

Mining heartland

The region's two principal iron mines are at El Pao and El Piar, south of Ciudad Guayana. Both are open-pit mines, the latter the entire top of a mountain called Cerro Bolívar.

In 1945, an expedition of US Steel geologists found the high-grade ore at Cerro Bolívar. Subsequent exploitation of iron ore here and at El Pao by Bethlehem and US Steel awakened the Venezuelan government's interest, resulting in nationalization of the mines in 1975.

In 1960, the **Corporación Venezolana de Guayana** (CVG) was created by presidential decree to develop the Guayana Region – initially just in Bolívar and Delta Amacuro, with later inclusion of Amazonas and even parts of Anzoátegui and Monagas. With the exclusion of petroleum, CVG controls the development of all the natural resources and basic industries in that region, as well as being responsible for development of public utilities, and economic, sporting, social and cultural affairs. 1997 was the year when privatization of some of the CVG companies began, principally in the area of the aluminum and steel industries.

Boom town

Ciudad Guayana ❸ was born in 1961, when the CVG fused Puerto Ordaz and San Félix with the industrial zone of Matanzas – at a sufficient distance west of Puerto Ordaz so that the city would not be affected by industrial contamination. The cities are linked by a double bridge over the Caroní River. The population of this thriving metropolis is now approximately 600,000 (expected to reach 2 million by 2030). Matanzas is the site of gargantuan steel, aluminum, and iron ore plants.

Puerto Ordaz was built in 1952 by the Orinoco Mining Company as its administrative headquarters for shipping iron ore abroad. At the wharf, you can see ore, which has been whisked by train from Cerro Bolívar, being loaded onto barges, and bauxite arriving from upriver at Los Pijiguaos. Many industrial executives make their homes in this part of town, while workers tend to live in San Félix.

Maps:
Area 274
City 276

From **Parque Cachamay** (closed Mon; token admission fee) which occupies 52 hectares (128 acres) next to the Hotel Inter-Continental Guayana, there is a great view of Cachamay and Llovizna Falls on the Caroní.

A visit to the very pretty **Parque Llovizna** (open daily; 9am–3pm; free), via the San Félix-El Pao road, offers a closer view of the falls. Nearby are the ruins of the **Caroní Mission Church**. The Spanish Capuchin monks who founded their first mission in the area in 1724 became successful cattle and horse breeders, and established towns and schools. These are all on land belonging to Edelca (Electrificación del Caroní) which keeps them beautifully maintained.

Downstream from Ciudad Guayana are the **Castillos de Guayana la Vieja ❹** (closed Mon; token fee), two forts built to protect San Tomé, Guayana's first Spanish settlement, against English, French and Dutch pirates. They are actually in Delta Amacuro state, but access is possible only by road from San Félix since their construction was designed to prevent access from the river.

The forts are poised on rocks high above the river. San Francisco was built 1678–84, on the site of the former monastery of San Francisco de Asís. The second fort, San Diego del Alcalá (or *El Padrastro* – the obstacle), built in 1747, is perched on a nearby hill. But even this was not enough of an obstacle to prevent pirate assaults, and eventually the settlement was moved up river for safety.

Giant dam

Another side trip from Ciudad Guayana follows the Ciudad Piar highway for about 90 minutes south along the Caroní River to **Guri Dam ❺**. Guayana's industrial development has relied on hydroelectric power provided by this giant, whose phased construction began in 1963. With the inauguration of Macagua II

BELOW: one of the many waterfalls near Puerto Ordaz.

Dam in 1997, another phase of the project, the complex's capacity is now 12,540 megawatts, among the world's largest. It supplies 70 percent of national electrical needs, including those of Ciudad Guayana's steel and aluminum plants, plus power for parts of northern Colombia. It will also soon supply Manaus, Brazil. Excellent free tours are available daily at Macagua II (10am and 2.30pm; it also has a visitors' center, open daily 10am–2.30pm, free) and at Guri (9am, 10am, 2pm, 3pm).

Guri's reservoir, the continent's fourth largest lake, is also a popular sport-fishing venue, featuring two of Venezuela's best freshwater game fish: feisty *pavón* (peacock bass) and *payara*.

A gold miner weighs his day's find.

Northwestern attractions

An enjoyable expedition can be made along the **Caura River**, where several tourist camps now operate, offering packages with rustic lodging, meals and excursions (the highlight of which is a trip to a waterfall called **Salto Para** by a Ye'Kwana indian community). This impressive cascade is reached via a three-hour trek through the jungle from a rustic base camp on a sandy river-front beach. As a bonus, at the indian settlement by the falls, visitors can buy exquisite, authentic crafts.

Continuing westward from Maripa (where the road crosses the Caura River) to Caicara de Orinoco, then south toward Puerto Ayacucho, you will see mammoth mountains of *laja*. In the area of the **Paraguaza River**, not far from the border of Amazonas state, there are various communities of Panare indians, most of whom wear traditional dress (men in what looks like a red diaper with a huge woollen pom-pom on each hip, and women with a short sarong-style skirt and bare-breasted). This road is paved and can be traveled in any car.

BELOW: an aerial view of the Guri Dam on the Caroní River.

En route to the Gran Sabana

From Ciudad Guayana to El Dorado is 296 km (184 miles). The latter is not only the last town of any size until you get to Santa Elena de Uairén near the Brazilian frontier, but marks the beginning of the count-down to the Gran Sabana.

Upata ❻ is basically a "dormitory" community of Ciudad Guayana, where many workers in the basic industries live. It is also considerably more economical, thus many travelers en route to the Gran Sabana choose to stay over in its large, comfortable but economical Hotel Andrea rather than in Ciudad Guayana (where options are quite expensive or quite ghastly).

Guasipati, El Callao, Tumuremo, and El Dorado are all "gold towns", getting progressively rougher as you proceed southward. Hotels, the few that are available here, are all pretty basic and generally do not cater for tourists.

El Callao ❼ enjoys two claims to fame – seemingly unrelated, but intimately linked: gold and Carnival. When news spread about incredibly high-grade ore found near the Yuruarí River in 1849, the gold rush was on. Prospectors established a settlement there in 1853 called Caratal, subsequently moved it to the banks of the Yuararí River and renamed it E

Callao. Among these fortune hunters were great numbers from the British and French Antilles who introduced their languages and customs. One of the latter was celebration of Carnival, an expression of their culture through the music and dancing of the calypso.

Gold has had its ups and downs, with exploitation ceasing for many years before recent revival. However, Carnival in El Callao has been an on-going tradition with lively calypso music; people dancing in the streets; the dark-skinned *Madamas* in elaborate dress typical of the islands; dozens of *comparsas* (extras) costumed according to particular themes; and an all-pervading party atmosphere.

El Dorado

Founded at the confluence of the Cuyuní and Yuruári Rivers, a basin containing Venezuela's most important gold deposits, **El Dorado** ❽ has always been linked with gold. Legends about gold here started long before the first actual discoveries by miners. Persistent stories about a lost Inca empire with a treasure-filled palace sent many of the conquistadores on the gold trail.

Today, a stroll through the town will show that gold reigns supreme. Nearly every establishment announces "Gold bought and sold", offers *bateas* (large shallow wooden bowls used for panning) and other equipment used by informal miners, or is a shop featuring gold jewelry. El Dorado's less glamorous side is its reputation as a dangerous place because of continual confrontations between formal and informal miners. It is also the site of the infamous maximum-security prison known as "Las Colonias", made famous by its imprisonment of Papillon nickname of Frenchman Henri Charrière, author of the famous autobiographical novel of the same name). Today, as then, it is considered a hell-hole. ❑

Map on page 274

At El Dorado, the kilometer markings on the road are "reset," starting at 0 km. From that point on, locations for all sites through Gran Sabana en route to Santa Elena de Uairén are indicated by their distance in kilometers from that point.

BELOW: a dip in the Orinoco.

LA GRAN SABANA

The Great Savannah, long the stuff of legends and novels, contains the dramatic Angel Falls and is full of magical landscapes. The big growth area today is adventure tourism

Map on page 286

Caracas

How could a place that contains the Angel Falls (the highest and longest free drop of water in the world); the imposing Roraima *tepuy* (inspiration for Sir Arthur Conan Doyle to write *The Lost World*); and has rivers flowing over beds of semi-precious jasper, not fail to act as a magnet for those seeking intimate contact with one of Mother Nature's greatest works? For this reason La Gran Sabana (the great savannah) and Canaima are two of Venezuela's most popular vacation destinations for adventure and ecotourism.

Identity crisis

Depending on the reference, prime attractions such as Angel Falls and Roraima *tepuy* are sometimes identified as being in La Gran Sabana, other times in Canaima – both are correct. The 3 million hectares (7.4 million acres) of **Parque Nacional Canaima** (decreed as such in 1962) overlap most of the vast area known as **La Gran Sabana**. Thus, many of the most famous sites in this zone of southeastern Bolívar state have the double identity as far as location is concerned.

"Jungle Rudy's" Campamento Ucaima, opening in the mid-1950s, was the pioneer camp in the area near the lagoon and tiny indian village which shared the name of Canaima. His camp was established on the banks of the Carrao River with majestic *tepuyes* in the background. Campamento Hoturvensa (more commonly referred to as Campamento Canaima) was established by Avensa airlines in 1979 at the edge of the lagoon, with an enviable view of the falls "thrown in." The camps by the village of **Canaima** are in the northwestern extreme of the national park.

The promotion by these two operators (especially that of Hoturvensa with the clout of an airline for widespread publicity) put Canaima on the map. So much so that, to most people, "Canaima" is not the entire national park, it is the Hoturvensa camp; while "La Gran Sabana" is everything else in southeastern Bolívar.

The popularly understood separation of the two is further accentuated by the fact that the only practical access to Canaima is by air, while "visiting La Gran Sabana" by any means other than by road (to be able to easily visit the beautiful waterfalls and other attractions along its full length) is not even considered.

Hoturvensa and Ucaima are considered the "premium" camps at Canaima. To provide less expensive alternatives, various others have opened (while labeled as "camps" they are really just *posadas*). In order of attractiveness, the best choices are **arakaupa** – run by one of Jungle Rudy's daughters with its own restaurant), **Churún Vena** (installing a

PRECEDING PAGES: the towering *tepuyes* on the savannah. LEFT: Kavac tourist camp at the foot of Auyántepui. BELOW: Pemón indian woman with her daughter.

American journalist and explorer Ruth Robertson made the first accurate measurements of Angel Falls in 1949 on an expedition sponsored by the National Geographic Society. She was also responsible for world-wide diffusion of the name Angel Falls.

restaurant); and, without their own eating facilities: **Wey Tepuy**, **Kaikusé**, an **Kusari** (arrangements can be made to eat at one of the above with dining ha or to use the **Restaurante de Simón** – next to Churún-Vena in the village which offers tasty, economical meals). All except Ucaima are within walkin distance of each other and of the airstrip.

The star attraction of the park is **Angel Falls ☉**, named after its discoverer, Jim mie Angel (*see page 288*), which makes its dramatic plunge off of the edge c **Auyántepui ☉**, the largest *tepuy* in the Gran Sabana park, covering 700 sq kr (270 sq miles). This cataract is renowned for being the highest (978 meters/3,21 ft) falls with the longest free drop of water (807 meters/2,648 ft) in the world.

In the language of the Pemón indians, *Auyántepui* means Devil's Moun tain. According to their mythology, a group of evil spirits called *marawitó*, live on the summit together with a higher spirit, *Tramán-chitá*. Angel Falls i *Parecupá-merú* (*merú* means falls); however, it is often mistakenly referre to as *Churún-merú* – the identification of another impressive cataract at th end of Devil's Canyon.

Canaima's camps are the departure point for excursions to Angel Falls but none has a view of them – or even Auyántepui, since they are about 5 km (30 miles) away. To see the famous cataract, you must sign up for a rive excursion or view it by plane in a fly-over.

The premium camps generally offer packages that include lodging, meals and excursions. All major travel agencies offer these, while those that are mor specialized in adventure travel (such as Roymar in Caracas; tel/fax: 58(2)57 6272) create a number of their own package deals which offer a variety of com binations and a wider range of prices – from backpacker specials, sleeping i

BELOW: climbing Auyántepui.

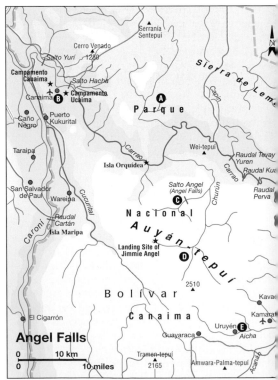

Map on page 286

hammocks and so on, to a far more luxururious option. Independent travelers can arrange tours in Canaima itself, with companies offering various combinations: as short as a half-day to those of several days.

Other northwest options

Uruyén ❺, near the southern base of Auyántepui (the opposite side from Angel Falls) has a simple but attractive camp (owned and operated by Pemón Indians) and an airstrip. This side is the departure point for travelers wishing to climb the *tepuy*. Previously the nearby camp of Kavac was heavily promoted by Aereotuy, with the highlight consisting of an excursion to a deep canyon (promoted as a "cave") with a beautiful cataract at the end. Sadly, due to lack of maintenance, the airstrip is now unusable, and the camp has been allowed to fall into a state of abandonment. Now, even tours to the "Cuevas de Kavac" depart from the nearby settlement of Uruyén.

Arekuna is a pretty premium camp operated by Aereotuy situated by the banks of the Caroní River, north of Canaima.

Route through La Gran Sabana

Before completion in 1991 of the excellent paved highway traversing the length of La Gran Sabana to Santa Elena de Uairén (now finished as far as Boa Vista in Brazil, too), a trip to La Gran Sabana was indeed an adventure. The first road was not cut through until 1973. Just dirt then, travel was possible only in caravans of several 4x4 vehicles to help each other in fording rivers or when stuck in deep sand or mud (and even then not during the rains).

Now, visitors in any normal city car can admire a marvelous variety of beau-

Camping en route to Auyántepui, a tough trek of at least 5 days to reach the summit.

BELOW: Angel Falls.

Jimmie Angel

The accidental discovery of the world's highest waterfall by the Missouri-born pilot Jimmie Angel has become an essential part of the mythology of the Gran Sabana. In 1921, Angel met the Alaskan geologist and explorer J.R. McCraken in a bar in Panama. McCraken told Angel about a mountain in South America with a river of gold. Angel told him he'd take him there for $3,000; to Angel's surprise, McCraken accepted. Angel landed in a remote spot in Bolívar state indicated by the Alaskan, who filled his sack with gold until Angel insisted on leaving as darkness was approaching.

Obsessed with the desire to find this treasure spot again, Angel dedicated the rest of his life in this pursuit.

McCraken had given only verbal directions as they flew, but Angel was sure the spot was on top of Auyántepui. In 1930, he returned with mining engineer Dick Curry, but couldn't land. On October 10 of that year, he tried anew, but foul weather again impeded landing.

In 1935, he convinced geologist F.I. "Shorty" Martin to get financing from the Case Pomeroy Company. They landed in Kamarata Valley and, on March 25, 1935, discovered the canyon of Auyántepui (now known as Devil's Canyon). "I saw a waterfall that almost made me lose control of the plane. The cascade came from the sky! But I still didn't have any luck in landing," said Angel.

However hard he tried, he couldn't find a place to land, so in 1937, he made an ascent accompanied by the Spanish sea captain and expert topographer, Felix Cardona Puig; and the engineer and explorer Gustavo Heny to survey possible landing sites. He then organized his fifth attempt, on this occasion accompanied by his wife Marie Sanders, Heny and Joe Meacham (owner of an Arizona nightclub). He landed on the top on October 9, 1937 in a Flamingo monoplane, Río Caroní. But it sank in the swampy ground, and he and his group had to hike down. The trek took them 11 days, but fortunately Heny was familiar with the route, and he led the group safely down to Kamarata.

Despite his continual search for the "river of gold", Angel never found the spot again.

He died in Panama in 1956 as the result of injuries suffered in a plane crash. He had left instructions that upon his death, he wanted to be cremated, with his ashes scattered over the falls that bore his name. This final, consoling wish was carried out.

In 1970, the Venezuelan Air Force (FAV) rescued his Flamingo in order to restore it for their 50th anniversary. It remained in the Museo Aeronáutico de Maracay until 1980, when it was moved to Ciudad Bolívar.

The American explorer and journalist Ruth Robertson, who made the first accurate measurements of the height of the falls in 1949, is credited with the naming of this natural phenomenon as "Angel Falls." Though much has been written about others who knew of the falls long before Jimmie Angel, he continues to be popularly credited with their discovery – perhaps because of his colorful character, or simply because this name best conveys a romantic image of the sparkling cascade of water, as if it were falling from the heavens. ❑

BELOW: Jimmie Angel's monoplane. After being rescued from the top of Auyántepui, it now waits to be returned to the spot where it landed.

Map on page 274

iful landscapes, unique flora, numerous waterfalls, and settlements of Pemón ndians on a comfortable, easy drive of just 227 km (141 miles) from Km 88 to Santa Elena de Uairén.

Major travel agencies offer all-inclusive tour packages for land travel, usually 3–4 days, typically including a visit to El Dorado and to a camp of informal gold miners, then on to hit all the standard stops en route to Santa Elena de Uairén.

If you are planning to fly to Ciudad Bolívar or Ciudad Guayana, then rent a vehicle there (normal car or 4x4); confirmed reservations paid well in advance are imperative, especially in high season. If driving, the ideal place to stay the night before starting through the Gran Sabana is in Las Claritas (Km 85). Although the town itself is the epitome of an Old West-style mining town, full of makeshift buildings and brothels, there are three good lodging options (all within walled or fenced compounds): Campamento Anaconda (tel: 086) 22 3130), Campamento Gran Sabana (tel/fax: (086) 22 8820), and El Chalet de Raymond (no phone).

The road enters the Canaima National Park and La Gran Sabana a short distance south of Las Claritas with the first landmark, **Piedra de la Virgen** ❾. Continue through the dense forest of the **Sierra de Lema**, and at Km 119.7 you will come to the **Salto de Danto** waterfalls.

Wide open spaces

As you emerge from the forest, the vast expanse of the high savannah stretches out in a breathtaking panorama: rolling hills covered with grasses, rivers bordered by *moriche* palms – and the first distant *tepuyes* to be seen on this drive.

All along the way are groupings (normally of extended families) of Pemón

The rainy season is the best time to visit the Angel Falls without risking the falls being reduced to a trickle. Climbing Auyántepui, however, is best done during the dry season, November to April.

BELOW: dining patio at Canaima jungle camp.

indian dwellings, along with various offerings of lodging (they are the only people permitted to reside in the national park or erect buildings), always located by a river to provide a source of water, including rustic camps with just empty *churuatas* to provide shelter from the elements for backpackers (Salto Kawi – Km 194.5; Quebrada de Pacheco – Km 238; Río Soroape – Km 243); ones with beds and some services (Salto Kama – Km 201.5); and even one place which not only has quite nice rooms with bath, but a large restaurant with good food, and a gasoline station (**Rápidos de Kamoirán** – Km 174; the only one with phone contact, tel/fax: 58(86)51 2729).

Near the National Guard outpost of **Luepa** (Km 147) is the side road to **Kavanayén** ⑩, with a relatively large Capuchin mission that offers basic dormitory-style accommodation. The route there is paved as far as the military airstrip, but a 4x4 vehicle is recommended to cover the rest. En route, a side road leads to **Iboribo**, the departure point in large motor-powered dug-out canoes for **Chinák-merú**, a beautiful falls on the Aponguao River, with a broad rock face over which a wall of water plunges.

The fragile landscape of the savannah hosts fascinating flora, including numerous carnivorous plants such as colonies of the tiny ruby sundew with its bright red "jaws", and huge expanses of vivid fuchsia-colored ground orchids.

Back on the main road, the next main attraction southward is **Salto Kama** ⑪ (Km 201.5). The waterfall faces west and is best photographed in the afternoon light, when there rainbows form in the mist produced from its high drop.

San Francisco de Yuruaní is the departure point for scaling **Roraima** ⑫ or **Kukenán** *tepuyes* – the latter is considered the hardest (it is obligatory to use the indigenous guides for both ascents). The normal round-trip excursion takes about six days, with different options and prices.

TIP

Roberto Marrero has spent years producing extremely detailed maps and guidebooks to this area, available at Tecni Ciencias bookstores in Caracas (CCCT, Centro Lido, C.C. Sambil).

BELOW: a low river level reveals a rich plant life.

Quebrada de Jaspe (Km 273.5) is among the most unusual places on this drive, with its river bed and base of the stair-step falls of semi-precious jasper. The water is shallow (mostly only knee-deep) and you can easily walk in the river to the base of the falls.

Santa Elena de Uairén ⑬ (first settled in 1922 and now with a population of some 5,000), besides having a military frontier outpost, is the source of supplies for local diamond miners and tourists. Santa Elena offers plentiful lodging and dining options.

Diamond territory

A popular trip from Santa Elena is to the diamond mining towns of **El Paují** ⑭ and **Icabarú** ⑮, 75 km (47 miles) and 115 km (71 miles) west, respectively. The famous 154-carat Bolívar diamond was found nearby in 1942. The dirt road (only for 4x4s) as far as El Paují has been improved recently, with driving time about 2.5 hours. The stretch between El Paují and Icabarú, however, is so bad that even most *Toyoteros* refuse to destroy their vehicles traversing it.

Toyoteros departing from Santa Elena's airport offer *por puesto* service to El Paují for about $8 per person each way. Rutaca provides air taxi service to both destinations daily, with flights from about 7am–5pm every time five passengers accumulate, for an extremely reasonable sum of about $15 per person each way.

Locals warn against visiting Icabarú, pointing out it is a very rough and dangerous miners' camp where tourists are not welcome.

El Paují, however, is quite a contrast – and a surprise. Rather than fortune-hunters, most of the residents are "refugees from stress" and artsy types: former high-pressure executives who came for a break – and decided to make the visit permanent; artists, musicians, dancers… who find endless inspiration in the tranquility and beauty of nature. These same people have opened some half dozen unique choices for comfortable lodging full of imaginative details. Most offer guided tours to visit local attractions.

Among the best choices in El Paují are Hospedaje Chimantá, Las Brisas, Campamento Manoa, Casa de Cultura y Posada Amariba. Since there are no telephones here, you should make arrangements via Anaconda Tours (tel: 58(88)95 1016), located next to the principal bakery (Panadería Trigopán) on Calle Bolívar in Santa Elena, which has radio contact. Via Icabarú, another good choice is Campamento Kawaik (tel/fax: 58(2)945 9806, 991 6854). All these camps are ecologically conscious.

Map on page 274

Roadside welcome.

Side trip to Brazil

Heading south from Santa Elena, you can cross over into Brazil to La Línea ("The Line") – aptly named being just across the international border between Venezuela and its neighbor. You may fancy a trip to La Línea to shop for Brazilian wines; macho, leather-sheathed Bowie knives, or to try a typical Brazilian *churrasco* – an all-you-can-eat meal, with large skewers of beef, pork, chicken and sausages served with a variety of side dishes, all washed down with liter-sized bottles of Antarctica beer. ❑

BELOW:
the road to Icabarú.

A CASTLE IN THE CLOUDS

Standing guard over the savannah like a medieval fortress, Mount Roraima harbors life-forms that inspired Conan Doyle to write "The Lost World"

Clammy mists swirl around labyrinths of blackened rocks sculpted into nightmarish shapes: bulbous heads, stretched and twisted limbs, spiny torsos and gaping jaws. This could be a Salvador Dalí landscape brought to life, or else a macabre graveyard of petrified Mesozoic reptiles.

In fact, this is the surface of Mount Roraima, the biggest and most famous of the hundreds of *tepuyes* (plateaus) that dominate the horizon of the Gran Sabana in southern Venezuela, and the source of inspiration for Arthur Conan Doyle's classic adventure story, *The Lost World*.

Elsewhere on Roraima are huge sinkholes, lined with spiky plants. A canyon on its eastern rim is carpeted with sparkling quartz crystals, earning the name *El Valle de los Cristales* (Crystal Valley). Providing a rare chance for hikers to wash in fresh water, another area has several pools in the rock, predictably nicknamed *El Baño* (The Bathroom). As for camping facilities on top of Roraima, visitors have to squeeze onto sandy ledges under narrow over-hangs, optimistically known as *El Hotel*. With only one known path in its entire perimeter, local guides are essential in this rocky maze – not just to get you up but to lead you back down. Roraima's splendid isolation is likely to remain safe for a few more million years.

▷ **LOCAL RESIDENTS**
A straw-roofed house of the Pemón indians,who are the only authorized guides to take you up the *tepuyes*, which they regard as sacred.

△ **VIEW FROM THE EDGE**
After one of the frequent rainstorms over Roraima, new waterfalls spring out from its rim and cascade onto the forest below.

▽ **ANCIENT OUTLINE**
Flying over the lush forest fringing the *tepuyes*, even the tannin-stained rivers seem to hint at the presen of prehistoric inhabitants.

△ **CLINGING TO LIFE**
Clusters of plants take root together in whatever crevice or patch of soil has survived the torrential rainfall on the summit of Roraima.

CARNIVOROUS PLANT LIFE

Roraima's rain-drenched surface supports few animals. Plant life up here, however, is plentiful and well adapted to the cold and wet climate. The black rock itself turns out to be pale underneath but coated with a species of algae that thrives in these sodden conditions. The heavy rainfall has washed away most of the soil and what little remains is low in nutrients. The plants that grow here are mostly insect-eaters, such as marsh pitchers, sundews and bladder worts, which cling to the crevices in the rock where soil has found a niche. One species of bromeliad has also evolved carnivorous habits, absorbing nutrients through its leaves from the bodies of insects drowned in pools formed in its vase.

PRIZE PLANTS
oggy sinkholes are filled
th plants, over half of
hich are unique species
d some of them exclusive
the summit of one *tepuy*.

◁ **TOWERING GIANTS**
A typical *tepuy* towers some 1,500 meters (5,000 ft) over the savannah, fringed by tropical forest.

▷ **NATURAL SCULPTURE**
The blackened rocks take on monstruous shapes as a result of millions of years of continuous erosion.

AMAZONAS

This spectacular state includes areas where only scientists and missionaries are allowed to travel independently. But camps allow others to explore the interior as packaged tourists

Map on page 298

Amazonas state, located in the southernmost extreme of the country, covers nearly 184,500 sq. km (71,000 sq. miles) yet has a population of only 120,000, the majority belonging to 15 indigenous groups. Bordered on the north by Bolívar state, with Colombia on the west, Brazil to the south, and Brazil and Bolívar state on the east, Amazonas includes rainforests sheltering exotic plants and rare animals, hundreds of rivers, and broad savannahs. Delicate border disputes have occurred more than once, and threats to its surprisingly fragile environment are always a concern – but, it is also a place where travelers can enjoy one of the world's great wilderness adventures.

Natural abundance

About 8,000 species of plants grow in Amazonas – 7,000 of them indigenous. Orchids, bromeliads and mosses drape the rainforest, with a canopy so thick and immense it seems impenetrable. Jaguars prowl deep in the jungle, along with ocelots, deer, tapir, giant anteaters, peccaries and half a dozen species of monkey – although you will not be likely to spot them. The fearsome bushmaster snake grows up to 4 meters (12 ft) in length; the deadly fer-de-lance and the better-known anaconda are not quite so long.

There are some 680 species of birds, including magnificently colored toucans, parrots and macaws. And here are insects galore: a hundred different families with their various relations, including brilliant, neon-colored butterflies and 6-inch (15 cm) cockroaches. Scorpions and tarantulas are found on the rain forest's floor, and its rivers harbor electric eels, piranha, alligators and crocodiles, *pavón* (peacock bass), fresh-water dolphin and the fast-disappearing Arrau tortoise, which is prized for its flesh.

Delicate ecosystem

Although Amazonas is teeming with life, the rainforest ecosystem is very delicate. If the land is cleared for large-scale farming, the shallow nutrients are leached out and washed away by the rains, leaving a desert-like landscape. Miners leave behind rivers contaminated with mercury and holes that fill with rainwater to become breeding areas for mosquitoes.

Nearly 6.3 million hectares (15.6 million acres) of the state are protected under special administration by the Environment Ministry: this includes 18 natural monuments (12 of which are *tepuyes*), four national parks, the Sipapo forest reserve, the upper Orinoco-Casiquiare biosphere reserve and the Cataniapo River protected hydrographic basin. (Unfortunately, actual protection is virtually non-existent due to the extreme difficulty of access to most areas.)

PRECEDING PAGES: bridge across a jungle river. **LEFT:** Yanomami indian children. **BELOW:** a screeching macaw.

Among these is the **Cerro La Neblina** (Mountain of the Mists), not only the highest point within the **Parque Nacional Serranía de La Neblina** but, at 3,014 meters (9,888 ft), the tallest peak in South America not in the Andes. Because of its remoteness along the southern border, it was not discovered until 1953.

Commercial resources

Amazonas contains a wealth of lumber, medicinal plants, dyes, resins, gums and fibers, and the rivers hold great hydroelectric potential. But such riches have been only marginally exploited. Amazonas also has the largest gold deposits in South America and has recently drawn thousands of miners – many coming over the border illegally from Brazil. Venezuela has not suffered the same sort of environmental catastrophe as its southern neighbor, but the situation is volatile.

Despite the difficulties, the area has attracted explorers for centuries. The Orinoco was probed as early as 1531 by conquistador Diego de Ordaz, who dreamed it would lead to El Dorado. Dozens of other explorers combed the 2,700-km (1,700-mile) river and its tributaries, but the source of the Orinoco remained a mystery until 1950. In that year, a team of Venezuelans, French and North Americans traced the last 190 km (120 miles) of the Orinoco's course to the Sierra Parima at the Brazilian border. The origin of the seventh largest river in the world is a stream that trickles from a mountain which expedition members named Delgado Chalbaud (elevation 1,047 meters/3,435 ft).

Amazing river

The Orinoco River exhibits a rare phenomenon in Amazonas. During certain times of the year, instead of receiving waters from the smaller Río Casiquiare, it feeds part of its own volume into this inferior channel. The Casiquiare then runs in the opposite direction from the Orinoco's main course, empties into the Río Negro and on into the Amazon. German naturalist Alexander von Humboldt (*see page 173*) documented this curiosity when he came to the area in 1800, and it amazes engineers even today.

Most travelers to Amazonas will be satisfied with tours organized by legally registered camps and travel agencies that offer anything from quick tours around Puerto Ayacucho to lengthy expeditions deep into the interior. To be avoided are tour offers by "pirates" – freelancers who often hang around in the airport to try to lure visitors with their low prices; they are neither legally authorized to offer these services nor equipped to handle any emergencies.

Anyone wishing to go into the interior independently must get authorization from the Office of Indian Affairs (ORAI), a lengthy and onerous process, which also involves approval from the Environment Ministry, National Guard and Amazonas State Government. Permission is normally granted only to scientists and missionaries.

Transportation in this remote region is mainly by air taxi and dugout canoes called *bongos* or *curiaras*. The only paved road is the highway coming to Puerto Ayacucho from Caicara de Orinoco in Bolívar state, which then continues southward to Puerto Nuevo, a

The same kind of pre-Cambrian plateaus known as tepuyes (from the Pemón Indian word for mountain) are usually called cerros *(Spanish for mountain) in Amazonas.*

BELOW: hiking through the rainforest.

Map on page 298

few kilometers beyond Samariapo and the Maipures Rapids. There is also a short spur northbound from the capital to Puerto Páez in Apure state.

Few towns

Arrows made by Yanomami indians from the Casiquiare River region.

The *criollo* towns are clustered along the Orinoco, Atabapo, Guanía and Negro rivers, bordering Colombia. **Puerto Ayacucho ②** is by far the biggest, with a population of about 80,000. The place where most travelers begin their journeys, Puerto Ayacucho was founded in 1924, and was originally the base camp for workmen building the road south to Samariapo. It links the two ports along a section of the Orinoco that cannot be navigated due to rocks and the treacherous Atures rapids. Being both a port on the Orinoco and a border post, Puerto Ayacucho has a heavy military and navy presence. The average temperature in Puerto Ayacucho is 27.6°C (82°F). In the dry season (December through April) the town gets very dusty, while during the rains it is extremely humid.

The airport offers daily flights to Caracas and other cities, while charter operators fly tourists, scientists and missionaries to the interior. Tourist information is available at the airport and at the tourist office in the Palacio del Gobierno on Avenida Río Negro, next to Plaza Bolívar. Look out for the free booklet, *Guía de Servicios Turísticos.*

Many indians live in Puerto Ayacucho or come to the market to trade. **Plaza Rómulo Betancourt** on Avenida Río Negro has become the port's informal indigenous market, where Guahibo, Piaroa, and Curripaco indians sell bead necklaces, carved wooden animals, and other crafts; most trading happens on Thursday, Friday and Saturday. Avenida Orinoco is the site of a daily market mainly focusing on food and clothing, which tends to be busiest on weekends.

BELOW: baby crocs.

Fresh produce and river fish, *tortas de casabe* (large circular cakes of the traditional bread made from grated yucca root), *katara* (a spicy sauce containing heads of *bachacos* – leaf-cutter ants with formidable mandibles, said to be an aphrodisiac), are all on sale here.

The **Museo Etnológico del Territorio Federal Amazonas**, facing the plaza, is outstanding, showing all aspects of everyday life and customs of the five ethnic families of Amazonas' indigenous peoples (open daily, Sun am only; small admission fee).

Jungle pleasures

There's much to see in this wild corner of the country. About 35 km (22 miles) north of Puerto Ayacucho is **Pozo Azul ③**, a deep, clear lagoon fed by a little stream. It's safe to swim here, but lately the area has not been well maintained. A much better choice is the popular **Tobogán de la Selva ④**, a natural rock slide in a river surrounded by jungle, the same distance in the opposite direction from the capital, just off the road to Samariapo. This 20-meter (60-ft) granite rock forms a natural slide and is set in a recreational area with nature trails and refreshment stands.

Cerro Pintado ⑤ has the largest known petroglyphs in Venezuela, including a 50-meter (164-ft) snake that is said to represent the Orinoco.

The paved road south from Puerto Ayacucho ends at Puerto Nuevo. Between this and another small port own, **Samariapo ❻**, several kilometers before it, are the impressive Maipures Rapids. At the southern extreme of these rapids, about 20 minutes by boat from Samariapo, is Isla Ratón, which is the largest land mass in the Orinoco River. It must also be one of the hottest places on earth: the sun beats down as its clusters of multi-colored houses stand unprotected against the burning rays.

Cerro Autana, the sacred mountain of the Piaroas, is 80 km (50 miles) southeast. This 1,200-meter (3,940-ft.) column of pre-Cambrian rock has a spectacular cave near its summit. Open at both sides, its galleries form a huge domed salon 40 meters (130 ft) high and 395 meters (1,300 ft) long.

Deep in Amazonas, along the Upper Orinoco, **La Esmeralda ❼** rests in the shadow of the Cerro Duida (2,396 meters/7,860 ft). Some 128 km (80 miles) upstream lies the Yanomami mission of **Platanal ❽**.

Tourist camps

All the tourist camps in the interior of the country offer all-inclusive packages for lodging, meals and excursions. They include: **El Yaví**, near Cerro Yaví, in the northeastern extreme of the state; **Yutaje**, some 40 km (25 miles) southwest of Yaví, near a pair of twin falls from which it takes its name; and **Camani** and **Junglaven**, both of which are near the headwaters of the Ventuari River in the northeast. These last two camps offer fishing packages, and Junglaven also specializes in bird watching. All the camps are in the zone of the Ye'Kwana (also known as Maquiritare) and Piaroa indians.

Camp **Mawadianajodo** is in the Ye'Kwana village of the same name, near the *tepuyes* Duida and Marahuaca in the center of the state. Camps in or near Puerto Ayacucho include Camturama, Tucán, Orinoquía, and Nacamtur. ❑

Map on page 298

TIP

Expediciones Aguas Bravas offers a unique adventure of rafting in the Atures rapids near Puerto Ayacucho – sitting in the front gives the wildest ride, and don't take a camera unless it is totally waterproof and shockproof.

BELOW: a red howler monkey.

Amazon Peoples

Only about 120,000 people live in Amazonas state, 40 percent of them members of 14 distinct indigenous groups in five linguistic families – Piaroa, Guahibo, Yanomami, Arawak and Ye'Kwana (the first three independent; the last pertaining to the Caribe family) – each with its own language and culture. Only the most isolated, the Yanomami for example, living deep in the jungle near Brazil, have been able to resist encroachment from the outside world. In 1991, in a precedent-setting decree, President Carlos Andrés Pérez set aside a large stretch of Amazonas as a permanent homeland for them: the Casiquiare–Alto Orinoco Biosphere Reserve. Nevertheless, to date the reserve exists only on paper, with no official demarcation, regulation of visitors or development plan – much less any consultation with the indigenous peoples it affects.

The Venezuelan indians have not faced the same systematic destruction as their coun-

terparts in Brazil, but many have suffered invasion of their lands by miners and ranchers, been poked and prodded in the name of science and urged by the government to assimilate into *criollo* society. Only a few groups are becoming politicized.

The Yanomami and other indian groups have been endangered by the white man's gold fever ever since the days of the conquistadores. More recently, since the late 1980s, illegal gold miners, primarily slipping across the border from Colombia and Brazil, have invaded the dense rainforests, looking for a latter-day El Dorado. Occasional violent clashes have occurred. Moreover, incursion by outsiders has often exposed these primitive populations to new diseases against which they have no immunity – such as yellow fever, an outbreak of which claimed the lives of numerous Yanomami in 1998.

Amazonas is also a battleground for souls. The first Catholic missionaries (Jesuits) arrived in the mid-1700s, followed by Capuchins and Franciscans. However, from 1845 until the arrival of the Salesians in 1933, the Catholic church was practically non-existent. In 1940 the Hijas de María Auxiliadora nuns arrived. Between 1976 and 1988, the Sisters of San José de Tarbes, Sisters of Nazareth, and Sisters of Madre Laura began working in the interior of the territory. In the 1940s, the Protestant New Tribes missionaries sent families to live in the indian villages. They learned the indigenous languages and have put five of them into written form. The government has taken advantage of this to communicate with the groups by printing booklets on health issues and other matters of social concern.

Visitors will have plenty of chances to see indians in their typical dwellings and engaged in their usual activities, but they may be surprised by what they see.

Publicity photos invariably show primitive **Yanomamis** – nearly nude, the females with thin sticks piercing their noses and the skin below their lower lip. But, because their remote southern homeland is in an area declared off limits to tourists, seeing them is unlikely. They belong to the Yanomama family – the first group to populate the continent and currently the most numerous indigenous population in the state, though, interestingly, their presence in Venezuela only dates from this century, having migrated from the bordering area of Brazil.

Farmers, hunters, fishermen and collectors, the Yanomami had, until recent times remained completely removed from the influence of modern culture (apart from the occasional brief encounter with a few explorers over the past several centuries). It has only been since 1950 that some of them have established relatively continual contact with the missionaries and scientists. For this reason, fascination is high with the group whose mode of living and customs have changed little since the Stone Age.

Guahibos (or *Hiwi*, in their own language) are primarily concentrated in Colombia, in the areas adjacent to the northwestern extreme of Amazonas state, but since the beginning of this century have expanded their presence to the east side of the Orinoco around Puerto Ayacucho, to become the second-largest indigenous group in Amazonas. They are known for their archery prowess, ceramics, and *katara* (hot sauce made with heads of *bachacos* – leaf-cutter ants).

Piaroa are mainly seen from the capital southward to the Sierra Guayapo and between Las Mercedes and San Juan de Manapiare along the Ventuari River, the extension of their population spreading progressively further east since the early 1900s.

In the Piaroa tongue, they call themselves *Uhuothoj'a*, meaning "people who live in the forest." And, indeed, the traditional lands of the Piaroa are the vast mountain forests, though they always build their palm-thatched *churuatos* (huts) in communities near rivers and their side-creeks, called *caños*.

Among the Piaroa crafts, the items most appreciated by collectors and tourists are the masks emulating animals (such as monkeys and peccaries), used in their *warime* ceremony. Though denominated "masks", they are worn on top of the head with the wearer's face covered by a long fringe of palm or bark, which is boiled until soft and used as a cloth.

The **Ye'Kwana** – aka Maquiritare or Makiratare – are known as expert boat-builders (using single hollowed-out tree trunks), and as navigators. They are also known for their

physical strength. Their territory extends from the headwaters of the Ventuari River south to the Orinoco. The Ye'Kwana have never lived in large concentrations, rather they have been strategically dispersed to make the most efficient exploitation of forest resources. They are particularly known for their highly democratic system and the tranquility of individuals – more likely to leave a community than provoke a confrontation.

Arawak, living along the southwest border from the Orinoco to Brazil, are known as collectors of jungle products, such as rubber.

Common traits are subsistence based on cultivation on small farms (*conucos*) cleared in the jungle; hunting, gathering wild fruits, and fishing; a rich magic-religious culture and shamanism (in which hallucinogens such as *yopo* are inhaled to induce supernatural visions); and multi-family living structures.

Unique to the Yanomami indians is the custom of grinding the bones of the dead after cremation, and consuming the powder in a special brew, believed to keep the spirit of the deceased with them. ❏

LEFT AND RIGHT: Piaroa indians.

INSIGHT GUIDES

Travel Tips

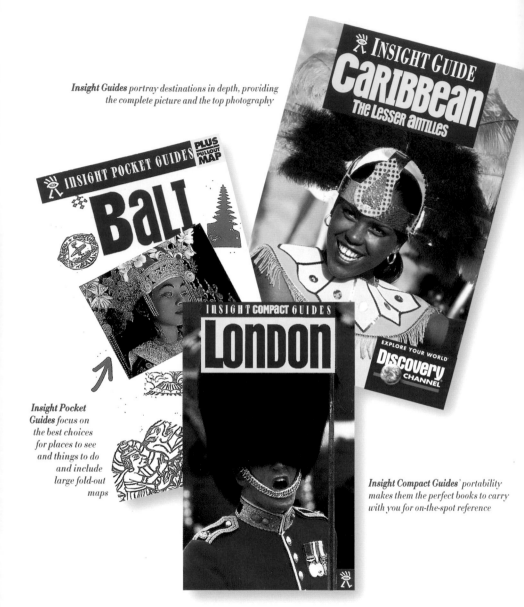

Insight Guides portray destinations in depth, providing the complete picture and the top photography

INSIGHT POCKET GUIDES PLUS PULLOUT MAP

BaLI

Insight Pocket Guides focus on the best choices for places to see and things to do and include large fold-out maps

INSIGHT GUIDE
CaRIBBeaN
THe LeSSeR aMTILLeS

EXPLORE YOUR WORLD
DISCOVERY CHANNEL

INSIGHT COMPACT GUIDES
London

Insight Compact Guides' portability makes them the perfect books to carry with you for on-the-spot reference

Three types of guide for all types of travel

INSIGHT GUIDES Different people need different kinds of information. Some want *background information* to help them prepare for the trip. Others seek *personal recommendations* from someone who knows the destination well. And others look for *compactly presented data* for on-the-spot reference. With three carefully designed series, Insight Guides offer readers the perfect choice. Insight Guides will turn your visit into an experience.

The world's largest collection of visual travel guides

CONTENTS

Getting Acquainted

The Place

Area: 916,442 sq. km (352,143 sq. miles), divided into 22 states, one Federal District, and 72 islands which are Federal Dependencies.
Capital: Caracas.
Population: 23 million.
Language: Spanish; 2 percent indigenous languages. Though English is a required school subject, one rarely finds anyone in the streets who speaks or understands it, particularly in the interior.
Religion: Roman Catholic (96 percent); complete religious freedom, with many different faiths represented; separation of church and state.
Time zone: GMT minus 4 hours; Eastern Standard Time plus 1 hour.
Currency: Bolívar.
Weights and measures: metric.
Electricity: 110 volts, 60-cycle system, with a single-phase AC current.
International dialing code: 00 58

Highlights

- Highest mountain: Pico Bolívar in Mérida state (5,007 m/16,427 ft).
- Longest (12.5 km/7.5 miles) and highest (4,765 m/ 15,630 ft) cable car in the world (in Mérida.)
- Longest river: Orinoco (2,574 km/1,600 miles).
- Largest lake in South America: Maracaibo in Zulia state; crossed by the longest pre-stressed concrete bridge in the world (8 km/4.8 miles).
- Highest waterfall in the world: Angel Falls (978 m/3,212 ft).

Public Holidays

January 1 New Year's Day
Carnival *Carnaval* – the Monday and Tuesday prior to Lent
Easter *Semana Santa* – Holy Week. Thursday and Friday of that week are holidays
May 1 International Workers' Day
June 24 Anniversary of the Battle of Carabobo, turning point in the War of Independence
July 5 Independence Day
July 24 Birth date of the Liberator, Simón Bolívar
October 12 *Día de la Raza*, Columbus Day
December 25 Christmas Day

Climate

Tropical climate predominates, making it a perfect year-round travel destination. Average daytime temperature is 27°C (80°F), varying only a few degrees from the "winter" (the seemingly backwards reference attributed to the rainy season – the *warmest* time of year, roughly May to October) to the coolest months (December to February) in the dry season. In the northern part of the country, rains in the wet season usually consist of a short downpour in the afternoon, with the sky quickly clearing again. Geographical situation, particularly altitude, affects the averages. Highest points in the Andes are perpetually covered with snow and anywhere in these mountains it gets cold at night even when days are hot. Average temperatures in January and July:
Caracas 18/21°C (65/70°F)
Mérida 18/19°C (65/67°F)
Puerto La Cruz 26/27°C (79/80°F)
Coro, in the driest state of Falcón, rarely gets rain. Meanwhile, Bolívar, Delta Amacuro and Amazonas states get the most; clearly the dry season is the best for comfort and photography. Any time is fine for the coast. The dry season is best for birding and exploring Los Llanos or the Gran Sabana, while the rainy season is the time to visit Angel Falls.

The Economy

Petroleum accounts for over half of the government's revenues, and about 25 percent of the GDP. With abundant raw materials and cheap electricity through the hydroelectric development of the Caroní River, aluminum, iron ore, and steel are other important contributors. Despite ideal conditions, not a fraction of the great potential of agriculture and tourism has been developed.

Since the early 1990s, Venezuela has been suffering a deepening economic crisis, spurred by "cures" as well as causes. The most recent problems were a plunge in the stock market in 1998, in line with other markets of the world following the Asian crisis, and political uncertainty prior to the 1998 presidential elections.

With salaries not covering even basic needs, some 51 percent of the workforce is employed in the growing underground economy. Over 80 percent of the population lives below the poverty level (minimum monthly wage was increased to Bs.75,000 in 1997, but the basic food basket for a family of four stood at Bs.145,000). The middle class has nearly disappeared and, for the first time in 30 years, even the rich are feeling the pinch.

The Government

A democratic republic since 1958, the president is chosen by direct popular vote every five years and can only be reelected after a lapse of 10 years. The president appoints all Cabinet members who hold the title of ministers. In 1989, the first direct elections were held for state and local officials. The legislative branch (Congress) consists of the Senate and Chamber of Deputies, with members elected at the same time as the president. The judicial system is based on Napoleonic law (no trials, rather hearings before a judge), with a Supreme Court and system of lower courts.

Planning the Trip

Visas & Passports

Regulations sometimes change overnight, so double check with your local travel agency or nearest Venezuelan embassy (*see* overleaf). At the moment, no visa is needed for tourists visiting from the United States, the United Kingdom, or Canada (a **tourist card**, valid for 60 days, is distributed by air or sea carriers or can be obtained at the immigration checkpoint); a visa *is* required for Australian tourists.

If a longer stay is anticipated, **tourist visas**, valid for up to one year, are issued at Venezuelan embassies or consulates abroad. Most nationalities are restricted to a maximum of three tourist cards or visas in one year. No inoculations are required.

Transient visas are required for anyone planning to work in Venezuela, even for a short period. They can usually only be obtained outside the country and visitors wishing to change from a tourist visa to a transient visa technically have to travel outside the country to obtain their papers from a Venezuelan consulate. Because of the delays involved, visitors wishing to remain in Venezuela for some time often arrive in the country with tourist cards, converting to transient visas by leaving and re-entering the country (usually by going to nearby Curaçao or Aruba) once their papers are ready. There are two types of transient visa: the **business visa** (*transeúnte de negocio*), which allows short-term business interests to be pursued, and the **regular transient visa**. The first is issued exclusively at Venezuelan consulates and is valid for 120 days or one year, at the discretion of the issuing consul and is not renewable in Venezuela. Regular transient visas must be applied for in Venezuela by a third party. These can be obtained by a company for a member of its staff, or by an individual seeking to bring a child or spouse to Venezuela.

Duty Free

The following may be brought in duty-free: – up to two cartons of cigarettes, 50 cigars or 250 grams (9 oz) of tobacco, any 2 liters (4.2 pints) of liquor, and personal possessions that are more than six months old, including items such as cameras, typewriters, tape-recorders, binoculars, and sports equipment. However, if they are new, they should not have a total value of over US$1,000 to be exempted from import duties. All receipts should be carried. The value of new goods must be detailed on a customs declaration form (*declaración de aduanas*) provided by airlines or travel agents. A reasonable amount of personal medications is permitted.

Customs

Prohibited

It is illegal to carry narcotics into Venezuela and penalties for foreigners are strict, ranging from immediate deportation to lengthy jail sentences. An ounce of marijuana is just as serious as a kilo of cocaine in Venezuelan courts. Also strictly prohibited from entry are firearms, ammunition, explosives (only Venezuelan citizens may apply for licenses to carry firearms), fresh flowers, sugar cane plants, citrus and other fresh fruits, cotton plant seeds, and pork.

Pets

Any pet entering Venezuela must have a general health certificate issued, signed, and stamped by a licensed veterinarian not more than 15 days prior to entry into Venezuela. Additional vaccination certificates, obtained within the preceding year, are also required, including an export permit, to be obtained 15 days before departure, with all documents in hand, from the Agriculture Ministry (Ministerio de Agricultura y Cría) in Parque Central, Caracas (tel: 02 509 0111).

Health

Diseases

Up to the 1930s, **malaria** claimed 10,000 lives a year from a population of some 3 million. By 1960, it had been eradicated from most of the country except for certain residual areas, mainly in Amazonas. Complacent that the disease had been licked, spraying for mosquitoes ceased and malaria stations were abandoned. The error of this move has now become evident with a resurgence not only of malaria, but also of **dengue fever**, also mosquito-borne.

The areas with the highest incidence of malaria during 1998 were Bolívar with 47.7 percent of the cases in Venezuela (the Gran Sabana area within Bolívar is particularly vulnerable), Sucre (21.6 percent) and Apure (6.3 percent). Areas with a lower risk are, in descending order, Táchira, Amazonas, Distrito Federal, Barinas, Delta Amacuro, Azoátegui, and Monagas. The only state with no reported cases was Yaracuy. Meanwhile, dengue (both classic and hemorrhagic) has had the greatest number afflicted in Distrito Federal (which includes Caracas and the Litoral Central), Monagas, and Aragua. Your physician may recommend anti-malaria prophylactics if you are planning extended visits to either Bolívar or Sucre. Otherwise, to combat both malaria and dengue (there is no vaccine or other similar prophylactic for the latter), the simplest protection is strong insect repellent both applied to the skin and sprayed on clothing wherever you are.

While few visitors enter the area of the upper Orinoco near La

Venezuelan Embassies Abroad

Australia (with jurisdiction for New Zealand and Fiji): 1st floor, Suite 106, MCL Tower Woden, ACT. 2606, Canberra. Tel: (61) 282 4827/4828; fax: 281 1969.
Canada:
Ottawa: – 32 Range Road. Tel: (613) 235 5151/5154.
Montreal: – 205 Peel St., Suite 400. Tel: (514) 842 3417/3418/0732.
United Kingdom: 1 Cromwell Road, London, SW7 2HW. Tel: (171) 581 2776, 584 4206/5375; fax: 589 8887.
Trinidad & Tobago: Venezuelan Centre, 16 Victoria Avenue,

Port of Spain, Trinidad. Tel: (62) 79 773/774; fax: 55 438.
United States:
Baltimore: 111 Water Street, Suite 402. Tel: (410) 962 0363
Boston: 545 Boylston Street, 6th floor, Suite 603. Tel: (617) 266 9355; fax: 266 2350.
Chicago: 20 North Wacker Drive, Suite 750. Tel: (312) 236 9659; fax: 580 1010.
Houston: 2700 Post Oak Boulevard, Suite 1500. Tel: (713) 961 5142; fax: 961 1485.
Miami: 1101 Brickell Avenue, Suite 901. Tel: (305) 446 2851; fax: 448 5699.

New Orleans: 1006–1009 World Trade Center, 2 Canal Street. Tel: (504) 522 3284; fax: 522 7092.
New York: 7 East 51st Street. Tel: (212) 826 1660; fax: 644 7471.
Philadelphia: Suite 303, New Market at Head House Square. Tel: (215) 923 2910; fax: 923 4722.
San Francisco: 455 Market Street, Suite 220. Tel: (415) 512 8340; fax: 512 7693.
Washington DC: Embassy of Venezuela, 1099–30th St N.W. Tel: (202) 342 2214, 242 6843.

Esmeralda and Parima in Amazonas, if you do, be aware that in late 1998 there was a serious outbreak of **yellow fever, leptopirosis**, and **hepatitis B** among the Yanomami Indians there.

Water
Urban water supplies are treated and chlorinated; however, it is still generally not advisable to drink tap water since most supply lines are in poor condition. Bottled water is available virtually everywhere in the country.

HIV/Aids
The Health Ministry reported that, as of 1996, Venezuela had half a million carriers of Aids (a figure which many sources consider conservative). If toying with the idea of a little Latin loving, do so only with adequate protection. Condoms are widely available; they are called *preservativos*, and are found in pharmacies and shops like Condomania in CCCT in Caracas – thanks to private initiative by concerned community and gay groups who have mounted their own "safe sex" campaigns.

Medication
No prescriptions are necessary to purchase any medications except those containing narcotics. Moreover, medications are generally

considerably cheaper in Venezuela than exactly the same ones abroad.

Money Matters

Because of the constantly changing rates of exchange, it is advisable not to change more currency into bolívars than you anticipate using imminently.

Cash is best to carry anywhere, preferably in small denominations since no-one ever seems to have change.

Outside of main hotels, restaurants, and expensive shops in the largest cities, few places accept travelers' checks, foreign currency, or credit cards. Even many of the major travel agencies in Caracas do not accept cards any more or, if they do, may add a surcharge of 3 to 15 percent since bank charges to businesses are now *at least* 10 percent. **ATMs** are widely available.

Cards accepted in Venezuela are: Visa, MasterCard, American

Lost Credit Cards

In Caracas (direct dial 02):
American Express (24 hours), tel: 206 0222;
Diners, tel: 503 2555;
MasterCard, tel: 607 7111;
Visa, tel: 501 0333.

Express, and Diners.

Currency Exchange
Currency can be changed at exhange bureaus known as *casas de cambio* (most banks only exchange currency for their clients). A set percentage is charged as commission, rather than a flat fee. Thus, you do not get hit with a fat "minimum commission", as is the case in many other countries. It is not recommended to exchange currency in hotels since they give notoriously unfavorable rates. There are several *casas de cambio* in the international airport in Maiquetía.

In Caracas, *Italcambio* is the main chain of exchange houses; its most convenient location is on Avenida Luis Roche, one block south of the Altamira Metro stop.

Emergency Money
Western Union "Money in Minutes" transfers are available through offices of DHL located in most principal cities in Venezuela. Offices in Caracas include:
Edif DHL (the headquarters), Av. Principal de Los Ruices, Monday–Friday 8am–8pm, Saturday 9am–1pm, tel: (02) 235 9080.
DHL Express Centers of Hotel Caracas Hilton and Hotel Tamanaco Inter-Continental, Monday–Friday 9am–1pm, 3–7pm, Saturday 9am–

1pm. For nearest location, tel:
(800) 34 592.

Tax

There is a 16.5 percent sales tax
applied to goods and services,
including plane tickets, lodging, and
tours. Sometimes it is included in
quoted prices, at other times not.
Be sure to ask, so as to avoid
surprises. (This sales tax is
normally charged only at higher-
priced establishments since its
application depends on the annual
sales of the business in question,
with those below a certain level
being exempt.)

Note on Prices

Because of the constant changes
in the value of the **bolívar** and
history of government-imposed
devaluations, prices in this guide
are given in **US dollar** equivalents
to try to provide as accurate
pricing as possible. Even many
hotels, travel agencies, and tour
promoters now quote all of their
prices in dollars "or the
equivalent in bolívars at the
exchange of the day" to avoid
problems with price quotations
when dramatic changes occur.

What to Bring

Clothes
Lightweight, casual clothing is best.
Venezuelans are very conscious of
looks and look smart even when
dressed casually. For evening dining
at formal restaurants and entry to
some Caracas discos, jacket and
tie are required for men. Bring a
sweater or light jacket for cool
evenings and overly air-conditioned
restaurants in any part of the
country. Heavier clothing is only
needed for high-mountain excursions.

Sun protection
If you have favorite brands, bring
strong sunscreen and insect
repellent, but you can easily obtain
high protection sunblock at any

pharmacy, and insect repellent
(Avispa and Osiris work best) in
grocery stores beside fly spray. A
hat and sunglasses are essential.

Wet weather gear
Bring a lightweight rain poncho for
the wet season or jungle trips, a
sturdy plastic bag for personal
belongings in the rain and in wet-
bottomed boats, and a compact
fold-up umbrella. Slip-on plastic
sandals are useful for wading from
boat to shore, dealing with sun-
baked sand and slogging through
rivers created in streets by
downpours.

Medicines
You are strongly advised to bring
any personal medications with you.

Film
Print film is widely available and
reasonably priced, but slide, black-
and-white or high-speed film is
normally difficult to find outside the
largest cities.

Getting There

BY AIR
The Simón Bolívar International
Airport is in Maiquetía, 28km (17
miles) from Caracas across a
mountain range. The airport has
separate terminals for international
and domestic flights, 400 meters
(437 yards) from each other. The
international terminal has a range
of facilities, including a tourist
office and *casas de cambio*.

Since dozens of major
international airlines offer services
to Venezuela, it is best to check
with your travel agent for the
options available.

Other cities which have
international airports include
Maracaibo, Valencia, Barcelona/
Puerto la Cruz, San Antonio de
Táchira, Las Piedras (Paraguaná
Peninsula), Falcón, Maturín.

Immigration & Customs
On arrival, tourists must present
their passport, visa or tourist card,
and entry card or customs
declaration. The last three are

Flying to Venezuela

Here are some of the principal
international airlines serving
Venezuela, with Caracas contact
numbers:
Air Canada: (02) 285 5127
Air France: (02) 283 5855
Alitalia: (02) 285 6108
American: (02) 209 8111
Avianca: (02) 953 5732
British Airways: (02) 261 8006
Continental: (800) 35 926
Iberia: (02) 267 8666
KLM: (02) 285 3333
TAP Air Portugal: (02) 951 0511
United: (02) 278 4545

normally distributed in the plane
before landing; otherwise, you will
have to seek them out at a
designated desk near the
immigration check-in counters.

In Maiquetía, there is a unique
system for checking out passengers
at customs. You press a button,
and if a green light comes on, you
pass through; if the light is red,
customs agents will go through
everything you have. As this system
is operated manually, one assumes
that the idea is that if someone
appears nervous the agents flash a
red light, since it's doubtful that the
button detects sweaty palms or
nervous twitches!

Airport Transfer
There are airport **shuttle buses**
which run between both terminals
and Caracas, with stops by the
Gato Negro Metro station (use this
stop only during daylight hours) and
at their terminal two blocks west of
the Bellas Artes Metro station and
Caracas Hilton (Calle Sur 17, in the
underpass below Av Bolívar.) The
fare costs less than US$2 and
generally takes just under an hour.
At weekends and during holidays
traffic jams can double that time.

The **taxis** which park at the curb
of the airport departure area have a
monopoly and charge nearly double
the going rate. Ask at the taxi desk
in the international terminal for the
official fare. Another option is to
call **Tele-taxi** on (02) 753

4155/9122 (pre-paid phone cards are sold in dispensers next to banks of phones in the terminal). This company has a stand at the airport's gasoline station, and they make pick-ups at curbside on the upper arrivals level (tell them what you are wearing and by which exit you will be standing). It costs about US$18 either way between the airport and Caracas Hilton. Pick-up at your place of lodging can also be arranged by phone with them or other radio contact taxi services (*see Getting Around on page 319*).

NEVER use the *piratas* who flood the terminal during times of incoming flights, offering "Taxi, taxi." They are operating illegally, most are not even licensed taxi drivers, and there have been many instances of hold-ups by them.

BY SEA

The waters of Venezuela are a favorite among visitors in yachts and sailboats – for the wonderful snorkeling and diving, beautiful islands, and the lack of tropical storms or hurricanes – *but* almost all have tales of problems with permits, port officials, and disasters which have occurred due to non-functioning lighthouses. For first-hand information, contact: *Mar y Tierra*, a Venezuelan-based newspaper in English directed to and written by sailors.Tel: (081) 65 0012; fax: (081) 68 82 43; e-mail: Compuserve: 102213,1634.
Chris Doyle, author of *Sailor's Guide to a Venezuelan Cruise* (inquiries: Nancy Scott, Cruising Guide Publications, Clearwater, Florida, tel: (813) 797 9576; or

Frances Punnet, St Vincent, W.I., tel: (809) 458 4246.
Falcón Ferrys offers vehicle and passenger services between La Vela de Coro (Falcón) and Aruba, Curaçao, Bonaire. Discounts for children and seniors. Tel: (068) 78 517, (016) 640 2944, e-mail: ferry@ telcel.net.ve.

New port

As of the end of 1998, all cruise ship lines had scratched **La Guaira** (near Maiquetía) off their itinerary, owing to continuing problems with strikes in the port and security problems in the area around the terminal (not safe for anyone going on foot). However, at the time of writing, the first phase of a new, very ambitious waterfront market-cruise port was nearing completion in **Porlamar** (Isla Margarita). Depending on the facilities and services installed, this could present new interest in Venezuela as a port of call.

BY ROAD

An entry permit is required for motorists intending to drive into the country. This can be obtained from your local consulate; when applying, take a photograph and money to cover the cost ($10).

Travel Agencies

The top seven travel agencies in the country (all based in Caracas, with direct dial code of 02) are:
Italcambio
Tel: 562 9555/9591
Fax: 562 9198.
Molina
Tel: 284 0022
Fax: 285 0224.
Omega
Tel: 285 3794/9783
Fax: 284 5753.
Quo Vadis
Tel: 263 0422, 261 7782
Fax: 263 1716.
Saeca
Tel: 954 1361/1337
Fax: 954 1348.
Turismo Maso Internacional
Tel: 267 3577/3600
Fax: 263 0638.

Specialist Tours

Alpi Tour, Caracas, tel: (02) 285 4116; fax: 285 6067, e-mail: alpitour@compuserve.com. Peacock bass fishing (catch and release) and numerous ecologically oriented tours (*llanos* camps for observation of fauna, hiking in the Andes, windsurfing), plus charter flights, yachts.
Anaconda Tours, Santa Elena de Uairén, tel/fax: (088) 95 1016. Excursions (including scaling the tepuyes) and camps throughout the Gran Sabana of Bolívar state.
Jesika Travel, Caracas, tel: (02) 762 4665, Litoral (031) 94 8534, Los Teques (032) 72 1856. Tours offered just for seniors (60+), with group excursions planned for all parts of the country; travel by air or land depending on destination.
Natoura Turismo Adventura, Mérida, tel: (074) 52 4216; fax: 63 44 44, e-mail: natoura@telcel. net.ve. Adventure and eco tours in the Andes, excursions by jeep and on horseback, mountain bikes, climbing, birdwatching and trout fishing, natural history tours, hang-gliding and paragliding, rafting in the rivers of Barinas, student discounts (office open 8am–7.30pm 7 days a week).

Paradise Expediciones, Caracas, tel: (02) 952 8617/2628. Dedicated exclusively to birdwatchers.
RAS Flying Safaris, through Alpiturismo, Caracas, tel: (02) 285 5116, e-mail: alpisafari@compuserve.com. Custom-designed air safaris in six-seater Aztec, geared to those who want to see the most possible in the shortest time with very personalized service; specialty of Guayana Region around Auyántepui/Angel Falls and Autana (with close-up flyovers), *llanos*; meals, beverages, lodging; land tours included.
Sesto Continente, Caracas, tel: (02) 74 3873. Specializes in organized diving trips to various diving spots.
Sociedad Conservacionista Audubon de Venezuela, Caracas, tel: (02) 993 2525/1727; fax: 993 9260, e-mail: audubon@telcel. net.ve. Handles bookings for ecotourism destinations, with emphasis on places for birding.
Tobogán Tours, Puerto Ayacucho, tel: (048) 21 700; fax: 21 600. Excursions to all parts of Amazonas, with over 30 years' experience in the area.

In the UK

A travel agency specializing in Venezuela is **Geodyssey**, based at 29 Harberton Rd, London N19 3JS, tel: (0171) 281 7788, fax: (0171) 281 7878, e-mail: enquiries@geodyssey.co.uk, web site: www.geodyssey.co.uk. With the popularity of the Internet, there are also many camps, hotels and tour operators that now have web pages which can be consulted.

Turisol
Tel: 206 4934/4935
Fax: 206 3978.

Traveling On

Flights: The airport in Maiquetía is the national hub for almost all domestic and international flights. Airport departure tax for international flights is the equivalent of about US$30; for national flights, roughly US$1. Reservations must be reconfirmed 72 hours ahead for international flights.

For national flights, you must be at the airport one hour ahead of departure, for international flights two hours. During peak season, add extra time for getting to the airport (especially on weekends), and also plan on arriving an extra hour early to deal with the chaos that prevails at the airports at that time. If you are not there on time, you lose your reservation.

Isla Margarita

This is a hopping-off point for nearby islands. Boats run to Coche and Cubagua, which are the other islands of Nueva Esparta state; and also to Los Testigos, Los Frailes and Tortuga.

Aereotuy offers flights from Isla Margarita to La Blanquilla, direct routes for day tours (or overnight) to Kavac and Canaima with fly-over of Angel Falls, and to Los Roques. International flights also originate and arrive here.

Practical Tips

Documents

Do not go *anywhere* without documentation (i.e. passport with tourist card or visa.) There are police checkpoints *(alcabalas)* all along the roads, where you may well be asked to show your documents; and checks are even made in the city, stopping buses or pedestrians. Such checks are aimed at picking up illegal aliens. If you do not have your documents, you will be taken to jail or at least held by the authorities until you can prove your legal status. Not a pleasant experience.

Make a photocopy of your passport (with visa) and any other important documents you are carrying with you, including your airline ticket and your driver's license. Make sure you also have a list of the phone numbers to call in case you lose your credit cards or traveler's checks. These should be guarded in a separate place from the originals.

Business Hours

Most offices and shops, and even many supermarkets, close for lunch, from around 11.30am to about 3–3.30pm. Most business offices begin work at 8–8.30am and end at 4.30–6pm.

Banks Many now have continuous hours: 8.30am–3.30pm; those which still maintain traditional hours are open 8.30–11.30am and 2–4.30pm, weekdays only. An exception to this are banks (such as Banesco and Interbank) with branches in the new Caracas mall, C.C. Sambil, which are open 365 days a year, Monday to Saturday, 10am–9pm; Sunday, open until

7pm, but starting between 11am and 1pm, depending on the bank. Also, during the Christmas shopping season, banks offer special extended hours (which are published in the local press). Some banks have external tellers offering service after normal closing hours.

Banks are often closed on Monday for "mandatory bank holidays" which don't necessarily bear any relation to national holidays.

Shopping Malls With the exception of C.C. Sambil in Caracas, and hypermarkets such as Makro, Rattan, and Construcentro, shops in malls normally don't open until 9.30–10am, close for lunch, end the day at 7pm, and are closed Sunday.

Important Numbers

Emergencies: **171**
Information: **103**
Long distance operator:
   national – **100**
   international – **122**
INDECU (institute for the defense and protection of consumers – where you can make complaints about abuses): **(800) 43 328**

Media

TELEVISION

The following are the commercial channels: 2 (Radio Caracas Televisión), 4 (Venevisión), 10 (Televen). Commercial pay-TV: 12 (Omnivisión). Government-owned: 8 (Venezolana de Televisión).

Just noting parabolic antennae on nearly every rooftop indicates the popularity of satellite TV. The service is now provided in nearly every larger hotel countrywide as well as in private homes. DirecTV is even available in places as remote as Santa Elena de Uairén in La Gran Sabana.

RADIO

AM stations tend to be oriented toward popular Latin music, while the repertoire of many FM stations is almost exclusively North American or European recordings.

Some stations with a difference:

Exitos FM 99.9: popular English-language songs of the 1960s, 70s and 80s.

FM 95.5: jazz.

Emisora Cultural FM 97.7: classical, jazz, and discussion programs (occasionally in English), with a limited number of commercials.

Radio Nacional FM 91.1: has a program in English, *¡Hola!*, hosted by Richard O'Brien on Sunday 6–7pm, with various topics.

KYS FM 101.5: the "station of contemporary adults" plays mostly English-language songs, and every Saturday at 10am and Sunday at 8pm features Casey Kasem's countdown of the American top 40.

PRINT

Newspapers

The only English-language newspaper published in Venezuela is *The Daily Journal*, available nationwide in the principal cities. (The 'Week in Review' supplement printed on Mondays provides a useful summary.)

The Miami Herald is on sale at some newsstands *(kioscos)* in Caracas. This, and various other English language papers such as *USA Today, The New York Times, Wall Street Journal* and *Financial Times* are often available (at more than face value) in the bookstores of Caracas' five-star hotels.

Magazines and Books

Newsstands of premium hotels plus large bookstores in major cities sell a wide selection of imported English-language magazines and some paperbacks, all at roughly double the normal price. Magazines include:

Business Venezuela (published monthly by the Venezuelan American Chamber of Commerce), in English, focuses on business themes, but also as an annual issue on tourism, usually in December.

Escape, an informative monthly tourism magazine with presentation in English and Spanish.

Entonces, a quarterly tourism and entertainment magazine, in combi-nations of English and Spanish.

VenEconomy (by subscription, tel: (02) 762 6142; fax: 762 8160), a monthly magazine printed in two versions (English and Spanish), plus weekly bulletins, focusing on the hot current economic topics.

Entertainment Guide

Every Friday included free in *El Universal* newspaper is an outstanding cultural guide (in Spanish), *Brújula,* which includes an exhaustive listing of events for the upcoming week: exhibitions, dance, museums, cinema, competitions, auditions, special events, children's activities, music, workshops, theater – for the entire country. Reviews of books, records, and videos are also included.

Telecommunications

Since privatization of CANTV, the national phone company, there has been a vast improvement in service.

Pay phones

Most pay phones accept only the pre-paid phone cards or *tarjetas teleflove*; these are sold at newsstands, by the blind – mostly at the entrances to Metro stations, at CANTV offices, hotels, and in many shops. Produced in various denominations up to about $10, they can even be used for making direct-dial national and international long-distance calls; you can also put in a new card without interrupting the connection.

Emergency phones: Phones exclusively for free emergency calls are found in many places, but

Telephone Cards

Buy two Bs.5,000 phone cards as soon as you arrive – one for general use, the other to keep in your wallet in case of emergency. If you should end up with a leftover unused or used card when you are ready to depart, don't worry, you can easily sell them to other arriving visitors or locals for the value left – which can be verified simply by inserting them in any card phone; the amount still available will be displayed in the window.

unfortunately these can be identified only by the message that shows in the window (*sólo llamadas de emergencia*).

Communication centers

Known as CANTV *Centros de Telecomunicaciones*, these offer services which can be paid for with credit cards as well as cash, for national and international calls, sending or receiving faxes, making photocopies, sale of pre-paid telephone cards, and providing information on car rental, hotels, airlines, and restaurants. They are generally open 8am–8pm, and can be found in the following places: the Símon Bolívar international airport in Maiquetía; Centro Plaza shopping center, Avenida Francisco Miranda, two blocks east of the Altamira Metro station, 5th level; and at the airports in Mérida (Mérida), San Cristóbal (Táchira), Porlamar (Isla Margarita), and Barcelona/Puerto La Cruz (Anzoátegui).

Collect Call Numbers

You can make collect calls (reversing the charges) from any private phone by dialing 122 (the international long-distance operator). Alternatively you can dial directly to an operator in the country you are calling:

Australia: (800) 1-1610
Belgium: (800) 1-1320/1321
Canada: (800) 1-1100
Germany: (800) 1-1490
Holland: (800) 1-1330
Hong Kong: (800) 1-1852
Israel: (800) 1-1390/1391
Japan: (800) 1-1810
Puerto Rico: (800) 1-1120/1122
Singapore: (800) 1-650/651
Switzerland: (800) 1-1410
UK: (800) 1-1440/1441
USA: (800) 1-1120/1121

The Internet

Premium hotels geared primarily toward business travelers have in-room plug-in facilities for computers to be able to transmit/receive email, etc

Cellular phones

Cell phones – with service provided by Movilnet (016 prefix) and TelCel (014) are used by everyone from executives to delivery boys. There are now also pre-paid phone cards available for certain models of cellular phones. In Caracas , cellular rentals are available through: Organización Rent-a-Phone, Hotel Caracas Hiton, tel: (02) 503 4329; fax: 503 4328, cell. (014) 921 8844. (For other cities, check Yellow Pages under *Teléfonos Celulares, Alquiler.*)

Postal Services

The mail service offered by IPOSTEL within Venezuela is less than reliable or speedy – particularly in Caracas (where letters can take months to move even between post offices just blocks away).

Outgoing mail however is relatively reliable. For Europe or the US, mail averages about 10 days. A few major hotels have mail drop boxes and sell stamps, but otherwise all mail must be taken to a post office for weighing, stamps, and posting. **Note:** No tape or staples may be used for closings on envelopes. For extra insurance, at a small extra charge, you can have your letter certified *(certificado)* or with return receipt *(con aviso de recibo).*

Express mail

IPOSTEL also offers an express service: EEE *(Envío Especial Expreso)* for mail within Venezuela, and EMS (Express Mail Service) for international mail, with dispatches of letters and documents sent sealed in a special waterproof, registered envelope; packages of up to 20 kg (9 lb), with tariffs cheaper than commercial couriers.

National delivery takes a day or two. For international mail: to America and Europe – 72 hours for capital cities, 96 hours for principal cities, 120 hours for rural zones; to Asia, Africa and Oceania – 96 hours capitals, 120 hours principal cities, 144 hours rural zones. All principal IPOSTEL offices in Caracas offer the services; for other locations call toll-free to the Unidad de Atención al Cliente: (800) 26 378, (800) 64 367.

Packages

All packages must be sewn inside solid-colored material, with the idea of discouraging pilfering. No string or tape can be used.

Private couriers

For important documents or packages, especially if speed and security are vital, national and international courier services are the method of choice, though costly. Some of the main agents in Caracas (in other cities check with the concierge at your hotel or in the phone book's Yellow Pages under *correspondencia internacional, servicios de),* all offering national and international door-to-door service unless otherwise noted.
Aerocav: tel: (02) 256 0111, 205 0511 (cargo and COD service too).
DHL Worldwide Express: tel: (02) 263 2122 (offices in Hotels Tamanaco Inter-Continental and Caracas Hilton, and in CCCT).
Domesa International: tel: (02) 693 0311 (an office in the Chacaíto Metro station).
FedEx: tel: (02) 22 0411 or toll-free 800-FEDEX (33 339).
Grupo Zoom: tel: (02) 242 7111.
World Courier: tel: (02) 953 2580/1128.
P.O. Box International: tel: (02) 993 35 49, 92 3492 (only international service, air and sea cargo).
United Parcel Service (UPS): tel: (02) 241 6454, 204 1353.

Local Tourist Offices

The offices of the **Tourism Ministry** and **Corpoturismo**, the National

Post Offices

The most convenient post offices *(correos)* in Caracas are in:
C.C. Arta, next to the Chacaíto Metro station.
Centro Ciudad Comercial Tamanaco (CCCT) in Chuao, close to the Hotel Euro-building, Hotel CCT (in the same building), Hotel Tamanaco Inter-Continental, and Hotel Paseo Las Mercedes.
Parque Central (by Residencias Anauco Hilton, the Hotel Caracas Hilton, and the Bellas Artes Metro stop).

Tourism Corporation, are located on the 35th–37th floors of the west tower of Parque Central in Caracas tel: 800-43 328. Amazingly, however, there is not a single tourist information kiosk anywhere in Caracas, and to obtain any maps, brochures etc, a written request must be submitted and appointment made! There is a booth in the international airport at Maiquetía, though, which is open every day, 8am–8pm.

Each state has its own tourism office, some of which are quite efficient (such as for Mérida and Yaracuy) and others practically worthless. The principal state tourism offices are as follows:
Amazonas:
• Dirección de Turismo, Av Río Negro, Palacio de Gobierno (next to Plaza Bólivar), tel: 21 0033/ 0371.
• Tourist kiosk in international terminal of airport (no phone).
Anzoátegui:
• Corporación de Turismo del Estado Anzoátegui (Coranztur), Calle Freites No. 2–45, opposite Plaza Nicolás Rolando, Barcelona, tel: (081) 77 7110/7034, 76 2827, fax: 76 2737.
• Tourist kiosk, Paseo Colón, Puerto la Cruz.
Apure: Edif. Julio Chávez, Mezanina B, Paseo Libertador, San Fernando de Apure, tel: (047) 24 827, 25 929, fax: 28 309.
Aragua: Museo Antropológico y de Historia, Plaza Girardot, Av Bolívar, Maracay, tel: (043) 45 3420/7308.

Barinas: Corporación Barinesa de Turismo, Av Marqués del Pumar, No. 5-42, tel: (073) 27 091, 28 162.

Bolívar: Gobernación Estado Bolívar Turismo, Av Táchira, Quinta Losuni, No. 42, tel: (085) 24 8803, 22 771.

Carabobo: Dirección de Turismo del Estado Carabobo, Calle Ricaurte con Anzoátegui, Puerto Cabello, tel: (042) 61 2975/2814/4622; fax: 61 3921.

Cojedes: Edif. Francis, Calle Ayacucho, San Carlos, tel: (058) 33 2786/0753; fax: 33 2025/0339.

Delta Amacuro: Edif. San Juan (2nd floor), Calle Bolívar, Tucupita, tel: (087) 21 9532/6852; fax: 21 1512/6853.

Falcón: Secretaria de Turismo y Recreación, Alameda de la Zona Colonial, tel: (068) 51 11 32; fax: 51 5327.

Guárico: Av Principal de La Morera, tel: (046) 31 0160; tel/fax: 31 0110.

Lara: All in Barquisimeto:
• Turismo y Recreación del Estado Lara, Av Libertador, Edif. Fundalara, Piso 2, tel/fax: 53 7544.
• Aeropuerto Internacional Jacinto Lara (no phone).
• Terminal de Pasajeros (no phone).
• Paseo Botánico El Cardenalito (*autopista* Dr Rafael Caldera at the entrance to Barquisimeto).

Mérida:
• City of Mérida: Cormetur (Mérida State Tourism Corporation), Av Urdaneta, con Calle 45 (next to the airport), tel: (074) 63 0814/5918/4701; fax: (074) 63 2782, (800) 63 743, with service of this toll-free number Monday–Saturday 8am–8pm, web page: http://www.cormetur.com, e-mail: promoción@cormetur.com
• Airport: tel: (074) 63 9330.
• Terminal de Pasajeros Sur: tel: (074) 63 3952.
• Jardín Acuario: Av Andrés Bello (across from Centro Comercial Las Tapias), tel: (074) 66 0143.
• Mercado Principal: Av Las Américas, planta baja (ground floor), tel: (074) 44 9366.
• By the cable car station: final Calles 24 y 25, facing Plaza Las Heroínas.

Foreign Consulates in Caracas

(Direct dial code 02)
Australia: Qta Yolanda, Av Luis Roche, entre 6ta y 7ta Transversales, Altamira. Tel: 261 4632, fax: 261 3448.

Canada: Centro Gerencial Mohedano, P.H., Av Los Chaguaramos, La Castellana. Tel: 263 0293/ 0473, fax: 263 8326.

Germany: Edif. Panaven, 2nd floor, Av San Juan Bosco con 3ra

• In the town of Santo Domingo: Calle San Gerónimo along the Transandean highway.
• Apartaderos: Transandean highway next to Hotel Turístico Apartaderos.

Monagas: Dirección de Turismo del Estado Monagas (Diturmo), Hacienda Sarripal, Avenida Alirio Ugate Pelayo, elevado de Boccarón (next to IPAN), Maturín, tel/fax: (091) 43 0798.

Nueva Esparta: State tourism office is in Centro Artesanal Gilberto Menchini, Local 18, Calle Jóvito Villalba, as you enter Los Robles. Tel: (095) 62 4194.

Portuguesa: Por Turismo – Dirección de Turismo, Calle 17, or entre Carreras 3 y 4, Guanare, tel: (057) 51 0324, 52 623.

Sucre: Directismo – Dirección de Turismo y Recreación, Calle Sucre No. 49, Cumaná, tel: (093) 24 449, 67 1022.

Táchira: Av Universidad con Av España, Complejo Ferial de Pueblo Nuevo, San Cristóbal, tel: (076) 56 2805, tele/fax: 56 2421.

Trujillo:
• Headquarters Corporación Trujillana de Turismo: Av Principal La Plazuela, Casa No. 1-23, Trujillo, tel: 36 1455/1277.
• Trujillo: Av Andrés Bello (no phone).
• Valera: Av Bolívar entre Calles 10 y 11, tel: 54 286;
Airport: Terminal de Pasajeros – Sector Plata 1, tel: 55 009, 52 724.
• Boconó: Oficina Municipal de Turismo de la Alcaldía, Calle Bolívar, tel: 52 3725/5554.

Transversal, Altamira Norte. Tel: 261 3253/0181.

Great Britain: Torre Las Mercedes (3rd floor), Av La Estancia, Chuao. Tel: 993 4111/52.80, fax: 92 3292.

Israel: Centro Empresarial Miranda, Ofic 4D, Av Principal, Urb. Los Ruices con Av Francisco de Miranda. Tel: 239 4921, fax: 239 4320.

Yaracuy:
• San Felipe: Fundación Yaracuyana de Turismo (Funyatur), Av Alberto Ravell, Centro de Prensa Henrique Tirado Reyes, tel: (054) 31 9255/ 9446/9955.
• Yaritagua: Centro Turístico Los Carrascosa, Carrera 8 con Calle 19, tel: (05) 82 3033/3781.

Women Travelers

As far as security is concerned, there is normally no problem for women travelers if you take normal common sense precautions.

Since old macho traditions die hard, it is still generally considered improper for a single woman to go into a bar alone. By night, even in the large hotels, a single woman going into a bar is normally viewed as being on the hunt – thus fair game for all wolves – or a prostitute. Many discotheques refuse entry to women on their own. Thus, most single women travelers prefer to choose restaurants or the theater for evening entertainment and to stay on business floors where the same stigma does not apply for using the bar of the separate executive lounge.

Traveling with Kids

Most lodgings offer discounts for children. In general, camps, ranches (*hatos*), and other adventure and ecotourism destinations are not appropriate for younger children. In fact some places flatly state no children under a certain age are allowed, either for safety reasons or out of consideration for other guests. At Hato Piñero for example, children are allowed only in low season, and not at all if they have birders booked.

One of the best destinations for children is the Andes, since there are many places to stop and let them run around, along with various attractions geared specifically to them (such as Valle Hermosa, tel: (074) 63 7561) or which are as enjoyable for kids as for adults (such as the reconstructed old Andean village, Los Aleros, or the science museum and aquarium in Mérida).

Business Travelers

Nearly all the five-star hotels have **Executive Floors** set aside for business travelers whose rooms are often outfitted with connections for computers, e-mail, etc., and which have their own lounge and bar where continental breakfast is often served. These all offer secretarial services; use of fax, photocopiers; rooms for small meetings, etc. The Caracas Hilton and the Tamanaco Inter-Continental also have Japanese-speaking personnel, and even have special Japanese menus. These hotels often have a weekly or monthly cocktail party specifically for business travelers.

Various suite-type facilities have come to be offered exclusively to corporate clients who make extended stays, where extras such as kitchen facilities are particularly appreciated. These include the following: **Altamira Suites** (tel: 02 284 0748, fax: 283 5574), **4ta Avenida Suites** (tel: 02 285 5252, fax: 285 5280) in Caracas and **Guaparo Suites** (tel: 041 25 0522, fax: 25 0412) in Valencia.

Corporate rates are normally available only to companies who have made a formal request in writing and who have a minimum number of room nights per year.

Chains such as **Inter-Continental** and **Hilton** afford priority treatment for frequent travelers. Maiquetía's international airport has several executive lounges at the disposition of frequent-flier card-holders of various airlines. **Aserca Airlines** specifically targets business travelers, offering all first-class service.

Travelers with Disabilities

Unfortunately, one finds very little consideration for the disabled in Venezuela, even in the capital; in the interior, it is nearly non-existent. Few sidewalks, and even fewer building entrances, are equipped with ramps, and sidewalks are often full of holes or obstacles, making wheelchair access difficult if not impossible. Few elevators have Braille indications on buttons. Few bathrooms have wheelchair access.

Tipping

A service charge (tip or *propina*) of 10 percent is normally added to all bills in restaurants. It is customary to leave 5–10 percent extra, depending on the quality of attention.

Taxi drivers are not usually tipped unless they carry bags or perform some special service.

Airport porters expect $1 per bag and in Maiquetía, this is a fee rather than a tip.

In top hotels, the standard for bellhops is $1–5, depending on the amount of luggage; for chamber staff the tip is the equivalent of $1 per night; for special services

Non-smokers

Venezuelans smoke a lot, and everywhere. Only a few of the five-star hotels have certain designated non-smoking rooms. It is very rare to find a restaurant which has a non-smoking section and, if it does, it is normally only a token gesture, without any physical separation from the smoking section. A few offices (principally those of foreign companies) are smoke-free.

performed by the *concierge* tip $3–5, though what you pay is likely to vary depending on the price of the place you are staying.

Medical Treatment

Good quality hotels have physicians on call. Check with the *concierge*. There are no specifically English-speaking medical facilities in Venezuela. However, many doctors and dentists, particularly special-ists, speak fluent English although English-speakers are more likely to be found in private clinics than public facilities. Public hospitals are more accustomed to handling emergencies, but some of the facilities can be sorely lacking in space, equipment, and even the most basic medical supplies.

In smaller towns in the interior of the country, there is normally only one hospital or *"ambulatorio"* – walk-in clinic. Anyone will be able to point you in the right direction.

Emergencies

The nationwide emergency phone number is **171** (when you dial, operators will direct your call to the appropriate service).

Pharmacies

An excellent system ensures that at least one pharmacy *(farmacia)* is open 24 hours in every sector of every town across the country – identified by a lighted *Turno* sign, and with the names of those *de turno* (on duty) in the vicinity posted on the doors of other pharmacies. Full lists are printed daily in Spanish-language papers.

Except for barbiturates, prescriptions are not required to buy any medications, and most major laboratories are represented here.

At the US Embassy, Health Unit personnel can offer advice about medications (locally available remedies for common ailments, Spanish terms for medicines and illnesses), and suggest English-speaking physicians.

Security & Crime

With the increase in the nation's economic problems, crime has likewise risen. Grim statistics of Monday morning body counts in Caracas newspapers are not representative of the general situation visitors are likely to encounter in areas frequented by most tourists, since 99 percent of these violent crimes are committed in slum areas.

Robbery

The targets of robbery, however, are more likely to be people who appear to be "good catches." Common sense is the best guideline for avoiding problems: do not flash your money around. If your hotel has secure safety deposit boxes with individual keys (not just a "place where it will be guarded"), leave any valuables you will not be needing there. Always carry your documentation, but leave photocopies in a secure place.

Men should always try to carry their wallets in front rather than in a hip pocket (many people prefer around-the-waist pouches). Women should hold purses firmly under an arm, and take special care with cloth bags – in *"Centro"*, the old downtown area of Caracas, people are particularly adept at slitting them with razor blades to remove wallets or other valuables without you noticing. Don't wear expensive jewelry (or fakes that look too real) or any other obviously valuable objects while out in the street. When not using them, tuck cameras in a carry bag or purse rather than hanging loosely around your neck.

Keep away from questionable areas in Caracas, even by day: any of the *barrios* (slum areas), anything west of Avenida Baralt, south of El Silencio, or north of Avenida Urdaneta; by night: Sabana Grande, any of Centro, or Plaza Venezuela.

Car Crime

When traveling by car, lock the doors. Be obviously aware of what is going on around you and who is nearby (not just for suspicious-looking characters on foot, but also motorcyclists who specialize in snatching purses, gold chains, etc. as they go by).

When you park, never leave anything inside. If you have to place objects in the trunk, do so before parking – so no one will see you "hiding" something, and never leave your vehicle unlocked in the street, even if it's "only for a minute." Should you be the unfortunate victim of a holdup, *do not* try to resist. The criminal is armed and has already been bold enough to face you, so would probably not hesitate to do you harm.

National Guardsmen

Visitors are often taken aback by the sight of police and National Guardsmen toting machine guns and automatic weapons. Not to worry, it's not the sign of an imminent insurrection, just the weapon of choice for national and local security entities.

Checkpoints (Alcabalas)

These are encountered along the highways throughout the country. Approach very slowly, watching for any indication to stop by the police or National Guardsmen manning them. If you are stopped, you will probably be asked for personal identification, driver's license, *carnet de circulación* (registration) for the vehicle, and requested to open the trunk for an inspection. Don't panic – this is a nuisance, but normal and legal. If they ask you to give them or someone else a ride (very common), you are neither obligated nor wise to do so; a polite refusal is not likely to cause offence.

Safety deposit boxes

Most places to stay either have in-room safety deposit boxes or ones available by the reception area. Use them to leave extra cash, tickets, credit cards, and other valuables you don't plan on using immediately.

Etiquette

Dress

Though shorts are now seen even on the streets of Caracas (formerly a real taboo except at beach towns), they are usually worn by young girls, and are still not considered in good taste. Topless sunbathing is theoretically illegal, but at some beaches on Margarita (such as El Agua and Caribe) a number of topless women are seen, though most are foreign tourists.

Form of address

Spanish-speakers from other countries are often surprised at the immediate use by many Venezuelans of "tú" (the familiar use of you) and being addressed with terms normally reserved for intimate relationships, such as "mi amor" (my love), even if they have just met the person or are talking to a total stranger on the phone. While this is a common practice, the well educated still consider it out of line. Thus, it is recommended that visitors stick to the more formal "usted" form of you and other addresses to avoid offence.

Photography

If you are planning to take a direct photo of a person, you should ask permission first. This is especially true in the case of indigenous people, who are often quite opposed to being photographed. You are more likely to be granted permission if you do not press the issue immediately, and then, ask the chieftain if it is all right.

Getting Around

By Air

For domestic travel, except for Delta Amacuro, every state has at least one airport for commercial flights. Tucupita's airport has been out of service for some years, so some travelers wishing to reach this state by air have to fly in to Monagas' Maturín airport, then use public transportation or rent a car to reach the delta.

Avensa/Servivensa and **Aeropostal** dominate the domestic market. However, a number of regional or specialized airlines now offer alternatives for specific routes and types of services on a regular basis (in addition to scores of charter services). It is best to check with a local travel agent to find out what lines are currently offering a service to your required destination, since there is often a surprising difference in prices.

By Bus

Because the majority of the population cannot afford private transportation, you will find frequent, cheap public transportation everywhere – even in the most remote areas.

In large cities, it is a breeze to get around. There are large buses (*transportes* or *colectivos*), *por puestos* (minibuses or cars which run on set routes and for which you pay by the seat), and *libres* (taxis), most of which circulate constantly.

Urban Buses

Buses and *por puestos* (super cheap: maximum to anywhere within a city about US$0.20) post main stops and end point of the route in the front window. Rates are controlled and posted for buses and *por puestos*.

Intercity Buses

Arrangements for interurban bus travel must be made at the **Terminal de Pasajeros** (passenger terminal), found in all towns and cities (except for the luxury lines, which have their own terminals – see opposite).

In Caracas, the former Nuevo Circo terminal used for all westbound buses (plus those going to El Litoral) was leveled in 1998, before a replacement had been contemplated, leaving the bus situation in chaos. At the time of writing a final location, **La Bandera**, at the junction of Avenida Nueva Granada and the El Valle autopista, near Los Próceres, had been chosen and was being reconditioned for use as the new westbound terminal. Some long-distance runs have only one or two scheduled departures per day, so call or check posted hours. But most buses and *por puestos* have no set departure time, leaving only when the last seat is filled. For some buses, you can buy tickets in advance (a must, if you can get them, for peak seasons of Christmas, Carnival and Holy Week, when huge lines and lack of seats are notorious).

The most common practice for popular destinations with frequent service is just to go to the terminal and take the next departing bus that looks to be in decent condition (dozens of hawkers for both buses

Caracas Bus Station

All eastbound interurban buses and *por puestos* use the new **Terminal del Oriente, General Antonio José de Sucre** (information, tel: (02) 243 2606/3253, daily 6am–11pm). It is located on the eastern outskirts of Caracas, on the freeway to Barcelona. The most convenient bus stop for transfers coming or going is at the Petare Metro station.

and *por puesto* cars shout out destinations, creating a circus atmosphere). Prices for buses are fixed.

Distances

If driving straight through, with only normal brief stops for gasoline or a quick bite to eat, and assuming that you take the most direct route, any major city in the country can be reached in one day's drive from Caracas. Flying time is under two hours for the most distant commercial flight from Maiquetía.

Luxury Buses

A welcome recent addition are the interurban bus services of "luxury" lines. They have fixed departure times, tickets can be purchased in advance, buses are new and air-conditioned, with TV or VHS, bathroom, and even trip attendants. The only drawback is that they have permanently closed curtains, making it impossible to view the landscape, so you are forced either to watch the TV or to sleep in the dark.

Aeroexpresos Ejecutivos
Av. Principal de Bello Campo, Caracas.
Tel: (02) 266 3601/2321/2214
Puerto La Cruz (081) 67 8855.
Runs a service between Caracas, Maracay, Valencia, Barquisimeto, Puerto La Cruz, Maturín.

Expresos Camargüi
Av. Principal de San Martín, behind Edif. Bloque Dearmas, Caracas.
Tel: (02) 471 7437.
Routes between Caracas and Puerto La Cruz, Cumaná, Cariaco, Carúpano, Punta de Mata, Maturín, Anaco, Cantaura, El Tigre, Ciudad Bolívar, Temblador, Tucupita, Ciudad Guayana. They also offer a taxi service to the terminal.

Peli Express
Behind Pro Venezuela, near Plaza Venezuela, Caracas
Tel: (02) 793 0830/0666, cell: (014) 980 3771.
Puerto La Cruz: (081) 81 8767/6286, 80 3772, cell: (014) 980 3705.

Offers a service from Caracas to Puerto La Cruz.

Expresos Los Llanos
Terminal del Oriente
Tel: (02) 243 3253/2606).
Has perhaps the most extensive service in the country, with routes connecting Caracas with all major coastal cities, from Maracaibo to Carúpano, and just about every point in the interior from San Antonio de Táchira and Mérida to Barinas, San Fernando de Apure, Barquisimeto, Ciudad Guayana, Santa Elena de Uairén, Tucupita, and Güiria – and points in between.

By Ferry

Conferry (Caracas, tel: (02) 782 8544) offers a service for cars/passengers between Puerto La Cruz (tel: (081) 65 3001) and Cumaná (tel: (093) 66 1903), and Isla Margarita (tel: (095) 61 9235). Buy tickets well ahead in peak season. You must line up two hours ahead if going by car (notoriously non-compliant with schedules)
Gran Cacique Express (Puerto La Cruz, tel: (081) 63 0935; Margarita, tel: (095) 98 339, fax: (800) 22 726, e-mail: naviarca@telcel.net.ve) has a passenger service only with transfer from Puerto La Cruz to Margarita in under two hours, VIP service.
Naviarca (tel: (093) 31 5577) has a car/passenger service from Cumaná to Araya (with car, best used morning only; as an open barge-like ferry,

afternoon winds and waves leave your car bathed with salt water) and Cumaná to Margarita.

There is a very inexpensive passenger-only service (no phone) between Chacopata (on the Araya Peninsula, Sucre state) and Coche Island, continuing to Margarita (landing in Porlamar, right by the main shopping area).

Driving

Driving in Caracas is an exercise in self-preservation and frustration, and a test of your nerve. The city is chaotic, congested, and filled with manic, aggressive drivers who consider traffic regulations (such as red lights, one-way streets) mere suggestions. However, once you escape this madhouse, driving in the interior is pleasant and roads are considered to be the best in Latin America.

In many areas, driving is not just the best, but the *only* way to really get a chance to see and appreciate landscapes, explore quaint villages, mingle with the people, check out crafts and foods sold along the roadside, all of which are missed if you fly or if you whizz by in a bus without stopping.

Night driving

Driving at night is not advisable, since lighting and lines defining lanes and warnings of obstacles are poor to non-existent, and there are frequently animals in the road.

Speed limits

Speed limits are all posted in kilometers per hour:
• Urban streets and roads: 40 kph (25 mph) – except near schools, hospitals or military installations, where the limit is 15 kph (9 mph).
• *Autopistas* (expressways): 80 kph (50 mph) in left lane, 60 kph (37mph) in right lane.
• Rural roads: 60 kph (37 mph) in daytime, 50 kph (30 mph) at night.

Traffic laws

Enforcement of driving laws has been notoriously non-existent in Venezuela. However, a new Ley de Tránsito (traffic law) may bring changes (especially since fines are viewed as an attractive source of income for local governments). Driving is on the right. Use of seat belts is required. Motorcyclists must wear helmets. Use of cellular phones by drivers in motion is prohibited.

Street Parking

Parking in the big cities, especially Caracas, is often next to impossible. For this reason, you see vehicles parked everywhere – on sidewalks, by fire hydrants, blocking driveways. Occasional *"operativos"* are carried out, towing away illegally parked cars and often legally parked ones too. They are

Taxis

Registered taxis have yellow license plates with black letters. and can be hailed in the street. Meters are not used, so agree on a price (bargaining is OK) before you get in. There is usually a minimum base price agreed upon by all the taxi lines in an area (even if you are only going a block), and the price goes up from there (in 1998, this was Bs.2,000 in Caracas). Even with traffic, no trip within the city with one of the circulating taxis should cost more

than the equivalent of about $8.

For your own safety, avoid the **piratas**, who are illegally operating freelancers (check for the yellow plates, since many mount the boxy "Taxi" signs on top of their car).

Taxis with *sitios* – lines which have a specific place they park (usually with a phone box there for clients to call them for pick-up) – charge more than those who simply circulate looking for fares. Taxi lines of the four- and five-star

hotels charge considerably more than other lines with *sitios*.

Longer Taxi Hire

You can also hire taxis by the hour or the day, for city sightseeing or for traveling to destinations (such as the beach for much less than renting a car, and you don't have to worry about getting lost, parking, or defensive driving. If you don't speak Spanish, check the "Language" section of this guide for some basic phrases.

supposed to write in chalk on the pavement the location of the official lots of the transit police where your car has been taken, but this is not always the case. Between this and the high incidence of car thefts (90 per day stolen in Caracas), it's worth using commercial enclosed parking lots/garages (*estacionamiento*).

Valet Parking Because of the ghastly parking situation in most popular restaurant zones, many establishments offer valet parking. While convenient, it is not necessarily safe: there have been many cases of items stolen from cars, keys duplicated and later used to steal the cars, and vehicles damaged by irresponsible driving of *parqueros*.

Car Rental

Car rental agencies have counters at all major airports and hotels. Those near "adventure areas" also rent out four-wheel-drive vehicles. During peak vacation periods, reservations should be made well in advance as demand far outstrips supply.

Rental fees are very high, with the lowest rate available for an economy compact about $50 per day. However, as compensation, gasoline is the cheapest in the world. Get full insurance coverage, since Venezuelans are aggressive drivers and are usually uninsured.

Make sure that they give you the *carnet de circulación* (registration documents) when you pick up the car, or you could run into problems

Car Rental Agencies

These numbers are available nationwide, some with toll-free for reservations:
Auto 727, tel: (800) 25 084
Avis, tel: (800) 12 016
Budget, tel: (800) 28 343
Hertz, tel: (800) 43 781
Other large agencies without toll-free numbers are:
Aco, tel: (02) 991 1054
Dollar, tel: (014) 927 2698

at the frequent *alcabalas* (police or National Guard checkpoints) scattered all along the nation's highways *(see page 318)*. Also check that the car has the required spare tire, jack, and emergency triangle required by law.

To rent a car you must have a credit card and valid driver's license (Venezuelan, international, or from the country of origin). The following companies have minimum age restrictions: 25 for Hertz; 23 with Avis.

Tours

Once in Venezuela, you will find that all major travel agencies (larger hotels all have them) offer numerous options for both local tours and trips further afield, and can arrange anything from just tickets to all-inclusive packages. This includes many all-inclusive charter flights, principally with the destination of Margarita. (*See "Specialist Tours" on page 312*)

Maps

Trying to find good road and city maps (or *any* maps) can be a challenge. One good source (and easily accessible) is the small shop, **Metro Guía**, in the La California Metro station in Caracas, just outside the turnstiles. They carry not only a wide assortment of maps, but also various guidebooks, Metro tickets and pre-paid phone cards.

Librería Tecni-Ciencias, one of the capital's most complete bookstores (CCCT, Centro Lido, near Chacaíto Metro; Torre Phelps, facing Plaza Venezuela; C.C. Sambil) also has many Venezuelan maps (including Roberto Marrero's series on the Gran Sabana).

Caracas A – Z

This section covers everything you need to know about visiting Caracas; it is followed by an A–Z of Isla Margarita *(page 327)*. For information about the rest of Venezuela, *turn to page 332*.

Choosing a Hotel

With the emphasis on business travelers (presumably with fat expense accounts), decent mid-priced lodging is difficult to find. Though dozens of two- and three-star hotels are found in the area from Plaza Venezuela to El Rosal, surrounding the popular Sabana Grande Boulevard, their use has come to be almost exclusively as by-the-hour places (with *por ratos* – just for a while – rates even clearly posted!) by prostitutes and clients. Going hand-in-hand with this, the zone changes dramatically by night. Hotels in Centro are likewise not recommended because of the high degree of insecurity at night.

HOTEL LISTINGS

Hotels are listed alphabetically. For price categories, see over.

Atlantida
Av La Salle, next to the Nunciatura Apostólica, Los Caobos
Tel: 793 3211
Fax: 781 3696
E-mail: j0016048001@cantv.net
Near Plaza Venezuela and Sabana Grande shopping and restaurant areas; fax, access to internet, and reception of e-mail for guests. **$$$**
Avila
Av George Washington, San Bernardino
Tel: 51 5155, 52 0170
Fax: 52 3021

A landmark (the first modern hotel built in Caracas, erected by the Rockerfellers), but remodeled with airy tropical furnishings; tranquil residential area, extensive garden-filled grounds, pool, tennis. **$$$**

Price Categories

Prices are quoted in US$, but payable in bolívars at the exchange rate of the day. Prices are based on double occupancy, standard room, without breakfast (unless otherwise noted).

$	under $60
$$	$60–100
$$$	$100–200
$$$$	over $200

CCCT-Best Western
Centro Ciudad Comercial Tamanaco (CCCT), Av La Estancia, Chacao
Tel: (800) 46 835, 959 5808
Fax: 959 6697/6409
In the huge, upscale CCCT shopping center; regular rooms plus suites with kitchen; swimming pool, gym, sauna, tennis; voice mail; rental of in-room faxes, computers, cellular phones. Exaggerated rates. **$$$$**
Centro Lido
Av Francisco de Miranda, El Rosal
Tel: 952 5040
Fax: 952 2944
In the sophisticated Centro Lido shopping center. "Boutique hotel" with emphasis on personalized attention. All rooms have two phone lines with voice mail, connections for fax and laptops, jacuzzi, spa. Three blocks from Chacaíto Metro. **$$$$**
Continental Altamira
Av San Juan Bosco, Altamira
Tel: 261 0044/0644
Fax: 262 0243
In the heart of one of the capital's best restaurant zones, two blocks above Plaza Francia and Altamira Metro; pool. **$$$**
El Cid
Av San Felipe, between 1ra and 2da Transversales, La Castellana
Tel: 263 2611
Fax: 263 5578
Modest, fully equipped (with kitchen) suites. Quiet side street in heart of La Castellana-Altamira

restaurant and banking district, opposite new Letonia Center, three blocks from Metro. Peruvian restaurant. **$$**
El Condor
3ra Av Las Delicias, Sabana Grande
Tel: 762 9911/7621
Fax: 762 8621
Easy access to shopping, Metro at east end of Sabana Grande Boulevard, by shops. Good Italian restaurant. **$**
Eurobuilding Caracas Hotel & Suites
Av La Guairita, Chuao
Tel: 907 1111
Fax: 907 2189
Great expanses of marble and glass give it an elegant but sterile look. Near Las Mercedes restaurant/gallery zone, CCCT mall. Three styles of Sunday brunch; Spanish nouvelle cuisine in luxury restaurant. **$$$$**
Four Seasons Caracas
Av Francisco de Miranda and Av Luis Roche, Altamira
Tel: 92 4122
Fax: 92 4377
Gigantic luxury facility (opening in 1999). Privileged location by Metro, prime restaurant zone. Rooms and kitchen-equipped apart-suites, business center, video conferencing salons, two pools, terrace with jacuzzi. **$$$$**
Gran Melia Caracas
Av Casanova and Calle El Recreo, Sabana Grande
Tel: (800) 63 542; 762 8111
Fax: 762 3737
Gigantic, new super luxury hotel of Spain's Sol Melia group, with 432 rooms, separate tower of apart-suites, convention area for 3,000; two pools. **$$$$**
Caracas Hilton
Av Libertador and Sur 25, El Conde
Tel: 505 5000; (800) 44 586
Fax: 503 5003
The best located lodging in the capital, facing the Bellas Artes (Fine Arts) zone, by a Metro station, just minutes from the financial district and freeway. Next door is the gigantic Parque Central complex, where they also have the four-star Residencias Anauco Hilton with rooms and apartment-style units. **$$$$**

Shopping Mall

C.C. stands for *Centro Commercial*, a Shopping Mall

Hotel Shelter Suites
Av Libertador and Calle José Félix Sosa, Chacao
Tel: 265 3866 to 69
Opposite the new C.C. Sambil; good Italian restaurant. Weekend discount. **$$**
Lincoln Suites
Av Francisco Solano López, between Av Los Jabilos and Jerónimo, Sabana Grande
Tel: 761 2727
Fax: 762 5503
In the heart of Sabana Grande boulevard shopping/restaurant area, classiest lodging in this zone. Special weekend rate. Near Metro. **$$$**

Hotel Discounts

When calling hotels for reservations, ask if they have any **special packages** on offer. They usually do – with great discounts and specific ground rules (by advanced reservation only, etc.) Among these are special weekend plans in hotels (such as the five-star chains) which normally cater to business clients, and weekdays for those geared toward tourists (principally beach hotels). Savings can be as much as 50 percent and often include a meal, welcome cocktail, or other extras.

Paseo Las Mercedes
Av Principal de Las Mercedes, inside C.C., Paseo Las Mercedes
Tel: 991 0033/0077
Fax: 993 0341
Great location in the heart of one of the city's principal zones for restaurants, nightlife, galleries. Pool. Weekend discount. **$$$**
Tamanaco Inter-Continental
Av Principal de Las Mercedes
Tel: 909 7111, (800) 12 132
Fax: 208 7116
"Grand dame" of the capital's luxury hotels, built in the 1950s when its

now-privileged location overlooking the bustling Las Mercedes zone of prime restaurants and galleries was "out in the country". It still enjoys a reputation as *the* status hotel for social and business affairs. **$$$$**

Restaurants

Caracas is reputed to have more restaurants per capita than any other city in Latin America. Thus, your problem will not be finding a place to eat, but to decide where! The two principal zones are **Las Mercedes** and the **Altamira-Los Palos Grandes-La Castellana** (the last three are essentially one area). **La Candelaria**, the Spanish sector in Centro, is known for its ethnic restaurants and *tascas*, but is best visited just for lunch since the zone is not safe by night. The same goes for **Avenida Francisco Solano** (which parallels the Gran Avenida of Sabana Grande) with many Italian and Spanish specialty eateries, among others. By day it's fine, but is an undesirable area by night. If you are into very serious sampling among the capital's hundreds of choices, you might pick up Miro Popic's annual Guía Gastronómica de Caracas (Spanish-English; available at bookstores, around $10) reviews virtually every place serving food in Caracas, and now includes nightspots and places in surrounding areas such as El Litoral.

RESTAURANT LISTINGS
Below is a sampler of the variety available, the best among all styles and prices ranges:

Ara
Centro Lido (8th floor), Av Francisco de Miranda, El Rosal
Tel: 953 3270
Menu combines Japanese (sushi bar) and "world cuisine." Rooftop setting complete with open-air oriental garden. Chic clientele. **$$$**

Arabica Café
Multicentro Los Palos Grandes, Av Andrés Bello, between Av Francisco de Miranda and 1ra Transversal
Tel: 285 6748

Estate-grown coffees, mouthwatering pastries, light fare. Nifty loft inside with newspapers and magazine for leisurely reading plus outdoor seating. Open daily 7am–11pm, candlelight by night. **$**

Bar Basque
Alcabala a Peligro, La Candelaria
Tel: 576 5955
Considered one of the best restaurants in Caracas. Tiny place with Basque home cooking; an institution for over three decades. Lunch only. Reservations a must. Closed Sundays, August. **$$**

Club Líbano-Venezolano
Calle Río de Oro, Prados del Este
Tel: 978 2368
Out-of-the-way location, but the restaurant (open to the public) of this private club serves excellent authentic Lebanese dishes. Closed Monday. **$$**

Price Categories

Prices are quoted in US$, but payable in bolivars at the exchange rate of the day. Prices are based on a three-course meal for one, without drinks.

$	under $10
$$	$10–20
$$$	$20–30
$$$$	over $30

Chez Wong
Av Francisco Solano, Edif Isabelita, Sabana Grande
Tel: 761 4194
Creative Chinese cooking head and shoulders above others of its genre, with regional specialties such as smoked duck with tea leaves and jasmine. Small locale with modern, refined interior. **$$$**

Da Guido
Av Francisco Solano nr. Las Acacias
Tel: 71 0937
Unpretentious but consistently good traditional Italian cooking; over 20 years with faithful following. **$$**

Das Pastellhaus
Calle La Paz and Calle Santa Rosalía (at the corner of the plaza), El Hatillo
Tel: 963 5486
Delicious calorie-laden German

pastries downstairs; upper terrace with both Italian and French-style (with white sauce rather than tomato sauce) pizzas. Closed Monday. **$$**

Tascas

Tascas are popular Spanish-style bars serving wine, beer and tapas.

Delicatesses Indú
Calle Villaflor, between Boulevard and Av Casanova, Sabana Grande
Tel: 762 0669
For years this modest place has maintained a standard of high quality Indian vegetarian cooking. No alcoholic beverages or smoking allowed. Economical fixed-price lunch. Closed Sunday. **$$**

El Buffet Vegetariano
Av Los Jardines, La Florida
Tel: 74 7490
Long-established, always faithful to healthy, generously served cafeteria-style vegetarian fare; family atmosphere. Fixed menu daily. No smoking or alcohol. **$**

El Portón
Av Pinchincha and Calle Guaicai-puro, El Rosal
Tel: 952 0027/0302
Traditional Venezuelan-style specialties, particularly beef; usually with live *música criolla* weekends and evenings. **$$**

Fuente de Soda Papagallo
C.C. Chacaíto, Chacaíto
Tel: 952 1008
An institution, with a huge selection of consistently tasty meals; fast service, excellent value. Good pizzas. Fixed-price lunch menu (under $5) is a real bargain. Great for people-watching. Open 8am–midnight. **$**

L'Attico
Av Luis Roche and 2da Transversal, Altamira
Tel: 261 2819
American-style casual restaurant (open-sided balcony is the best spot) and lively bar with occasional live music. Great burgers, varied menu; Sunday brunch. (Check out their Boston Bakery downstairs.) **$$**

Le Petit Bistrot de Jacques
Av San Felipe, La Castellana (facing McDonald's)
Tel: 263 8595
Traditional French bistro which has won a faithful following for its authenticity and consistency. Closed Sunday. **$$$**

Maute Grill
Av Río de Janeiro, Las Mercedes
Tel: 991 0892
Skip the American West air-conditioned bar and head to the rear for the restaurant part surrounding a traditional Venezuelan-style tree-filled patio. Excellent beef, perfectly cooked, generous portions. **$$**

Nomad
Multicentro Los Palos Grandes, Av Andrés Bello, between Av Francisco de Miranda and 1ra Transversal, Los Palos Grandes (no sign, next to Arabica Café)
Tel: 286 1849
What it lacks in atmosphere Nomad makes up for with its succulent authentic Moroccan cuisine. **$$**

Samui
Multicentro Los Palos Grandes, Av Andrés Bello, between Av Francisco de Miranda and 1ra Transversal, Los Palos Grandes (no sign, next to Arabica Café and Nomad)
Tel: 285 4600/4603
Rated by Florence Fabricant in *The New York Times* as "the best Thai restaurant in South America" with good reason. Beautiful interior and food presentation; outstanding food. Closed Sunday. **$$$**

Urrutia
Av Francisco Solano, Esquina Los Manguitos, Sabana Grande
Tel: 71 0448
More than 30 years of consistent excellence, serving traditional Spanish dishes, with an emphasis on seafood. Closed Sunday. **$$$**

Nightlife

As in most places, the main time for enjoying nightlife is on weekends. But, in Caracas, bars, discos, and other hangouts for *parranderos* (people who like to party) also do a healthy business any night of the week.

Night Centers
Along with traditional discos and bars, an interesting assortment of businesses catering to "night people" has emerged – most combining shopping and R&R activities. Be aware that the night scene only warms up after 11pm.

In Las Mercedes, **Le Monde de l'Image** (Calle Madrid, between Mucuchíes and Monterrey) combines, in one large open space, a bistro (with live music Thur–Sat from 9pm), ample bookstore, record shop and gallery (closed Mon; opens 10am until 10–11pm on Tues/Wed, and 2am or so Thur–Sat; Sun, open 1–8pm). At **El Chavo del Ocho** (C.C. El Mirador, Lomas de San Román), by night, three restaurants, Lectovideo book/video store and Jazzmania record shop "start their motors" when the other traditional merchants close their doors, and stay open, depending on demand, as late as 3–4am. **Café con Leche** combines a café with a boutique featuring designer clothing, Bonnet Diseños (Av Libertador, Edif Libertador, one block west of PDVSA, El Bosque; Mon–Thur, 10am–3am; Fri–Sat, until 4am; closed Sun), and does a booming business in the wee hours.

Bars and Music
For more traditional nightlife of dancing, drinking, music, and cafés, **Las Mercedes** is the best area, with a great number and variety of dynamic places, and with the best security. *Caraquiños* are a fickle audience, always seeking something new, different, and with infallible service. If a place begins to slack, you can be sure it will be gone soon. In Las Mercedes, there is every type of place – from **Taz Sports Bar** (open 24 hours a day) to a score of *terrazas* (open-air cafés which don't come alive until late at night), such as Mexican cuisine specialist **El Tajín**, or a growing number of places with gourmet ice cream such as **4-D, Bravíssimo**, and **Gelatería Parmalat**.

While an older audience hits places like **Tapas de Madrid** for the evening, the younger crowd is out cruising to see where the action is, very likely changing places several times in an evening, depending on the crowd or their mood. This is definitely the zone to check out what's new and who's who.

Best Nightspots
El Sarao
C.C. Bello Campo, basement
Tel: 267 2503
Overflowing on weekends with people who love to dance to salsa, merengue, and other infectious Latin rhythms.

Juan Sebastián Bar
Av Venezuela, El Rosal
Tel: 951 5575
The clientele comes for the music provided by top jazz bands, not to see and be seen.

Pal's Club
CCCT, Level C-1 (entrance from parking lot), Chuao
Tel: 959 1690
Elegant place for upscale crowd. Includes cyberbar, dining area, bar, dance floor.

Patatu's Drive Pub & Grill
C.C. Los Chaguaramos
Tel: 662 5085
Tex-Mex cooking; live '60s music (and interior decoration to match) Tues–Thur, and Sat. Ladies Night 7.30–9.30pm, Wed–Thur. Music for three generations on other nights. Closed Sun.

Stage
Av Luis Roche, entre 1ra y 2da Transversales, Altamira
Tel: 286 8717, (800)78 243
Blues and jazz specialties, but other live music featured. The best sound in the city. Kitchen open until the wee hours.

Weekends
Av San Juan Bosco, Altamira.
Tel: 261 3839
Going strong for more than a decade. TVs everywhere showing sports and MTV, loud music, many levels and frequent special events.

Night Delivery Service
Vip-Vip (tel: 993 6822/8763); provides a motorcycle delivery service for dozens of businesses from sushi bars and numerous

restaurants to liquor stores, pharmacies, and florists, 365 days a year, 24 hours a day.

Publications

For the latest "in" spots, keep updated with publications like the weekly *Date en Caracas* guide or *El Nacional* newspaper's Sunday supplement, *Feriada*, which has a fixed section on what's new and hot.

Cultural Activities

Caracas has a dynamic cultural agenda; to find out what's going on, check the free weekly calendar, *Brújula*, published Fridays in *El Universal*. *The Daily Journal* carries a Calendar of events (in English) every day – with its Friday edition being the most exhaustive. There are also culture/events pages published daily in the Spanish-language newspapers.

Theater

The majority of live presentations take place in the complex of the Bellas Artes zone in Los Caobos;
Ateneo de Caracas
Tel: 573 4622
Theater, films, gallery, music.
Casa del Artista
Tel: 577 2923, Boulevard Amador Quebrada Honda.
Rajatabla
Tel: 572 6109
Alternative theater
Teatro Nacional
Tel: 41 5956, Esquina Los Cipreses, Av Vicente Lecuna - Este 10 y Av Sur, El Silencio.
Newly restored.
Teatro Teresa Carreño
Tel: 800-67372; 239 8622
The country's principal theater, which features anything and everything from opera to rock concerts.

The venue for larger events (especially pop concerts) is usually the **Poliedro** (tel: 681 3333); take La Rinconada exit from westbound El Valle autopista, indicated as the route for Maracay.

The principal salons of five-star hotels also hold concerts.

Art

The greatest concentration of private galleries is in **Las Mercedes**, with Sundays (roughly 11am–2pm) being the principal day for openings, and the favorite time for art lovers to make the rounds (mainly because you can park in this sector on Sundays).

The **Bellas Artes** zone offers the following important galleries (for further details, *see page 140/41*):
Museo de Arte Contemporáneo de Caracas Sofía Imber
Tel: 573 8289
One of the best art galleries on the continent.
Museo de Bellas Artes
Tel: 571 1819
Features mainly temporary exhibitions. Excellent views from the rooftop terrace.
Galería de Arte Nacional
Tel: 587 1118
Four centuries of Venezuelan art.

Other important sites for art and cultural events scattered through the city include:
Casa Rómulo Gallegos
Tel: 285 2990, CELARG – Av Luis Roche y 3ra Transversal, Altamira.
Museo Alejandro Otero
Tel: 682 0941, La Rinconada.
Fundación Corp Group Centro Cultural
Tel: 206 3246, Torre Corp Banca, La Castellana.
Museo de Arte Colonial Quinta de Anauco
Tel: 51 8517, Av Panteón, San Bernadino.
Sala Mendoza
Tel: 571 7120, Av Andrés Bello, Edif. Las Fundaciones, PB, Local 10. Gallery with over 40 years in the spotlight, bookstore focusing on international art publications, café.
Centro de Arte La Estancia
Tel: 208 6972, Av Francisco de Miranda, La Floresta.

General Information

El Nacional newspaper publishes a weekly magazine (sold separately at newsstands for about US$1), *Date en Caracas*, which, along with information about upcoming events,

gallery shows and TV programming, also includes comprehensive listings of restaurants, bars, cafés, ice cream shops, with reviews; plus listings of hotels, transportation services, emergency numbers, shopping destinations... in other words, everything at your fingertips and updated weekly!

The monthly *Exceso* magazine includes reviews of all the principal restaurants, cafés, and nightspots in Caracas.

Festivals

There are many annual festivals as well, ranging from dance, theater, and jazz to Latin and chamber music fests. Dates and locations vary, so keep an eye out for announcements in the local media and banners strung across principal avenues.

Children

Caracas provides a fair number of activities specifically geared towards children; various restaurants, for example, (such as **Cristal Ranch**, Av Principal, Las Mercedes) have clowns and other entertainment for kids on Sunday afternoons.

Museo de los Niños (Wed–Sun, closed noon–2pm) is the capital's most outstanding offer for kids and is fascinating for adults, too. This enormous hands-on children's museum in Parque Central should not be missed. (*See page 140*)

Parks such as **Caricuao Zoo** (with a kids' petting zoo) and **Parque del Este** are ideal destinations. **Parque Los Caobos** nearly always has informal performances by clowns on Sundays, along with plenty of space for working off excess energy. **Teatro Tilingo** (tel: 793 7570; Av Andrés Bello, Parque Arístides Rojas, Meripérez) offers theater for kids every weekend (Saturday, 3pm; Sunday, 4.30pm); as does **Sala Cadafe** (tel: 208 8355; Saturday, 4pm; Sunday, times vary – best to call; Edif. Cadafe, Av Sanz, El Marqués). The **Cinemateca Nacional** (tel: 576

1491, Galería de Arte Nacional, Los Caobos) offers films especially for children on Sundays, 11.30am.

Emergency Services

MEDICAL

Aeromed Aeroambulancias: Transfer of patients in critical condition on national and international routes in airplanes specially equipped for intensive care; transfer on land by ambulances to assistance center. 24-hour emergency service. Tel: 993 2541, 92 8980, 74 6311, Cell. (016) 625 1391.
Centro Móvil de Medicina Permanente is an emergency service with doctors who make 24-hour house calls if a patient can't be moved. Tel: 483 7021/6092.

Hospitals include:

Clínica El Avila: Av San Juan Bosco con 6ta Transversal, Altamira. Tel: 208 1111/1001/1003 (private).
Clínica Cardiológica San Pablo: Calle La Peña con Calle La Guairita, Lomas de Las Mercedes. Emergency tel: 991 2121/5454.
Clínica de Emergencia Infantil (children's emergencies): Edif. Topacio (4th floor), Av Avila, between Av Caracas and Gamboa. Tel: 51 6111/7531 (private).
Hospital Universitario: Universidad Central de Venezuela. Tel: 606 7111 (public).

DENTAL

With some English-speaking staff:
Centro de Especialidades Odontológicas: Av Principal, Chuao. Children's services: tel: 991 6122/6801; adult services, tel: 991 6422/6877.
Clínica Odontológica Oreadi: CCCT, Ofic 218 (2nd floor), Chuao. Tel: 959 1948/1971.
Centro Odontológico El Prisma: El Pirámide (same exit as for C.C. Concresa, right next door), Prados del Este (ground floor by the gasoline station). Tel: (016) 625 1795 or 979 4280/2245. 24-hour emergency service.

Transportation

THE METRO

The Metro (subway) is the pride of Caracas. Three lines provide stops all along the main corridors for business, shopping and cultural attractions. A complementary system of Metrobuses combines Metro travel with buses which cover extensive routes from each subway stop.

Tickets can be purchased singly for Metro alone or *combinado*, good for a Metro ride and continuing service on Metrobus (or vice versa). Much more economical are *multi-abono* and *multi-abono combinado* tickets, good for 10 rides for a flat fee. Tickets are also sold at many newsstands (identified with a large 'M').

The Metro runs from 5am to 11pm (with the exception of a few stations in grotty areas which close earlier) and is very clean, with excellent security day or night.

Tourist Information

Contact **Corpoturismo** (the national tourism ministry), Torre Oeste (West Tower), 37th floor, Parque Central (1 block south of the Bellas Artes Metro station). Call the same toll-free number as the consumer protection unit, Indecu, tel: (800) 43 328. *See page 315 for further details.*

TAXIS

For reliable late night/early morning taxi service in Caracas (such as at the door pick-up to get you to the airport for an early-morning flight, or pre-arranged pick-ups from isolated areas at specific times) there are several 24-hour service radio-link taxi lines.
Coventaxis, tel: 576 6865/6533
Taxi Móvil-Enlace, tel: 575 0767, 577 0922/3344/4940.
Taxitour, tel: 794 1264/1365.
TaxiVen, tel: 985 0296/5715.
TeleTaxi, tel: 753 9122/4155.

If speed is of the essence and traffic is at a standstill, another option is **Pronto Taxi**, which

pioneered motorcycle taxi service in Caracas (passengers are provided with helmets and raincoats and even use of an enclosed compartment for personal items if the weather changes), tel: 793 4981, 263 7959. Other moto-taxis include **Lion Taxi**, tel: (016) 709 7730, and **Moto Racing**, tel: (02) 74 6889. One of the main places where they all gather is at the east end of the Chacaíto pedestrian boulevard.

Shopping

SHOPPING MALLS

There are numerous shopping malls (*centros commerciales*) in Caracas. The biggest and best are:
C.C. Sambil (Av Libertador) and **Centro Ciudad Comercial Tamanaco (CCCT)**, both in Chacao. The first, reputed to be the largest in Latin America, along with 540 shops has a marine aquarium; an annex of the Museo Jacobo Borges (art museum), recreation center with 24-lane bowling alley, enormous Play Adventure amusement park, Tierra Increíble (with "galactic adventure," robot dinosaurs, an interactive part for kids to manipulate robots), discotheque, multiple theaters, etc.

CRAFTS

For gorgeous museum-quality Venezuelan crafts, try **Casa Caruba** (tel: 283 9368; open Mon–Sat 10am–7pm; Av Andrés Bello, between 1ra and 2da Transversales, Edif. Everi, Los Palos Grandes). Rather than the often mass-produced pieces sold as "typical crafts" at many places, these are more aptly works of art created by fine Venezuelan craftsmen – with everything from wood carvings and hammocks to jewelry and furniture.

The colonial village of **El Hatillo** (Metrobus service from the Altamira Metro stop) is the best place in the Caracas metropolitan area to spend a full day leisurely browsing on foot. For several blocks in each direction from the traditional Plaza Bolívar (with requisite colonial church facing one side and a pair of sloths living in the treetops) the vintage buildings are jammed with small shops that house everything from mini-galleries and workshops of one-of-a-kind gold jewelry, to places with ceramics, books, unique clothing, spices, and antiques. A prime attraction is **Hannsi**, indisputably the place with the best selection of Venezuelan handicrafts in the country (its representation of indigenous art is outstanding). But remember that almost every place is closed Monday. Unfortunately, a number of unscrupulous tour operators purposely choose this day to offer visits to El Hatillo – since it's easiest to park then!

A bonus is that El Hatillo is packed with restaurants to suit every taste and most pockets. Here are a few to choose from: **Sake** (Japanese), **Casaccia** and **La Terraza** (Italian), **L'Arbalette** (Swiss), **Houllhan's** (American), **Don Juseff** (Arabic), **Mi Fogic** (Venezuelan), **La Romana Hatillana** and **Hatillo Grill** (meats), **Papasitos** and **Padrisimo** (Mexican), some half-dozen pizza places, **Sukothai** (Thai), **Vara Grill** (shish kebabs), **El Gratín** (Antillian), **Oker's** (Basque), **Mantuán Café** (continental), etc.

Isla Margarita A – Z

Choosing a Hotel

Your choice of accommodation here is more varied than anywhere else in the country.

Most of the large hotels and resorts offer rock-bottom bargains to boost occupancy. Since these offers are constantly changing, it is best to consult local travel agencies. These special deals are usually all-inclusive packages with meals, and often tours and airline ticket thrown in.

Among the travel agencies most frequently offering special plans are: **Aseyreca-A-1 Tours**, tel: (02) 62 8860/2328, 61 8427; after 7pm, (02) 61 0808, (014) 927 7051. **Holiday Tours**, tel: (095) 61 1311, 64 1311, fax: 64 2992. **Liberty Tours & Travel**, tel: (02) 952 2833/4070, fax: 952 2427. **Oiota Tour Operators**, tel: (02) 761 9511. **Party Tours**, tel: (095) 61 0390/0035, fax: 61 0080. **Toromaima Tours**, tel: (02) 263 5833/5710, fax: 264 0082. **Trotamundos Internacional**, tel: (02) 285 2410/5237, fax: 285 2498. **Turitalia**, tel: (02) 263 1633/1723, fax: 263 5210. **Unitón Tours**, tel: (02) 501 7019/7085, fax: 501 8245.

Most of the places listed below are alternatives to the large resorts heavily promoted by most agencies.

As in other areas of the country, choices of decent mid-priced traditional hotels are sadly wanting. A number of entrepreneurs are now offering small *posadas* (lodges) with personalized service aimed at independent travelers looking for something different from all-inclusive packages with homogenized meals and group tours. For value for money, these options offer a far better deal than cheap hotels.

The capital is listed first, then other resorts in alphabetical order.

Hotel Listings

PORLAMAR

Aguila Inn
Calle Narváez (five blocks north of Av 4 de Mayo)
Tel: 61 2311
Fax: 61 6909
Uptown location near duty-free shopping, restaurants. Swimming pool, bar, restaurant, satellite TV.

Howard Johnson Tinajero Suites & Beach Club
Calle Campos, between Marcano and Cedeño, Sector Bella Vista
Tel: 63 9503/9163;
reservations Caracas
Tel: (02) 241 7321/4302/0591
Three blocks from 4 de Mayo (one of the main streets for shops and restaurants), yet on a quiet side street. Suites with one or two bedrooms, fully equipped kitchen, jacuzzi, satellite TV. **$$$**

Price Categories

Prices are quoted in US$, but payable in bolívars at the exchange rate of the day. Prices are based on double occupancy, standard room, without breakfast (unless otherwise noted).

$	under $20
$$	$20–50
$$$	$50–100
$$$$	over $100

Margarita Princess Suites
Av 4 de Mayo
Tel: 63 6777, 61 8732/3476
Fax: 63 0222
Downtown location. Suites with one or two bedrooms, one or two bathrooms (one with jacuzzi and hairdrier), cable TV, balcony, restaurants, bar, in-room fridge, travel agency, pool, executive services. Breakfast included. **$$$**

La Samanna
Av Bolívar and Francisco Esteban Gómez, Urb. Costa Azul
Tel: 62 1204/1267
Fax: 62 5466;
reservations Caracas
Tel: (02) 284 9006
Fax: 285 7352
Luxury lodging aimed toward clients using their Thalassotherapy Center for seawater treatments to counteract stress or physical ailments, and for beauty treatments. Four restaurants including Japanese and dietetic, piano bar; 25 shops. $$$$

Price Categories

Prices are quoted in US$, but payable in bolívars at the exchange rate of the day. Prices are based on double occupancy, standard room, without breakfast (unless otherwise noted).
$ under $20
$$ $20–50
$$$ $50–100
$$$$ over $100

COCHE ISLAND
Isla de Coche Hotel
San Pedro del Coche
Tel: (014) 99 1431/1435
Fax: (014) 99 1132
Aimed principally at windsurfers, on the beach but with pool as well. Restaurant, TV.
Coche Speed Paradise
Playa La Punta
Tel: (014) 995 2182/2183
This spot is also geared toward windsurfers, but offers other watersports too. In beachfront location with pool. 48 rooms with rustic-style decoration.

JUANGRIEGO & VICINITY
Apartments of Marie-Noelle
Casa No. 11, Calle La Marina, Playa Zaragoza, Pedro González
Tel: (016) 81 8119
Two very attractive beachfront apartments, fully equipped kitchen and dining area; every imaginable detail to make you feel at home (huge stacks of towels, books, coffee, tea, etc.). French spoken. $$

Dunes Hotel & Beach Resort
Playa Puerto Cruz, Pedro González
Tel: 63 1333
Huge resort sold in all-inclusive packages. Beachfront, tennis, gym, diving lessons in the pool, boat excursions to nearby beaches, kids' club. $$$$
Isla Bonita Hotel & Golf
Playas de Puerto Viejo y Puerto Cruz, Pedro González
Tel: 65 7111
Fax: 63 9068;
reservations Caracas,
Tel: (02) 781 8591, 793 1659
Modern, new prestige hotel offering a spectacular beach on one side and a top-flight 18-hole golf course on another. $$$$
Laguna Honda Inn B&B
Urb. Laguna Honda on main road from Juangriego to La Asunción
Tel: 53 1150
Very warm, homey setting. Delightful owners (firebrand *venezolana* and her British spouse) personally attend to guests. Comfortable, spotless rooms. Central atrium with excellent restaurant, bar, living area. Tours. Breakfast included. $$

PAMPATAR
Lagunamar
Apostadero, via Guacuco north of Pampatar
Tel: 62 0711
Large rooms and suites, enormous grounds, beach, watersports, huge swimming pools, tennis, gym. Set in an isolated location, so without private transportation you have to take taxis. All-inclusive. $$$$
Posada La Bufonera
Calle Almirante Brión, Pampatar
Tel/fax: 62 8418
Very pretty beachfront rooms with rustic-style, well equipped kitchen, in-room safes, beach chairs and umbrellas; enclosed compound. Quiet setting off main streets. Restaurant next door. $$

PLAYA EL AGUA & VICINITY
Hotel Coccoloba
North end of waterfront street, Playa El Agua
Tel/fax: 49 0353

Large attractive rooms and bungalows with sunken bar by the pool, small refrigerator, terrace with hammock, safety deposit box, sound equipment, hair drier. Breakfast included. $$$
Hostería El Agua
At 31 de Julio, by the south entrance to waterfront boulevard of Playa El Agua
Tel/fax: 49 7297

PLAYA EL YAQUE
Las Brisas del Yaque
End of waterfront street then half a block to left
Tel: (014) 995 6504
Fax: (014) 995 0908
A walled complex with 10 four-person villas – modern tropical-style, with fully equipped kitchen and two bedrooms, two bathrooms. Half a block from the beach. Price 50 percent more in high season than low season. $$$–$$$$
Yaque Motion-Windsurfer's Guest House
Waterfront street
Fax: 61 8956
Enclosed compound. Attractive rooms; upper terrace with restaurant, bar. Guests can use equipped kitchen. Mountain bike rental. Camping allowed. Breakfast included in high season. German and English spoken. $$

PLAYA FERMÍN/EL TIRANO
Hostería & Pensión Casa Maya
Half a block east of the plaza, El Tirano
Tel/fax: 48 187, (014)995 0079
German chef, Andreas Höschele, runs this intimate *posada* in a restored colonial house. Four double rooms, two with air-conditioning, private bath, two with shared bath, fan. Optional tours. German and English spoken. $$
Hostería Marymonte
In front of Playa Fermín, via El Cardón
Tel: 48 066
Fax: 48 557
Internet: http://comucen.com/mym/
Nine pretty cabins; each has private terrace with hammock. Pool, restaurant. French, German, English, and some Italian spoken.

Sun umbrellas and chairs to take to the beach. **$$**

PLAYA PARGUITO

Casa Blanca
One block from the beach, huge sign marks turn from El Tirano-Playa El Agua road
Tel: (014) 995 0290
Fax: (095) 48 631
Eight extremely attractive villas (for two to eight people) with fully equipped kitchen, terrace, satellite TV, sound system, air-conditioning. Pool, bar; lush gardens. French, English, German spoken. **$$$**

ROBLEDAL

L'Auberge L'Oasis
Calle El Tanque (south edge of Robledal, on the Macanao Peninsula)
Tel/fax: reservations: 91 5339
The only lodging on Macanao Peninsula. Ideal for sailors, with a calm bay in front. Inviting inn, comfortable, spotless rooms. Restaurant open to public (excellent French cooking). Breakfast included. French and English spoken. **$$**

Restaurants & Nightlife

The greatest concentration of restaurants, clubs, bars, bingo halls, discos, and other spots for nightlife is on Avenida 4 de Mayo and Avenida Santiago Mariño. This is particularly convenient for visitors without private transportation, who can either check out the options on foot or easily hail a passing taxi or *por puesto* bus. A good number of the restaurants are known as much for nightlife as for dining: the emphasis is on food during the day and early evening, but from 11pm or so until dawn, the focus shifts to the bar, music (live or recorded), and dancing.

All of the five-star hotels have their own discotheques and usually feature theme nights (Pirate Night, Caribbean Night, etc.), with appropriate music and show or activities with an older clientele.

At Playa El Agua, casual open-sided restaurants line the beach,

many with live music, most featuring seafood. In Juangriego, the beachfront likewise has the best restaurants. Playa Caribe has become a very popular place with the young crowd for night entertainment in its casual, open-sided waterfront bars (most with music and dancing after dark). But it is very isolated, and private transportation is a must for getting back to your hotel.

Places where you have to dress up are practically unheard of – even the Hilton is without any fancy restaurant, acknowledging that people come to Margarita specifically to relax and to get away from the formalities of ties and high heels.

The free promotional literature passed out to arriving passengers at the airport and in various free magazine-style guides available in hotels. often contain special coupons for restaurants and night spots good for discounts, such as free drinks or snacks, entry without cover charge. Since people tend to go out late, most places have a happy hour around 7–8pm.

Price indications apply only to restaurant service.

Price Categories

Prices are quoted in US$, but payable in bolívars at the exchange rate of the day. Prices are based on a three-course meal for one, without drinks.

$	under $10
$$	$10–20
$$$	$20–30
$$$$	over $30

PORLAMAR

Cheers
Av Santiago Mariño
Tel: 61 0957
Ample, and divided into several different sections (but still usually packed). Casual place. Good food by day; good for mixing at night, live music in many styles. In an area with various popular spots where people do a lot of bar-hopping. **$$**

Cocody
Av Raúl Leoni, sector Bella Vista
Tel: 61 8431
A taste of France in the Caribbean; romantic terrace with tropical atmosphere. **$$$**

Da Gaspar
Av 4 de Mayo
Tel: 61 3486
Seafood specialties, with attached art gallery. **$$**

Gold Fingers
Av 4 de Mayo
Tel: 61 5557
Strippers, table dancing, VIP rooms for private parties and stagnights. **$**

La Atarraya de las 15 Letras
Calle San Rafael at Charaima
Tel: 61 5124
Typical *margariteña* and *criolla* cuisine. **$**

Mosquito Coast Bar & Grill
Av Santiago Mariño, Paseo Guanaguao
Tel/fax: 61 3525
The most popular spot on the island for years. Older crowd comes early, for Tex-Mex food and the 7–8pm happy hour. Younger crowd drifts in around midnight for energetic dancing in a more wacky atmosphere than usual, and dark discos. Open 7pm–dawn. **$$**

Piano Blanco
Calle J.M. Patiño (half a block from Av Santiago Mariño)
Tel: 64 0936
Long-standing piano bar, drawing a slightly older crowd than the current "in" places, traditionally featuring *boleros*, salsa, music of the 1960s. Restaurant with French and Italian specialties. Open noon–3am, Sundays from 6pm. **$$$**

El Remo
Av 4 de Mayo
Tel: 61 3197, 63 4048
The downstairs restaurant is known for its paella. Upstairs is the bar and dance floor, open until 4am. **$$**

Señor Frog's
Av Bolívar, C.C. Costa Azul, Local 1
Lively bar/restaurant with crazy atmosphere, loud music, dancing, margaritas by the pitcher, BBQ ribs, etc. Cover charge. **$$**

Sevillanas
Av Bolívar, sector Bella Vista
Tel: 63 8258

Spanish cuisine with live music and flamenco dancing. $$$

PLAYA CARDON/PLAYA FERMIN

La Langouste del Cardlión
Boulevard Playa Cardón
Tel: 48 550
Tanks with live lobsters to eat all year long, haute cuisine, French wines. $$$$
La Trattoría al Porto
Calle La Marina, El Tirano
Tel: 48 208
Removed from the usual restaurant areas, but with a virtual cult following for its authentic Italian food. Pretty, fresh decoration with homey atmosphere. $$

PLAYA EL AGUA

Mambo Tango Beach Club
Playa El Agua (in front of Flamenco Hotel)
Tel: 49 1207
Fax: 49 0107
By day it is a beach club, offering chairs, sun umbrellas, restaurant with beach service, Sunday brunch, lockers and showers. From 8pm, dinner and Caribbean Show package; dancing in Disco Tropical 'til dawn. $$

PLAYA CARIBE

Mosquito Beach Club
Playa Caribe (2 km east of Juangriego)
Located by the beach, where the young and beautiful go to play. Restaurant features seafood, burgers, salads. For beach-goers: bathrooms, changing rooms, showers, chairs and sun shades. Music and dancing by night. Bilingual staff. $$

Consulates

Canada, tel: 64 1404/0086
Denmark, tel: 74 1975
France, tel: 61 8431, 64 1425
Germany, tel: 61 5212/5331
United Kingdom, tel: 62 4665
Italy, tel: 61 0213
Spain, tel: 64 1771
Switzerland, tel: 62 8682/5672

Currency Exchange

Caribe Express: Av Santiago Mariño, C.C. Fermín, Local 4, Porlamar. Tel: 63 9051/9153.
Cussco: Calle Velásquez con Santiago Mariño, Porlamar. Tel: 61 3379.
Febres Parra: Hotel Bella Vista, lobby, Local 21, Porlamar. Tel: 63 3811.
For You: Av Santiago Mariño, Porlamar. Tel: 61 4442.

Tourist Information

Corporación de Turismo de Nueva Esparta, the state tourism office, is located in the Centro Artesanal Gilberto Menchini, Los Robles. Tel: 62 3638.
FONDENE (Fund for the Development of Nueva Esparta State). Headquarters in the old customs house in Pampatar, by the fort. Tel: 62 2494/2342, fax: 62 2814. It also has a tourist information stand at the airport (tel: 69 1394).
INDECU (consumer protection institute), Av Constitución, Gobernación del Estado Nueva Esparta, 7th floor, La Asunción. Tel: 41 505.

PUBLICATIONS

Mira is a free English newspaper, available at major hotels and other spots frequented by visitors. It is famous for its out-spoken opinions, and attempts to provide visitors with current, useful information about the tourism and general scene in Margarita.
La Guía – Margarita Tourist Guide (with information in English, Spanish, and German), is published each trimester and is free, widely available at hotels, restaurants and shops on the island. While the information is more commercial than objective, it is comprehensive.

Emergency Services

MEDICAL
Centro Diagno Esteban Gichi, Calle Díaz con Calle Marcano, Porlamar. Tel: 63 2778.
Pediatric emergencies.

Hospital Luis Ortega, Av 4 de Mayo con Calle San Rafael, Porlamar. Tel: 61 6508/6646/2212. Public.
Centro Clínico Margarita, Calle Marcano con Calle Díaz. Tel: 61 5635/4611. Private.
Centro Médico Nueva Esparta, via La Sierra, La Asunción. Tel: 42 0011/0822. Private.

DENTAL
Dr Salomon Klugermann DDS
Calle Petronila Mata, Quinta No. D-12, Urb Playa El Angel, Pampatar. Tel/fax: 62 5146/1301.
Emergencies and regular care, English and German spoken.
Dr Lorena Godoy, Av Francisco Esteban Gómez con Av Bolívar, C.C. La Samana, Local 27, Porlamar. Tel: 62 7563
Emergencies tel: (016) 681 6008. English and French spoken.

Fun for Kids

Play Aventura, entertainment center in C.C. Rattan Plaza, Pampatar, has special areas for kids (huge play-park with slides, labyrinths, tubes, "swimming pool" filled with plastic balls; video games) and for teens (with video games, simulators, pool tables, air hockey, music, etc.).

Outdoor Activities

You can take a ride in an **ultralight** plane in Porlamar (Tues–Thurs) or at Playa El Agua (Fri– Sun). Tel: 62 5030, 61 7632.
Parasail – the Flyer offers parasailing from the beach in front of the Margarita Hilton, Playa Moreno. Tues–Sun 10am–4pm. Tel: 82 1904.
Operators offering **diving** are:
Margarita Divers, contact Aldonza Manrique, tel/fax: 62 1289 or (016) 995 3341.
Scuba Doo Diving Center, tel: 64 6272, fax: 61 8258; e-mail: octupus@enlared.net.
Diverland, via Porlamar–Pampatar is a large amusement park, open Wednesday–Friday, 7pm–1am, weekends 11am–1am. Single price

admission for unlimited use of all the rides.

Windsurfing is the name of the game at Playa El Yaque (its waters rated third best in the world), with numerous shops offering rental of equipment and lessons.

Horseback Riding Cabatucán offers riding in the rugged Macanao Peninsula presented in a package with French dinner while watching the sunset. Reservations through Holiday Tours, tel: 61 1311, 64 1311, fax: 64 2992.

Tours

C.C. Tours, Calle Tubores, Porlamar.
Tel: 64 0297.
Jeep safari of Macanao Peninsula with bilingual guide, insurance, visit to La Restinga, Museo Marino, lunch, open bar.
Fiesta Caribe
Tel: 63 9811
Fax: 64 1455.
Offering all-inclusive day tours (including champagne and oyster bar) to Coche Island, daily departures.
Cata Fiesta
Contact Catatumbo
Tel: 63 1072, 64 2772
Fax: 63 2080.
Their mini-cruise ship offers full-day, all-inclusive (lunch, drinks and live music) trips to Cubagua.
Aereotuy
Tel: 63 2211/2094/0307
Fax: 61 7746.
Offers numerous tours, including from Margarita to Los Roques, La Blanquilla Island, Canaima and Angel Falls, Canaima National Park, Delta Amacuro, and Grenada and Tobago in the Caribbean.
Rutaca
Tel: 69 1447/1346.
Offers day tours from Margarita to Canaima-Angel Falls, Uruyén, Los Roques, Trinidad, Tobago; plus flights to Barcelona, Güiria, Ciudad Bolívar, Carúpano.

Sundays

Sunday is *not* a good day for public transportation. Many drivers traditionally take the day off to be with their families, so buses and trains are few and far between.

Sundays, holidays, and at night, taxis charge 25 percent over the normal day rate.

Transportation

Along with a multitude of taxis, both circulating and with *sitios* (fixed stands), which can be contracted for single rides or by the day, there is an ample service of *por puesto* cars and buses, which are much less expensive.

BUSES

The following are the principal bus routes, with departures from various points in Porlamar – all next to or near the Plaza Bolívar. Routes are usually posted in the front window; fares to any destination are under $1. The name of the bus company is in italics:

La Asunción, Playa Guacuco: *Línea Matasiete* on Calle Fajardo, entre Av 4 de Mayo y Calle Igualdad.
Playa Parguito, Playa El Agua, Manzanillo: *Línea Antonín del Campo*, Calle Guevara, entre Calles Marcano y Cedeño.
Tacarigua, Santa Ana, Juangriego: *Unión Juan Griego*, Av Miranda, entre Calles Igualdad y Marcano.
El Valle, Las Piedras: *Línea Mariño*, Calle Marcano entre Calle Guevara y Av Miranda.
La Guardia: *Línea La Guardia*, Calle La Marina, entre Calle Libertad y Calle Arismendi.
San Juan, Fuentideuño: *Unión de Conductores San Juan*, Calle San Nicolás, entre Calles Arismendi y Mariño.
Ferry Terminal in Punta de Piedras: *Unión Tubores*, Calle Manciro, entre Calles Mariño y Arismendi.
Laguna de La Restinga, Península de Macanao: *Línea La Restinga*, Calle La Marina, entre Calle Mariño y Boulevard Guevara.

TAXIS
Taxi Impacto, tel: 63 7798/7113.
Taxi.net, tel: 64 2114/4103.

CAR RENTAL
Avis, tel: airport, 69 1236; Hotel Bella Vista, 61 8920.
Beach Car Rental, tel: 63 1005, 61 7753.
Budget, tel: 61 6413.
Hertz, tel: 02 3333.
Miami Car, tel: airport, 691483/1253; Hotel Bella Vista, 61 2490.
Oriental Car Rentals, tel: airport, 69 1284; Playa El Agua, 49 0029; main office tel: 74 3192, fax: 74 1448.
Rojas Rental Car, tel: 69 1442.

FERRIES
Conferry, tel: 61 9235/6780, fax: 61 4364; (800) 33 779. You can reserve and request tickets through their toll-free (800) number.
Gran Cacique II, tel: 98 339/430. Service between both Cumaná and Puerto La Cruz-Margarita.

MOTORCYCLES
A number of companies rent out motorcycles. Some locations include:

Airlines

Aereotuy, tel: airport, 69 1129/1480; Porlamar, 63 2211/0307.
Aeroejecutivos, tel: Pampatar, 63 2642.
Aeropostal, tel: airport, 69 1172/1374.
Aserca, tel: airport, 69 1460.
Avensa, tel: airport, 69 1301 to 05; Porlamar, 61 7111.
Avior, tel: airport, 69 1314/1014.

Laser, tel: airport, 69 1329/1216; (800) 52 737.
Oriental de Aviación, tel: Porlamar, 69 1054, 61 2019, fax: 69 1254; (800) 67 436.
Rutaca, tel: airport, 69 1346/1245.
Sasca, tel: airport, 69 1070/1170; Porlamar, 62 7156.
Zuliana de Aviación, tel: Porlamar, 63 2852/2936.

Hotels Bella Vista Cumberland (in the parking lot)
Tel: 61 7222, ext. 260
La Perla
Tel: 63 5902, ext. 3009
Crystal Garden
Tel: 62 0211
Port L'Mar Suites
Tel: 61 7444, ext. 734
Nicol's Rent Motors
Av 4 de Mayo at Calle Amador Hernández.
For Harley-Davidsons, the exclusive concessionaire is:
C.C. Buena Ventura
Av 4 de Mayo (in front of Tropi Burger), Porlamar
Tel: 61 8178.

Casinos and Bingo

Casino of the Margarita Hilton
Playa Moreno
Tel: 62 3333/ 4111.
Bingo Reina Margarita
Av 4 de Mayo, Porlamar
Bingo Charaima
Av 4 de Mayo, Porlamar
Huge bingo parlor that also features a salsa show, live music and dancing.

Shopping

The principal area for **duty-free shopping** in Porlamar is along Avenida 4 de Mayo and the down-town area centered around the huge Rattan hypermarket (Av 4 de Mayo near Santiago Mariño).

Various large new malls and shopping centers have developed around Los Robles and Pampatar on the eastbound extension of 4 de Mayo. There are duty-free shops in Juangriego, too, but, on the whole, the quality and variety of the merchandise is inferior to that in Porlamar.

Opening Hours

Most shops are open Monday to Saturday 9am–1pm, 3–7pm; but in high season Monday–Saturday 9am–7pm (during Christmas season, many are open until much later), Sunday 9am–1pm.

Where to Stay

Choosing a Hotel

Corpoturismo (the National Tourism Corporation) has a **star rating system** (one to five) which has been applied to most hotels. Suites, *posadas* (inns), and other distinct options, however, are normally not officially graded. There is generally a significant gap between quality of four- to five-star hotels and three-star or below. Most one- to two-star choices would be considered only if you are happy with basic accommodation.

Filling the gap has been a strong entrepreneurial movement to offer "alternatives" to traditional hotels, where smaller size and personalized service are emphasized, and where the value is usually much better for cost. These are primarily in the form of *posadas*, cabins, and camps. They come in all styles and price ranges, from extremely basic and inexpensive to truly exceptional offers with service and facilities that put five-star hotels to shame.

Reservations

All camps, *hatos* (ranches) and places with meals included require advanced reservations. In any case, it is always best to call ahead in case deposits are required, to check availability, to get specific directions for arrival, etc. This is particularly true during the high season, the timing of which can vary depending on the location: all places are busy over the Christmas period, for example, while the *llanos* camps are busy in the dry season; carnivals and special regional fairs will also affect availability.

Guide to Information

The order of regions follows that of the Places section in the main book. Caracas and Isla Margarita are listed separately:
Caracas: *see page 321*
Isla Margarita: *see page 327.*

El Litoral

This is the area of the Caribbean coast nearest Caracas and the National and International Airport in Maiquetía which serves Caracas.
Gran Hotel Caribe
Sector Caribe, Caraballeda
Tel: (031) 94 555; (800) 62 747
Formerly called the Melia Caribe. Access to beach, tennis, popular discotheque, gym, sauna, directed activity for kids and adults. Frequent discount packages for holidays. $$$$
Hotel Tojamar
Calle El Medio con Calle Regenerador, Macuto
Tel: (031) 44 232
Nicest of the economical small hotels, clean modern lines, air-conditioning, *tasca* (Spanish-style bar), restaurant. Two blocks from the swimming beach. $$
Hotel Las Quince Letras
Av La Playa con Calle San Andrés, Sector Punta Brisas
Tel: (031) 46 1551; (014) 930 4982
Fax: 44 1432
Facing the water, but with no swimming beach; restaurant/bar at the water's edge. $$
Hotel Puerto Viejo
Av Principal Puerto Viejo, entre 3ra y 4ta Transversales, Sector Playa Grande (al oeste de Catia La Mar)
Tel: (031) 52 4044
Fax: 52 1311
Nice hotel and the only lodging close to the airport, but in a rather grotty area. All the amenities of a five-star hotel plus beach front, three swimming pools (including a saltwater pool), tennis, satellite TV, marina. $$$$
Hotel Royal Atlantic
Av Costanera, El Caribe
Tel: (031) 94 1350/1361

Good choice for budget-minded travellers. Two blocks from the beach, restaurant, bar. Many restaurants and shops nearby. **$$**

Hotel Santiago
Av La Playa con Calle 2, Macuto
Tel: (031) 46 1754/1915; (014) 922 3168
Facing the water, but no swimming beach. Restaurant, bar, suites have jacuzzi. **$$**

Aloe Spa
Between La Sabana and Caruao on the dirt road east of Los Caracas
Tel: Spa (014) 934 0954; Caracas (02) 952 3741
Great place for total relaxation. Massage, steam baths with aromatic herbs, hydrotherapy, clay treatments and hatha yoga. Gourmet vegetarian cuisine. Beach, nearby hot springs. Plan includes meals and treatments. **$$$**

Los Roques

Because new construction is prohibited due to the archipelago's national park status, all lodging is in the form of *posadas*, which have been installed in former houses of local fishermen. Except for a handful of extremely basic options with shared bath, lodging is generally very expensive compared to other locations in Venezuela – even considering the fact that meals are included, and most also provide a cooler with lunch to take to the beach – and some will even provide transport for guests to go to nearby cays or beaches. The average is around $60–200 per person/per night, not including the cost of the flight (about another $100). Many offer a discount in low season.

Aereotuy Posadas
Tel: (800) 23 736
This airline has five *posadas* with pretty, airy rooms, two different pricing categories, and offers packages with flight and excursion to nearby cays included. **$$$$**

Posada La Corsaria
Tel: (014) 930 0796; (02) 267 6321
Handsome decorating with vivid tropical colors, lots of artistic details. Excursion to nearby cays. **$$$$**

Posada Mediterráneo
Tel: (014) 929 3305;
Agencia Elero in Caracas (02) 975 0906/0082/0237
Streamlined Mediterranean look, rooftop terrace with bar and telescope. Bone fishing packages available. **$$$$**

Posada Gremary
Tel: Posada (014) 927 8614; reservations La Guaira (031) 72 2765
Simple rooms but with cute decorative touches, some with private bath and plans to install them in the others. Shared living room with DirecTV. **$$$**

Hoteles del Amor

Throughout the country, you will find *hoteles del amor* or "love hotels" (usually referred to as "motels"). Some are enormous, very showy, and easily identified by their separate entrance and exit, with the "reception" just a booth to pay at the entrance.

These are not brothels (you bring your own partner). Rather, they are places where lovers can go for a private encounter in surroundings that are often surprisingly luxurious. They have come about because most young adults live with their parents (even once they marry), with no private space for intimate encounters, and also because of the high level of extramarital activity.

You can stay a full night (although it is preferred that you don't), but you cannot come and go. In many destinations, they are the best-value option as long as you are without kids, don't need a receipt, and understand the ground rules.

All have room service, with reasonably priced food but expensive booze, delivered through a double door pass-through so no faces are seen.

Price Categories

Prices are quoted in US$, but payable in bolívars at the exchange rate of the day. Prices are based on double occupancy, standard room, without breakfast (unless otherwise noted).
$ under $20
$$ $20–50
$$$ $50–100
$$$$ over $100

Posada El Canto de la Ballena
Tel: (016) 630 2420
Facing the sea, two rooms form Oriental-style combo boutique-restaurant, the Madrugada. Attractive rooftop terrace. Italian and English spoken. **$$$$**

Posada Acuarela
Tel/fax: (014) 932 3502;
reservations Caracas
Tel: (02) 793 7117
Fax: (02) 781 5756
Rustic furnishings and imaginative decor such as wooden fish mobiles. Transfer to cays, cooler with snacks, beer for lunch. Italian, French and English spoken. **$$$$**

Guaicamar
Tel: (02) 235 2250/2350; (014) 922 4965
Fax: (02) 234 3279
Rooms on a 23-meter (76-ft) yacht – three cabins, each with double bed, private bath, hot water, central air-conditioning. All meals, snacks and open bar. Sailing through cays, equipment for snorkeling and underwater photography. **$$$$**

El Oriente

ANZOATEGUI
Píritu
La Morenita
Av Principal Píritu-Puerto Píritu
Tel: (081) 41 2579
Fax: 41 0783
Walled compound with three extremely appealing two-bedroom cabins, fully equipped kitchen, great attention to detail, surrounding a pool. Very personable owners. **$$$**

La Posada de Alexi
Sector El Tejar
Tel: (081) 41 0469/3754;

Caracas, (02)52 5668; (016)622 5084; (014)629 5753
Plain but large and comfortable rooms in the owners' huge house (independent entrance); quiet residential area, game room with pool table, terrace with BBQ, fenced parking. Breakfast available. **$$**

Lecherías-El Morro
Golden Rainbow Maremares Resort & Spa
Av Américo Vespucio and Av R-17, El Morro
Tel: (800) 73 766; Caracas, (02) 564 0604/0630
Fax: 564 5502;
Puerto La Cruz
Tel: (081) 81 1011/3022
Fax: 81 3028.
Mega-resort with several lagoon-sized pools, golf (though the course is in poor shape), various restaurants, bars, nightclub, complete health spa facilities includes gym and sauna, shops, marina. Reduced price for guests over 55. **$$$$**

Price Categories

Prices are quoted in US$, but payable in bolívars at the exchange rate of the day. Prices are based on double occupancy, standard room, without breakfast (unless otherwise noted).

$	under $20
$$	$20–50
$$$	$50–100
$$$$	over $100

Puerto La Cruz
Gaeta Hotels
Beach, tel: (081) 65 18 22/5922
Fax: 65 0065;
city, tel: 65 0536
One facing the beach, on Paseo Colón, another two blocks south of the beach (defined as the "city" hotel and slightly cheaper). Plain but comfortable rooms, good location, continental breakfast included. **$$–$$$.**
Hotel Cristina Suites
Av Municipal
Tel: Puerto La Cruz, (081) 67 4712
Fax: 67 5058;
Caracas, (02) 953 7122

Eight blocks from beach. 236 junior and luxury suites, mini-bars in all rooms, satellite TV. Piano bar/disco, two pools, gym, sauna, game room, laundry, shops, babysitting, emergency medical center, organization of excursions. **$$$$**
Hotel Rasil Cumberland
Paseo Colón
Tel: (081) 67 2422/2535
Fax: 67 3121; reservations Caracas, (02) 761 1425/0923; (800) 72 745
Large "anchor" hotel of west end of Paseo Colón, near the ferry terminal. Terrace pool, large shopping arcade. **$$$**
El Dorado Suites
Av Principal Mesones and Calle 2, Zona Industrial Mesones, vía Distribuidor Los Mesones-Barcelona
Tel: (081) 76 9166/9245
Fax: 76 9366
Rooms and suites (with jacuzzi), swimming pool, restaurant, bar. While it has attractive services (gym, sauna) and prices, it has the aspect of a by-the-hour place. **$$$**
Hotel Caribe Mar
Calle Ricaurte No. 12, half a block from Hotel Rasil
Tel: (081) 67 3291/4973/5722/5846
Fax: 67 2096
Good option for tight budgets in generally expensive city; 73 rooms and suites, room service, satellite TV, basement parking garage, restaurant, bar, safety deposit boxes for rent. Near ferry terminal, Paseo Colón. **$$**
Hotel Turístico Puerto La Cruz
Paseo Colón
Tel: (081) 65 1393/3402
Formerly the Meliá PLC, first of the luxury hotels built in Puerto La Cruz. Only hotel on the beach (but water's not good for swimming), next to the marina, large pool, various restaurants, very popular bar, disco, shopping arcade. **$$$$**

Route of the Sun: PLC-Cumaná
Colorado Bungalo's Hotel Club
Urb. Playa Colorado
Tel: (014) 981 3966
Eight spacious and very attractive three-level bungalows for four with fully equipped kitchen, two bath-

rooms, covered parking for each unit. Swimming pool, BBQ. **$$**
Quinta Jaly B&B
Calle Marchant, Urb. Playa Colorado
Tel: (016) 681 8113
Comfortable rooms, some with private bath, others shared; AC or fan. Honor system for beer, pop from fridge. Full breakfast included. French spoken. **$**
Chez Federic et María
Las Colinas de Santa Cruz
Tel: (014) 980 3751
Twelve rooms on a hillside with short path to the beach of Playa Santa Cruz. Swimming pool, excursions for diving, beaches, mountains available. French and English spoken. Restaurant with breakfast, dinner. **$$**
Cafe del Mar
Santa Fe
Tel: (093) 21 0009
Right on the beach. Small, casual restaurant (open from 2pm) in front, very handsome double rooms in rear, all with sliding glass doors. German spoken. **$**
Villa Majagual
Punta Majagual (6.5 km/2.5 miles east of Santa Fe)
Tel: (093) 33 2120; (02) 976 2117
One of the best places in Venezuela. Six cabins on private unspoiled peninsula, French chef, impeccable service, small beach where dolphins frolic, option of yacht for "beach hopping." Price includes all meals (outstanding), and alcoholic as well as non-alcoholic beverages. **$$$$**
Posada Gaby
Final Av Principal de Mochima
Tel: (014) 993 2725;
Cumaná, fax: (093) 33 0462
Best option in Mochima. On the shoreline with own dock; optional boat trips, rental of diving and snorkeling equipment, pedal boats, and "banana." Breakfast available. **$$**

Cumaná
Hotel Los Bordones
Av Universidad
Tel: (093) 65 3555/3622
Beachfront. Tropical-style decor, rooms and suites with satellite TV, mini-bar. Daily aerobics by pool shops, tennis, disco, dining, bar,

tennis. Low season discounts up to 50 percent. **$$$**

Hotel Minerva
Av Cristóbal Colón
Tel: (093) 31 4471
Fax: 66 2701
Faces shoreline, but not a swimming beach. Restaurant, bar, small pool, satellite TV. **$$**

Bubulina's Hostal y Restaurant
Half a block west of Iglesia Santa Inés
Tel/fax: (093) 31 4025
Excellent choice for colonial zone location. Very pretty rooms in pair of colonial houses, outstanding traditional recipes of inviting restaurant/bar. Breakfast included in price. **$$**

Types of Lodging

Not all lodging is in hotels in Venezuela. Especially in the interior, the alternatives are more common than traditional hotels. These include:
cabase cabin, cottage
campamento camp
hato cattle ranch
posada inn, small and usually family-run lodging characterized by personalized attention
churuata indigenous-style dwelling, usually with earthen walls, palm thatch roof (often used for restaurants, bars, social areas too)
caney Like a *churuata*, but without side walls.

Araya Peninsula

Medregal Village
On Los Cachicatos-Guacarapo highway
Tel: (014) 993 0700
Attractive beachfront compound with social buildings (large restaurant, poolside bar, etc.) in palm-roofed *churuatas*; emphasis on water sports plus ultralights. Handsome rooms. Breakfast included. **$$**

Posada Araya Wind
Village of Araya
Tel: (093) 71 442
Next to photogenic ruins of colonial fort and beautiful beach, aimed

mainly at windsurfers. Comfortable rooms, pretty rustic style. Restaurant/*tasca* bar in back garden. **$**

Carúpano

Posada Nena
Playa Copey
Tel: (094) 31 7624
Fax: 31 7297
E-mail: posadanena@cantv.net
Extremely attractive, cozy place facing the beach. Grounds paved with seashells, shaded by palm trees; outstanding food, intimate bar. Pool table. Upper rooms in rear with screened walls are of note. Unique tours offered. German and English spoken. Excellent value. **$$**

Posada La Colina
Calle Boyacá No. 52 (behind Hotel Victoria)
Tel: (094) 32 0527
Fax: 32 2915
Pretty, rustic style, hilltop setting with sea view. Rooms with handsome bentwood furniture, tropical-style decor. Casual poolside dining, formal restaurant, *tasca* bar. Breakfast included. **$$**

Río Caribe

Hotel Mar Caribe
Av Rómulo Gallegos
Tel/fax: (094) 61 494
Walled compound next to the beach in the heart of town, rooms surround large pool, restaurant, bar frequently with live music. **$$**

Posada Caribana
Av. Bermúdez No. 25
Tel: (094) 61 162/242; reservations Caracas, tel: (02) 265 9150, 263 3649
Restored colonial house with very stylish rooms, central open courtyard, inviting shared living area. Restaurant/bar in rear with dining on terrace or inside with AC. American breakfast included. **$$$**

Playa Medina

Cabañas Playa Medina
On the beach.
Tel: reservations Encuentro Viajes y Turismo (094) 31 5241/2067
Fax: 31 2067
On one of the most beautiful beaches in Venezuela. Very appealing rustic-style cottages amid

palm trees, most with two levels, living room, separate bedrooms, fridge. Plan includes meals, drinks, transfer from/to Carúpano airport. Optional tours. **$$$$**

Via El Pilar-Bohordal

Campamento Agro Ecológico Río de Agua
Near Bohordal
Tel: reservations, Encuentro Viajes y Turismo (094) 31 5241/9124
Fax: 31 2067
Unique camp on large water buffalo ranch, with emphasis on ecotourism. No TV, phones, or electric generators. Energy from solar panels, bio-gas plant. Abundant wildlife observed during tours by dugout canoe. Lodging in *churuatas*. Meals, juices, tours included. **$$$$**

MONAGAS

Caripe & Vicinity

Cabañas Bellerman
On San Agustín-Teresén highway
Tel: (092) 51 326
Seven km (4.2 miles) from Guácharo Cave. Very pleasant cabins (one or two bedrooms) on wooded hillside, equipped kitchen. Playground, shop with homemade liqueurs, jams. Pets allowed. Friendly owners. **$$**

Hacienda Campo Claro
Teresén
Tel: (092) 55 1013
A 70-hectare (173-acre) functioning farm; visitors can explore the farm, hike in hills, ride horseback. Nice stone cabins with equipped kitchen, individual room, BBQ, meals available. Rooms **$**, cabins **$$**

Cabañas Niebla Azul
Via Mirador de Caripe, Sector Las Delicias
Tel: (092) 51 501
Fax: 42 4789/6674
Cabins (for up to six, two bedrooms) with front terrace, to enjoy great view of entire valley, fireplace, equipped kitchen, mini-bar, TV with VHS. **$$$**

Maturín

Chaima Inn
Av Raúl Leoni (next to Sigo), via San Félix

Tel: (091) 41 5955/6062
Fax: 41 8881
Discotheque and restaurant in part closest to street, motel-style connected rooms in an arc around pool in rear. **$$**

Hotel Morichal Largo
Via La Cruz, Km 3
Tel: (091) 51 4222/6122
Fax: 51 5544
On the outskirts of the city. New luxury hotel with all the usual five-star amenities but rather cold aspect. Two huge pools, tennis, gym, racquetball, sauna. **$$$$**

Hotel Stauffer Maturín
Prime location, next to new mega-mall. Very attractive low-rise design. Central pool with ample gardens, large handsome rooms. European-style service. **$$$$**

Posada Rancho San Andrés
Via Aribí, off Via San Félix (20 minutes south of Maturín)
Tel: (091) 43 0298, (06) 691 1067, (014) 760 0094.
Very pretty new camp on 1,000 hectares (2,500 acres), with cozy rooms, large *churuata* restaurant next to pool, excursions to observe fauna, horseback riding, bicycles to use. French and English spoken. Breakfast included. **$$**

Midwest

ARAGUA
Colonia Tovar
Cabañas Breidenbach
Sector El Calvario
Tel: (033) 51 211
Modern, cozy apartment-style units for 2–6, some with fireplaces and fully equipped kitchen and TV. **$$**

Hotel Selva Negra
One block from the church.
Tel: (033) 51 415/072
Fax: 51 338
Pioneer hotel in the colony, founded in 1936. Regular rooms and cabins spread over extensive wooded grounds, traditional design, highly regarded restaurant with typical German cuisine. **$$**

Posada Don Elicio
Sector La Ballesta
Tel: Posada (033) 51 254
Tel/fax: 51 073;

reservations Caracas
Tel: (02) 286 0464, 284 5310
Fax: 284 2429
Among the most beautiful places to stay in Venezuela, extremely cozy, decorated in the best of taste. Excellent food (breakfast, dinner included in price), terrace seating or inside dining, extensive grounds, intimate bar. **$$$$**

Maracay
Hotel Pipo Internacional
Av Principal El Castaño
Tel: (043) 41 3111
Fax: 41 6298
The best in the city. Cooler mountain location, just minutes from entrance to Henri Pittier National Park. Twelve-story tower, many thoughtful details (bedside control switches, phone in bathroom), large pool, gym, sauna, disco. **$$$**

Byblos Continental
Av Las Delicias (opposite Redoma del Toro)
Tel: (043) 41 5111
Fax: 41 0335
In the heart of the main street for restaurants, nightlife and shopping; near the zoo. Eighty-seven attractive rooms in tower, plus suites, small pool, disco, restaurant, bar. **$$$**

Hotel Princesa Plaza
Av Miranda, entre Fuerzas Armadas y Bermúdez
Tel: (043) 33 2357; 32 1454
Excellent central location just one block from the Plaza Bolívar and Teatro de la Opera, with the added benefit of being on quiet side street. Disco, restaurant with international and French cuisine, satellite TV, beauty salon. **$$**

Via El Limón-Cata-Cuyagua
Posada Boconó Club
El Playón
Tel: Posada (043) 93 1443
Fax: (043) 45 1473; reservations Valencia (041) 32 0038; (014) 945 1819; (016) 640 8003
The only *posada* in town right on the beach. Simple but comfortable rooms, huge log cabin with restaurant, land and boat excursions available. Price includes breakfast and dinner. **$$**

Posada Cuyagua Mar
One block from the main plaza in Cuyagua
Tel: (02) 861 1465; (016) 620 4491; (014) 937 4507
Surprisingly large with 26 simple, pleasant rooms surrounding tree-filled grounds, terrace, restaurant. Price includes breakfast and dinner. Short drive to beach – one of the best in Venezuela for surfing. **$$**

Via Las Delicias-Choroní-Puerto Colombia
Casa Vacacional El Portete
Calle El Cementerio, between Choroní and Puerto Colombia
Tel: Posada (043) 91 1255; (014) 945 7768;
reservatios Maracay
Tel: (043) 45 9271/0734
Complex on 60 hectares (150 acres) including Playa El Diario, with swimming pool, children's play area, video room, DirecTV, conference area, restaurant, bar, stage for live performances. Plans with one, two, or three meals. **$$$**

Posada La Casa de Los García
Calle El Cementerio, between Choroní and Puerto Colombia
Tel/fax: (02) 662 2858
Tel: (043) 91 1056; (016) 635 6894
E-mail: pogarcia@caracas.c-com.net
A 300-year-old house converted into a *posada*, maintaining its traditional styling; flower-filled center court-yard. Nicely furnished rooms. Price includes breakfast. **$$$**

Posada La Mesón Xuchitlán
Calle Principal de Puerto Colombia
Tel: (043) 91 1234;
reservations Caracas
Tel/fax: (02) 977 1794; (014) 928 0952
Gorgeous Mexican hacienda-style architecture, furnishings, antiques and original art. Suites have private garden patio with jacuzzi; family-style rooms have two levels. Price includes ample breakfast buffet. **$$$**

Posada Parchita
Calle Trino Rangel, Puerto Colombia.
Tel: (043) 91 1259.
On quiet side street, traditional architecture with pleasant rooms

opening out to garden courtyard. Reduced rate weekdays. Breakfast included weekends. **$$**

CARABOBO

Valencia

Apart-Hotel Ucaima
Av Boyacá, by C.C. La Viña Siglo XXI, La Viña
Tel: (041) 22 7011/4853/7381
Fax: 22 0461
Next to shopping center. Rooms and large suites (only slightly dearer than rooms) with kitchen, lighted tennis courts, swimming pool, satellite TV, restaurant, bar, parking garage, room service. **$$$$**

Guaparo Suites
Between Guaparo–Redoma Freeway
Tel/fax: (041) 24 3182/7978, 25 0522
Appealing new suites with fully equipped kitchenette, AC, TV, nice furniture, in-room safe. Roof-top terrace with jacuzzi, bar, game room with pool tables; buffet style American breakfast included. By main restaurant/shopping zone. **$$$$**

Hotel Coronado Suites
Calle 149 and Av 101, Urb. Carabobo
Tel: (041) 21 8255.
With 48 suites (small refrigerator, hair drier, bathtub) and 40 regular rooms, satellite TV, restaurant, bar, room service. Rooms **$$**, suites **$$$**

Hotel Don Pelayo
Av Díaz Moreno, between Calle Rondón and Vargas
Tel: (041) 57 9372/9378
Fax: 57 9384
143 pleasant rooms and suites, satellite TV, air-conditioning, restaurant, coffee shop, bar, parking garage; but avoid walking around this area at night. **$$**

Hotel Inter-Continental Valencia
Av Juan Uslar, La Viña
Tel: (041) 21 1533/1681/1033
Fax: 21 1151; (800) 12 132.
The most prestigious in the city. Mainly a business traveler hotel, but also popular for entertainment with frequent top name presentations. Quiet residential zone. **$$$$**

Hotel Paris
Av Bolívar and Calle 128
Tel: (041) 21 5655; 22 4757

Centrally located economical choice on main shopping and restaurant street. **$$**

Hotel Stauffer Valencia
Av Bolívar Norte, El Recreo
Tel: (041) 23 4022/6633; reservations 23 5197
Fax: 23 5044
Ideal for visitors without private vehicle: on principal avenue of Valencia for restaurants and entertainment. Shopping center in the base of the tower, plus restaurants and cinema. Pool. Free early-bird continental breakfast. **$$$**

Puerto Cabello

Hotel Suite Caribe
Av Salóm No. 21 (the continuation of the freeway entering the city), Urb. La Sorpresa
Tel: (042) 64 3276/3568
Fax: 64 3910
Tower hotel with regular rooms and two-room suites, satellite TV, disco, pool, sauna, gym, various restaurants, bar. A good choice. **$$$**

Bejuma-Aguirre

Posada La Calceta
Bejuma
Tel/fax: (049) 92 522, (014) 940 3254
In a large working hacienda in the mountains. Large, well-appointed rooms with great attention to detail, tasty meals included plus tours. Huge pool, horseback riding. German and English spoken. **$$$$**

Hacienda La Concepción
At entrance to Aguirre
Tel: Spa (014) 941 9999;
reservations Caraca
Tel: (02) 993 4410
Fax: 993 5275.
Spa under the direction of Dr Efraín Hoffmann, specialist in alternative medicine. Various anti-stress, beauty, detoxification programs. Attractive rustic-style buildings set in beautiful tropical gardens. **$$$$**

YARACUY

Campamento Ecoturístico El Jaguar
Via Duaca-Aroa
Tel: (051) 334064, 52 0235, (016) 50 3632

Simple lodging, all with shared bath, in a marvelous setting atop a hill within extensive virgin forest. Trails for observing wildlife, and horseback riding. Meals, tours included. French spoken. **$$$$**

Posada Turística Granja Momentos
Via Club La Montaña, San Felipe
Tel: (054) 31 0153
Very inviting option, enhanced by extremely friendly owners/hosts. Two separate cabins plus two rooms (shared bath) in their home. Large *churuata* (palm-roofed hut) where delicious meals are available. Pool, BBQ. **$**

Price Categories

Prices are quoted in US$, but payable in bolívars at the exchange rate of the day. Prices are based on double occupancy, standard room, without breakfast (unless otherwise noted).

$	under $20
$$	$20–50
$$$	$50–100
$$$$	over $100

FALCON

Tucacas

Aparto Posada del Mar
Calle Páez and Av Silva
Tel: (042) 83 0524, (014) 940 7836, (016) 642 1817
Very handsome, spacious apartments for four to six with fully equipped kitchen, penthouse with private terrace, BBQ. Beach front, *caney* (open-sided native-style hut) with BBQ, pool with jacuzzi, sauna with ocean view, boat service to cays. **$$$**

Hotel Sunway Morrocoy
Carretera Nacional
Tel: (042) 83 1138/1333/1652/1912
Most luxurious facility in Tucacas, but lacks atmosphere; three pools, lighted tennis courts, gym, four restaurants, disco, shops, satellite TV, all rooms with balcony. No elevator to 2nd floor. Plans with or without meals. **$$$$**

Posada Johnatan
Calle Sucre and Calle Principal
Tel: (042) 83 0239.

Simple but comfortable and economical rooms, plus a suite with equipped kitchen. **$**

Between Tucacas & Chichiriviche
El Solar de la Luna
Bella Vista
Tel: Posada (016) 647 2741; Caracas (02) 986 2861
Outstanding. Beautiful rustic-style house with five guest rooms, each a work of art with vivid colors, crafts, paintings. Terrace with dining area and garden centered by jacuzzi with panoramic view of the coast. Excellent food. Everything first class, including the charming owner/hostess Bertapaula. Breakfast and dinner included. **$$$** per person
La Pradera
Sanare
Tel: (016) 642 2014; (014) 943 2339
Extremely cozy rooms, all with either four-poster bed or bunks. Terrace with pool table. Restaurant with imaginative menu. Breakfast, dinner included. **$$** per person

Chichiriviche
Villa Marina Apart-Hotel
Vía Fábrica de Cemento, Sector Playa Sur
Tel: (042) 86 759/411
Fax: 86 503
Large, attractive complex with huge pool as focal point. 40 apartments with fully equipped kitchen. Pool tables, covered children's playground, ample gardens and plants everywhere. **$$$**
Posada Alemana
Vía Fábrica de Cemento
Tel: (042) 86 639; (016) 741 1765
Six pleasant rooms with private bath, giant thick towels. Deep lot filled with coconut palms, upper terrace, BBQ for use by guests, books, games. Breakfast and tours available. German and English spoken. **$**

Via Chichiriviche-Coro
Hacienda El Ojito
Tocópero
Tel: (068) 74 1050/1057
Very appealing compound with quality

throughout. Ten rooms with central AC, DirecTV, hammocks in deep porch. Pool, short walk via palm grove to beach, German, French and English spoken. Restaurant and bar only for guests. **$$**

Coro
Hotel Intercaribe
Av Manaure con Calle Zamora
Tel: (068) 51 1811/1944/1955
Fax: 51 1434
Near historic zone, simple but comfortable rooms, satellite TV, small swimming pool, ice cream shop, restaurant, *tasca* bar, barber, room service, video games, playground, secretarial service. **$$**
Hotel Miranda Cumberland
Av Carnevalli
Tel: (068) 52 4724
reservations Caracas
Tel: (02) 761 1662
Fax: 761 6681
Excellent location in front of the airport, and within walking distance from the heart of the colonial zone. Has been handsomely remodeled; pool. **$$$**
Posada Corocororico
Intercomunal, Sector La Sabana
Tel: (068) 78 517
Near Xerophytic Garden. Rather plain but clean, economical option. Restaurant, bar, room service. **$**

Paraguaná Peninsula
Hotel Península
Calle Calatayud, next to Club Centro Hispano, Punto Fijo
Tel/fax: (069) 46 6708/5983; 45 9776/9734/9847
Enclosed compound, rooms with satellite TV, mini-bar. Laundry and fax service, *tasca* bar, restaurants, room service, gym, sauna, pool, jogging track, playground, shops, multi-purpose sports areas. **$$$**
La Troja
Calle Santa Ana, No. 2, Adícora
Tel/fax: (069) 88 048; (02) 952 8352
Large, very pretty, enclosed complex. Cabins for up to eight plus large dorms for summer camps, meetings. Restaurant. Volleyball, basketball, BBQs, mini-zoo. Breakfast, dinner, excursion included in high season. **$$$**

Vacaciones Mostacho
Adícora
Tel: (069) 88 210
Fax: 88 054
E-mail: nhardin@conicit.ve
Five options in the heart of the colonial zone of xxxxxxxxxxxx, with individual rooms, studios with kitchenette, large fully equipped apartments with kitchen; some on the beachfront, others several streets back from the sea. Seaside restaurant and club, shop, rental of windsurf equipment, tours available. All lodging includes welcome cocktail, discounts in the shops, use of beach chairs. German and English spoken. **$$–$$$**

Lara

Barquisimeto
Hostería El Obelisco Hotel y Hostería Plaza
End of Av Libertador, opposite Obelisco
Tel: (051) 41 0311; 42 2233/ 2011/0711
Fax: 42 2133
Within one complex, the Obelisco has only twin-bed and single rooms; the newer Plaza has only double-bed rooms. Satellite TV, pool, five minutes from airport or industrial zone. Obelisco **$$**, Plaza **$$$**
Hotel Barquisimeto Hilton
Carrera 5, between Calles 5 and 6, Urb. Nueva Segovia
Tel: (051) 54 3201/2945
Fax: 51 8404, 544365; (800) 44 586
E-mail: hbhilton@sa.omnes.net
Great view over valley of Turbio River, both from back rooms and its popular poolside restaurant; lighted tennis courts, disco, spa (beauty treatments only), sauna, steam bath, access to private golf course (15 minutes from hotel), quiet residential neighborhood. **$$$$**
Hotel Principe
Calle 23, between Carreras 18 and 19
Tel: (051) 31 2111/1131
Fax: 31 1731
In the heart of the banking district, just blocks from the historic zone

and government offices. 150 rooms, satellite TV, pool, shops and services from pharmacy to travel agency. Restaurant, bar. **$$**

Hotel Yacambú
Av Vargas, between Carreras 19 and 20
Tel: (051) 52 1077/4272; 51 3022/3229
Fax: 52 2474
With 48 rooms and suites (some impressive bathrooms considering its three star status, with bidets, sinks in separate anteroom from shower/toilet, etc.) Cable TV, restaurant, bar. **$$**

Cubiro
Hotel Centro Turístico Cubiro
Av Principal ("La Vuelta")
Tel/fax: (053) 48 155
Regular rooms plus cabins for six with two bedrooms, TV, private terrace with great view of the valley, BBQ, table and benches. Restaurant service until 8pm, bar open much later. Rooms **$$**, cabins **$$$**

Sanare
Posada Los Cerritos
Los Cerritos colonial zone
Tel: (053) 49 0016
In the midst of the restored colonial zone and near entrance to Yacambú National Park. Attractive complex built in traditional style, with simple but comfortable rooms. Large pleasant restaurant, bar. **$**

Carora
Posada Madrevieja
Av Francisco de Miranda (main street entering town)
Tel/fax: (052) 21 3787
Large, inviting, open-sided restaurant (with good food) is closed to street, separate building in back houses clean, comfortable rooms. **$$**

Northern Zulia

Maracaibo
Astor
Calle 78, No. 3H-37 (opposite Plaza La República)
Tel: (061) 91 4530/4510
Very modest rooms (with AC, cold water only; private parking), but very convenient location surrounded by

many restaurants, shopping, discotheques and bars. **$**

Apart Hotel Suite Golden Monkey
Calle 78 (Dr Portillo) between Av 10 and 11
Tel: (061) 97 3285/6462/7423; (014) 961 7440
Fax: 97 1040
Regular rooms plus apartments with kitchen (without utensils). Restaurant and bar. Rooms **$$**, apartments **$$$**

Hotel Del Lago Inter-Continental
Av 2 El Milagro
Tel: (061) 92 4022/4222
Fax: 91 4551; (800) 12 132
On the shore of Lake Maracaibo, next to new shopping center. Popular poolside BBQ with live entertainment is a weekend gathering spot; night club, piano bar, gym, racquetball, shopping arcade. **$$$$**

Hotel El Paseo
Av 1B and Calle 74, Sector Cotorrera
Tel: (061) 92 4422/4114/1929
Fax: 91 9453
Tower topped by the country's only revolving restaurant (with bar and small dance floor) offering fabulous view over city and Lake Maracaibo. 53 large suites, satellite TV, pool. **$$$$**

Hotel Kristoff
Calle 67 and Av 8 (Santa Rita)
Tel: (061) 97 2911–13; 97 2919
Fax: 98 1614; reservations, (800) 57 478
Handsome alternative with full facilities but more economical than other four-star hotels; rooms, suites, and *cabañas* (larger suites) with mini-bar, satellite TV; nightclub, pool, playground. **$$$**

Marriott Maruma International
Av Circunvalación 2
Tel: (061) 36 3622/0022; reservations Caracas
Tel: (02) 752 0009
Fax: 751 2579
Near airport/industrial zone. Elegant public areas, shopping arcade, pool, jogging track, gym, sauna, tennis, horseback riding, racquetball courts. Weekend packages with greatly reduced rates. **$$$$**

Los Andes

This region has more lodgings than anywhere else in Venezuela, the majority in the form of cabins or small *posadas*. Thus, the list following barely scratches the surface of a multitude of excellent options available. Reservations are almost always necessary, because of great demand everywhere in high season, and for places including meals.

TRUJILLO
Boconó & Vicinity
Posada Turística Estancia de Mosquey
Guanare-Boconó highway, a short distance before Boconó
Tel: (071) 52 1555/1886
Pleasant rooms, tranquil setting with extensive lush gardens, covered terrace with BBQ for guests to use, kiddie pool, game room. Restaurant service 8am–6pm. Attended by friendly owners. **$$**

Price Categories

Prices are quoted in US$, but payable in bolívars at the exchange rate of the day. Prices are based on double occupancy, standard room, without breakfast (unless otherwise noted).
$ under $20
$$ $20–50
$$$ $50–100
$$$$ over $100

Hotel Campestre La Colina
By the river at northern exit of Boconó
Tel/fax: (072) 52 2695/1960
Quiet setting, extensive lawn areas (great for kids). Rooms plus handsome cabins with separate bedrooms, private verandah. Restaurant/bar. Rooms **$$**, cabins **$$$**

Trujillo
Hotel Trujillo
Av Carmona, at exit of downtown via Monumento Virgen de la Paz
Tel: (072) 33 952/576
Fax: 33 942

The fanciest among the few offers in town, with tranquil setting; pool. **$$**

Posada La Troja: El Portal del Encanto
Via Monumento Virgen de la Paz
Tel: (014) 971 2990; (014) 723 1959
Unique alternative in rustic artisan style with lots of imaginative decorative details; separate units with sleeping lofts (trojas) are the highlights. Popular restaurant in front terrace. **$–$$**

Valera-La Puerta & Vicinity
Camino Real
Sector La Plata, Valera
Tel: (071) 52 260
The best on offer in the state's largest and most important city. Tower hotel in the center of town. Refined restaurant/bar. **$$$**

El Nidal de Nubes I
Via Valera-La Quebrada-Jajó
Tel: (014) 961 3213
Spectacular mountaintop setting with panoramic view true to its name ("nest in the clouds"). Super cozy, imaginative rooms, restaurant, bar. Grounds overflowing with flowers. Meals included. Tours. **$$$**

Hotel Guadalupe Resort
Av Principal, La Puerta
Tel: (071) 83 294/825/703
Large resort (also time-sharing) with rooms plus apartments with equipped kitchen. Tennis court. Tours available. **$$$**

Casa Agripina
La Flecha (just south of La Puerta).
Tel: (071) 83 957
A delight! Very handsome units, most with fully equipped kitchen (including fireplace); each with its own private area in central terraced garden brimming with flowers. Very personable owner. **$$–$$$**

MERIDA
Santo Domingo & Vicinity
La Trucha Azul International Resort
Av Principal, Sto Domingo
Tel: (073) 88 066/150/079
Fax: 88 067;
reservations Valencia, (041) 21 9296.
Very pretty, large rustic-style resort, with a creek amid lush vegetation.

Elegant furnishings, first class service. Regular rooms plus suites with fireplace. Hairdriers, mini-bar. Tours. Midweek special includes continental breakfast, welcome cocktail, kids under 10 free. **$$$**

La Sierra
Av Principal, Sto Domingo
Tel: (073) 88 110/113
Fax: 88 050;
reservations Caracas, (02) 575 4835, fax: 575 4853
Luxury look throughout this compound with brick suites, the largest (for six) with fireplace. Restaurant with great view of valley, tasca (Spanish-style bar), sauna, lush flower-filled gardens. Low-season discount. **$$**

Hotel Los Frailes
Via Santo Domingo-Apartaderos
Tel: Hoturvensa (02) 564 0098; 562 3022
Extremely pretty complex incorporates buildings of vintage farm on site of, and following style of, 1642 monastery in center of the páramo. Excellent restaurant (except during Christmas; when only buffet service is offered) and cozy bar with huge fireplace. **$$$**

Price Categories

Prices are quoted in US$, but payable in bolívars at the exchange rate of the day. Prices are based on double occupancy, standard room, without breakfast (unless otherwise noted).

$	under $20
$$	$20–50
$$$	$50–100
$$$$	over $100

Timotes-Mérida
This area of the páramo is one of the most picturesque in the country with beautiful mountains and ancient farmhouses.

Hotel Las Truchas
At northern entrance to Timotes
Tel/fax: (071) 89 158
Beautifully maintained and family-run for over two decades. Rooms and cabins (some with fully equipped kitchens, all with fireplace). Restaurant with typical

Andean dishes, super cozy bar. **$$–$$$**

Posada San Rafael del Páramo
Just north of entrance to San Rafael de Mucuchíes
Tel: (074) 82 4198
Very pretty hand-built house, with original part erected in 1868 by father of famous local artisan Juan Félix Sánchez. Filled with imaginative decorative details, eminently cozy. Meals available. **$$**

Hotel Castillo San Ignacio
At north entrance to Mucuchíes
Tel: (074) 82 0021/0751
Mammoth stone castle that people love or hate since it is not at all "typical", but with incredible workmanship, medieval-style architecture with huge beams, etc. Each room different with first-class bathrooms, elegant aspect. Excellent restaurant and inviting bar. **$$$**

Hotel/Restaurant El Carillón
South exit of Mucuchíes
Tel: (074) 82 0600
Enormous, elegant suites feature beautiful and unique hand-crafted furniture, parquet floors, writing nooks. Low season discount. **$$$**.

Hacienda Escagüey
Main highway, Escagüey
Tel: (014) 974 9712; reservations Caracas, (02) 963 5608/7951
Two distinct options: rooms in a 1878 hacienda house, or beautiful cabins built nearby in a high valley surrounded by flowers. Breakfast and dinner included. Tours available. Rooms **$$$**, cabins **$$$$**

Cabañas Micatá
Near Escagüey
Tel: (014) 974 1277; (014) 974 0700
Fax: (074)52 5360
Handsome log cabins with first-class features, refrigerator, most with fireplace, surrounded by lawn and flowers, pool, restaurant, bar, pool table, table soccer, fireplace; satellite TV. Breakfast and dinner included. **$$$**

Cabañas Mucuratay
Tabay
Tel: (014) 974 0769
Large, inviting cabins (for 7–10 occupants), with outstanding workmanship, fully equipped

kitchen, hilltop setting. Restaurant, gym. Low season discount. **$$$**

Posada Turística la Casona de Tabay
Tabay
Tel: (074) 83 0089; 52 8727
Tranquil hillside setting, style of traditional colonial homes with open central courtyards, rustic tile floors, beamed ceilings, flower-filled gardens. Restaurant service by prior arrangement. **$$**

Via El Valle-La Culata
El Riacho
El Valle, Sector El Playón
Tel: (074) 44 4624; (014) 974 3025
By advance reservation only. Extensive walled compound of forested land and gardens with four top-class cabins (separate bedrooms, TV, fully equipped kitchen, fireplace). Playground, gazebo with BBQ, river. **$$$**

Riverside
El Valle, Sector El Playón
Tel: (074) 44 6639
Pretty, well-kept, and very homey cabins set in impeccably maintained garden, fenced compound. Sauna. Friendly European owner sells great homemade sausages, jams and dried fruit. Low season discount. **$$**

City of Mérida
For less expensive lodging here, you are better off in *posadas* than the city's cheaper hotels.

Park
Calle 37, in front of Parque Glorias Patrias
Tel: (074) 63 7014
Fax: 63 4582
One of the best options downtown: 125 rooms and suites in tower hotel, with restaurant, bar, disco, travel agency, shops. **$$$**

La Sevillana
Final Av Principal La Pedregosa
Tel: reservations, Fontina Tours, (074) 66 3225;
La Sevillana, tel: 52 0955;
tel/fax: 52 3051
One of the best in Venezuela. Marvelous tranquil wooded setting, yet minutes from downtown Mérida, gorgeous rooms, excellent food,

spa. Social area with fireplace, bar. Beautiful gardens, hiking paths. Breakfast included (also plans with all meals available), discount in low season. With breakfast **$$$**, with all meals **$$$$**

Posada de Luz Caraballo
Av 2, No. 13-80, opposite Plaza Sucre (Milla)
Tel: (074) 52 5441
Forty simple but immaculate rooms with TV and hot water; consistently dependable, friendly service year after year; restaurant with bar service, snack bar. Parking for only five cars. Low season discount. **$**

Posada Los Bucares de Mérida
(formerly Los Compadres), Av 4, No. 15-5, con Calle 15
Tel/fax: (074) 52 2841
Typical vintage house with central patio, spotless comfortable rooms with hot water, some with TV; use of refrigerator; artesanía shop and snack bar in front; ample private parking. Very friendly owners. **$**

Posada La Casona de Margot
Av 4, entre Calles 15 y 16
Tel: (074) 52 3312
Vintage house with central patio, handsomely decorated, telephone for phonecards, friendly staff. **$**

Residencias Agua Blanca
Urb. Alto Chama, Calle Las Peatones
Tel: (074) 71 2443/2723
Fax: 71 0846
In a suburb at south end of Mérida. Apartments with fully equipped kitchen for up to six, TV, lobby with VHS to offer English movies, transportation service, 24 hour concierge. English spoken. Low season discount. **$$**

SOUTHERN MERIDA
Jají
Hostería Hacienda El Carmen
Aldea La Playa, 2 km from Jají
Tel/fax: (074) 63 5852
E-mail: hostecar@telcel.net.ve
Active 19th-century coffee hacienda with attractive guest rooms. Excellent food, bar; social area with satellite TV, pool table, museum. Price includes welcome cocktail, coffee from the hacienda, plantation tour, horseback riding for kids. Plans with one to three meals. **$$–$$$**

Posada Papá Miguel
Calle Piñango, No. 1, La Mesa de Los Indios (5 km from Ejido)
Tel/fax: (074) 52 2529
Delightful vintage house plus additions in same style, restaurant with delicious home cooking, bar, BBQ, shop with handmade crafts, special programs, traditional Christmas dinner; friendly owner speaks some English. Includes welcome cocktail, breakfast, and dinner. **$$**

El Tao
Near La Azulita
Tel: (014) 960 5888
Fax: (074) 97 040
Unique ecological farm with emphasis on natural health programs, appreciation of nature, relaxation. Guests can use pretty cabins as *posada* or as part of programs. Excellent birdwatching. Without meals **$$**; with programs, meals **$$$**

TACHIRA
Northern Táchira
Finca La Huerfana
Páramo El Zumbador, via El Cobre-La Grita
Tel: (014) 979 5350
A real gem! Located in 80 hectares with river, forest, *páramo* with many trails. Extremely pretty, widely spacious cabins, rustic style, fireplace. Inviting restaurant (emphasis on natural foods), bar. English spoken. **$$–$$$**

Western Táchira
La Posada de la Abuela
Peribeca
Tel: (076) 88 0595
Restored, beautifully decorated vintage house on the plaza done in the best of taste in this delightful village. Inside restaurant with creative menu, bar, café; informal country-style restaurant in back. **$$**

Mi Viejo San Juan
North edge of San Juan de Colón
Tel: (076) 85 392, 93 040
Huge complex with manicured gardens, restaurant, game room, horseback riding, live entertainment, various bars, picnic kiosks. Unique cabins with *bahareque* (earthen walls) handsome interiors. **$$**

Hotel Aguas Calientes
Via Principal Ureña-Aguas Calientes
Tel: (076) 87 2450/1291
Fax: 87 1391
The principal draw is that 34 of the 36 rooms have natural "hot tubs" fed by thermal springs. Large pool with normal water, expansive grounds, massage. 15 minutes from San Antonio airport. **$$$**

Posada Paseo La Chiriri
Calle Los Morales, San Pedro del Río
Tel: Posada (014) 700 3447; reservations (076) 44 9403
Simple but pleasant rooms in traditional house in picturesque restored village. Central garden with breakfast area, ice cream and handicrafts shop. Outdoor crèches throughout the town in Christmas season. **$**

Price Categories

Prices are quoted in US$, but payable in bolívars at the exchange rate of the day. Prices are based on double occupancy, standard room, without breakfast (unless otherwise noted).

$	under $20
$$	$20–50
$$$	$50–100
$$$$	over $100

San Cristóbal
Castillo de la Fantasía
Redoma España
Tel: (076) 56 4492/4959
Fax: 56 4847
Definitely different! Built in the style of a European chateau. Each room is distinct – from streamlined modern to rococo with ornately carved furniture, crystal chandeliers; huge bathrooms, most with jacuzzi, elegant restaurant, inviting bar. **$$$–$$$$**

Posada Los Pirineos
Av Francisco Cárdenas, Quinta El Cerrito, No. 16-38, Urb Los Pirineos
Tel: (076) 55.65.28
Fax: 55.83.66
Nicely decorated rooms, small refrigerator, AC, phone, guests can use kitchen, inviting second-story terrace; breakfast and laundry service available. **$$**

Hotel Del Rey
Av Ferrero Tamayo
Tel: (076) 43 0561/2703
Fax: 46 3704 (the same as for Hotel Corinú, specify Del Rey)
Good-sized suites with full kitchen but no utensils, TV, underground parking, surrounded by area of small shops, bakery. **$$**

Los Llanos

Packages at the *hatos* (cattle ranches) all include lodging, meals, drinks, excursions with bilingual guides (by boat, horseback, photo safari trucks). By reservation only.

Hacienda Turística Ecológica Chinea Arriba Dude Ranch
5 minutes from Calabozo, Guárico state.
Tel: (02) 781 9684/4241
A 600-hectare ranch 3.5 hours from Caracas. Not as much fauna as others, but good for weekend outing. Unique outdoor natural jacuzzis. All-inclusive package. **$$$**

Hato El Piñero
Vía El Baúl, Cojedes state.
Tel: Bio Tours (02) 991 1135/8935
E-mail:
hatopinerovzla@compuserve.com
Pioneer among hatos in the llanos (plains) accepting tourists. Very pretty lodging in colonial-style building amid 80,000 hectares, top-notch service, wildlife reserve, biological station, fauna checklist. No children under 12. You can drive there in city car (5½ hours from Caracas). **$$$$**

Hato El Cedral
Between La Ye and Elorza
Tel: reservations Caracas (02) 793 6082
Fax: 781 8995
Former King Ranch with 50,000 hectares. Incredible quantity and variety of wildlife, especially birds. Simple cabins with AC, swimming pool, fauna checklist. Best to visit in dry season. Access by car. **$$$$**

Posada del Cabestrero
Guanare, estado Portuguesa
Tel: (057) 53 0101
Within the grounds of the Museo de los Llanos complex. *Posada* built in typical rustic ranch style, ample room with private patio/garden with

hammock, cable TV, small fridge. Price includes breakfast. **$$**

Guayana Region

DELTA AMACURO
Prices are for one person per night.
Delta Orinoco Lodge
Caño Guamal, northern part of delta
Tel: reservations Tucupita Expeditions, (087) 21 2986/1953
Tel/fax: 21 0801; (014) 989 0334
The most attractive camp in the delta. Some 25 individual cabins with private bath built like native-style *churuatas* with palm roof, all connected by elevated boardwalk. Meals, excursions included. **$$$$**

Campamento Boca de Tigre
Boca de Tigre, northern part of delta
Tel/fax: (091) 41 7084/6566
Built in Guyanese style, Large buildings with 25 rooms. Option of arrival by seaplane from Maturín. Meals, tours included. **$$$$**

BOLIVAR
Western Bolívar
Prices are for one person per night.
Hato Las Nieves Lodge
River valley of Las Nieves in La Cerbatana mountain range (1½-hour charter flight from Caracas)
Tel: reservations HAMAC. Tours (02) 993 9991/0591/3440
Fax: 993 5084
Top-class camp on water buffalo ranch, four suites (with terrace/living area), 12 rooms. Excellent food and service. Poolside bar, tennis, private landing strip (since the lodge is accessible only by charter flight). Excursions with horses, mountain bikes, canoe, kayak, motor boats, 4x4s. Geared toward adults only. **$$$$**

Campamento Río Caura
Las Trincheras, on banks of Caura River (4½ hours by boat west of Ciudad Bolívar)
Tel: reservations Cacao Expeditions (02) 977 1234
Fax: 977 0110
Sleep in hammocks in indigenous-style *churuata* (with shared bath) or in beds in cabins (private bath). Optional tour to Salto Para is a highlight: by river, camping on

beach, hike through jungle to reach beautiful falls next to Ye'Kwana Indian community. Multiple plans: lodging only, with some or all meals, with one or more tours. German and English spoken. **$$$**

Ciudad Bolívar

Laja Hotels
La Real: Av Jesús Soto, facing the airport
Tel: (085) 20 813, 27 955/944
Large pool, gym, excellent restaurant, piano bar, disco, shops, and pre-check-in service available for flights. **$$$**
Laja City: A few blocks from Laja Real (Av Bolívar entre Táchira y Germania).
Tel: (085)29 920
Fax: 28 778.
Guests may use the facilities at La Real. **$$**

Ciudad Guayana

Hotel Inter-Continental Guayana
Av Guayana, Parque Punta Vista
Tel: (086) 23 0011/1711
Fax: 23 1914
E-mail: guayana@interconti.com
Great location overlooking river and Cachamay Falls, next to Cachamay Park (connected by jogging path). Private dock and boats for river tours, pool, business center, weekend discounts. **$$$$**
Hotel Rasil
Centro Cívico
Tel: (086) 23 5096/4881/3626
Fax: 22 7703
In a good location for those without private transportation. There are 287 standard rooms plus suites and 32 apart-hotel units, bar, disco, restaurants, small pool, all one block from large shopping center. **$$$**

Upata

Hotel Andrea
Av Raúl Leoni (south exit of town)
Tel: (088) 21 3656
This is a good alternative to the expensive lodging of Ciudad Guayana for people heading for the Gran Sabana. Simple but comfortable rooms, Chinese restaurant/bar, shops, guarded parking. **$$**

Route of La Gran Sabana

La Montañita
Km 70.
(No phone)
Simple but comfortable, well-maintained spot, built and run by Pemón Indian couple. Rooms with private bath in straw-roofed churuatas; meals, tours available. Pool table, bar, VHS for guests only. Camping allowed. **$**
Campamento Anaconda
Las Claritas (Km 85)
Tel: (086) 22 3130/2864
Ideal place to stay for independent travelers before exploring Gran Sabana (starting at Km 88). Enclosed compound lodging alone available in nice cabins, or full packages with excursions and meals. Lodging only **$$**, all-inclusive (minimum two nights/three days). **$$$$**
Alligatour Mobile Camp
Tel: reservations, Caracas (02) 793 2419
Fax: 782 7719
Ciudad Guayana
Tel: (086) 22 9270.
Five or more days touring the Gran Sabana in minivans and camping, with all equipment supplied from tents to towels plus portable toilets and electric generator; meals. **$$$$**
Rápidos de Kamoirán
Km 174
Tel/fax: (086) 51 2729; (016) 686 5297
Twenty-five simple but very pleasant rooms with private bath, electricity 6pm–midnight. Restaurant with surprisingly ample menu, best food in the area. Small shop with basic supplies. Gas pump. **$**

Santa Elena de Uairén

Cabañas Freidenau
Av Principal Urb. Cielo Azul
Tel/fax: (088) 95 1353
Large fenced compound in pleasant grounds on edge of town, with various sized cabins and mini-suites (for three, with covered parking) up to nine (these have kitchens, but no utensils). Owners also organize guided hikes up Mount Roraima. Suites **$$**, cabins **$$–$$$**

Campamento Ya-koo
Via Sampay
Fax: (088) 95 1332
E-mail: yakoo@telcel.net.ven
Situated on the outskirts of town. Handsome churuata-inspired cabins with nice view from hillside, restaurant/bar for guests, many reference books about the area, tours available. German spoken. **$$**
Hotel Lucrecia
Calle Perimetral
Tel: (088) 95 1130/1385
Convenient in-town location. Simple but comfortable rooms with private bath, hot water, TV. Restaurant, bicycle rental. **$**
Villa Fairmont
Urb. Akurima
Tel: (088) 95 1022
Spacious triple rooms with DirecTV, small fridge. Large restaurant in churuata with bar, pool tables, wood-fired pizza oven. Tours available. **$$**

Hotel Addresses

There is only one main road through La Gran Sabana. Where no other address is given, hotels can be located using the distance (kilometer), based on the El Dorado fork at 0 km, and running southwards to Santa Elena, by the Brazilian border (316 km).

El Pauji

Hospedaje Las Brisas
Eastern outskirts of El Pauji
Tel: 088) 95 1030
To make the most of the beautiful surrounding landscapes, picture windows have been installed in main room of cabins; you can look out even as you take a refreshing shower. **$**
Hospedaje Chimantá
At the only intersection in the village, near the airstrip
Tel: (088) 95 1994
Fax: 95 1431
Comfortable rooms furnished with many attractive and imaginative details such as use of bateas (wooden bowls used for panning gold) for sink basins. **$**

Canaima

Prices at camps are per person per night, flight *not* included.

Campamento Ucaima (Jungle Rudy's)
600 m/yards from Hacha Falls
Tel: reservations, Caracas (02) 693 0618
Fax: 693 0825
This very inviting camp was established by Dutchman Rudy in the mid-1950s. On banks of the Carrao River with *tepuyes* in background. Extensive lawn and tropical flora; spacious rooms, very intimate feel and personalized treatment. Meals, tour included. **$$$$**

Hoturvensa (Campamento Canaima)
Tel: Caracas (02) 562 3022, 564 0098
Fax: 564 7936
At edge of Canaima Lagoon, with Hacha Falls and *tepuyes* in background. Huge camp with 115 rooms in cabins. Cafeteria-style meals. Plan includes meals, boat ride in lagoon; all tours extra. **$$$$**

Campamento Parakaupa
Tel: (086) 61 4963/2605; (014) 986 4821
Fax: (086) 61 4963
Short walk from Canaima airstrip, view of Canaima Lagoon, Hacha Falls, *tepuyes*. Run by Jungle Rudy's daughter. Eight comfortable rooms, porch with hammock in front. Tasty meals included, not tours. **$$$$**

Wey-Tepui
In the Pemón village of Canaima behind Hoturvensa camp. Simple rooms with private bath. Restaurant. Optional tours offered. (Price per room.) **$$**

Other Options

Campamento Arekuna
Northwestern corner of Canaima National Park, by banks of Caroní River. Attractive native-style cabins. Private landing strip. Some attractions can be visited on foot. Optional boat tours to falls and petroglyphs, Intimate feel and personalized treatment. Includes flight (from Porlamar or Ciudad Bolívar), meals, tours. **$$$$**

Amazonas

Puerto Ayacucho & Vicinity

Camps are definitely the best option in Puerto Ayacucho. The hotels are quite poor, and the residences (aimed principally at backpackers and use-by-the-hour) are cheap – but you definitely get what you pay for.

Hotel Apure
Av Orinoco, Edif Servicentro Apure, Puerto Ayacucho
Tel: (048) 21 0516
Fax: 21 0049
Noisy location on the main street above various commercial establishments, bar, etc., but convenient for tourists without transportation, with restaurants and shops within walking distance. **$$**

Price Categories

Prices are quoted in US$, but payable in bolívars at the exchange rate of the day. Prices are based on double occupancy, standard room, without breakfast (unless otherwise noted).

$	under $20
$$	$20–50
$$$	$50–100
$$$$	over $100

Guácharos Amazonas Resort
Where Calle Evelio Roa meets Av Amazonas, Puerto Ayacucho
Tel: (048) 21 0328
Large hotel (but hardly of "resort" category). Plain rooms, pool, restaurant. **$$**

Residencia Internacional
Av Aguerrevere No. 18
Tel: (048) 21 0242
Considered slightly better than the rest, but still very basic; 30 rooms, most with private bath. Some with AC. Small TV area and bar. **$**

Nacamtur
Vía Pto. Ayacucho-Samariapo, 13 km after the exit for Camturama take the road for El Retiro/Gavilán
Tel: (048) 21 2763/4255 (answer machine)
Fax: 21 0325
Tel: 21 4066 (Anunción Cobos)
Best alternative to Puerto Ayacucho

hotels if you have a vehicle. Paved access. Attractive compound. Large suites in brick cabins, air-conditioning, hot water. Huge restaurant, *tasca*, disco, pool table, Short walk to caves and petro-glyphs. Tours available. English and Italian spoken. **$**

Camps with packages

All include transfer between airport, lodging, meals, local tours. Prices per person per night.

Campamento Tucán
Behind Terminal de Pasajeros, Punto Ayacucho
Tel: no phone at camp; reservations, Alpiturismo Caracas (02) 285 4116/5116
Puerto Ayacucho
Tel: (048) 21 1378 (Luis González)
Large fenced compound within the city, access by paved road. Lodging in rooms or cabins set back in wooded property (some with AC, all with cold water only). If the camp has space available or in low season, rooms alone can be rented directly with them for about $15. **$$$**

Camturama Amazonas Resort
Km 20 via Samariapo, Sector Garcitas
Tel: camp (048) 21 0266; reservations, Caracas (02) 941 8813
Fax: 945 6160
Geared to those who prefer not to rough it. Modern cabins with AC, hot water. Restaurant. Large entertainment center with bar, disco, game with pool tables, etc. Without any excursions **$$$**, with tours **$$$$**

Campamento Orinoquía
Km 20 via Samariapo, Sector Garcitas (next to Camturama)
Tel: Cacao Expediciones (02) 977 1234
Fax: 997 0110
On banks of Orinoco, individual cabins with private bath, or triple rooms next to huge *churuata* social building (dining, bar, living area). German and English spoken. Plans with lodging plus two meals, or various full packages with tours. **$$$**

Note. To reach the following camps, there is an air taxi service from the airport in Puerto Ayacucho by Aguaysa (048) 21 0020/0026/0443 and Wayumi (048) 21 0635.

Campamento Yutaje
Northern Amazonas, north of San Juan de Manapiare.
Tel: (048) 21 2550.
Cabins and *churuatas* in large cleared area surrounded by woods, and a river. Private landing strip. Abundant fauna observed on river excursions. Fifty percent discount August/September. **$$$$**

Campamento Camani
On banks of Ventuari River, near San José de Camani
Tel: (048) 21 4865
reservations, Porlamar
Tel: (095) 62 7402
Fax: 62 9859
Internet:
http:www.enlared.net/camani
E-mail: camani@enlared.net
Short distance from airstrip. Native-style cabins, pool. Social building with restaurant, bar, Betamax. Horseback riding. Optional sport fishing plans. Drinks included in price. **$$$$**

Where to Eat & Nightlife

In the smaller towns and cities, there is usually not sufficient potential clientele for venues to dedicate themselves solely to nightlife. Thus, many places lead a "double life," being popular as a restaurant during the day and early evening; but, by night, putting on a different face – often with the addition of some form of entertainment or space cleared for a dance floor. For this reason, restaurants and nightlife have been placed under the same headings.

Because of the fact that most discotheques charge cover and/or require *consumo mínimo* (ie. the purchase of at least half a bottle of liquor, with no sale of individual drinks, beer, or wine), many people prefer to simply go to a pleasant bar for nightlife, rather than costly discos or nightclubs.

Eating Out

With the exception of coffee shops in premium hotels, it is rare to find any restaurant open for breakfast. Venezuelans either eat at home or will stop at a *panadería* (bakery) for juice, coffee and *cachitos* (ham rolls), *pastelitos* (pastry turnovers with ham or cheese inside), or similar fast food; or at an *arepera* for a *tostada* (an *arepa* filled with anything from grated cheese to quail eggs or octopus), or at street stands for *empanadas* (deep-fried turnovers with different fillings).

Most formal restaurants close after lunch, around 3pm, and do not re-open until 7–8pm, with dinner service until nearly midnight. Venezuelans usually have their evening meal late,

whether at home or in restaurants, rarely sitting down to eat before 8.30–9pm.

Many places offer a *Menu Ejecutivo* (along with their regular menu) as lunch option. This is a fixed-price menu, including soup or appetizer, main hot dish, dessert, and beverage – usually a great bargain and with service much faster than à la carte orders.

In many villages in the interior, the best places to eat are not necessarily formal restaurants, but private homes where *la señora* prepares tasty home cooking which she also serves to the public to bring in extra cash or fill a need in places where no restaurants exist. You will often find hidden gems by asking for advice of where to go at the place where you are staying (particularly at *posadas*) since they are most familiar with the local offers.

El Litoral

Come with a desire for fruits of the sea, since this is the emphasis in nearly every restaurant throughout the area.

Alamo
Av La Playa, Macuto
Tel: (031) 44 884
Divided into two parts: great location with tables in open air under the shade of trees and sea grapes at the edge of the sea (very romantic under the stars), but forgettable, over-air-conditioned interior restaurant. Seafood is the specialty. **$$**

El Bodegón de Lino
Av Principal Urb Caribe, Caraballeda
Tel: (031) 94 4992
One of the best choices in this tourist area; international menu, but emphasis on fish and seafood, most of which is prepared on a central grill in view of diners. Informal, lively setting. **$$$**

El Mesón del Faro
Av Principal de Puerto Viejo, Catia La Mar
Tel: (031) 51 1435
Though the neighborhood is less than appealing, this is the best option on the central coast, with excellent Spanish cuisine

emphasizing fish and seafood; attentive service. **$$$**

Sevilla
Sheraton Macuto Resort, Urb. Caribe, Caraballeda
Tel: (031) 94 4300
Elegant, refined restaurant of this five-star hotel, with outstanding French cuisine prepared by a top chef, Michele Catalá. **$$$$**

Yacht Club Cruise
Av La Playa, Caraballeda.
This bar is in a ship anchored along the shore and restaurant in a *churuata* directly on the beach. Order your seafood in the bar and they call by radio when your order is ready so you can move to your table. **$$**

El Oriente

ANZOATEGUI
Puerto La Cruz
The area in the center of Puerto La Cruz, by Hotel Meliá, on Paseo Colón and the block to the south and west is solid with bars, discotheques, cafés, restaurants. With the great number of offers on this boulevard and the pleasant area for strolling, most people prefer to simply stop at whatever place strikes their fancy, rather than heading for a specific destination.

Brasero Grill/La Boite del Brasero
East end of Paseo Colón
Tel: (081) 67 4850
Restaurant features beef and seafood. Large, yet cozy bar with lots of dark wood making it a good place to start or finish a night out. Upscale, older crowd. **$$$**

El Bacha
Paseo Colón
Tel: (081) 65 0206
Mouthwatering Arab pastries, Middle Eastern espresso. **$**

El Parador del Puerto
Paseo Colón
Tel: (081) 65 0391/3950
Seafood is the specialty; attractive rather elegant-looking dark interior. **$$– $$$**

El Rancho del Tío
East end of Paseo Colón
Tel: (081) 65 3677
Huge place with a variety of areas; an open-sided terrace, an air-

conditioned enclosed section with live music, a separate bar and a room for large private functions. Prices a bit higher than in nearby places. Beef and seafood specialties. **$$–$$$**

Fornos
Paseo Colón
Tel: (081) 65 3860
Handsome, rather formal interior, appealing antipasti cart, Italian kitchen. **$$–$$$**

Fuentemar
Paseo Colón
Tel: (081) 68 7623
Long-established place on the beach side, with both inside and outside seating – outside has a distinct soda-fountain-style menu. The more formal interior features seafood, as do most of its neighbors. **$$**

Lecherías-El Morro (Barcelona)
Caffé L'Ancora
Av Americo Vespucio (opposite Maremares), Complejo Turístico El Morro
Tel: (081) 81 0090
Popular casual setting with Italian

Note

Most restaurants, bars and other places with public restrooms do *not* provide toilet paper (or, if they offer it, you have to pay for it); thus you should always carry this necessity with you.

specialties, pizzas (white and red sauces), fajitas, interesting sandwiches, special desserts. Open 9am–midnight daily. **$$**

La Churuata del Morro
Via Principal del Morro, Playa Cangrejo
Tel: (081) 81 7486
Casual waterfront setting. Beef, seafood specialties. Live music Tuesday–Saturday, from 8pm; Sunday, 4pm. Closed Monday. **$$**

La Crêperie de Philippe
Av Principal de Lecherías
Tel: (081) 81 6695
For a change from the seafood which dominates local menus, try their variety of crêpes. **$$**

La Terraza Bar & Grill
C.C. Punta Marina, Av Americo Vespucio, Via Maremares
Tel: (081) 81 8212
Very pretty outdoor setting on a large terrace, protected by giant umbrellas, overlooking the canals. Salads, BBQ ribs, pizza, fajitas, gourmet hamburgers, etc. **$$**

Puerto Grill Steak House
Calle Arismendi and Calle Las Peñas, Urb. El Peñonal, Lecherías (next to C.C. Plaza Mayor)
Tel: (081) 86 8969/8218
Featuring prime rib, T-bone steaks, tenderloin and other succulent beef cuts, plus lamb chops, veal roast, and grilled Norwegian salmon. Reasonable bar prices. Open setting with sail-like blue glass roof. Live music Thursday–Sunday. **$$$**

Sushi Chef Japanese Restaurant
Av Principal de Lecherías
Tel: (081) 86 2424
Taking advantage of the plentiful fresh seafood – but presenting it with a different twist. In the principal restaurant and shopping area. **$$$**

SUCRE
Mochima
El Mochimero
On the waterfront, a few doors down from the parking lot. Pleasant, casual setting with open sides looking for view out over the water. Very tasty food with many creative touches. Great collection of jazz recordings for background music. **$–$$**

Cumaná
El Rancho E'Morris
Av Universidad, Sector San Luis
Tel: (093) 65 2866/2966
Waterfront setting with focus on authentic and delicious Italian cuisine that makes a change from the norm, prepared by Italian owners. **$–$$**

Restaurant & Hostal Bubulina
Callejón Santa Inés and Callejón El Alacrán (half a block west of Iglesia Santa Inés)
Tel/fax: (093) 31 4025
In the heart of the historic zone in a converted colonial house, with extremely appealing interior;

outstanding menu featuring traditional dishes of yesteryear. Definitely worth seeking out. Closed Sunday. **$$**

Restaurant El Navegante
Marina Cumanagoto, Av Perimetral
Tel: (093) 31 5023
Casual open-sided restaurant overlooking the marina, very popular with sailing crowd. Seafood. **$$**

Carúpano

Restaurant Rancho Grande
Carretera Cumaná-Carúpano, opposite Carúpano industrial zone
Tel: (014) 994 0962
Large *churuatas* house family-run restaurant featuring standard beef, chicken and fish choices, but very well prepared; good service, music, recreation area. **$$**

Posada Nena
Playa Copey
Tel: (094) 32 0527
Inviting setting with restaurant (open breakfast, lunch, dinner) in *churuatas* shaded by palms, sea shells underfoot. Savory food, varied menu with many creative touches, occasional German dishes. **$–$$**

MONAGAS

Maturín is not known for its great choice of dining spots, with the majority leaning to family-oriented pizza parlors or no-frills *pollo en brasa* (spit-roasted chicken) places with plastic chairs and formica table tops. The smartest places are the restaurants of the Morichal Largo and Stauffer.

Agora
Av Alirio Ugarte Pelayo.
Mixed bag: popular discotheque, but also pool tables; open from 9pm.

El Portal Maya
Behind the cathedral
Tel: (016) 691 3244
Good Mexican food, reasonable prices. **$–$$**

La Curagua
Hotel Morichal Largo, Km 3, vía La Cruz
Tel: (091) 51 4222/4322
The most formal restaurant of those offered in this hotel (though still more resort-style dress than

coat and tie). Frequent gastronomic festivals. **$$$**

Meeting Place
Av Ugarte Pelayo
Popular pool place with bar, videos, music, games.

Río Macho Café
Opposite Banco Provincial, between Av Bolívar and Av Luis del Valle García
Very casual meeting place. Serves hamburgers, BBQ meats, shish kebabs. Live music weekends.

Whisky's
Hotel Morichal Largo, Km 3, vía La Cruz
Tel: (091) 51 4222/4322
Bar with music and dance floor of the city's only five-star hotel, geared to a more up scale and older audience than other local offerings for nightlife.

Yarúa Internacional
Carrera 7, No. 64.
Considered one of the best places in town. Decent food but huge warehouse-like dining room and AC set at deep freeze level. **$$**

Guyana Region

DELTA AMACURO

Tucupita
Hotel-Bar-Restaurant Pequeña Venezia
Sector San Salvador
Tel: (087) 21 0777/0578
The specialty of the house is indeed unique: *costillas de morocoto* – unusual because *morocoto* is a huge local fish and the ribs (*costillas*) are the size of pork ribs with very tasty meat the flavor of chicken! **$$**

BOLIVAR

Puerto Ordaz
The greatest concentration of long-standing restaurants and bars are to be found in "Centro" – in the area in the immediate vicinity of C.C. Trébol and the Civic Center. With the numerous new shopping centers which have developed in the Alta Vista, various modest offers are beginning to open; however, these are geared toward daytime shoppers looking for a quick lunch.

Continental Café y Pizzería
C.C. Continental (near the CADA)
Tel: (086) 61 7671/7456
Popular café in the lower covered passageway (away from the sun and traffic noise) of this shopping center, open Monday–Saturday, 7am–11pm; Sunday, noon–11pm. **$**

El Churrasco
Carrera Upata at Calle El Callao
Tel: (086) 22 5939
Good pizzas and typical BBQ meats grilled over a wood fire. **$**

Ercole
Torre Loreto, vía Colombia
Tel: (086) 23 3356, 22 3319
One of the best-stocked wine cellars in Venezuela, gourmet dining in elegant Art Deco setting. Private club, but the Guest Relations person at the Hotel Inter-Continental Guayana can make reservations for visitors. **$$$–$$$$**

Price Categories

Prices are quoted in US$, but payable in bolívars at the exchange rate of the day. Prices are based on a three-course meal for one, without drinks.

$	under $10
$$	$10–20
$$$	$20–30
$$$$	over $30

La Cuisine Express
C.C. Anto, Carrera Tumeremo con Av Las Américas
Tel: (086) 23 4076
Wide variety of interesting deli fare, cheeses, mouthwatering pastries along with outside tables; open Monday–Saturday, 7am–8pm; Sunday, 7am–1pm. **$**

La Forchetta de Oro Ristorante (Da Sergio)
Edif. Royal, Calle Tumeremo
Tel: (086) 22 6384
Good choice for pinched budgets. Homemade pasta; live music. **$**

La Llovizna
Hotel Inter-Continental Guayana, Parque Punta Vista
Tel: (086) 22 2244; 23 0722/0011
Gourmet international menu, with a beautiful view of Llovizna Falls in an elegant dining room. **$$$–$$$$**.

El Tascazo
C.C. El Trébol III, PB
Tel: (086) 22 9851
Popular discotheque and *tasca*;
also with restaurant specializing in
seafood. **$$**
Piano Bar-Restaurant Miuty
Edif. La Meseta, Local Sótano,
Calle Guasipati
Tel: (086) 23 4690; 22 0485
International cuisine in its
restaurant, but more popular for its
night action in the bar and for its
large dance floor. **$$**

Price Categories

Prices are quoted in US$, but
payable in bolívars at the
exchange rate of the day. Prices
are based on a three-course
meal for one, without drinks.
$ under $10
$$ $10–20
$$$ $20–30
$$$$ over $30

Santa Elena de Uairén
El Churanay Akurima
Villa Fairmont, Urb. Akurima
Tel: (088) 95 1022
Huge log cabin with various levels
suggesting divisions between
inviting restaurant (featuring
delicious meat dishes, seafood,
and pizzas baked in wood-fired
oven), from popular bar, and wing
with pool tables. **$$**
Restaurant El Quixote
Calle Icabarú, vía La Línea
Pleasant dining spot removed from
the congested downtown area,
offering meat and some Spanish
dishes. **$–$$**

El Pauji
Restaurant-Bar La Comarca
At the only intersection, in the
center of the village.
Limited menu, but food is well
prepared. However, the reason to
make a bee-line for this place is the
fantastic bread (full of whole grains
and honey – moist and heavy),
which is baked fresh for each meal
by owner Luis Scott. **$**

Midwest

ARAGUA
Puerto Colombia
Pizzería
Av Principal
While it is identified simply as the
"pizzería", this place has a large
variety of very creative salads and
other light fare which depart totally
from the usual carbon copy menus.
Open from 7pm. **$**

Maracay
Bodegón de Sevilla
Av Las Delicias
Tel: (043) 41 8410
Handsome and very popular
Spanish *tasca* bar and restaurant in
the heart of Maracay's restaurant
zone. **$$**
Label's
Av Las Delicias, sector La
Rinconada
Tel: (043) 41 8401/3189
French and Spanish menu in the
sleek contemporary interior of its
restaurant, with adjoining *tasca* and
disco with faithful night crowd. **$$**
La Terraza del Vroster
Av Las Delicias
Tel: (043) 32 1528
An institution in Maracay for its
consistency and good value. Huge
informal restaurant with ample
menu emphasizing meat and
Venezuelan specialties. Generous
portions, rapid service. **$$**
Los Caneyes
Hotel Pipo Internacional,
Av Principal El Castaño
Tel: (043) 41 3111
Very pleasant casual restaurant in
the rear of the hotel, with service in
individual caneyes surrounded by
tropical gardens. Meat is their
specialty. **$$**

CARABOBO
Valencia
Al-Ferdaus
Av Carlos Sanda, El Viñedo.
Arabic meals and sweets, all made
in-house. **$$**
Asociación de Ganaderos
Av Claudio Muskus, Guaparo
Tel: (041) 23 9770
As one would suppose, this
restaurant of the cattlemen's club

has outstanding beef: their *lomito*
piece – section of whole tenderloin
done to perfection and thin crispy
onion rings – is legendary. Casual,
open-sided. **$$**
Bar Camoruco
Hotel Inter-Continental Valencia,
Av Juan Uslar, La Viña
For years one of the favorite spots
for dancing; good house band
alternating with disco music of all
styles; ample dance floor, no cover
or minimum, guarded parking and
safe area.
Casa Valencia
End of Av Bolívar Norte, near
Redoma de Guaparo
Tel: (041) 23 4823/9517
Very pretty large building in the style
of a vintage house with each room
used as a different dining area.
Traditional *criolla* fare, meats. **$$$**
Central Social Chino Valencia
Urb. La Trigaleña Sur (entrance off
the main Lomas del Este-El Trigal
highway)
Tel: (041) 42 1677
Impossible to find more authentic
Chinese fare than within the private
club of the city's large Chinese
community. Restaurant/bar open to
the public. **$$**
La Cueva de Luis Candela
Av Bolívar, C.C. Los Sauces in the
basement, entry from the south
side
Tel: (041) 21 5028
Liveliest Spanish-style bar in town,
with clients of all ages and social
groups thanks to years of
consistently fast, friendly service,
reasonable prices, generous drinks,
good food, and live music at night;
the owner is present to make sure
everyone is happy. **$$**
La Grillade
Callejón Peña Pérez (half a block
east of Av Bólivar)
Tel: (041) 21 6038
The place to go for a special meal.
Elegant, French specialties but also
excellent grilled meats, ample salad
bar. Bar is a very popular evening
gathering spot. **$$$**
La Villa de Madrid
Av Bolívar NP 152-75
Tel: (041) 21 5681
One side is a popular Spanish
restaurant; the other side an

equally favored bar with dancing at night (combo of live music, disco). **$$**

Marchica
Av Bolívar Norte No. 152-210 (next to Centro Comercial y Profesional Av Bolívar Norte)
Tel: (041) 22 5288
Traditional lair of business leaders and political movers and shakers. Emphasis on seafood. **$$$**

Ristorante Villa Etrusca
Av Principal de Matrusca
Tel: (041) 42 2886/2998
Large, very formal Italian restaurant attracting the who's who of Valencia society. **$$$**

Puerto Cabello

Mar y Sol
Calle El Mercado
Tel: (042) 61 2572
Long-standing favorite. View from terrace or interior air-conditioned part of the port's beach and waterfront. Lobster specialty. **$$$**

Marisquería Venezuela
Calle El Aguila
Tel: (042) 61 8466
Western extreme of colonial zone. Emphasis is seafood, but they also feature good selection of antipasti. **$$**

Restaurant Lanceros
Malecón
Tel: (042) 61 8920
In the heart of the restored colonial zone with view of the water (upstairs is best for this). Pleasant informal atmosphere, seafood specialties. **$$**

YARACUY

San Felipe

Misión Nuestra Señora del Carmen
Sector La Marroquina
Tel: (054) 41 565
Fabulous setting in an impeccable reconstruction of a former 1720 mission that stood on this site. Gourmet restaurant Los Borbones featuring "Euro-Yaracuyana" cooking; El Monje Piano Bar with live music (jazz and romantic ballads); and casual El Trapiche restaurant in the patio (BBQ beef). **$$-$$$**

FALCON

Tucacas

Tuca Café
Calle Páez
Tel: (042) 83 3739
Very pleasant surprise in an area with few decent options. Gallery in the front. Restaurant in back opens to garden. Creative touches to menu, good salads. Gathering place for artists, musicians and intellectuals. **$**

Venemar
Av Principal opposite the docks
Tel: (042) 83 0532
Surprisingly elegant-looking restaurant (complete with waiters in tuxedos) for an area where everyone lives in shorts and swimsuits. Seafood featured, with lobster a specialty. Deep freeze-level air-conditioning. **$$-$$$**

Sanare

La Pradera
On the left, just south of the split for Coro-Chichiriviche
Tel: (016) 642 2014; (014) 943 2339
Recently expanded to better serve clientele appreciative of cooking with interesting sauces and combinations that depart from the usual grilled meat, fish and chicken of the area. **$**

Sierra de San Luis

Falconés
Vía Soledad-Curimagua (just east of Curimagua)
Tel/fax: (068) 51 8271
People come from all around the area to this hotel for its delicious meals served family-style. **$$**

Cumarebo

La Fuente
West side of Cumarebo, on the north side of the highway
Tel: (068) 72 141
This is the best option in the zone with international menu, but particular emphasis on seafood. Be sure to order their arepas of maize pilado (stuffed savory rolls made of coarsely pounded maize) served with nata (a cross between sour cream and butter). **$-$$**

PARAGUANA PENINSULA

Adícora

Club de Playa Moustacho
On the beach, 50 m from the National Guard station
Tel: (069) 88 210
Pleasant enclosed compound with large, tree-shaded central garden area with kiddie pool, bar, casual restaurant; terrace dining as well. **$**

Cabo San Ramón

Marisquería/Cervecería San Ramón
From Pueblo Nuevo, head north to Cabo San Ramón via Voz de Venezuela. Then take the road passing behind the huge radio tower another 3 km/1.8 miles. Here, right on the water, you will have the most wonderful lobster (**$$$**) you've ever tasted. Taken from the sea and prepared to order for you. Their fish (**$**) is likewise as fresh as it comes.

Via Adícora-El Hato

La Pancha
On the left side of the highway, just a short distance outside of Adícora in this direction.
Tel: (014) 968 2640.
In a handsome colonial-style house perched atop a small hill, with duck pond in front, and garden court inside. Filled with antiques (probably why no children under 16 allowed)! Catalan and French cooking with criollo touches (where "you will never find the standard grilled chicken or fish of every other place!" assures the owner). Open weekends only. **$$**

Lara

Barquisimeto

Bacarat
Carrera 21 between Av Morán and Calle 9
Tel: (051) 52 2754/0403
Very popular large bar, disco, with live shows; open to the public from 8pm Tuesday–Saturday.

Barquisimeto Hilton
Carrera 5, between Calles 5 and 6, Nueva Segovia
Tel: (051) 53 6022
Three offers of the hotel are very

popular with locals: **Le Provençal** gourmet French restaurant (**$$$$**); **Valle del Turbio** restaurant on a terrace overlooking the Río Turbio valley (weekend BBQ from noon; Wednesday from 7pm, typical Larense night with live music; **$$$**); and **Disko Laser**, considered the best discotheque in town.

Bourbon Street Café & Bar
C.C. Ciudad París, Nivel El Parque, Local 2-1, Av Los Leones
Tel: (051) 54 0018
In new shopping center, featuring deli sandwiches, salads, open Tuesday–Sunday from 6pm; live music Friday–Saturday. **$**

Café 90
C.C. Paseo, Av Lara and Los Leones
In principal shopping zone, popular coffee bar, with pizzas and pasta. **$**

Círculo
Centro Financorp, Carrera 2, Nueva Segovia
Tel: (051) 54 0975
Excellent creative continental cuisine at very reasonable prices. Sophisticated contemporary setting where all the movers and shakers gather. **$$**

Eros Sports Bar
Av 20, between Av Morán and Vargas. Pool tables, live music and dancing, bar; minimum consumption (*consumo mínimo*); open from 4pm.

La Piazza Ristorante
C.C. Plaza Sevilla, Av 20 and Av Morán
Tel: (051) 51 8067
Classic Italian cuisine. **$$**

La Trattoría
Hotel Principe, Calle 23, entre Carreras 18 y 19
Tel: (051) 31 2111
Handy downtown location, near area of museums as well as financial and shopping zones. Italian. **$$**

Pastelería/Café Majestic
Carrera 19, entre Calle 30 y 31
Tel: (051) 31 7687
Very pretty and ample seating area with elegant furniture, lace curtains and thoroughly tempting pastries. Open Monday–Saturday, 8am–8pm. **$**

Tequila Club
Carrera 18, entre Calles 31 y 32
Tel: (051) 32 2434/1314
The club holds special nights:

University Tuesday; Vikings night Wednesday; Tequila Thursday with *mariachis* (Mexican musicians) and surprises.

Tiuna
Final Av Lara Este
Tel: (051) 54 6471/2832
Long-established casual place with restaurant specializing in grilled meats; while its bar side is a popular spot for its *tasca* (Spanish bar) and dancing. **$$**

Villa del Mar
Av 20 con Calle 9
Tel: (051) 51 1079
Huge seafood restaurant; its bar offering live music and dancing nightly 8.30pm–midnight.

Northern Zulia

Maracaibo
The largest concentration of restaurants is in the area by the junction of Calle 77 (Av 5 de Julio) and Av 4 (Bella Vista).

Babelonia
Av 9, between Calle 78 (Dr Portillo) and 79
Tel: (061) 98 1318
Good Arabic food, open lunch and dinner. **$$**

Bibas "El Café del Teatro"
Calle 70 con Av 3F (next to Centro de Bellas Artes)
Tel: (061) 92 8791; (061) 961 4485
Popular spot after events in the adjacent Bellas Artes center. Cocktails, grill, salad bar; live jazz on Wednesdays. Open from 5pm Monday–Saturday (but people don't start showing up until around 7–8pm). **$$**

Celia
Calle 75, between Av 3F and 3G, Edif Marsans
"Fit for life" low-fat selections, good vegetarian dishes. Open for lunch only. **$**

Chilanaga
Calle 72, between Av 3G and 3H
Tel: (061) 92 1309
Offering tasty Mexican cuisine, with fajitas served on sizzling cast iron. Inside dining for lunch and dinner, with a terrace open for evening meals. **$$**

Da Maurizio
Av 4 (Bella Vista), No. 68–30, between Calles 67 and 68.
Handsome setting, authentic Italian cuisine, Owner Maurizio Lombardo speaks fluent English and is always on the premises. **$$**

El Gaucho
Av 3Y, between Calle 77 and 78
Tel: (061) 98 2110
Featuring Argentine-style mixed grill. Indoor/outdoor dining. Open 5pm–2am daily. **$$**

El Payés
Av 3Y (San Martín), No. 80–23
Tel: (061) 91 7033
Continental cuisine, and crepes are a specialty. Attentive service and owners speak English, French and German. **$$**

El Zaguán
Calle Carabobo (Calle 94) and Av 6, No. 6-15
Tel: (061) 23 1183
Traditional Venezuelan fare, lively bar, seating in garden where live music is sometimes presented. **$$**

Fein Kaffe
Calle 78 and 3F
Tel: (061) 91 4296
As pleasant for the art everywhere – from tabletops to walls – as for the wide assortment of light American-style deli fare and pastries; adjoining gourmet shop.

Hotel San José
Av 3Y and Calle 82, No. 82-29
Tel: (061) 91 4647/4714; (014) 961 8549
Not a hotel, but on the former site of one. Now a unique entertainment spot with each room serving a different function, with jazz bar, disco, restaurant, and art gallery all under one roof. **$$**

Mi Vaquita
Calle 76 and 3-H
A fixture in Maracaibo since 1963, as popular for its beef specialty restaurant (American cuts, baked potatoes) as for its large, lively bar with music and dance floor. **$$$**

Mandarin
Calle 68A, No. 3H-08
Tel: (061) 91 7209/2120/0060
Elegant Cantonese and Mandarin cuisine. Karaoke happy hour in bar Monday–Friday, 3–7pm; Thursday–Saturday, 11.30am–3am. **$$–$$$**

Sal y Pimienta
Calle 71, between Av 3F and 3G
Tel: (061) 91 1476
Appealing, casual setting in old house, with each room a small dining area. Family owned and operated. Daily specials range from BBQ spare ribs with baked beans to Mexican and Colombian dishes. Popular for Sunday brunch. Closed Monday. **$–$$**

Torremolinos
Av 9B and Calle 75
Tel: (061) 98 8034
Tasca-restaurant with wide variety of food (paella is a specialty), live music with Mexican (*mariachis*), flamenco show, dance music. **$$**

Price Categories

Prices are quoted in US$, but payable in bolívars at the exchange rate of the day. Prices are based on a three-course meal for one, without drinks.

$	under $10
$$	$10–20
$$$	$20–30
$$$$	over $30

Los Andes

TRUJILLO

Boconól

La Vieja Casa
Calle Miranda (half a block west of the Plaza Bolívar)
Tel: (072) 52 2496
Delightful combination museum-restaurant featuring savory typical Andean home cooking. Each room of the converted old house is a separate dining room packed with memorabilia. Open daily 3–7pm. Closed Tuesday. **$$**

City of Trujillo

Bar/Restaurant Bella Vista
Av La Paz
Tel: (072) 32 956
Casual open-sided restaurant with varied menu focusing on meats. Nice view. **$–$$**

MERIDA

Fresh trout is a particular specialty throughout Mérida, prepared in many different forms. Smoked trout is also available at many roadside shop, and makes a fabulous snack while you are driving. On the route through the *páramo*, nearly every restaurant features "typical Andean cooking" – a good opportunity to try it, since, once in the larger towns, the emphasis is on international fare.

Timotes

Hotel Las Truchas
North entrance of town
Tel: (071) 89 158/ 88 066
Pretty restaurant serving typical Andean fare; super cozy bar which makes a good choice for a quiet romantic encounter, rather than lively nightlife. **$$**

Via Santo Domingo-Apartaderos

Los Fralles
Tel: Hoturvensa (02) 564 0098/ 562 3022
Beautiful dining room with Old World feel – soaring ceilings with rough-hewn beams, handsome traditional furnishings. Focus on typical local dishes, very well prepared and presented. **$$**

Mucuchíes
For a break from "typical Andean dishes" that dominate the menu of every place in the *páramo*, these two places in Mucuchíes provide a most definite change – in terms of both architecture and food.

Castillo de San Ignacio
Northern entrance to town
Tel: (074) 82 0751/0021
The unique atmosphere of a medieval-style castle, with waitresses in period dresses, and a menu featuring varied international dishes, offer diners a unique experience. **$$–$$$**

El Carillón
Southern exit of town, on the right
Tel: (074) 82 0600
A far cry from the rustic-style places that predominate in this area. The interior is like that of an elegant European villa. Ornate furniture, huge murals and beamed ceiling painted with intricate designs. Italian cuisine. **$$–$$$**

City of Mérida

There are a great many restaurants concentrated along Avenida Los Próceres and its northern extension, Via Chorros de Milla, with more modestly priced ones found throughout the heart of Centro, in the vicinity of the Plaza Bolívar.

Bingo Royal
Hotel La Pedregosa, Av Los Próceres (southern end), Urb. La Pedregosa
Tel: (074) 66 0177
Electronic bingo, slot machines, plus bar/restaurant service.

El Bodegón de Pancho
Av Los Américas, C.C. Mamayeya, PB, Local C-1
Tel: (074) 44 9819
Huge place, generous bar, friendly crowds, mostly in the 21–35 age range. Good music for dancing (mostly merengue and salsa), though the dance floor is tiny.

El Oso Polar
Via Pedregosa
Modest-looking place with the appearance of a common beer hall from the outside, but with faithful clientele from university students to diplomats. Tasty yet inexpensive food, cozy bohemian atmosphere. **$**

La Chivata
Pasaje Ayacucho (two blocks from cable car)
Tel: (074) 52 9426
Divided into several inviting intimate dining areas, plus bar, with lots of art and creative menu with reasonable prices. **$–$$**

La Cucaracha
C.C. Las Tapias, Av Andrés Bello
Tel: (074) 66 1312
Four options under one roof: *tasca* bar, pub, pool, and discotheque (primarily American rock music).

La Fonda de Tía Mila
Calle Chorros de Milla
Tel: (074) 44 3308
Popular, casual place featuring *carne en vara* (beef roasted on a spit over a wood fire) and trout. **$–$$**

La Fonda Vegetariana y Restaurant El Tinajero
Calle 29 entre Av 3 y 4
Tel: (074) 52 2465
Fixed-price menu of the day or à la

carte. Falafels, vegetable *hallacas* (savory pasty), whole wheat *arepas* (stuffed rolls) with cheese, *empanadas* with vegetables, herb infusions, etc. Open 7am–9pm. **$**

La Gitana
C.C. San Antonio, Av Andrés Bello (frente a la Plaza del Ejército).
Tasca with formal atmosphere, older crowd, drinks, good tapas. Live background music weekends.

La Patana
C.C. San Antonio, Av Andrés Bello (opposite Plaza del Ejército)
Tel. (074) 66 2746
Favorite night spot with wide age-span of clientele due to its varied program. Live music (primarily for listening) nightly – boleros (Tues), Jazz (Thurs), etc.

Los Tejados de Chachopo
Via Chorros de Milla
Tel: (074) 44 0430
Interior filled with antiques and memorabilia, waiters dressed in vintage fashions; divided into many rooms and specializing in typical Andean fare. Fun place. **$$**

Price Categories

Prices are quoted in US$, but payable in bolívars at the exchange rate of the day. Prices are based on a three-course meal for one, without drinks.

$	under $10
$$	$10–20
$$$	$20–30
$$$$	over $30

TACHIRA
San Cristóbal

For restaurants and nightlife, the two areas with the greatest concentration of choices are on Avenida Libertador in the Las Lomas Sector, and Barrio Obrero in the area around Plaza Los Mangos (between Calles 10–14 and Carreras 22 and 23). In the latter zone, there are more than a dozen popular pubs, restaurants, and discotheques. Among those with the greatest following are **Mario's Discoteca, Pietro Restaurant and Tasca**, and **La Pícola Tábola**. Also drawing large weekend crowds are

La Hormiga Pub, Barra Pub Bla Bla, D'Cachett, and **Cigogne Restaurant** (French cuisine), to name a few.

Several large shopping centers and a number of unique shops add to the interest of this area.

Discoteca Tempest
Edif. Primo Centro, Sótano, Av Libertador.
Popular discotheque with mostly young crowd, current hits.

Hato Viejo
Barrio El Lobo (off Av Los Agustinos)
Tel: (076) 56 4251
Large casual place with faithful clientele, divided into bar and restaurant; meat is a specialty. **$–$$**

La Vaquera
Av Libertador, Sector Las Lomas (access only from Avenida Libertador southbound)
Tel: (076) 43 6769
Popular for years for its seafood and beef. **$$**

Nuevo Nan King
Av 19 de Abril, Sector La Concordia
Tel: (076) 46 5357/4433
Huge Chinese place with the look of a temple. A fixture in the capital since 1967. **$–$$**

Amazonas

Puerto Ayacucho
Discoteca Hot City
Av 23 de Enero, Centro.
Located in the front of Hotel City, with deafening decibel level that appeals primarily to a young crowd.

El Rincón de Apure
Av Orinoco
Tel: (048) 21 2212
Large place and long popular for both its bar and restaurant featuring beef. Often with live music on weekends (but just for listening – there is no dance floor). **$$**

El Sharazad
Av Aguerrevere con Río Negro
Tel: (048) 21 0874
Arab restaurant with the pleasing combination of good food, huge portions, and very reasonable prices. **$**

Mi Jardín
Av Orinoco (opposite Hotel Apure)
Tel: (048) 21 0658

Second-story location with view out to the street. Not at all fancy, but a favorite with locals for its home cooking with popular prices. **$**

Vía Puerto Ayacucho-Samariapo
Nacamtur
13 km after the exit for Camturama take the road for El Retiro/Galiván
Tel: (048) 21 2763
Though outside Puerto Ayacucho, Nacamtur is very popular for its much classier ambience and variety of entertainment than in-town offers: Huge restaurant, *tasca*, discotheque, pool table. **$–$$**

Los Llanos

With population centers few and far between, restaurants tend to be scarce, and those you find are all about the same, without any particular distinction to single them out; all with beef as the usual principal offer. *Carne en vara* (large pieces of beef skewered on a long pole and roasted over a wood fire) is a particular specialty. Many of these places have live *música criolla* (Venezuelan-style country and western music) on weekends.

Language

It is very rare to find anyone among the general public in Venezuela who can speak or understand any language other than Spanish – even in Caracas. Thus, if you are a non-Spanish speaker, it is best to be armed with a basic dictionary and willingness to do a bit of acting out to make yourself understood. Fortunately, most Venezuelans bend over backwards to facilitate communication if you make any attempt at all to speak their language.

Pronunciation & Grammar Tips

Unless an accent mark indicates otherwise, stress on all words ending in vowels, "n" or "s" is on the penultimate syllable; while all words ending in other consonants are stressed on the last syllable.

"You" has both familiar (*tú*) and formal (*usted, Ud.*) forms in the singular, while *ustedes* is used for "you" plural for both.

VOWEL PRONUNCIATION
a – as in rather, bar.
e – at the end of a word is pronounced like the "e" in they, but in words that end with a consonant like the "e" in set or wet.
i – as a cross between the "i" in tip and the "i" in machine.
o – as in *hole*.
u – as in *rude*, but silent after "q" and in the groups "gue", "gui", unless marked by a diaresis (*antigüedad, argüir*) when the sound is like "gway" or "gwe").

CONSONANTS
These are pronounced more or less like those in English, the main exceptions being:

b and **v** – are usually pronounced the same (just as with **ll** and **y**, which are both pronounced as "y" in yes (unless the y comes at the beginning of a word, when it is usually pronounced as the "j" in Jordan).
c – before a, o, or u is like the "k" in keep; before i or e, like the "s" in same (as opposed to the Castilian pronunciation; most Venezuelans don't say they speak Spanish – *español*; rather, they say they speak *castellano* – Castilian). Thus, *censo* (census) sounds like senso.
g – before e or i sounds like a guttural h (as the "ch" in the German *Achtung*); at the start of a breath group and after n (*gloria, rango*), the sound is that of the g in get; in other positions it is like the "g" in go.
h – is always silent.
j – has a strong guttural sound like the "ch" of the German word *Achtung*, except at the end of a word (*reloj*) when it is silent.
ll – sounds approximately like the "lli" in million (though it is often pronounced like a j).
ñ – sounds like ny, as in the familiar Spanish word *señor*.
q – is followed by u as in English, but the combination sounds like "k" in kick instead of like "kw" since the u is silent. ¿*Qué quiere Usted?* is pronounced: Keh kee-ehr-eh oostehd?
r – has a single trill or vibration, though it is often rolled for effect at the start of a word.
rr – is always strongly trilled or rolled.
x – between vowels sounds like the "x" in box, or like the "g s" in big stick.
y – alone, as the word meaning "and", is pronounced "ee"; but when indicated as the letter, or the indication of a split in a road, or at the beginning of a word it is pronounced like the "j" of Jordan; while in the middle of a word it sounds like the "y" in yes.

Note that **ch** and **ll** are each considered to be a separate letter of the Spanish alphabet; phone books now have ch and ll in normal English alphabetical order, however in dictionaries, ch follows all other c entries. The same applies to ll.

NOUNS
Nouns are either masculine or feminine. Masculine nouns usually end in "o"; with article *el* for singular, *los* for plural and adjectives usually with corresponding "o" singular or "os" plural ending. Feminine nouns usually end with "a"; with article adjective *la* for singular, *las* plural and adjectives usually with corresponding "a" singular or "as" plural ending.

Basic Communication

Yes *Sí*
No *No*
Thank you *Gracias*
You're welcome *No hay de que/ Por nada*
Alright/Okay/That's fine *Está bien*
Please *Por favor*
Excuse me (to get attention) *¡Perdón!/¡Por favor!*
Excuse me (to get through a crowd) *¡Permiso!*
Excuse me (sorry) *Perdóneme, Discúlpeme*
Wait a minute! *¡Un momento!*
Could you help me? (formal) *¿Puede ayudarme?*
Certainly *¡Claro!/¡Claro que sí!/ ¡Por cierto!*
Can I help you? (formal) *¿Puedo ayudarle?*
Can you show me...? *¿Puede mostrarme...?*

Subject Pronouns

Subject pronouns are often eliminated (except for emphasis) since the verb ending indicates whether you are indicating I (*yo*); you singular, familiar (*tú*); you formal (*usted*, often written as *Ud.* – always with U capitalized if abbreviated); he (*él*), she (*ella*), it (*ello*); we (*nosotros*); you plural (*ustedes*); they (*ellas* – f., *ellos* – m.). For example. *Soy americano* (instead of *Yo soy americano*) – I am American.

I need... *Necesito....*
I'm lost *Estoy extraviado*
I'm sorry *Lo siento*
I don't know *No sé*
I don't understand *No entiendo*
**Do you speak English/French/
German? (formal)** *¿Habla inglés/
francés/alemán?*
**Could you speak more slowly,
please?** *¿Puede hablar más
despacio, por favor?*
Could you repeat that, please?
¿Puede repetirlo, por favor?
Slowly *despacio/lentamente*
here/there *aquí* (place where), *acá*
(motion to)/*allí, allá, ahí* (near you)
What? *¿Qué?/¿Cómo?*
When? *¿Cuándo?*
Why? *¿Por qué?*
Where? *¿Dónde?*
Who? *¿Quién(es)?*
How? *¿Cómo?*
Which? *¿Cuál?*
How much/how many? *¿Cuánto?/
¿Cuántos?*
Do you have...? *¿Tiene...?/
¿Hay...?*
I want.../I would like.../I need...
Quiero.../Quisiera.../Necesito...
**Where is the lavatory (men's/
women's)?** *¿Dónde se encuentra
el baño (de caballeros/de damas)?*

Titles

Venezuelans tend to be very title
conscious. Take a clue from the way
a person presents him/herself or
how the person is presented by
another and address him/her in
kind. Then, if they wish to be more
informal, they will usually so
indicate. But some people can get
very touchy if you ignore their title
when addressing them, particularly
upon first meeting.

Doctor (male) or *Doctora* (female)
is used for lawyers as well as
physicians. People who have
doctorate degrees usually use the
title *Doctor* as well. While people
who have earned an undergraduate
university degree use the title
Licenciado/a (Lic). When in doubt
about their degree, you're better off
using *Doctor*.

Some other professions given
titles are *Economista* – economist;
Arquitecto/a – architect;

Ingeniero/a – engineer; *Poeta* –
poet; *Maestro/a* – for educators,
well-known artists and musicians.
Thus, a person is addressed as
Ingeniero José López, if they use
these titles, always use them in
formal correspondence.

Men or women who have passed
beyond 50 are often addressed
affectionately with a title of respect:
Don (masc), *Doña* (fem). In this
case, in conversation, it is usually
with first name only: *Don Pedro*, or
Doña Blanquita. *Doña* is also often
used alone by strangers addressing
an older woman when they do not
know her name.

Unless you are sure a young
woman is married, address her as
Señorita (Miss) rather than *Señora*
(Mrs), since the latter is used for
women who are no longer virgins,
thus, presumably only married
women.

Greetings

Hello! *¡Hola!*
Hello (Good day) *Buenos días*
Good afternoon/night *Buenas
tardes/noches*
Good-bye *Ciao/¡Adios!*
My name is... *Me llamo...*
What is your name? (formal)
¿Cómo se llama usted?
Mr/Miss/Mrs *Señor/Señorita/
Señora*
Pleased to meet you *¡Encantado!*
**I am English/American/Canadian/
Irish/Scottish/Australian** *Soy
inglés(a)/norteamericano(a)/
canadiense/irlandés(a)/
escocés(a)/australiano(a)*
Do you speak English? (formal)
¿Habla inglés?
I'm here on holiday *Estoy aquí
para vacaciones*
It is my first trip to Venezuela *Es
mi primer viaje a Venezuela*
Do you like Caracas/ my city?
¿Le gusta a Caracas/mi ciudad?
I like it a lot *¡Me gusta
muchísimo!/¡Me encanta!*
It's wonderful *¡Es maravilloso(a)!*
How are you? (formal/informal)
¿Cómo está? ¿Qué tal?
Fine, thanks *Muy bien, gracias*
See you later *Hasta luego*
Take care (informal) *¡Cuídate!*

Telephone Calls

The area code *El código de área*
**I'd like to make a reverse charges
call** *Quisiera hacer una llamada
que paga el destinario*
**Where can I find a telephone that
takes pre-paid cards?** *¿Dónde
puedo encontrar un teléfono que
toma tarjetas?*
**Where can I buy/do you sell
telephone cards?** *¿Dónde puedo
comprar tarjetas telefónicas?/¿Se
venden aquí tarjetas telefónicas?*
**May I use your telephone to make
a local call?** *¿Puedo usar su
teléfono para hacer una llamada
local?*
Of course you may *¡Por supuesto
que sí!/¡Como no!/¡Claro!*
Hello (on the phone) *¡Aló!*
May I speak to...? *¿Puedo hablar
con...* (name)*, por favor?*
Sorry, he/she isn't in *Lo siente, no
se encuentra*
Can he/she call you back?
¿Puede devolver la llamada?
Yes, he/she can reach me at... *Sí,
él/ella puede llamarme en* (number)
I'll try again later *Voy a intentar
más tarde*
Can I leave a message? *¿Puedo
dejar un mensaje?*
Please tell him/her I called *Favor
avisarle que llamé*
Hold on *Un momento, por favor*
Can you speak up, please? *¿Puede
hablar más fuerte, por favor?*

In the Hotel

Do you have a vacant room?
¿Tiene una habitación disponible?
I have a reservation *Tengo una
reservación*
I'd like... *Quisiera...*
**a single/double (with double bed)/
a room with twin beds** *una
habitación individual (sencilla)/una
habitación matrimonial/una habitación doble*
mosquito netting *mosquitero*
for one night/two nights *por una
noche/dos noches*
**ground floor/first floor/top
floor/with sea view** *una habitación
en la planta baja/en el primer
piso/en el último piso/con vista al
mar*

Does the room have a private bathroom or shared bathroom? ¿Tiene la habitación baño privado o baño compartido?
Does it have hot water? ¿Tiene agua caliente?
Does it have a kitchen (with utensils)? ¿Tiene cocina (equipada)?
Could you show me another room, please? ¿Puede mostrarme otra habitación, por favor?
Is it a quiet room? ¿Es una habitación tranquila?
What time do you close (lock) the doors? ¿A qué hora se cierren las puertas?
I would like to change rooms Quisiera cambiar la habitación
This room is too noisy/hot/cold/small Esta habitación es demasiado ruidosa/caliente/fría/pequeña
How much is it? ¿Cuánto cuesta?
Okay, I'll take it Está bien
Is everything included? ¿Es un paquete todo incluido?
Does the price include tax/breakfast/meals/drinks? ¿El precio incluye el impuesto/desayuno/comidas/ bebidas?
Do you accept credit cards/travelers' checks/dollars? ¿Se aceptan tarjetas de crédito/cheques de viajeros/dólares?
I need a bell hop Necesito un botón
What time is breakfast/lunch/dinner? ¿A qué hora está servido el desayuno/almuerzo/la cena?
Please wake me at... Favor despertarme a...
Come in! ¡Pase!, ¡Adelante!
I'd like to pay the bill now, please Quisiera cancelar la cuenta ahora, por favor
Can you call me a taxi, please? ¿Puede llamarme un taxi, por favor?

Tasca bars

A tasca is a Spanish-style bar, where appetizers are usually available with the drinks. These bars are popular throughout Venezuela, and particularly in Caracas.

USEFUL WORDS

Bath el baño
Dining room el comedor
Elevator/lift el asensor
Key la llave
Push/pull empuje/hale
Safety deposit box la caja de seguridad
Soap el jabón
Shampoo el champú
Shower la ducha
Toilet paper el papel higiénico
Towel la toalla

Swearing

Startling to many visitors, even natives of other Spanish-speaking countries, is to hear swear words (groserías) and vulgarities seemingly in every other sentence by the majority of the population – even children – for whom ¡coño! and ¡no joda! ("f—!" and "don't f— around!") are more common than "damn" or "really?!" in English.

Drinks

What would you like to drink? ¿Qué quiere tomar?
coffee... un café...
    American-style guayoyo
    with a lot of milk con leche
    with a little milk marrón
    strong fuerte
    cappuccino capuchino
    small/large pequeño/grande
    without sugar sin azúcar
tea... té...
    with lemon/milk con limón/leche
herbal tea té manzanilla
hot chocolate chocolate caliente
fresh orange juice jugo de naranja natural
orangeade naranjada
soft drink refresco
mineral water still/carbonated agua mineral sin gas/con gas
    with/without ice con/sin hielo
cover charge entrada
minimum consumption consumo mínimo
beer hall/pub cervecería
discotheque disco/discoteca

nightclub club nocturno
a bottle/half a bottle una botella/media botella
cocktail un cailo
a glass of red/white/rosé wine una copa de vino tinto/rosado/blanco
beer una cerveza
Is service included? ¿Incluye el servicio?
I need a receipt, please Necesito un recibo, por favor
Keep the change Es completo
Cheers! ¡Salud!
ice cream helado
sandwich sandwich
turnover (filled with meat, cheese, etc.) una empanada

IN A RESTAURANT

I'd like to book a table Quisiera reservar una mesa, por favor
Do you have a table for...? ¿Tiene una mesa para...?
I have a reservation Tengo una reservación
breakfast/lunch/dinner desayuno/almuerzo/cena
I'm a vegetarian Soy vegetariano(a)
Is there a vegetarian dish? ¿Hay un plato vegetariano?
May we have the menu? ¿Puede traernos la carta (o el menú)?
wine list la carta de vinos
What would you recommend? ¿Qué recomiende?
home-made casero(a)
fixed price menu menú ejecutivo/menú de degustación
special of the day plato del día/sugerencia del chef
The meal was very good La comida fue muy buena

Menu Decoder

EXTREMESES, PRIMER PLATO (FIRST COURSE)

sopa/crema soup/cream soup
hervido de res/ pescado/ pollo broth with large chunks of meat/fish/chicken and vegetables
mondongo tripe soup
sopa de ajo garlic soup
sopa de cebolla onion soup
ensalada... salad...
    mixta mixed
    de palmito with palm hearts

ensalada de aguacate con tomate **avocado and tomato salad**
pan con ajo **garlic bread**

SEGUNDO/PLATO PRINCIPAL (MAIN COURSE)

crudo **raw**
vuelta y vuelta **rare**
término medio **medium rare**
tres cuarto **medium**
bien cocida **well done**

La Carne (Meat)

a la brasa/a la parrilla **charcoal grilled**
a la broaster/en vara **spit roasted**
a la plancha **grilled**
ahumada **smoked**
albondigas **meat balls**
asado(a)/horneado(a) **roasted**
cerdo/cochino/puerco **pork**
chivo **goat**
chorizos **Spanish-style sausage**
chuleta **chop**
conejo **rabbit**
cordero **lamb**
costillas **ribs**
empanizado(a) **breaded**
frito(a) **fried**
guisado(a) **stewed**
hamburguesa **hamburger**
higado de res **beef liver**
jamón **ham**
lengua **tongue**
lomito **tenderloin**
milanesa **breaded and fried thin cut of meat**
pernil **leg of pork**
rebosado(a) **batter fried**
riñones **kidneys**
salchichas/perros calientes **sausage or hot dogs**
ternera **veal**

Aves (Fowl)

alas **wings**
chicharrón de pollo **chicken cut up in small pieces and deep fried**
muslo **thigh**
pato **duck**
pavo **turkey**
pechuga **breast**
piernas **legs**
pollo **chicken**

Mariscos/Pescado (Fish/Seafood)

almejas, guacuco **clams**

anchoa **anchovy**
atún **tuna**
bacalao **cod**
bagre **catfish**
botuto **conch**
calamares **squid**
cangrejo **crab**
caracoles **snails**
carite **mackerel**
cazker **baby shark**
corvina **blue fish**
langosta **lobster**
langostinos **prawns**
lebranche **black mullet**
lenguado **sole or flounder**
lisa **silver mullet**
mariscos **shellfish**
mejillones **mussels**
mero **grouper, sea bass**
ostras **oysters**
pargo **red snapper**
pulpo **octopus**
salmón **salmon**
sardinas **sardines**
sierra **king mackerel**
trucha **trout**
vieras **scallops**

Ordering Beef

Note: Steak tends to be cooked one notch rarer than American style. (If it comes too rare, ask: *¿Puede cocinarla un poco más, por favor?*)
bistec **thin cut of beef**
brocheta/pincho **shish kebab**
carne (carne de res) **beef**
churrasco **a large boneless steak, usually rump, round, or chuck**
punta trasera **rump roast or steak**
solomo **chuck**

Vegetales (Vegetables)

ajo **garlic**
ajoporro **leeks**
alcachofa **artichoke**
auyama **pumpkin or yellow squash**
batata **sweet potato**
berenjena **eggplant**
brócoli **broccoli**
calabacín **zucchini**
caraotas **black beans**
cebolla **onion**
coliflor **cauliflower**
endivia **endive**

espárrago **asparagus**
espinaca **spinach**
guisantes **peas**
hongos, champiñones **mushrooms**
lechuga **lettuce**
maiz, jojoto **corn (corn on the cob)**
pepino **cucumber**
pimentón **green (bell) pepper**
remolacha **beets/beetroot**
repollo **cabbage**
vainitas **green beans**
zanahorias **carrots**

FRUTAS (FRUIT)

aguacate **avocado**
cambur **banana**
cereza **cherry**
ciruela **plum**
dátil **date**
fresa **strawberry**
guayaba **guava**
higo **fig**
lechoza **papaya**
limón **lime**
mandarina **tangerine**
manzana **apple**
melecotón **peach**
melón **cantelope/melon**
mora **blackberry**
naranja **orange**
parchita **passion fruit**
patilla **watermelon**
pera **pear**
piña **pineapple**
platano **plantain**
toronja **grapefruit**
uvas **grapes**

MISCELLANEOUS

arróz **rice**
azúcar **sugar**
espaguetis **spaghetti**
guasacaca **sauce made with avocado, onions, parsley, coriander, etc.**
huevos (revueltos/fritos/hervidos) **eggs (scrambled/fried/boiled)**
mantequilla **butter**
mermelada **jam**
mostaza **mustard**
pan **bread**
pan integral **wholewheat bread**
pan tostado **toast**
pasticho **lasagna**
pimienta negra **black pepper**
queso **cheese**
sal **salt**
salsa de tomate **ketchup**
salsa picante **hot sauce**

tocineta **bacon**
tortilla **omelette**

Tourist Attractions/ Terms

aguas termales **hot springs**
artesanía **handicrafts**
balneario **swimming spot**
campamento **camp**
capilla **chapel**
castillo/fortín **fort**
catedral **cathedral**
cayo **cay/key**
centro **(historic) center of town**
cerro **hill**
comunidad indígena **Indian (indigenous) community**
convento **convent**
galería **gallery**
iglesia **church**
isla **island**
jardín botánico **botanical garden**
laguna **lagoon**
lago **lake**
mar/Mar Caribe **sea/Caribbean Sea**
mercado **market**
mirador **viewpoint**
montaña **mountain**
monumento **monument**
oficina de turismo **tourist information office**
parque de atracciones **amusement park**
parque infantil **playground**
parque **park**
pico **(mountain) peak**
piscina **swimming pool**
playa **beach**
plaza **town square**
postal **postcard**
puente **bridge**
quebrada **stream**
río **river**
ruinas **ruins**
sanctuario **sanctuary**
teleférico **cable car**
tepuy **mesa of ancient rock found in Bolívar and Amazonas**
torre **tower**
zona colonial **colonial zone**
zoológico **zoo**

Road Signs

alcabala, punto de control
police/military checkpoint
autopista **freeway**

bajada/subida peligrosa
dangerous downgrade/incline
calle ciega **dead-end street**
calle flechada **one-way street**
canal derecho **right lane**
canal izquierdo **left lane**
carretera **highway, road**
carretera negra **paved highway**
cauchero **tire repair shop**
cede paso **yield/give way**
circunvalación **by-pass road**
conserve su derecha **keep to the right**
conserve su canal **do not change lanes**
cruce de ferrocarril (sin señal)
railway crossing (without signal)
despacio **slow**
desvío **detour**
distribuidor **freeway interchange**
doble vía **two-way traffic**
Enciende luces en el túnel **Turn on lights in the tunnel**
encrucijada **crossroads**
entrada prohibida **entrance prohibited**
estacionamiento **parking lot**
fuera de servicio **not in service**
hundimiento **sunken road**
intercomunal **interconnecting freeway between two close towns**
no estacione/prohibido estacionarse aquí **no parking**
no gire en U **no U-turn**
no hay paso, vía cerrado **road blocked**
no hay salida **no exit**
no pare **no stopping here**
no toque la coroneta **no horn honking**
¡ojo! **watch out!**
pare **stop**
paso de ganado **cattle crossing**
paso de peatones **pedestrian crossing**
peaje **toll booth**
peligro **danger**
pendiente fuerte, curva fuerte
steep hill, sharp curve
redoma **roundabout**
reductor de velocidad, obstáculos en la vía, muros en la vía, policia acostada **speed bump(s)**
resbaladizo al humedecerce
slippery when wet
salida/próxima salida **exit/next exit**
semáforo **traffic light**
sólo tránsito local **local traffic only**

tome precauciones **caution**
un solo canal **single lane**
velocidad controlada **speed controlled or restricted**
vía en reparación/en recuperación
road under repair
zona de construcción **construction zone**
zona de derrumbes **zone of landslides**
zona de niebla (neblina) **fog zone**
zona de remolque **tow zone**
zona escolar **school zone**
zona militar **military zone**

Traveling

4x4, double-traction vehicle, 4-wheel drive vehicle rústico
airline línea áerea
airport aeropuerto
arrivals/departures llegadas/ salidas
bus stop parada (de autobus)
boat dock for small boats/large boats embarcadero/muelle
bus terminal terminal de pasajeros
bus transporte, autobus
car carro, automóvil
car rental alquiler de carros sin chofer
charter flight vuelo charter
connection conexión
dug-out canoe without motor/with motor curiara/bongo
ferry ferry
first class/second class primera clase/segunda clase, clase de turista
flight vuelo
luggage, bag(s) equipaje, maleta(s)
mini-bus or car with passenger service on a fixed route, with passage sold by the seat por puesto
Next stop please (for buses) En la próxima parada, por favor
one-way ticket boleto de ida
open barge-like ferry chalana
platform el anden
round-trip, return ticket boleto de ida y vuelta
sailboat velero
ship barco
subway Metro
taxi taxi, libre
traditional fishing boat peñero
yacht yate

Terms for Addresses/Directions

a la derecha **on the right**
a la izquierda **on the left**
al lado de **beside**
alrededor de **around**
arriba/abajo **above/below**
avenida (Av) **avenue**
calle/carrera **street**
cerca de **near**
cruce con/con **at the cross of (two streets)**
cruce hacia la izquierda/la derecha **turn to the left/right**
debajo de **under**
delante de **in front of**
derecho **straight ahead**
detrás de **behind**
edificio (Edif) **highrise office building**
en frente de/frente de/frente a **in front of**
en **in, on, at**
en la parte de atrás **in the rear area (as behind a building)**
encima de **on top of**
entre **between**
esquina (Esq) **corner**
PH – penthouse/PB – planta baja/PA – planta alta/mezanina/sótano **penthouse/ground floor/upper floor (of 2)/mezzanine/basement**
residencia (Res) **residential tower, small pension**
torre **tower**
transversal(es) **crossroad(s)**
una cuadra **a block**

At the Terminal, Airport, or Travel Agency

customs and immigration *aduana e inmigración*
travel/tour agency *agencia de viajes/de turismo*
ticket *boletos pasaje*
I would like to purchase a ticket for... *Quisiera comprar un boleto (pasaje) para...*
When is the next/last flight/departure for XXX? *¿Cuándo es el próximo/último vuelo/para XXX?*
What time does the plane/bus/boat/ferry leave/return? *¿A qué hora sale/regresa el avión/el autobus/la lancha/el ferry?*

What time do I have to be at the airport? *¿A qué hora tengo que estar en el aeropuerto?*
Is the tax included? *¿Se incluye el impuesto?*
What is included in the price? *¿Qué está incluido en el precio?*
departure tax? *¿el impuesto de salida?*
I would like a seat in first class/business class/tourist class *Quisiera un asiento en primera clase/ejecutivo/clase de turista*
lost luggage office *oficina de reclamos*
on time *a tiempo*
late *atrasado*
I need to change my ticket *Necesito cambiar mi boleto*
How long is the flight? *¿Cuánto tiempo es el vuelo?*
Is this seat taken? *¿Está ocupado este asiento?*
Which is the stop closest to XXX? *¿Cuál es la parada más cerca a XXX?*
Could you please advise me when we reach/the stop for XXX? *¿Por favor, puede avisarme cuando llegamos a/a la parada para XXX?*
Is this the stop for XXX? *¿Es ésta la parada para XXX?*

Driving

Where can I rent a car? *¿Dónde puedo alquiler un carro?*
Is mileage included? *¿Está incluido el kilometraje*
comprehensive insurance *seguros comprensivos*
spare tire/jack/emergency triangle *caucho de repuesto/gato/triángulo de emergencia*
Where is the registration *¿Dónde se encuentra el carnet de circulación*
Does the car have an alarm? *¿El carro tiene alarma?*
a road map/a city map *un mapa vial/plano de la ciudad*
How do I get to XXX? *¿Cómo se llega a XXX?*
Turn right/left *Cruzar (or girar, doblar) hacia la derecha/izquierda*
at the next corner/street *en la próxima esquina/calle*
Go straight ahead *Siga derecho*
You can't miss it *No hay perdida*

You are on the wrong road *No está en la vía correcta*
Please show me where am I on the map *Por favor, indíqueme dónde estoy en el mapa*
Where is...? *¿Dónde se encuentra...?*
Where is the nearest...? *¿Dónde se encuentra el/la XXX más cerca?*
How long does it take to get there? *¿Cuánto tiempo requiere para llegar?*
driving license *licencia de conducir*
service station, gasoline station *estación de servicio, bomba de gasolina*
My car won't start *Mi carro no prende*
My car is overheating *Mi carro está recalentando*
My car has broken down *Mi carro está accidentado*
tow truck *una grúa*
Where can I find a car repair shop? *¿Dónde se encuentra un taller mecánico?*
Can you check the...? *¿Puede revisar/chequear...?*
There's something wrong with the... *Hay un problema con....*
oil/water/air/brake fluid/light bulb *aceite/agua/aire/liga para frenos/ bombillo*
trunk/hood/door/window *maletín/capó/puerta/ventana*

The Car

...accelerator *el acelerador*
...alternator *el alternador*
...battery *el acumulador, la batería*
...brakes *los frenos*
...carburator *el carburador*
...clutch *el embrague*
...engine *el motor*
...fanbelt *el correo del ventilador*
...gear box *la caja*
...headlights *los faros*
...radiator *el radiador*
...shock absorber *el amortiguador*
...spark plugs *las bujías*
...starter *el arranque*
...steering wheel *el volante*
...tire(s) *los cauchos*
...windshield *la parabrisa*
...wires *los cables*

Note: If you call the **171** nationwide emergency number, they will dispatch the appropriate emergency personnel. Before you call, however, verify the exact address where you are located to be able to tell them. If you are in a traffic accident, NEVER move your vehicle, no matter how much you are blocking traffic, until the traffic police (*tránsito*) have arrived and indicated you can do so. If you have a rental vehicle, call the company immediately in case of breakdown, accident, or theft for instructions on what to do.

Emergencies

Help! *¡Socorro! ¡Auxilio!*
Stop! *¡Párate!*
Watch out! *¡Cuidado! ¡Ojo! ¡Epa!*
I've had an accident *He tenido un accidente*
Call a doctor *Llame a un médico*
Call an ambulance *Llame una ambulancia*
Call the... *Llame a...*
...police *la policía* (for minor incidents)
...transit police *la policía de tránsito* (for traffic accidents)
the fire brigade *los bomberos*
This is an emergency, where is a telephone? *Es una emergencia. ¿Dónde se encuentra un teléfono?*
Where is the nearest hospital? *¿Dónde se encuentra el hospital más cerca?*
I want to report a robbery (something stolen when you were not present) *Quisiera reportar un hurto/un robo*
Thank you very much for your help *Muchísimas gracias por su ayuda*

Health

shift duty pharmacy *farmacía de turno*
hospital/clinic *hospital/clínica*
I need a doctor/dentist *Necesito un médico/dentista (odontólogo)*
I don't feel well *Me siento mal*
I am sick *Estoy enfermo*
It hurts here *Duele aquí*
I have a headache/stomach ache/cramps *Tengo un dolor de la cabeza/del estomago/de vientre*
I feel dizzy *Me siento mareado*

Do you have (something for)...? *¿Tiene (algo para)...?*
a cold/flu *gripe/virus*
diarrhea *diarrea*
constipation *estrenamiento*
fever *fiebre*
aspirin *aspirina*
heartburn *ácidez*
insect/mosquito bites *picaduras de insectos/mosquitos*

Shopping

antiques shop *antigüedades*
bakery *panadería*
bank *banco*
barber shop *barbería*
beauty shop *peluquería, salón de belleza*
bookstore *librería*
butcher shop *carnicería*
currency exchange bureau *casa de cambio*
delicatessen *delicatesses*
department store *tienda por departamentos*
florist *florestería*
gift shop *(tienda de) regalos*
greengrocer's *frutería*
hardware store *ferretería*
shopping center *centro comercial, mall*
jewelry shop *joyería*
laundry *lavandería*
library *biblioteca*
liquor store *licorería, distribuidor (de licores)*
market *mercado*
newsstand *kiosco*
pastry shop *pastelería*
post office *correos*
shoe repair shop/shoe store *zapatería*
small grocery store *bodega, abasto*
small shop *tienda*
supermarket *supermercado, automercado*
toy store *juguetería*

Useful Phrases

What time do you open/close? *¿A qué hora abre/cierre?*
Open/closed *Abierto/cerrado*
I'd like... *Quisiera...*
I'm just looking *Estoy sólo mirando, gracias*
How much does it cost? *¿Cuánto cuesta?*

It doesn't fit *No queda bien*
Do you have it in another color? *¿Tiene en otro color*
Do you have it in another size? *¿Tiene en otro talla* (clothing), *tamaño* (objects)
smaller/larger *más pequeño/más grande*
It's too expensive *Es demasiado caro*
Do you have something less expensive? *¿Tiene algo más económico?*
Where do I pay for it? *¿Dónde está la caja?*
Anything else? *¿Quiere algo más?*
a little more/less *un poco más/menos*
That's enough/no more *Está bien/no más*

Colors

light/dark *claro/oscuro*
red *rojo*
yellow *amarillo*
blue *azul*
brown *marrón*
black *negro*
white *blanco*
beige *color crema*
green *verde*
wine *vino tinto*
gray *gris*
orange *color naranjo*
pink *rosada*
purple *púrpura*
silver *plateado*
gold *dorado*

Numbers

1 *uno*
2 *dos*
3 *tres*
4 *cuatro*
5 *cinco*
6 *seis*
7 *siete*
8 *ocho*
9 *nueve*
10 *diez*
11 *once*
12 *doce*
13 *trece*
14 *catorce*
15 *quince*
16 *dieciséis*
17 *diecisiete*
18 *dieciocho*

19 *diecinueve*
20 *veinte*
21 *veintiuno*
25 *veinticinco*
30 *treinta*
40 *cuarenta*
50 *cincuenta*
60 *sesenta*
70 *setenta*
80 *ochenta*
90 *noventa*
100 *cien*
101 *ciento uno*
200 *doscientos*
300 *trescientos*
400 *cuatrocientos*
500 *quinientos*
600 *seiscientos*
700 *setecientos*
800 *ochocientos*
900 *novecientos*
1,000 *mil*
2,000 *dos mil*
10,000 *diez mil*
100,000 *cien mil*
1,000,000 *un millón*
1,000,000,000 *mil millones*
1,000,000,000,000 *un millardo*
NOTE: In Spanish, in numbers, commas are used where decimal points are used in English and vice versa. For example, in English: $19.30 = in Spanish: $19,50; 1,000 m = 1.000 m; 9.5% = 9,5%.

Days and Dates

morning *la mañana*
afternoon *la tarde (noon–7pm)*
late afternoon, dusk *atardecer*
evening *la noche (7pm–midnight)*
midnight-sunrise *la madrugada*
sunrise *amanecer*
sunset *puesta del sol*
last night *anoche*
yesterday *ayer*
today *hoy*
tomorrow *mañana*
the day after tomorrow *pasado mañana*
now *ahora*
early *temprano*
late *tarde*
a minute *un minuto*
an hour *una hora*
half an hour *media hora*
a day *un día*
a week *una semana*
a year *un año*

weekday *día laboral*
weekend *fin de semana*
holiday *día feriado*
long weekend *un puente*

Months

January *enero*
February *febrero*
March *marzo*
April *abril*
May *mayo*
June *junio*
July *julio*
August *agosto*
September *septiembre*
October *octubre*
November *noviembre*
December *diciembre*

Days of the Week

Monday *lunes*
Tuesday *martes*
Wednesday *miércoles*
Thursday *jueves*
Friday *viernes*
Saturday *sábado*
Sunday *domingo*

Conversion Charts

Metric–Imperial
1 centimeter = 0.4 inch
1 meter = approx. 39 inches
1 kilometer = 0.62 miles
1 gram = 0.04 ounces
1 kilogram = 2.2 pounds
1 liter = 1.76 UK pints
1 hectare = 2.47 acres
Imperial–Metric
1 inch = 2.54 centimeters
1 yard = 0.9 meters
1 mile = 1.6 kilometers
1 ounce = 28.35 grams
1 pound = 0.45 kilograms
1 pint = 0.47 liters
1 acre = 0.4 hectare

Clothing/Shoe Sizes

North American	European or South American
Shirts (Men)	
15	38
15 ½	39
16	40
16 ½	42
17	43
Blouses (Women)	
10	38
12	40
14	42
16	44
18	46
Shoes (Men)	
8	41
9	42
10	42
11	44.5
12	46
Shoes (Women)	
6 ½	36.5
7	37
8	38
8 ½	38.5
9	39

Further Reading

There is a notable lack of current comprehensive information in print in English about Venezuela. However, there are numerous photographic/"coffee table" books (nearly all produced by foreigners). Many have English and both Spanish captions. These are available in all major bookstores.

General

Guide to Venezuela, by Janice Bauman and Leni Young, Ernesto Armitano Editor (1989). While much of the general travel information is totally out of date, one of the book's most interesting aspects is the multitude of historical notes that are well researched, and also written in a readable style.
Living in Venezuela, published in English biannually by the Venezuelan American Chamber of Commerce (tel: (02) 263 0833). This is the most complete and up-to-date orientation book available about Venezuela, covering every possible aspect: vital statistics, history, government, economic overview, geographic regions, getting around, community organizations, education, clubs, health services and issues, legal matters, communications, leisure and travel, and more.

Nature

Birding in Venezuela, by Mary Lou Goodwin (1998), is published by, and available through, Venezuela's Audubon Society, tel: (02)92 3268/ 2812. Written with a very personal approach by a founding member of South America's oldest Audubon Society, this is not only the definitive guide to exactly where to go to see certain species (down to exactly which path to take and what tree they are usually seen in), but is full of useful suggestions for

lodging, places to eat, names and phone numbers of local birders, and comments about ecological issues. Technical, helpful, entertaining, all in one package.
A Guide to the Birds of Venezuela, by Rodolphe Meer de Schauensee and William H. Phelps, Jr.; Princeton University Press (1978). The bible for birdwatchers, with detailed descriptions and illustrations for all entries.
In the Rainforest, Catherine Caufield (1991). Commentaries about life and nature in the rainforest.
Churún Merú, Ruth Robertson (1975). Recollections of the American journalist and adventurer who was the first person to measure the height and drop of Angel Falls accurately.

Politics and Economy

Indictment of a Dictator: The Extradition and Trial of Marcos Pérez Jiménez, by Judith Ewell (1981).
Venezuela, the Democratic Experience, edited by John D. Martz and David J. Meyers (1986).
Venezuela's Voice for Democracy: Conversations and Correspondence with Romulo Betancourt, by Robert J. Alexander (1990).
Venezuela's Movimiento al Socialismo: from Guerrilla Defeat to Innovative Politics, by Steve Ellner (1988).

Fiction

Lost World, by Sir Arthur Conan Doyle. A classic portraying an imaginary world on the summit of Roraima tepuy where, because of its isolation, dinosaurs continued living after their disappearance from the rest of the world.
The General in His Labyrinth, by Gabriel García Márquez (1990). Novel about the final days of Simón Bolívar by the famous Nobel Prize-winning Colombian writer.
The Man from Maracay, by Barry Oldham (Industrias Capsvar S.A. 1998). Action thriller written by a long-time British resident and

journalist about the intrigue of kidnappings and confrontations with guerrillas along the Venezuelan-Colombian border.

Other Insight Guides

There are nearly 200 titles in the Insight Guide series, with the same high standard of text and photojournalism. Insight Guide titles on South American destinations include Argentina, Buenos Aires, Brazil, Rio de Janiero, Chile, Ecuador, Peru and South America. There are also titles on Central and North America, including Belize and Costa Rica, Mexico and Mexico City, and a number of Caribbean titles including Trinidad and Tobago and Cuba.

Insight Pocket Guides are a companion series in which local host authors show you specific itineraries that will make the most of your stay. The books come with a full-size fold-out map. Among the 100-plus titles are Jamaica, Bermuda, Bahamas, Puerto Rico, Mexico City and the Baja and Yucatán peninsulas.

ART & PHOTO CREDITS

Photography by EDUARDO GIL except for
Thomas Altinger 4BL, 51, 83, 195T, 255T, 277, 286, 287T, 291, 291T
Ask Images/Art Directors & Trip 4/5, 4BR, 17, 272/273, 278T
M Barlow/Art Directors & Trip 132, 132T
André and Cornelia Bärtschi 101, 253, 256, 257, 297, 300, 301
R Belbin/Art Directors & Trip 243
Charles Brewer-Carias 296
Marvi Cilli 111, 114
R Daniell/Art Directors & Trip 251
Alain Dhone/Sipa Press/Rex Features 53
Ray Escobar 50, 68/69, 140,
Veronica Garbutt 49, 142T, 151
John Gottberg 90, 107
Andreas M Gross 173
Dave G Houser 20, 289
Volkmar Janicke 1, 2B, 5BR, 126/127, 128, 135L, 137T, 144, 204T, 206T, 231T, 237T
Elizabeth Kline 24, 32, 80, 81R, 81R, 95, 104, 105, 108, 131, 138T, 146, 147T, 163T, 168T, 171T, 172, 176, 179T, 181, 184T, 196, 197, 198T, 199, 200, 201, 208, 209, 210, 211, 212, 212T, 213, 218T, 222T, 229, 242, 243T, 244
Courtesy of *Lost World Adventures* 287, 299
Francisco Márquez/Naturpress 191
Buddy Mays/Travel Stock 269
Keith Mays 10/11, 16, 34, 54, 94, 96/97, 99, 100, 102, 103, 106, 109, 120/121, 129, 133, 190, 193, 202, 224/225, 248
B Masters/Art Directors & Trip 300T

S Mead/Art Directors & Trip 2/3, 271
P Musson/Art Directors & Trip 21, 181T, 227, 232, 235
Fernando Ortega/Naturpress 155, 156T, 157, 162T, 230, 245
Mike Osborne 110, 113, 115
Tony Perrottet 18/19, 39, 88, 116/117, 141, 143, 145, 154, 216, 275, 278, 280T, 288, 304
RCTV 70, 71, 73
Brian Rogers/Biofotos 250
Matthew Stockman/Allsport 98
Topham Picturepoint 8/9
Eduardo Vigliano 74, 75
Graham Wicks/Cephas 264, 266/267

INSIGHT GUIDE
Venezuela

Cartographic Editor **Zoë Goodwin**
Production **Stuart A Everitt**
Design Consultants
Carlotta Junger, Graham Mitchener
Picture Research **Hilary Genin, Monica Allende**

Picture Spreads

Pages 84-85
All pictures by Elizabeth Kline
except bottom right-hand corner:
Volkmar Janicke
Pages 186-187
Top Row, left to right: P Musson/Art Directors & Trip, Volkmar Janicke, Volkmar Janicke, M Cerny/Art Directors & Trip
Centre Row, left to right: Volkmar Janicke, P Musson/Art Directors & Trip
Bottom Row, left to right: Elizabeth Kline, P Musson/Art Directors & Trip, Thomas Altinger
Pages 258/259
Top Row, left to right: Fernando Ortega/Naturpress, Fernando Ortega/Naturpress, Elizabeth Kline, Mireille Vautier
Centre Row, left to right: Brian Rogers/Biofotos, Fernando Ortega/Naturpress
Bottom Row, left to right: Thomas Altinger, Thomas Altinger, Thomas Altinger
Pages 292/293
Top Row, left to right: Thomas Altinger, Huw Hennessy, Thomas Altinger
Centre Row, left to right: Huw Hennessy, Huw Hennessy
Bottom Row, left to right: Thomas Altinger, Huw Hennessy, Elizabeth Kline, Huw Hennessy

Maps Colourmap Scanning Ltd
© 1999 Apa Publications GmbH & Co.
Verlag KG (Singapore branch)

Index

Numbers in italics refer to photographs.

The Insight Approach

The book you are holding is part of the world's largest range of guidebooks. Its purpose is to help you have the most valuable travel experience possible, and we try to achieve this by providing not only information about countries, regions and cities but also genuine insight into their history, culture, institutions and people.

Since the first Insight Guide – to Bali – was published in 1970, the series has been dedicated to the proposition that, with insight into a country's people and culture, visitors can both enhance their own experience and be accepted more easily by their hosts. Now, in a world where ethnic hostilities and nationalist conflicts are all too common, such attempts to increase understanding between peoples are more important than ever.

Insight Guides:
Essentials for understanding

Because a nation's past holds the key to its present, each Insight Guide kicks off with lively history chapters. These are followed by magazine-style essays on culture and daily life. This essential background information gives readers the necessary context for using the main Places section, with its comprehensive run-down on things worth seeing and doing.

Finally, a listings section contains all the information you'll need on travel, hotels, restaurants and opening times.

As far as possible, we rely on local writers and specialists to ensure that information is authoritative. The pictures, for which Insight Guides have become so celebrated, are just as important. Our photojournalistic approach aims not only to illustrate a destination but also to communicate visually and directly to readers life as it is lived by the locals. The series has grown to almost 200 titles.

Compact Guides:
The "great little guides"

As invaluable as such background information is, it isn't always fun to carry an Insight Guide through a crowded souk or up a church tower. Could we, readers asked, distil the key reference material into a slim volume for on-the-spot use?

Our response was to design Compact Guides as an entirely new series, with original text carefully cross-referenced to detailed maps and more than 200 photographs. In essence, they're miniature encyclopedias, concise and comprehensive, displaying reliable and up-to-date information in an accessible way. There are almost 100 titles.

Pocket Guides:
A local host in book form

However wide-ranging the information in a book, human beings still value the personal touch. Our editors are often asked the same questions. Where do *you* go to eat? What do *you* think is the best beach? What would *you* recommend if I have only three days? We invited our local correspondents to act as "substitute hosts" by revealing their preferred walks and trips, listing the restaurants they go to and structuring a visit into a series of timed itineraries.

The result: our Pocket Guides, complete with full-size fold-out maps. These 100-plus titles help readers plan a trip precisely, particularly if their time is short.

Exploring with Insight:
A valuable travel experience

In conjunction with co-publishers all over the world, we print in up to 10 languages, from German to Chinese, from Danish to Russian. But our aim remains simple: to enhance your travel experience by combining our expertise in guidebook publishing with the on-the-spot knowledge of our correspondents.